A BASEMENT SEAT
TO HISTORY

A BASEMENT SEAT TO HISTORY

Tales of Covering Presidents
Nixon, Ford, Carter and Reagan
for the Voice of America

Philomena Jurey

Linus Press   Washington, DC

Linus Press
Washington, D.C.

Library of Congress Catalog Card Number 95-76896

Printed in the United States of America

Chapter 7 is an expansion of "China and the Voice of America: A Reminiscence" published in the Fall 1990 issue of *Delos*, a journal of world literature.

Jurey, Philomena
A basement seat to history: tales of covering Presidents Nixon, Ford, Carter and Reagan for the Voice of America
Includes index.

ISBN 0-9647015-0-2

Memoir—journalism—United States. U.S. international broadcasting—Voice of America—History. Presidents and press—United States—History. Foreign affairs—United States—History.

First edition: October 1995

In memory of
Francis and Fortunata Sparano, my parents
Jack Jurey, my husband

Acknowledgments

In writing this memoir, I was fortunate to have the advice and encouragement of many friends and former colleagues. Of enormous help were four special people: Edward Bliss Jr., Vera Dickey, Theda Parrish, and Edith Sherbine. They lived through the book with me, reading the chapters as they emerged from my Macintosh, and made suggestions that greatly improved the manuscript. I am indebted to them.

I also treasure the advice given by Charles McCarry, who read my first rough attempt at a memoir years ago and told me what I needed to do to turn a draft into a book. "Tell stories," was one of the things he said in steering me on my way. In making the transition from writing broadcast news reports to the far different discipline of writing a book, I was helped immensely by Reed Whittemore, who showed me how to use details in telling stories and furthermore gave advice on how to structure the book.

Others who made useful and valued suggestions were Corinne Condé, Bernard H. Kamenske, Dina Modianot–Fox, Lee Hall Valeriani, and Carol Woodard. I also had the benefit of the sharp eyes and editing skills of Ada Kimsey and Peter H. Silberman, and very helpful editing advice from Hans N. Tuch. Of great assistance were Eva Jane Fritzman and Myrna Whitworth, to whom I turned when I wanted updates on developments at the Voice of America. Additional help came from Elizabeth Knisley, who provided recent VOA press releases.

I am grateful to all of them. Any shortcomings in the book are mine.

Many others were supportive of my efforts in producing this book. David Shears of Starfish Press was always ready to answer my questions. The Reagan, Ford and Carter Libraries, and the Nixon Presidential Materials Staff at the National Archives, were responsive to my requests for photos. Morris Cobern of Allied Printing was indispensable in guiding the book through the production process. And plaudits to Marla Rosenthal, for her skill at the computer.

Finally, many thanks to my former colleagues at the Voice and in the White House press corps for the experiences that we shared and made this memoir possible.

Contents

Front cover photo: President Reagan sees off Presidents Ford, Nixon and Carter, October 8, 1981, for their trip to Cairo to represent him at President Sadat's funeral. (Courtesy Ronald Reagan Library)

Back cover photo: Jurey at work on a camera platform at the Aswan, Egypt, airport, January 4, 1978. (Photo by E. Allen Brown, VOA)

1
Scenesetter

The headline in the Tokyo newspaper *Mainichi Daily News* said: "Famous VOA Unknown Retires." It appeared over an Associated Press story on my retirement from the Voice of America, the U.S. government's global radio station. The headline made me laugh, but it was an apt description of VOA's broadcasters and VOA itself: famous abroad, unknown at home.

This was my major frustration in working for VOA: Americans don't know enough about it. They don't because VOA is barred from beaming its programs to Americans under the 1948 Smith-Mundt Act. The purpose of the statute was to forestall any attempt by the government to propagandize the American people. VOA is even prohibited from disseminating transcripts of its broadcasts within the United States.

Scholars and reporters are allowed to visit VOA's offices in Washington and examine its material on the premises, and a few have published scholarly works and magazine articles containing examples of VOA broadcasts. Newspapers occasionally carry stories about VOA, but still the Voice of America remains largely unknown in America.

Because it is a government radio, the assumption is that it is a propaganda agency broadcasting slanted news. In this personal account, a memoir of what it was like working at the Voice, I hope to shed light on how we reported the news, particularly in the 70s and 80s when I covered the White House. Was I a propagandist?

I never thought of myself as a cold warrior. I was a reporter and that's all there was to it. This is the way I felt in the 28 years I spent at VOA. I traveled at least a quarter of a million miles overseas, covering a secretary of state and then four presidents, and was treated abroad as a celebrity. One reason for this glorified status was that people in other countries are intensely interested in everything about America, and I was the conveyor of news about its leaders.

The main reason, I like to think, is that I came through to listeners as a reporter, trying to do an honest job of reporting. In my mind there was no conflict between being a reporter and a government-employed journalist at the same time. What better example of the freedom in America than for the government's overseas radio to operate in the tradition of its free press.

I had always wanted to be a reporter, ever since I was in grade school in New Castle, Pennsylvania, and wrote items for the Mahoning School's little mimeographed news bulletin. My father read the New Castle, Pittsburgh, and Youngstown, Ohio, newspapers avidly, encouraged me to read them, and bought me a Remington portable typewriter so I could peck out my school reports. Neither he nor my mother had much formal education, but they fostered my love of books and were determined to send me and my younger sister and brother to college.

Papa came to America from the poor Calabrian region of southern Italy at the age of 15, and Mama was the American-born daughter of an immigrant from Calabria. From my parents I inherited a singlemindedness of purpose and what Norman Douglas, in his book *Old Calabria*, called the "straightforward" character of the Calabrians.

I studied journalism at the University of Missouri, graduating in June 1949 with a B.J. degree and with "accuracy, accuracy, accuracy" drummed into me. From Missouri I took with me the Journalist's Creed, which says: "I believe that clear thinking and clear statement, accuracy, and fairness, are fundamental to good journalism."

My reporting career was launched at *The Southwest Times* in Pulaski, Virginia, a pretty little town at the foot of Draper Mountain in the southwestern part of the state. I was one of two reporters and covered everything from the courts to a communist attempt to infiltrate the local electrical workers union.

From Pulaski I went to Roanoke, Virginia, to work for *The Roanoke Times*, where blustery, beer-bellied W. (Bill) Atkinson, the managing editor, taught me how to write in plain language. I started as a writer for the women's section, whose editor, Mrs.

Anne Nelson Montgomery, was a pioneer in the transformation of traditional society pages into sections of broader interest. In time I became the paper's first woman reporter.

In Virginia I learned just how unconscionable racial segregation was. Growing up in a largely Italian section of New Castle, I was more aware of discrimination against "dagos" and other ethnics than against blacks. In Pulaski, I was appalled that the doctrine of separate facilities even included Draper Mountain, where the viewing site for whites was at the top, the one for blacks lower down the slope. But I also learned in Virginia that not all southerners should be tarred as bigots. Many of those who worked at the paper were in favor of desegregation.

On return to the North in 1952 I was hired by the Youngstown paper, *The Vindicator*, to substitute for vacationing correspondents in its regional bureaus, then as New Castle correspondent, finally as a general assignment reporter. Youngstown was a great training ground for a reporter. It was a center of the nation's iron and steel industry, a city where you could smell and see the odor of steel plants working, gray in the daytime, open hearth red at night. It was a commercial center, a city of ethnic communities with roots in more than 50 countries, a microcosm of the 1950s with the inner city beginning to crumble. And it was a center of illegal gambling and other unlawful enterprises, with warfare among racketeers spawning a series of bombings.

For a time I was on the "obits and late cops" beat, writing obituaries in the morning and covering the police department in the afternoon. In writing obits, I kept in mind an experience in the New Castle bureau. In a hurry one morning I asked a funeral director, "Anybody important?" His reply was a humbling reminder: "Everyone is important to someone."

I was *The Vindicator's* second woman police reporter. The first was Ann Przelomski, a teacher who went to work temporarily for the paper during World War II when male reporters were in the service. She was asked to stay on and eventually rose to managing editor. The paper's star columnist was Esther Hamilton, a gruff no-nonsense person and a legend for her coverage of famous cases, including the Lindbergh kidnap trial. There were other women on the staff too, but I don't think any of us thought of ourselves as feminists, blazing trails in the man's world of journalism. Yet it *was* largely a man's world; most newspapers and broadcast news organizations didn't hire women as reporters then.

While working for *The Vindicator* I met the man who would become my husband and the center of my life. Jack Jurey was the paper's labor editor and top investigative reporter, hired away from the city's major radio station, WKBN, where he had been news director. He was passionate in his beliefs about justice, life, and the news; he believed journalism was a public trust. When we married I took my husband's name and changed my newspaper byline from Philomena Sparano to Philomena Jurey. In doing so I felt no loss of identity; I was the same person, and cherished as well.

With Jack I attended my first presidential press conference. We were on vacation in Washington in October 1956, and the Bascom Timmons Bureau, which covered local–angle Washington stories for *The Vindicator* and other newspapers, arranged for us to be invited as visiting journalists. We even were given printed vellum invitations signed by President Eisenhower's press secretary, James C. Hagerty, to the session in the ornamental Indian Treaty Room of the Old Executive Office Building, next to the White House. I was thrilled to be seeing a president in person for the first time.

Then 65, Eisenhower had undergone surgery for ileitis five months earlier, and the year before had had a heart attack. From our back row seats, he looked good to us. We wrote a page one feature story for *The Vindicator*, which began: "Although President Eisenhower's health is a matter of public concern, in person he looks as well as any man, unlike TV pictures which tend to make him appear wan and drawn." Television then was in black and white, but when color eventually came to TV it still couldn't beat seeing a president in the flesh.

Along about that time Jack was writing editorials for the paper and I was covering the county courthouse. In reporting on court trials, I learned to expect the unexpected. And in reporting on the doings of the county commissioners, I learned that officials sometimes lie.

The Vindicator newsroom was a journalistic way station for us and some of the lifelong friends we made there. Among them was Charles McCarry, with whom I shared amused looks when an editor erroneously accused him of splitting infinitives. He would become one of the nation's finest writers of novels and nonfiction books.

A turning point and blessing in our lives came when Jack won a fellowship to Harvard and we went off to Cambridge, Massachusetts for the 1957-58 academic year. It was a golden, intellectually intoxicating time for us both. Jack had a Ford Foundation Mass Media grant but he and two other grantees, Phil Kerby of *Frontier* magazine and University of North Carolina journalism professor Walter Spearman, took part in the Nieman Fellows program through the kindness of its curator, the beloved Louis Lyons. The Nieman group included reporters destined for distinguished careers in the national press, like Tom Wicker, Simmons Fentress, John Lindsay, Peter Kumpa and Stanley Karnow. We all became good friends.

The times we spent with the Fellows and their spouses — only one woman was a Nieman then and her husband cheerfully joined the "wives" — were exhilarating. A passage in Edith Wharton's *The Age of Innocence* sums up how I felt: "Ah, good conversation — there's nothing like it, is there? The air of ideas is the only air worth breathing."

I took two evening courses in philosophy and accompanied Jack to some of his classes, including a lecture on the consequences of nuclear attack, by a professor with a German accent named Henry Kissinger. And I found a job at the college newspaper, *The Harvard Crimson*, as a secretary handling bills and subscriptions. My bosses were undergraduates who called me Mrs. Jurey, out of politeness and not, I hoped, because of my age, nearly 30. I enjoyed seeing them put out the paper, especially the top editors, Adam Clymer and George Watson. They too would have successful careers in news.

I did keep my hand in as a reporter, by freelancing feature articles to *The Boston Globe*. I was paid $15 for each but much more in pride. What a boost it was to take the subway into Boston for the symphony and see riders reading one of my bylined stories.

Jack and I returned to Youngstown enriched, and with two Harvard chairs, in May 1958, but in a few months moved to Washington. He had won an audition as a newscaster at WTOP Radio and Television (Channel 9), CBS affiliates then owned by the Washington Post Company. Within a year he began writing and delivering daily editorials. He was one of the pioneers in television editorials, winning national recognition, and later was news director as well. I was so proud of him and wrapped up in his career.

Our life revolved around our home (Jack's daughter from his previous marriage came to live with us when she was 14), our friends, playing bridge (including spirited games with network correspondent Paul Niven and a young WTOP reporter, Sam Donaldson), books, and of course the news.

As for my own career, I had been unsuccessful in finding work as a reporter and had taken a job in the Washington bureau of *The London Daily Telegraph* as a secretary. I stayed there until I joined the Voice of America in 1961.

The foregoing is, then, a scenesetter. For in reporting the news at VOA, I was shaped by the influences of my parents and husband and by my early experiences. In telling the reader about the Voice, personal reminiscences are part of the story.

2
Tea with the Brits
Baptism as a VOA Correspondent
Diplomacy and Bridge

We had tea every afternoon at 4 o'clock in *The London Daily Telegraph* office in Washington's National Press Building. I brewed it, with Crosse & Blackwell teabags, as part of my "Girl Friday" duties, and then the bureau's two correspondents and I settled back in our swivel chairs for enjoyable discussions of literature, history, and social and political customs.

The chief correspondent was Denys Smith, a rumpled grandfatherly–looking man who had been based in Washington for 30 years. He wrote a book, which I helped type, about the forthcoming 1960 presidential election, explaining how the American electoral process differs from the selection of British prime ministers. The book, *Polls Apart*, was a good read, with lines like: "Every American presidential election is an adventure into the great unknown."

Working for the London paper taught me how to look at America and its institutions from the perspective of a non–American. I saw that in reporting American news to people overseas, the stories often must include explanations of our society and system of government.

My major duty was to attend the noon briefings at the State Department and type up copious notes. Denys used the notes in writing his dispatches and in checking the stories filed by the wire service diplomatic correspondents. Seeing their "hard leads" as the stories chattered out on the teletype machines in the bureau was an education for me in how to pick one's way through diplomatic obfuscation under deadline. I also learned briefing rules. When an official speaks "on background," he can't be quoted by name. "Deep background" means no attribution at all; a reporter makes use of the information at his or her own risk. And "off the record" means the information imparted is "for guidance" and not supposed to be printed or broadcast at all.

Denys Smith was responsible for my observing Richard Nixon in person for the first time. The vice president and Mrs. Nixon were preparing for a visit to London and invited the Washington–based British correspondents and their wives to their home in the upscale Spring Valley section for drinks and conversation in advance of the trip. Denys said that since I was on his staff the invitation included me and my husband. I went out and bought a new dress. How often does one get to meet the vice president, a controversial figure like Richard ("Tricky Dick") Nixon at that, and in his own home! The Nixons were gracious hosts and it was a proper evening. Nixon was more human, more forthcoming than I expected him to be. The session was bland in terms of producing news but the Brits were happy. The foreign press in Washington doesn't often get such attention from a vice president, or any high U.S. official.

During the evening Mrs. Nixon showed the women guests some of the clothes she planned to wear in London, including a gown made of material similar to a sari, which I mentioned in a feature I wrote for the paper. To my dismay, the headline on the story went beyond what I'd written, and trumpeted that she would "wear a sari." I hoped she never saw it.

Besides writing occasional pieces for the paper, I freelanced feature articles to the North American Newspaper Alliance, including a series based on interviews I had with cabinet wives in the Eisenhower administration. But I longed to return to hard news, and in October 1961 became a news writer at the Voice of America.

I was leary about going to work for a government agency and knew next to nothing about VOA. In Youngstown, I had heard of an American overseas broadcast station, Radio Free Europe, because a friend of my husband's, Paul Smith, headed up the local Crusade for Freedom fundraising campaign for RFE broadcasts to Eastern Europe. None of us knew RFE was a CIA-financed covert operation. That wasn't disclosed until the early 1970s, after which RFE and its sister station broadcasting to the Soviet Union, Radio Liberty, were funded by congressional grants.

New friends in Washington told me VOA was not the same as RFE, and wasn't like other government agencies but was a legitimate broadcaster of news. On joining the Voice, I found that its newsroom was peopled on the whole with professional journalists who knew their stuff, from News Division Chief Bob Goldmann, who hired me, on down. I was impressed with their knowledge of national and international affairs and the straightforward way in which they wrote the news for broadcast to international audiences.

The newsroom operated 24 hours a day, seven days a week. News items were distributed on internal teletype machines to Worldwide English and 35 language services for their newscasts. To be sure the stories were accurate the newsroom had a "two source rule," which meant that the facts in them had to be based on at least two independent sources, usually the wire services, unless the information came from a VOA correspondent on the scene or from an original source such as a speech or press conference. Great care also was taken to be sure the news items contained enough explanatory material so they'd be understandable to overseas audiences.

One of the staffers, Richard Engel, a German emigré and sweet man, would come up to me and other writers on occasion to say, "In your otherwise excellent story. . .," and proceed to point out where the story lacked necessary details.

The language services, too, kept us aware of the need to be explicit, especially in stories from one part of the world being broadcast to another. One day a fellow in the Portuguese to Brazil service phoned me with a query on a news item about Burma. "What," he asked, "is a Rangoon?" I rewrote the story to insert "the capital" after Rangoon.

News writers and editors signed off each item with their initials, and I became the newsroom's PJ. One of the editors was CC, Corinne Condé, a legend at VOA for challenging an edict on reporting the Soviet launching of Sputnik in October 1957. First some explanatory background: During World War II VOA was part of the Office of War Information; after the war it was deposited in the State Department, and in 1953 President Eisenhower transferred it to the newly created U.S. Information Agency. At the time of Sputnik's launching, the VOA newsroom was in the USIA building on Pennsylvania Avenue, a block from the White House.

When Corinne went to work that night, she was greeted with a "policy note," from a USIA official, that said VOA could not lead its newscasts with Sputnik. She phoned the official, who said this word was relayed by Lewis Strauss, the head of the Atomic Energy Commission, and that he, the official, assumed it came from "the highest authority." As Corinne recalled, she replied, "In the news business you never assume anything, as you would almost always be wrong." She told the USIA official she would lead the newscasts with Sputnik, "but if 'the highest authority' was serious he could make a personal appearance in the newsroom and tell me himself, and I would argue with him."

Corinne was right, and her decision was not disputed. Although she was wispy in appearance, everyone knew she was made of steel. She demanded excellence from the writers and tore up their copy if it wasn't satisfactory. We called her the Dragon Lady, with admiration and affection.

The guidelines under which the newsroom operated were rooted in a pledge VOA made when it went on the air for the first time, in World War II. The broadcast on February 24, 1942, in the German language, promised: "Daily at this time we shall speak to you about America and the war. The news may be good or bad. We shall tell you the truth." The guidelines were eventually spelled out in a VOA Charter that was developed within the Voice during the latter part of the Eisenhower administration.

It was drafted by Jack O'Brien, the deputy director, and Barry Zorthian, the program manager. The aim, as described by Zorthian at a symposium in 1990, was "a Voice of America charter that would provide continuity and a basis for response to criticisms and pressures." He recalled the "devastating period for the Voice" in the early 1950s when Senator Joseph McCarthy was accusing VOA editors of communist sympathies.

When I joined VOA, Zorthian had left for assignments overseas, but I heard a lot about him. During the McCarthy era he had fought for VOA staffers who were threatened with being fired. As program director, he raised professional standards and developed new programming, including the inauguration in 1959 of VOA's popular Special English, which broadcast news and information in simplified language, using a vocabulary of 1,300 words (later 1,500).

The VOA Charter served to protect the integrity of the news but did not have the full force of law for over 15 years. It was written into law by Congress under the leadership of Senator Charles Percy of Illinois and Representative Bella Abzug of New York, with input from dedicated VOA staffers like Bernard H. Kamenske and Alan L. Heil, and signed by President Gerald Ford on July 12, 1976. Here is the Charter in full:

"The long–range interests of the United States are served by communicating directly with the peoples of the world by radio. To be effective, the Voice of America must win the attention and respect of listeners. These principles will govern VOA broadcasts. (1) VOA will serve as a consistently reliable and authoritative source of news. VOA news will be accurate, objective and comprehensive. (2) VOA will represent America, not any single segment of American society, and will therefore present a balanced and comprehensive projection of significant American thought and institutions. (3) VOA will present the policies of the United States clearly and effectively, and will also present responsible discussion and opinion on these policies."

The Charter mandate was, I thought, not unlike the Journalist's Creed I learned at the University of Missouri. And I liked what President John Kennedy and his USIA director, the icon of broadcast journalism, Edward R. Murrow, said about VOA.

Murrow: "The Voice of America stands upon this above all: The truth shall be the guide. Truth may help us. It may hurt us. But helping us or hurting us we shall have the satisfaction of knowing that man can know us for what we are and can at least believe what we say."

Kennedy: "We seek a free flow of information across national boundaries and oceans, across iron curtains and stone walls. We are not afraid to entrust the American people with unpleasant facts, foreign ideas, alien philosophies and competitive values. For a nation that is afraid to let its people judge the truth and falsehood in an open market is a nation that is afraid of its people. The Voice of America thus carries a heavy responsibility. Its burden of truth is not easy to bear. It must explain to a curious and suspicious world what we are."

They spoke at a ceremony marking VOA's 20th anniversary in 1962 at its headquarters on Independence Avenue S.W. The VOA director was Henry Loomis, whom I also admired. He was appointed by Eisenhower to head the Voice in 1958 and presided over the development of the Charter and of a worldwide transmitter network, expanding the reach of VOA broadcasts.

During the Cuban missile crisis in 1962 I worked on the Latin American desk in the newsroom, under BHK, Bernie Kamenske. We were dismayed when a USIA official was installed in the newsroom to read our copy. We were writing the stories with extreme care and felt that USIA's action at the least showed a lack of confidence in our work and at the most amounted to censorship. Looking back on those frightening days on the edge of nuclear confrontation between the United States and the Soviet Union, I can understand why the parent agency took such a precaution, but I still think it was unnecessary.

After the crisis, one of my jobs in the newsroom was to write fast bulletins on Kennedy's televised press conferences. These were broadcast live by Worldwide English, but bulletins had to be run on the house wire so that language services could translate them for broadcast in their upcoming newscasts. It was easy, and fun, to write the bulletins because Kennedy was so accomplished in his answers, and handling the press.

I was working on the national desk on November 22, 1963, and had just finished writing a "hold for release" news story on the advance text of a speech Kennedy would be delivering in Dallas, when a newsroom colleague, Van Seropian, came tearing in from the wire room housing the news agency teletype machines. "Kennedy's been shot," he cried out. I began writing bulletins on the terrible news from Dallas, with the first ragged effort printed on the VOA house wire at 1:54 p.m. Eastern Standard Time:

"President Kennedy was shot today as he rode through Dallas in an open automobile. He was rushed immediately to a hospital. It is not known at this time whether the president survived the assassin's bullets. We will keep you informed of developments as they are learned."

Jerry Thiese, the newsroom chief, was editing the copy as we pieced together information from the wire services and television broadcasts and churned out "adds" to our running bulletin story, conscious of the responsibility we bore in reporting the anguishing news to listeners around the world. At one point, in an attempt to provide some recent historical background as we awaited further information, I wrote a sentence that we agonized over and re-wrote and re-wrote. I got VOA into trouble with the sentence, which said: "Dallas of recent months has been the scene of extreme right wing movements." This was before Lee Harvey Oswald was arrested. The sentence was deleted 11 minutes after it was printed on the house wire. Some members of Congress criticized VOA for having written it, and the venerable *New York Times* columnist Arthur Krock was indignant.

In his "In The Nation" column published November 26, Krock cited the facts known about Oswald — that he "was a Marxist; at least a sympathizer with the religion of Communism; emigrated to and married in the Soviet Union; and was trying to return" — and went on to say: "This is certainly not the dossier of the 'Right Wing extremists,' a stigmatic label of Dallas which some members of the Administration are too prone to affix. That inclination was revealed by the Voice of America broadcast at 1:59 P.M. last Friday of the ghastly tragedy in the city. 'Dallas,' the V.O.A. explained to the world, 'is the center of the extreme Right Wing.' This gratuitous, and as it proved, false, suggestion that such was the affiliation of the assassin was deleted from the broadcast at 2:10 P.M. but it was grist to Moscow's mill, which has been grinding it ever since."

Some members of Congress demanded the name of the person who wrote the offending sentence, but VOA management wouldn't say, although I was willing to be named. I don't think the sentence was unwarranted. It was, in hindsight, irrelevant, but it wasn't false. Other news organizations included background on rightist activity in Dallas in their stories, including *The New York Times*. Tom Wicker, in his masterly account of the assassination, described the enthusiastic crowds in downtown Dallas before Kennedy was shot, and added this background: "The turnout was somewhat unusual for this center of conservatism, where only a month ago Adlai E. Stevenson was attacked by a rightist crowd. It was also in Dallas, during the 1960 campaign, that Senator Lyndon B. Johnson and his wife were nearly mobbed in the lobby of the Baker Hotel."

Throughout that afternoon I wrote the story. "President Kennedy is dead. The president of the United States was shot down as he rode through downtown Dallas in an open automobile. . ." — and updated it — "President Kennedy is dead — the victim of an assassin's bullet. And the new president of the United States is Lyndon Johnson. . . ." All the time that I was writing, I operated automatically, thinking only of getting out the facts as they became known. The enormity of the loss hit me when another shift took over in the newsroom and I went home.

VOA was without a reporter in Dallas because it did not always send its White House correspondent with the president when he traveled. But from then on, the VOA White House correspondent or a substitute went on presidential trips, in what is frankly known as "body coverage."

During the Johnson administration I continued to write fast bulletins on presidential press conferences, and wrote and edited news stories on international and national developments, including the civil rights and anti–Vietnam war demonstrations.

On the civil rights struggle, the Voice tried to report the good as well as bad, carrying stories for instance whenever a black person achieved prominence in one field or another. There was more bad than good to broadcast in the early years and VOA was criticized for its uneven coverage. Naturally it was uneven; our newscasts were reflecting the way things were. We tried hard to be accurate, and our "two source" rule governed our output. For instance VOA did not carry an AP–only dispatch which reported, erroneously, that James Meredith was killed at the University of Mississippi.

Many of the stories that writers turned in to me as copy editor dealt with the growing conflict in South Vietnam. So when my husband asked if I'd like to accompany him on a trip to Vietnam in 1965 for a series of editorials he would be doing on the war, I jumped at the chance to get some first–hand knowledge and arranged to go on vacation. I'd been interested in Saigon since 1953 when a hometown friend, Edith Sherbine, was working at the U.S. aid mission there. She wrote me letters describing the cosmopolitan city with its "French Foreign Legionnaires, Vietnamese officers, Indians in their sarongs, Chinese, cyclo pedalers in only shorts, Europeans in tropical helmets and shorts, Americans in their usual summer attire, French ladies in sheer blouses, servants in their white blouses and black pajamas." Edith also wrote about the Viet Minh guerrillas, the deteriorating French military situation, and the fear of venturing into the countryside, and said an American journalist told her "the French would never win."

This was seven or eight months before the defeat of the French at Dienbienphu in May 1954. With Vietnam subsequently divided into North and South, the United States increased aid to South Vietnam, and the guerrillas fighting against the Saigon government were called the communist Viet Cong instead of Viet Minh.

Saigon in May 1965, when Jack and I were there, was the cosmopolitan city Edith had described, with cyclo pedalers and so on, but with Americans replacing French Foreign Legionnaires. There was, too, the fear of driving outside the city at night. The night we arrived we were driven into town from the airport with the car lights off, the driver flashing them on only when he divined an oncoming vehicle. I wasn't sure whether I should be more scared of being hit by a car or by a Viet Cong sniper.

We attended the famous "Five O'Clock Follies," the briefings held by JUSPAO, the Joint U.S. Public Affairs Office (I finally met Barry Zorthian of VOA fame who was running JUSPAO); we discussed the war with reporters at meals and over drinks in the Caravelle Hotel bar; and Jack interviewed American and South Vietnamese officials and went to the Mekong Delta and Da Nang.

In one of his editorials filmed on the Caravelle roof Jack said: "Discussing the ugly, uncertain war in South Vietnam, there seems to us to be both an official and unofficial failure to emphasize one aspect clearly enough. That is the extreme likelihood that, having entered this struggle, the United States will be unable to withdraw from it for a considerable number of years."

The number of Americans on duty in South Vietnam at the time was around 37,000; the first U.S. combat troops had landed at Da Nang two months earlier. By the end of 1965, U.S. troop strength was nearly 200,000.

The trip, with stops in Tokyo, Hong Kong and Bangkok, was a help to me in my work at VOA. Now I knew something of the region, and I knew what the JUSPAO briefings were like, the latitude reporters had in going out into the field to see things for themselves, the views of officials and journalists on the scene, the taste and feel of Saigon. The trip also underscored for me the value of shortwave radio and of VOA newscasts in informing overseas listeners on developments around the world. We had bought a shortwave radio and listened to the news on VOA in our hotel room at the Caravelle. One night after the newscast, we heard a good discussion on civil rights by a Washington panel that included one of our Nieman friends, Simmons Fentress of *Time* magazine. The impact of a familiar voice broadcasting to distant places was something I would remember.

I was comfortable working in the VOA newsroom and progressed to coverage editor assigning correspondents. I had no thought of being a correspondent myself, no desire for any assignment that would involve travel away from my husband. If Jack had not died, I am sure I would have stayed put, with my career probably following the executive track. He was hospitalized in February 1969 and cancer was discovered. I brought him home in April; he died in May, barely three months after his 45th birthday. There were hundreds of tributes to him, from grade school children to Chief Justice Earl Warren, who wrote me that his editorials were "always in the best interests of good government and the advancement of justice. We shall miss him greatly. . . ." Lyndon Johnson, in retirement at his Texas ranch, sent me a telegram and then a letter.

While LBJ was president, he phoned our house several times to compliment Jack on his editorials. I'll never forget the first time, in September 1965. I was in the back yard with our two dachs-hunds when the phone rang. Jack answered it in the kitchen and called out, "Philomena, come quick." As I rushed in, he cupped his hand over the mouthpiece and whispered, "It's the president!" Johnson had seen his editorial on TV that evening and told him, "You've got guts over there." When Jack became ill, a Washington friend and fellow New Castle native, Carol Woodard, informed Johnson. He wrote to Jack and sent him a book, and a photo of himself and Lady Bird at the ranch. This was a side of LBJ, so often portrayed as boorish, that I choose to remember.

In Jack's illness and death, family and friends sustained me, and the people at VOA, WTOP television and radio, and *The Washington Post* could not have been more supportive. Katharine Graham was especially kind.

I went back to work right away and soon was promoted to shift chief, in charge of the newsroom from 4 p.m. to midnight. For a vacation in 1970 I visited my stepdaughter Diane in Nicosia, Cyprus, where her husband, a Navy enlisted man, was attached to the U.S. embassy, and from there she and I traveled to Lebanon, Algeria and Morocco. It was a rewarding trip for a reporter.

Visiting Cyprus was an education in the uncompromising attitudes of the Turkish Cypriots and Greek Cypriots, their unreasoning hatred dividing that lovely island. Beirut was a cosmopolitan city that pulsed with commerce, entertainment, learning, and Arab wealth. In that tranquil period we visited the serene campus of the American University of Beirut and walked about the ancient ruins of Baalbek. We also saw the Palestinian refugee camps near the airport, and that was depressing.

The visit to Algiers was sentimental; Jack had been stationed there in World War II and I wanted to see it. The Algerians were warm and kind to us, though diplomatic relations with the U.S., broken by Algeria in the 1967 Arab–Israeli war, had not yet been restored. The young women we met wore veils in public, but removed them in our private conversations and wanted to know all about America.

During the Algerian War of Independence from France, I had written news items for VOA about the nationalist stronghold at Tizi Ouzou, so we took a side tour to see it, and the residents there were hospitable too. In Morocco we went to Casablanca, more European, more French, than I thought it would be, and I took a drive to Rabat to visit USIS. USIA posts overseas are known as USIS, for U.S. Information Service. They distribute literature and films about America; make available texts of speeches by the president and other high U.S. officials, the "wireless file" of the agency's press service, and other USIA publications; they also sponsor exhibits and events, and maintain libraries, where local people read American books and magazines.

On my return to Washington I was assigned to cover a trip by Mrs. Nixon to Peru in late June. It was my baptism as a broadcast correspondent.

The First Lady was flying there to deliver relief supplies to the victims of the worst earthquake in Peruvian memory. The 1970 trip was her first journey abroad on her own, and my first for VOA. I flew to Lima by commercial airline in time for Mrs. Nixon's arrival on Air Force One from California, where she'd been at the Western White House with her husband. The presidential plane was accompanied by a C–130 cargo plane and both were crammed with tents, blankets, winter clothing and other supplies donated by American citizens and voluntary organizations. The May 31st earthquake had killed an estimated 50,000 people and left more than 700,000 homeless. Worst hit was a valley, Callejon de Huaylas, known as the Switzerland of Peru. Now it was being called the Valley of Death.

Mrs. Nixon and Mrs. Juan Velasco, the wife of Peru's president, made a helicopter tour of the valley after a hairy flight on the C-130 between towering mountain ranges to an airstrip at Anta. This was a base of relief operations by Peruvian and U.S. helicopter pilots. I was in the press pool in Huey choppers that followed the First Ladies on their tour. We saw towns that had been ruined, homes left in splinters, cracks in mountainsides, and the terrible residue of mud and rock slides.

The First Ladies made a stop at Huaraz, a town that was 80 percent destroyed, with up to 16,000 people killed. The helicopters landed on a soccer field and we reporters and camera crews scurried out beneath still-whirling blades to follow Mrs. Nixon in a swarm. She shook hands and talked with townspeople, letting them know that the people of the United States cared about them. This was not the woman who had been labeled "Plastic Pat." She was genuinely warm and outgoing, offering comfort to the bereaved.

In leaving Huaraz, the first Huey press chopper took off with not every seat filled, so there wasn't enough room on the remaining Huey for the rest of the press party. We were promised another chopper would come from Anta to retrieve those who couldn't get seats, a small group that included CBS White House correspondent Bob Pierpoint and me. Both of us were worried about missing deadlines. The afternoon waned, and we worried some more. We had been told the helicopters wouldn't fly after sunset. Would we be left behind and have to spend the night in a temporary shelter? As the sun was sinking, the helicopter arrived. I rushed aboard, secured my seatbelt and hugged my gearbag and typewriter to me. In semi-darkness the Huey climbed into the Andes, the sides of the mountains frighteningly close, close enough to touch, I thought, close enough to crash. My knees were still shaking that night when we returned to Lima.

In missing the deadlines for VOA's newscasts to Latin America, I learned a lesson. I should have filed a "holding spot" before going to the valley, so that the newscasts would have had something from

VOA's correspondent on the scene. Too late to do anything about that, I filed a quick report for broadcasts to other areas. In Huaraz, I had used what little Spanish I remembered from high school to interview quake survivors for VOA's Spanish language service. They were an engineer, an art student, and two teachers whose school had been destroyed. As I reported, they were hopeful about the future and said they were happy about Mrs. Nixon's visit and the concern shown by the U.S. When I cued the tape to transmit to Washington, there was nothing on it. My recorder had failed. It had been jostled from my shoulder by a cameraman and dropped in the scramble to follow Mrs. Nixon, and I hadn't checked to see if it was okay. More lessons: Always check out equipment, never cover a trip without an extra tape recorder, and stay out of the way of camera crews.

With those lessons in mind, I took two tape recorders with me when I was assigned to the State Department beat in August 1971 and began covering Secretary of State William P. Rogers. U.S. attitudes toward Communist China were changing then, with "ping pong diplomacy" a catchy phrase, inspired by an American table tennis team's visit there in April.

On July 15, after a secret Kissinger trip to Peking, President Nixon broke the news that he had accepted an invitation to visit the Peoples Republic of China "at an appropriate date before May 1972." Two and a half weeks after Nixon's announcement, Rogers unveiled a new American policy on Chinese representation at the United Nations: The U.S. would support admission of the PRC but oppose moves to expel the Republic of China, the Nationalist Chinese government on Taiwan.

Rogers traveled to New York to press the case at the U.N. for dual Chinese representation. On September 25, after a round of lobbying, he said the U.N. General Assembly vote would be close "but we think we'll win." In my report for VOA I added a line that was necessary to tell the complete story, that the secretary of state was disputing "forecasts that the American effort is on the road to defeat."

The forecasts were well-based. At dinner with several diplomatic correspondents one evening well before the vote, Peter Kumpa of *The Baltimore Sun* listed the U.N. delegations and we all gave our assessments on which way they were leaning. The list added up to membership for and only for, Communist China. On October 25 the General assembly voted to expel Nationalist China, a member of the U.N. since its founding in 1945, and to admit the PRC.

In early May 1972 Rogers flew to Europe for an eight-day trip to brief the NATO allies in advance of Nixon's visit to Moscow for his initial summit meeting with Leonid Brezhnev. The first stop was Reykjavik, Iceland, where it took me a couple of frustrating hours to get a clear-enough telephone line to VOA in Washington to report on his arrival and upcoming talks. It is maddening to have material to file and yet be thwarted by phone problems. Eventually, with the alligator clips on a cord from my tape recorder securely fastened to the innards of a telephone at the Hotel Saga, I got an acceptable connection and fed my report. I joined the other correspondents at dinner and relaxed, looking out of the Saga dining room's huge picture windows as the long Icelandic day came to an end with a glorious fiery sunset.

Only three other diplomatic correspondents were on the trip; Rogers didn't attract much press, the limelight was occupied by Kissinger. The three, however, were among the best of the State Department press corps and I was pleased to be their colleague: Bernard Gwertzman of *The New York Times*, Hank Trewhitt of *Newsweek*, and Darius Jhabvala of *The Boston Globe*. From Reykjavik we went on to London, Brussels, Luxembourg and Bonn. We arrived in the West German capital May 6, looking forward to the next day when Rogers and his party were to go on a boat ride on the Rhine River.

Two hours before our cruise, we reporters were told to pack our bags. Rogers had been summoned back to Washington by the president. No details, just that it was in connection with the situation in Southeast Asia. On the flight home we were the only passengers besides Rogers and his wife, Adele; Robert McCloskey, the State Department's chief spokesman, and a few security men.

Rogers had left the rest of his official party in Bonn to wait for further word.

We rattled around on the big Air Force plane, with the secretary of state entertaining us by telling jokes and juggling oranges and apples. And then I was summoned to his cabin to be a fourth at bridge, partnered with Bob McCloskey against Rogers and his wife. Rogers was an excellent bridge player, a serious but genial adversary — he didn't seem to mind when I blurted out at one point that he'd played out of turn. While the game went on, I was conscious that Bernie, Hank and Darius were wondering if I was learning anything about this sudden call home. Alas, not a clue. As Bernie wrote in a story datelined "Aboard Air Force 86971, over the Atlantic, May 7 —," the secretary of state "could only speculate along with other passengers on what was on Mr. Nixon's mind." His story also mentioned the bridge players, and of course I mailed it to my parents in New Castle.

The night after our return, Nixon announced intensified military moves against North Vietnam, including the mining of Haiphong Harbor.

Rogers was back in Bonn again in late May to brief NATO allies after the Moscow summit. A Washington contingent, including Mrs. Rogers, flew there ahead of him, and while waiting for the secretary to arrive I covered her activities, taking advantage of the opportunity to go with her on that Rhine River cruise that we'd missed on the aborted previous trip. Tough assignment that, gliding along the river looking at old castles on shore.

On that same trip, the press accompanied Rogers to Berlin for the signing of an agreement to reduce tensions in and around the divided city: the Final Protocol to the four-power Berlin Agreement. Time was limited at the ceremony in an unimposing and crowded room at the Allied Control Authority Building and I scribbled a story during the remarks by the four foreign ministers: France's Maurice Schumann, the Soviet Union's Andrei Gromyko, Britain's Sir Alec Douglas-Home, and Rogers — who pointedly noted "barriers which too long have divided this continent and this city."

After the ceremony, Rogers met with West Berlin's mayor, and then took a drive across communism's barrier into East Berlin. The press had not been told he was going to cross the Berlin Wall, and we had gone to the airport. Nobody in the official party would answer our questions about the secretary of state's whereabouts, not until he showed up and the plane took off. Charlie Bray, his spokesman, gave us the news. I phoned my office from the plane — a new experience, filing a story while airborne — and reported that Rogers was the first American secretary of state to cross the wall for a visit to the Eastern Sector of Berlin. My report, I learned when I got home, was not airworthy for shortwave radio, but at least VOA had the information for its next hourly newscast.

Later in 1972 I left the State Department beat to become deputy chief of the newsroom. But in January 1973 I pulled rank to be a correspondent again, briefly, so I could cover the signing of the Vietnam peace agreement, the result of four and a half years of negotiations in Paris, including secret negotiations held since early 1970 by Henry Kissinger and North Vietnam's Le Duc Tho.

Nixon announced the agreement January 23, a Tuesday night, after Kissinger returned to Washington from initialing it with Le Duc Tho earlier in the day. Friday morning Rogers flew off to Paris to sign it, accompanied by a batch of reporters. How great, I thought, to be able to witness the ending of the "ugly, uncertain war." But when we arrived, VOA's Paris correspondent John Bue told me the disappointing news: Space for the press was limited in the International Conference Center salon where Saturday's signing ceremonies would be held, and VOA had only one pass. There was no question in my mind about it; John had covered the negotiations all those years and was entitled to see the signing in person.

So I watched the ceremonies — there were two — on a television monitor in a press room at the conference center, the former Hotel Majestic. Actually, this was an advantage, as I had a telephone on my desk and was able to file instantly. "The four parties to the Paris talks on Vietnam now have formally committed themselves to ending the war," I reported after the first one. "The United States and South Vietnam signed English and Vietnamese copies of the agreement and protocols on one page, and North Vietnam and the Viet Cong signed them on another. The atmosphere was businesslike as the four foreign ministers wrote their names: America's William Rogers, South Vietnam's Tran Van Lam, North Vietnam's Nguyen Thuy Trinh, and the Viet Cong's Madame Nguyen Thi Binh. Mr. Rogers and Mr. Trinh will sign the agreement again in afternoon ceremonies, a procedure devised because South Vietnam and the Viet Cong do not recognize each other. . . ."

The ceasefire in Vietnam went into effect Saturday as Rogers was flying back to Washington. At the moment it began — we were over Atlantic City — we raised champagne glasses in a thankful toast. During the flight we were shown the U.S. copies of the documents, bound in handsome blue leather. "The secretary's signature, William P. Rogers, is in a flowing script," I reported. "Mr. Lam's is sort of scratchy, like most of our signatures when we have to write them so many times. Madame Binh left out her middle name in her signature, and North Vietnam's foreign minister signed his name simply Trinh."

On returning home I was asked to do a first person "mood piece," and wrote: "This war — America's longest and most difficult — did not end with jubilation and smiles of victory. The end was subdued, with the only sounds the turning of pages as the Paris Agreement on Ending the War and Restoring Peace in Vietnam was signed. The war was officially over. . . ." The piece ended with: "I'll always remember what kind of a day it was in Paris on January 27th, 1973. In the morning it was raining and it was gray, although not dreary. Then the rain stopped and the sun came out — weakly at first, gathering strength through the hours but never brilliant. It was nothing spectacular. The whole day was not spectacular. But it was peace at last. And certainly there were prayers that peace will last." Looking back I guess I was naive.

American troop strength in Vietnam had been reduced to 23,700 from its 1968 peak of 540,000 under Johnson. Two months after the signing of the agreement, the last American troops left

Vietnam. Two years later, on April 29, 1975, the last American civilians were evacuated from Saigon.

Covering the State Department was a plum assignment at VOA, since any foreign policy pronouncements or comments by the secretary of state and department spokesmen about other countries naturally are of interest to overseas listeners. Reports by the diplomatic correspondent are aired around the world, around the clock, and although they're directed to non–American audiences, they are also followed by Americans overseas. In visits to Brussels to cover NATO meetings, for instance, American reporters based in Europe told me they listened to my reports.

I liked and respected the diplomatic correspondents. Only one other woman was covering State on a full–time basis while I was there, Marie Koenig of USIA's press service, a very able and conscientious reporter. VOA and USIA outpaced the commercial broadcast media in advancing women. The male diplomatic reporters treated Marie and me as their equals; no discrimination against us because of our gender, or because we were employed by the government. I believe we were the first women voted into membership by the State Department Correspondents Association.

I also liked and respected Rogers, and when I left the State Department beat I sent him a note telling him about my new job at VOA. He wrote back: "While we will certainly miss you around the Department, I want you to know how pleased I am for you. This sounds like a challenging assignment and I wish you all success."

Bill Rogers was one of the most decent figures in public life that I covered. And a class act in forbearance. If he was upset over being shunted to a secondary role in making foreign policy, I never saw a hint of it. He left office at the end of August 1973, succeeded by Kissinger, and in a "remembrance" of him for VOA I wrote that he "gave the appearance of being unflappable" and "was always circumspect." Rogers had "the air of a person who feels that problems can be solved if people just sat down and tackled them sensibly. . . . He is human, a gentle man."

In my new job I was deputy to the News Division chief, Philip W. Carroll, a USIA Foreign Service officer. The staff at VOA was a mix of Civil Service employees and Foreign Service officers and some of the latter didn't understand news or broadcasting. But Phil Carroll did, and we developed projects to improve news gathering and news writing. Much of my work dealt with administrative and personnel issues which were, yes, challenging, but not my cup of tea.

Although I was a news executive, I felt removed from news and wanted to go back to reporting. When Phil Carroll left for an overseas post, I served temporarily as acting chief of the News Division until BHK, Bernie Kamenske, took over. A former AP staffer, Bernie was a strong defender of the newsroom's integrity and one of those rare individuals with the ability to interpret trends and deploy resources for developments that would require full-court coverage. He was, for example, one of the early ones who deduced the scope of Mao's Cultural Revolution in China.

With my duties as acting chief behind me, I was to become a national correspondent, reporting on stories of my choosing. But Bernie asked me to cover the White House instead, succeeding the respected W.B. Sprague. As a reporter, I couldn't have picked a better time to start on the White House beat: April 1974.

I stayed there 14 years and never got over the rush of emotion I felt in walking up the White House driveway to the West Wing to go to work, not so much because the White House is the seat of power, the center of news. I thought of my father — how glad I was that before he died he got to see his daughter covering the president, and I thought of my husband — he had been so supportive of me and always confident in my abilities.

I was prepared for the new assignment. In addition to everything learned in my previous jobs, I had continued to take private lessons in broadcasting techniques from a skilled instructor, Lillian Brown, who also did the makeup for television correspondents and a succession of presidents. She taught me not to be declamatory, had me record newspaper stories over and over, and would gently suggest places where I was "just a bit high-pitched" and should try again. She also taught me how to pace myself. At VOA, broadcasters speak at a slower pace than do those on American radio and television, so as to be understood more easily by listeners for whom English is a second language, and because of atmospherics in shortwave. I have Lillian to thank for those letters in which listeners referred to my voice in such terms as "golden" and "cool, calm and reassuring."

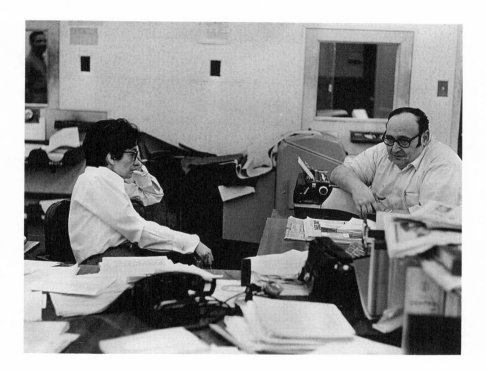

Seated near old teletype machines in VOA's basement newsroom in the early 1970s, Jurey and Bernie Kamenske review coverage. The newsroom later was moved to windowed space on the third floor of VOA's headquarters at 330 Independence Avenue S.W. in Washington.

3
Nixon and the Middle East
King Faisal Startles Reporters
The Washington Post March

I was riding on the "zoo plane" accompanying President Nixon on his way to the Middle East. Of course I was excited; this was my first White House trip abroad and it was a big story. He was making an unprecedented tour of four Arab countries and Israel — and furthermore at a time when the House of Representatives Judiciary Committee was holding hearings on whether to impeach him.

The June 1974 trip began a little over two months after my initiation as a White House correspondent in places like Bad Axe, Michigan, and Key Biscayne, Florida. In Bad Axe, I wasn't fast enough to claim a telephone in the press center and missed the chance to file a story. Fay Gillis Wells of Storer Broadcasting offered counsel: You have to be fleet of foot on White House trips; there are never enough telephones at the filing centers, and those who grab them first don't usually let loose of them. At the next stop, in Cass City, Michigan, I made a successful dash, captured a phone, and filed. On every trip since, I ran.

On Nixon's trips to Key Biscayne, hardly anyone in the press corps bothered to drive out to the airfield to see him arrive and leave because reporters knew he wouldn't say anything and there wouldn't be any news. But UPI's Helen Thomas and AP's Fran Lewine did, and they took me with them. You never miss an opportunity to see the president, they said. Correspondents need to see a president as often as they can to gauge his mood or the state of his health, and besides, something might happen.

Nixon was spending the Memorial Day weekend in Key Biscayne when reporters learned that he might make a trip to the Middle East in addition to his planned visit to the Soviet Union for another summit with Leonid Brezhnev. Secretary of State Kissinger was shuttling between Israel and Syria trying to negotiate a disengagement agreement in the aftermath of the October 1973 Arab–Israeli war. He'd successfully negotiated one between Israel and Egypt earlier in 1974. By May 31 the Israeli–Syrian agreement was signed, and on June 4 the White House announced Nixon would leave June 10 for visits to Egypt, Saudi Arabia, Syria, Israel and Jordan, stopping first in Salzburg, Austria.

In the scant time we had to prepare for the trip, I put together a file of material on the issues and countries, wrote scenesetters, packed an extra tape recorder and other equipment, and went shopping. A White House notice had advised the accredited traveling press (115 men/7 women): "Generally speaking, conservative clothing is appropriate in all the countries to be visited. In Saudi Arabia, women should take particular care to dress conservatively. Sleeveless dresses, pantsuits and short skirts are strongly discouraged."

Forewarned, I bought a cotton dress with long sleeves, buttons up to the neck, and a skirt that was long by the standards of the mini–skirts then in fashion. Connie Chung of CBS didn't have enough time to shop and was mini–skirted in Jidda. The Saudis didn't seem to mind. In my scenesetters, I reported to VOA listeners that the trip would "dramatize the improved relations between the United States and Arab nations." But to tell the whole story, I also reported that "critics of the president have said he should not be traveling abroad while the impeachment inquiry is going on" and that some had contended the trip "might be an attempt to divert attention from his domestic difficulties." Omitting these would have been remiss journalistically, shortchanging listeners. I gave the administration's case as well, quoting Vice President Ford as saying he preferred "to believe the president will make another breakthrough in the search for a new world order of compassion and cooperation."

Nixon left Washington on the morning of June 10, a Monday, after a departure statement in which he referred to his successful 1972 visits to China and the Soviet Union and called the Mideast trip "another journey for peace." The White House–chartered Pan

American "zoo plane" and TWA "writers' plane" were already airborne on the eight and a half hour flight to Salzburg.

When a president travels, the press flies ahead of him in order to be in place to cover his arrival at the airport. The zoo plane, always the first to arrive at the destination, carried television camera crews (with their cameras occupying some of the seats), network producers, radio technicians and still photographers, all of whom needed time to set up at the airport. It was so named because they were presumably less decorous than the reporters. Correspondents were aboard the writers' plane, but some who needed to file quickly to meet deadlines elected to take the zoo plane. I chose to do so; VOA has deadlines every hour, and I liked to be first, remembering the lesson learned in Bad Axe.

On both Boeing 707s, White House Press Office staffers distributed the detailed trip schedule, called "bible," and sometimes the advance text of the president's arrival remarks. The press corps traveled first–class, with the fare paid by our news organizations including an additional amount to cover the costs of press buses and filing centers.

A small press pool, composed of representatives of the various news media, traveled with the president aboard Air Force One, which Nixon called "The Spirit of '76." He was accompanied by Mrs. Nixon and an official party that included Secretary of State Kissinger, White House Chief of Staff Alexander M. Haig Jr., and Major General Brent Scowcroft, the deputy assistant for national security affairs.

Salzburg was in essence a rest stop, but any thought of rest vanished when word began sweeping through the press center that Kissinger was about to call a press conference. He did, and it was news. Visibly angry, he responded to "innuendoes" that he had given misleading testimony to the Senate Foreign Relations Committee about national security wiretaps in 1969, denied any "illegal or shady activity," called on the committee to review his testimony, and threatened to resign.

"I do not believe," he said, "that it is possible to conduct the foreign policy of the United States under these circumstances when the character and credibility of the secretary of state is at issue. And if it is not cleared up, I will resign." After filing a bulletin I wrote fuller reports with background details: The wiretaps involved "electronic eavesdropping on a number of people including members of his own staff when he was the president's national security advisor" and "were used to investigate leaks to the press." In Washington later that day the Foreign Relations Committee agreed unanimously to review Kissinger's testimony.

On presidential trips abroad domestic stories tag along. I was glad VOA's European correspondent David Lent was also covering the Salzburg stop. He filed stories on European matters covered in Nixon's talks with Austrian Chancellor Bruno Kreisky, while I concentrated on the Kissinger flurry and Mideast scenesetters.

The next morning the Nixon party, intact, left rainy Salzburg for Cairo, where leading Egyptian newspapers carried banner headlines over stories heralding the importance of the talks President Anwar Sadat would have with President Nixon. He was the first U.S. president to make an official visit to Egypt, and as noted in the English language *Egyptian Gazette*, the first to visit "since the late President Roosevelt visited Cairo during World War II in 1943 and then again in 1945 on his way back to Washington after attending the Yalta conference."

President and Mrs. Sadat were at the airport and after their greeting the two presidents got into an open limousine for the motorcade to Qubba Palace, where the Nixons would stay. "Throngs of arm–waving, chanting, smiling Egyptians lined the streets of Cairo to give President Nixon what is described as the greatest reception ever given here to a foreign leader," I reported on VOA. It was said to be the largest turnout since President Nasser's funeral in 1970. Press Secretary Ron Ziegler estimated the number at over two million.

An Egyptian ministry official said "I've never seen anything like it." Nor had I, riding on one of the press buses far back in the motorcade. Crowds of people, sometimes standing six and seven deep, lined almost every bit of the 12 kilometer route (7.2 miles; VOA used kilometers in its reporting). They chanted "Long Live

Nixon!" "Long Live Sadat!" and they carried signs, "Egypt Land of Peace Welcomes Nixon" and "God bless Nixon." Aboard my press bus, we discussed the likelihood that the welcomers included "rent-a-crowds," since we could see buses on sidestreets that obviously had brought them out, but we agreed the enthusiasm was genuine.

The White House "bible" estimated the drive to Qubba Palace at 20 minutes, but it took nearly an hour to get there. At the formal arrival ceremony at the palace, the two presidents spoke from a balcony as the afternoon sun beat down on the press standing below. Sadat said he was confident Nixon's visit would be "a milestone in the shaping and evolution of American–Egyptian relations. . . in a manner that I hope would compensate for the long years of strain and lack of understanding." U.S.-Egyptian relations were broken in the June 1967 Mideast war and were not resumed until early 1974.

The White House press included top print reporters like John Herbers of *The New York Times*, Carroll Kilpatrick of *The Washington Post*, Peter Lisagor of *The Chicago Daily News* and PBS's "Washington Week in Review," and television anchormen Walter Cronkite of CBS and John Chancellor of NBC. Chancellor was a friend, introduced to my husband and me by Pete and Mimi Kumpa, and my boss for two years when President Johnson persuaded him to be VOA's director. Chancellor brightened up VOA's programming and instituted a sprightly version of its "Yankee Doodle Dandy" theme. He has said ruefully that he will be remembered, however, as the director "who moved the VOA newsroom to the basement." The move gave the news staff more space but was not universally welcomed. The newsroom later was relocated to its present windowed quarters on the third floor.

The international contingent in the traveling press included Pierre Salinger, Kennedy's White House press secretary, who was covering the trip for the French journal *L'Express*, five correspondents from the Japanese news media, and a reporter for *The Iran Times*. Australian newspaper correspondent Roy McCartney, of *The Age* and *Sydney Herald*, carried a shortwave radio and tuned in

VOA at all our stops, recording its newscasts and playing them back so we could keep up with events outside our trip–constricted orbit.

In Cairo the Voice had a team of reporters covering the visit along with me: Beirut–based Don Burgess, Sam Hilmy of the Arabic service in Washington, Ibrahim Abdin, the Arabic service's Cairo reporter, and Munich–based Eugene Nikiforov who reported in Russian. We filed our stories from the Cairo Broadcasting Center, a short taxicab ride from the White House press center at the Nile Hilton — and a breathless hike when we couldn't get a cab and had to rush on foot to meet deadlines for two–way radio circuits that were booked in advance.

Filing was not easy and I was thankful for the expertise of Burgess and Abdin, old hands at dealing with the frustrations of delays and atmospheric problems in transmitting reports via two–ways. And I was grateful for the unfailing help of the network radio technicians, CBS's Norm Hannen, ABC's Bill Barry and NBC's Aldo Argentieri, in trying to establish airworthy circuits. The Voice did not send a radio engineer on presidential trips then — VOA's management was always citing budget problems — and I felt like a poor cousin for having to rely on the kindness of the network fellows. I resolved to make a pitch for assigning VOA techs to future trips abroad. Eventually management agreed, most of the time.

From Cairo, Sadat and Nixon traveled by train to Alexandria, preceded by a special press train. The ride through the fertile Nile Delta lived up to my colleague Don Burgess's billing: "Some of the most lush farmland in all of the world." Farmers working in the fields waved at us, and crowds were already gathered at railway stations and in villages waiting for the presidents' train. The two and a half hour ride was marvelously smooth. I wasn't the only one who thought the operators of America's deteriorating railroads could learn a thing or two from the Egyptians.

Aboard the presidential train, pool reporters had a question–and–answer session with Nixon and Sadat in their Victorian era car, built in 1900 in Britain. Nixon was asked what he thought of the car. He liked it, he said, "but what I like better is the roadbed because, as I told President Sadat, the roadbed between Cairo and Alexandria is infinitely better than the roadbed between Washington and New York. . . that is almost an obsolete roadbed. . . ." He added that when he got home he would "tell some of our people" that the railroads ought to improve it.

In Alexandria, the American president got another tremendous reception, surpassing the one in Cairo. Immense crowds, including many more women and children than there had been in Cairo, flowed from the sidewalks into the street and draped the seawall along the route from the train station to Ras–el–Tin palace where the Nixons would spend the night.

"An outpouring of affection and warmth," I reported. "This Mediterranean resort city has a population of two million and it seemed that almost all of them were lining the streets of the motorcade." An Egyptian official estimated the turnout for the entire day, including the train ride, at three and a half million people.

Alexandria was appealing, an ancient city and a popular summer resort, but there was no time to see anything but people and palm trees. At the press center we all had trouble filing but I did get through to VOA in Washington and at the same time to Burgess in Cairo on a noisy radio circuit and gave them information for the newscasts. Then I recorded a report in the quiet of an empty dining room, and gave the tape cassette to an NBC courier who was taking television film by helicopter to NBC's film room in Cairo. There Burgess would pick up my cassette. On presidential trips the television networks performed logistical feats, deploying large staffs and hiring transport to get pictures out for their news shows. While I was recording that report, a waiter came in, plopped himself in a chair at the table and stared at me. After I finished he told me he admired Americans and was familiar with VOA.

The press assembled in late afternoon to take our special train back to Cairo, leaving behind a pool that would cover the Nixons' dinner for the Sadats and their return to Cairo by helicopter the next morning. Curiously the ride to Cairo was unsmooth. As the

Huge crowds turned out for President Nixon's visit to Egypt during his unprecedented Middle East tour in June 1974. (Courtesy, Nixon Presidential Materials Staff, National Archives)

train rocked along, I tried to type a story but my Olivetti portable slid from my lap with every bump. Was the difference in roadbed linked to the presidents' return by helicopter instead of by train?

The next morning, the Sadats served as tour guides for the Nixons in a visit to the Pyramids under sunny skies. Before that, however, the White House issued the advance text of a statement, Principles of Relations and Cooperation Between Egypt and the United States, embargoed for release at 1 p.m. Cairo time (6 a.m. EDT), when the two presidents would sign it. It contained a section that said "the two governments will begin negotiation of an Agreement for Cooperation in the field of nuclear energy under agreed safeguards. Upon conclusion of such an agreement, the United States is prepared to sell nuclear reactors and fuel to Egypt, which will make it possible for Egypt by the early 1980s to generate substantial additional quantities of electric power to support its rapidly growing development needs."

This obviously was important and we reporters needed background details. But no briefing was held and, adding to the frustration, there wasn't time to track officials down because we had to file stories quickly and board press buses for the Pyramids.

There, the American helicopter carrying the two presidents and their wives landed on the Giza desert virtually at the foot of one of the Pyramids. In a sidebar feature I reported to VOA listeners that "those of us who had never seen these 5,000–year–old monuments, numbered among the seven wonders of the ancient world, just stood there and gazed at them. In turn Egyptians who are used to seeing the Pyramids were looking at the American president. And just about everybody took pictures." Shortly after we flew to Saudi Arabia.

At the arrival ceremony at Jidda airport King Faisal, dressed in a long dark robe fluttering about his ankles in a gentle breeze, welcomed Nixon, the first American president to visit Saudi Arabia, and then escorted the U.S. party to the main salon for Arabic coffee. The press waited in a lounge, with our Australian colleague playing his latest tape of a VOA newscast.

Nixon also got a warm welcome from applauding, cheering and whistling crowds as his motorcade traveled from the airport through the Saudi diplomatic capital to the royal guest house on the Red Sea. His visit, I reported to VOA listeners, came a week after the signing in Washington of a Saudi–U.S. agreement that provided for joint economic cooperation and security cooperation commissions. The agreement would help Saudi Arabia with technological know–how so that it "can best use its large income from oil production to further its economic development and industrialization. The accord is also viewed as an incentive to Saudi Arabia to increase its oil production to help meet international energy needs." An Arab ban on oil exports to the U.S. that was imposed during the October 1973 war lasted until March 1974.

The press was comfortably quartered at the Kandera Palace Hotel, where our filing center had only three international telephone lines. VOA, however, had arranged two–ways for Sam Hilmy and me at the Saudi Arabian Broadcasting building. It had a beautiful interior with thick golden–hued carpeting, but thin communications facilities. Sam spent hours there trying to establish contact with Washington while I returned to the hotel and finally got a broadcast–quality telephoned report out at 1 a.m. The Saudi men at the hotel and the broadcasting building were courteous to me and didn't show any sign of the anti–female bias we'd heard about. Maybe it was because they were fascinated by the White House press corps; maybe it was because they listened to VOA; maybe it was because of my age, 46 then.

The Saudi monarch and the president wrapped up their talks on a sweltering mid–June day at the king's Riasa Palace office. The press was outside in a courtyard, consuming gallons of lemonade as the temperature climbed and we wilted. King Faisal made up for it. When the two leaders came out and addressed us, the king praised Nixon effusively for trying to improve U.S.–Arab relations, then startled us out of our lethargy. "But what is very important," he said, "is that our friends in the United States of America be themselves wise enough to stand behind you, to rally around you, Mr. President, in your noble efforts, almost unprecedented in the history of mankind, the efforts aiming at securing peace and justice in the world."

Press jaws dropped and notebook pages filled. For the leader of a country to make such comments on the internal affairs of another was exceptional. King Faisal had not specifically referred to the scandal swirling around Nixon but as I wrote in reports for VOA that would be beamed back to Saudi Arabia and broadcast around the world, the Saudi leader was urging Americans to rally around the president "at a time when he is embattled at home because of Watergate and the impeachment inquiry." The king "made news by seeming to inject himself into the American domestic controversy."

In a side-note to that day, a pool report on the beginning of the Faisal–Nixon meeting said the president "looked a bit tired." Ziegler was asked about Nixon's physical condition later in the afternoon by the Air Force One pool on the flight from Jidda to Damascus and said, "I think he's holding up quite well." We didn't know it then, but the president was suffering from phlebitis, the inflammation of a vein in his left leg, throughout the Middle East tour.

President Hafez al Assad, Syria's ruler since 1971, was at the Damascus airport to greet President Nixon and together they rode in a motorcade to the Government Guest House through streets where American flags were flying for the first time since the June 1967 war. Syria had been one of the most scathing critics of U.S. policies, which made the sight of the U.S. flags waving in the breeze that day in Damascus so extraordinary, and splendid. The crowds along the motorcade route were friendly, with the turnout estimated by a Syrian official at between 350,000 and 400,000, not bad for a city with a population then of 1.2 million.

VOA's Beirut bureau chief, Dave Roberts, preceded the Nixon entourage to Damascus and reported the city had undergone a face-lifting operation in the past three days, including installation of a fountain illuminated by red, white and blue lights. Dave and Arabic reporter Fawzi Tadros, also from the Beirut bureau, met me in the cramped press filing center at the Semiramis Hotel, and we reviewed the "bible" to plan our coverage. A group of us listened to a VOA newscast, and it was pleasing to hear other reporters compliment our newscasts and Watergate coverage.

That night Assad and his wife gave a state dinner in honor of the Nixons at the fashionable Orient Club. In an exchange of toasts, the Syrian leader said that if there is to be lasting peace in the Middle East, Israeli occupation must be ended and the "legitimate national rights" of the Palestinians ensured, the same points made by the Egyptian and Saudi leaders. Nixon replied that finding a permanent and equitable peace would have to be a step-by-step, case-by-case process. He also announced re-establishment of cultural exchanges between the United States and Syria.

Nixon began his toast by noting that President Assad had told him "a Syrian saying to the effect that the guest's respect and admiration for his host is directly measured by the amount of food the guest consumes at the host's dinner." To appreciative laughter, he added: "I can now see why Henry Kissinger gained seven pounds in his 13 trips to Damascus in the last 30 days."

State dinners were covered by pools representing the entire traveling press, and those not in pools listened to the toasts piped into the filing center by the White House Communications Agency. Broadcast reporters and technicians recorded the speeches by plugging cords from tape recorders into the "mult box," a device with multiple outlets. The toasts invariably came late at night, and Damascus was no exception.

My post-midnight dinner was an enjoyable get-together with other correspondents around a sidewalk table at an accommodating and very good restaurant. We all expected, and reported, that the U.S. and Syria would shortly be announcing resumption of diplomatic relations. The announcement by the two presidents was made the next day, Sunday June 16, a couple of hours before Nixon boarded his plane for the half-hour flight to Israel.

At Ben Gurion Airport, President Ephraim Katzir welcomed the U.S. party "with a very warm Shalom" and said "blessed are you who come in the name of peace." Nixon was the first U.S. president to visit Israel, but had been there in 1966 and at the end of the June 1967 war and was regarded as a friend. The crowds that

turned out along the 31-mile motorcade route to Jerusalem —
through landscape ranging from rugged terrain to neat farms —
were friendly, and estimated at between 150,000 and 200,000.

In Jerusalem the Nixons stayed at the King David Hotel, where
the president immediately went into talks with Prime Minister
Yitzhak Rabin, a former ambassador to Washington. The press
stayed at the Kings Hotel, where the filing center on the lobby
level was accessible to curious Israelis who walked in freely to
observe us at work. One couple came up to Dan Rather, seated at
a worktable just behind me, and said, "Oh, Mr. Kalb, it's such a
pleasure to meet you." Dan thanked them with good grace, never
letting on that he wasn't Marvin Kalb, the CBS diplomatic
correspondent who'd been in Israel many times covering Kissinger's
shuttle diplomacy.

Israeli officials were concerned about the news that the United
States was prepared to sell nuclear reactors and fuel to Egypt, and
Kissinger quickly met with them to give assurances that such aid
would be limited to peaceful purposes. And in the evening at a state
dinner, as I reported on VOA, Nixon "assured Israel's leaders that
the fact that the United States is seeking better relations with some
of its neighbors does not mean its friendship and support for Israel
is any less."

The traveling press was awakened the next morning before 6 by
telephone calls from White House press office staffers notifying us
that Kissinger would hold a briefing at 8 a.m. A story in *The
Jerusalem Post* provided the reason. It reported that a joint
communique to be issued later in the day was expected "to
announce an American undertaking to supply Israel too with a
nuclear power station and the enriched uranium required to fuel
it." Kissinger's briefing remarks were guarded but pointed us in the
right direction, and as I reported for VOA, he "indicated that the
United States is prepared to provide nuclear energy assistance to
Israel." Within a few hours Nixon and Rabin announced their
governments would negotiate a nuclear energy cooperation
agreement. Their joint statement also devoted considerable

attention to peace in the Middle East. But it was the nuclear issue that dominated the Jerusalem stop.

VOA's regular Jerusalem stringer, the respected Charles Weiss, who later became a full-time correspondent for us, was in the hospital at the time of Nixon's visit, but his wife Harriet was an enormous help. Numerous times, day and night, she drove the VOA team back and forth between the press center and the Weiss home so we could use Charlie's excellent filing facilities to feed our reports to Washington. His broadcast "studio" was in the kitchen, and Harriet energized us with her strong coffee and keen insights.

From Israel we flew to Jordan, our final stop in the Middle East. At the Amman airport, a Jordanian military band entertained the press waiting for the president's arrival. As Air Force One touched down, the band ironically was playing a spirited rendition of John Philip Sousa's "The Washington Post March." It's a great march, a favorite of military bands, and the Jordanians undoubtedly were unaware that *The Washington Post* was a detested name at the Nixon White House because of its Watergate coverage.

After the airport welcome — a dashing affair with smartly stepping soldiers, bouncy band music, and swooping jets flying in formation overhead — King Hussein and his wife, then Queen Alia, and the president and Mrs. Nixon rode in a motorcade through Amman. In describing the crowds along the route, the travel poolers said "it probably would not be exaggerating to say that from 80,000 to 100,000 turned out." A Jordanian security official, unconcerned about exaggerating, put the estimate at 200,000.

Street banners were in abundance, with messages like "Jordan Salutes President Nixon and the American People," "Watany Sporting Club Welcomes President Nixon," "Arab Bank Welcomes President Nixon," and so on. When the motorcade reached the guesthouse for the Nixons, a mountaintop villa 15 miles outside of Amman, a military ceremony was held, and at one point the band played "The Washington Post March."

The press stayed at the Grand Palace Hotel, where Dave Roberts, Fawzi Tadros, Sam Hilmy and I teamed up again. Seated in the spacious lobby's comfortable lounge chairs and sipping soft drinks, we reviewed the schedule for the evening, when King Hussein, Jordan's head of state since 1952, would host a dinner for the Nixons. Nixon and Hussein had known each other since 1959, when Nixon was vice president and the king, then only 23, visited Washington at President Eisenhower's invitation. The Nixon trip to Jordan was the first by an American president.

In my thoughts the king was "Mr. King" as I recalled my husband's interview with him in Amman just after the 1967 war. Jack and cameraman Leo Pitts were among the first newsmen, if not the first, to arrive in the Jordanian capital once the airport runways were repaired. The half–hour TV film, "Conversation With A King," won an Emmy award, but beyond that, it was special to me because my egalitarian husband said he was worried throughout the interview that he would inadvertently address Hussein as "Mr. King." So the thought of "Mr. King" accompanied me to Amman. And the suitcases I took with me were the same gray tweed canvas bags that I'd bought for Jack for his trip seven years earlier.

The highlight of our stay in Amman was a superb performance of "Beating the Retreat" by the Jordan Armed Forces Band in honor of the Nixons. The some 225 band members marched in precision, with a difficult heel–toe–step, and played slow and quick marches and selections ranging from Jordanian and Bedouin folk songs to Scottish and American tunes — among the latter, "Yankee Doodle" and yes, "The Washington Post March."

The performance was a rousing finale to the Amman visit and the Mideast tour. At the airport, Nixon said "This is the last stop on a very long trip, but it is only the beginning of a much longer journey" toward the goal of "a just and lasting peace. . . ." Hussein called Nixon "one of the greatest men of our time."

As Air Force One flew to the Azores for a rest stop at Lajes Air Force Base, leased by Portugal for American use, Press Secretary Ziegler summed up the trip for the pool reporters who were aboard. Based on what he told them, one of my VOA stories filed from Lajes that night reported: "President Nixon believes his journey has strengthened relations between the United States and the nations of the Middle East, and that it has established a framework in which negotiations for peace in the area may go forward." In another story I reported Ziegler's response when asked what effect the Mideast trip would have on Watergate: "The American people have to be the judges."

Ziegler also told the pool that at the end of the 14,775-mile trip, Nixon "will have traveled 137,500 miles on foreign trips, making him the most widely traveled president." The record was broken by President George Bush in 1991.

The next morning Nixon met with Portugal's President Antonio Spinola and then headed home to resume preparations for his trip the following week to Brussels for a NATO summit and to Moscow for his summit with Soviet leaders. Six days after returning to Washington, I was on the zoo plane again.

The 1974 Mideast trip was exhausting, particularly for the Press Office secretaries who worked far into the night typing and mimeographing transcripts and other handouts, and pool reports. These pool reports are indispensable, for the large press corps traveling with a president doesn't get to cover all the events on his schedule, mostly because of limited space. The pools are the eyes and ears for the rest of the press, supplying descriptions, quotes and background essential for comprehensive stories reflecting the dynamics of an event. Serving on a pool gives a reporter a chance to see the president and other leaders up close. I resolved to try to get VOA included in pools in the future.

The Mideast and Soviet trips were, as I reported to a VOA staff meeting, "a reminder that we do have listeners — real, live people who know us, know our names and know what we do, and depend on us for news." Les Janka of Kissinger's staff told a colleague of mine a story that was illustrative of VOA's listenership. He said he talked to more "locals" on the Mideast trip than in previous visits to the area because he mentioned to them that he was "a friend of Mrs. Jurey with VOA, and that opened doors."

Nixon's motivations for going to the Middle East were questioned in light of Watergate but I believed then and now that his opening to the Arab countries was an initiative well worth taking. It was the undergirding for future efforts to negotiate peace in the region.

The Mideast tour demonstrated that Nixon was seen overseas as a statesman. But he was in trouble at home — a fact that VOA didn't gloss over, to the credit of the U.S. government's overseas radio. When the trip was over, I reported that the president "returned to plaudits in Washington for his successful tour, but he also returned to his Watergate difficulties — with yet another former aide sentenced to jail."

4
With Nixon in the Soviet Union
Pulling the Plug on the White Line
The Velvet Season

Nixon's trip to the Soviet Union was what he called "another journey for peace." It was a story of superpower summitry, and more. The rhetoric of detente and the reality of Soviet dissidents and Soviet censorship. The depressing atmosphere of Moscow and the delightful ambience of Yalta. And again the view of Nixon abroad contrasted with the view of him at home. The baggage of Watergate went along on the trip.

He flew first to Brussels to confer with other leaders of NATO countries. Aboard Air Force One, "a high White House official" acknowledged to pool reporters that Watergate posed problems. Speaking on background, he argued that "history would never forgive" Nixon if he halted his foreign policy efforts. The Moscow summit "had to be held. If we did not go to the summit we would be saying we are not a functioning government." The official was Kissinger, identified later by *Newsweek*. In Brussels, well–wishers shouted "Welcome Nixon" as he took a walk from the U.S. Embassy to the Royal Palace two blocks away. In Washington the same day the House Judiciary Committee announced it would make public the record of its impeachment inquiry. That night at a briefing for the traveling press, Kissinger was asked if Nixon would be inhibited in the Moscow summit negotiations in light of the committee's action.

My report for VOA reflected the tenor of the questions and his replies: "Some critics of the president's trip to the Soviet Union contend he will be in a weakened position because of Watergate, and others have advanced the theory that he would take a hard line in bargaining in order to hold on to conservative support. Dr. Kissinger told newsmen presidential decisions at the summit will not be on the basis of domestic necessity but on the basis of judgments as to national interest."

VOA's Mark Hopkins, meanwhile, was reporting from Moscow that "the Soviet press, reflecting official opinions, is welcoming the forthcoming talks as another major step in Soviet–American detente." He added, "There is virtually no press reporting of Watergate here," and said "Soviet opinion is being concentrated on pursuing better relations with the United States."

The pursuit of better relations was not evident, however, when the White House press planes arrived at Moscow's Vnukovo–Two airport on the afternoon of June 27. The network radio correspondents and I were to share broadcast booths set up in an airport building so we could cover Nixon's arrival and we were supposed to be given Soviet press credentials on landing. But there were no credentials, and Soviet security men would not let us through a chain–link fence to the building.

These fellows were not people one would want to tangle with. It made no difference to them that we were accredited by the White House and that arrangements had been made for broadcasting the arrival. Andy Falkievicz of USIA, who was on detail to the White House, saw our standoff and came to the rescue. He somehow convinced them we had permission, and pulled a few of us through a gate in the fence. I ran across to the building, found the booth marked VOA and CBS, and stationed myself at a microphone, breathless but in place in time.

Nixon's visit was for his third summit with Soviet leaders. In 1972 in Moscow the first strategic arms limitation agreement, SALT I, was signed, and in 1973 Leonid Brezhnev visited the U.S. Brezhnev was at the airport to welcome him and Mrs. Nixon, along with Premier Alexei Kosygin and President Nikolai Podgorny. The collective leadership continued to be on display during the summit, though Brezhnev clearly was the main man.

At the Intourist Hotel, the headquarters for the White House press (142 men/11 women), I joined Mark Hopkins in the filing center. A Soviet affairs scholar who understood Russian and a former *Milwaukee Journal* reporter, Mark followed Soviet developments from VOA's bureau in Munich. VOA did not have a resident correspondent in Moscow until 1989, after the Soviets finally agreed to let us open a bureau.

Filing reports from the Soviet Union was far easier than filing from the Middle East because there had been time to set up a "white line." This was the name given a special broadcast line via satellite leased by news organizations that were members of the U.S. Radio Pool. The radio pool, not to be confused with White House coverage pools, used the white line to transmit speeches, press conferences and correspondent reports to home offices in New York and Washington. Pool members — for this trip ABC, CBS, NBC and VOA — shared the costs of the line and other pool facilities. The networks took turns running the white line and for the Soviet trip it was ABC's turn, with the efficient Joe Keating in charge. Soviet technicians, with Russian interpreters, were assigned to work with ABC's pool technician, Doug Allmond. Doug quickly became a buddy of the Soviet techs by accepting an invitation to drink vodka with them.

The radio pool was set up outdoors on the third floor terrace of the hotel, and we filed our reports in pleasant, breezy weather. Each pool member had a work area with a closed circuit television monitor for viewing summit ceremonies and two "unilateral" telephone lines, for use in discussing coverage with home offices and as a backup for filing reports in case the white line was occupied with feeding other material or was down.

At a banquet on the first night of the visit, Nixon and Brezhnev predicted progress would be made at the summit. Brezhnev used the occasion to scold those "who favor whipping up the arms race and returning to the methods and procedures of the cold war," which I reported was "an obvious reference to American critics of the strategic arms limitation negotiations." Nixon said the agreements negotiated in the previous summits were possible because of a "personal relationship" between himself and Brezhnev.

A translation of Nixon's remarks by the Soviet news agency Tass got considerable attention the next day because Tass used the word "mutual" instead of "personal." As Mark reported, this led to "widespread speculation that the Soviets were trying to disassociate themselves from a personal relationship with the president under investigation for Watergate." At a joint press conference with White House Press Secretary Ziegler, the Soviet government spokesman, Tass Director General Leonid Zamyatin, denied any political significance and called the wording in the Russian text simply a matter of translation. Both he and Ziegler emphasized the "personal" relationship between the two leaders. Their joint briefings throughout the summit came to be known as The Ziggy and Zaggy Show.

The flap over the Tass translation was part of a long day that began in the early morning hours with an insistent tapping on the door of my Intourist room. I opened it a crack. A woman stood there, middle-aged, in undistinguished dark clothing, with both hands grasping a large valise-like handbag. "You are the VOA correspondent?" With my cautious "Yes," the woman began to speak rapidly, a flood of Russian. Perhaps she thought I understood her — my reports were translated and broadcast in Russian — but I knew not a word. "I have a VOA colleague who knows Russian," I said, "maybe I can call him." She raised her hand and pointed up. She must have known Mark Hopkins had a room on a floor above mine. "Maybe the lady down the hall can help," I said, referring to the woman who collected and gave out the keys to rooms and kept an eye on the comings and goings of the occupants. At that, my visitor vanished. I phoned Mark, we met at the filing center, and he told me the woman had shown up at his room and given him a handwritten letter addressed to President Nixon.

Mark phoned Mike Hoffman, a member of the team of USIA, White House and Embassy staffers who coordinated arrangements for press coverage during the visit. Mike joined us and reviewed the letter, a rambling narrative that seemed to be a plea for help, though it wasn't clear exactly what the writer was asking. He told us the letter might be an attempt to compromise us, and that we, because we worked for VOA, were probably the most vulnerable members of the press corps. He took the letter to pass on to the U.S. consular staff. We didn't see the woman again and heard nothing more about the letter.

Could it have been a legitimate plea for help? Did she know our names because she'd heard our broadcasts, and did she think VOA's White House correspondent could deliver the letter personally to the president? On the other hand, how did she find our rooms and get by all the Soviet security people in the hotel, to say nothing of the vigilant lady collector of keys? The idea of American reporters being vulnerable to a Soviet trap didn't seem farfetched, given the atmosphere of suspicion in U.S.-Soviet relations.

In any case, the encounter was merely puzzling, and I concentrated on the summit, after what was a memorable breakfast at the Intourist: an assortment of canned green peas, cold cuts, hardboiled eggs, pickles, tinny tomato juice and thick coffee strong enough to dissuade a second gulp. Meals were uniformly unsatisfying at the Intourist. The bar set up at the hotel for the visiting press was another matter. It was clearly a place where Soviets could try to propagandize and pick the brains of American reporters, but it provided welcome nourishment when a Russian bartender, with some coaching and in the spirit of detente, learned how to make martinis.

For Nixon the day's events began with a ceremony at the Tomb of the Unknown Soldier where he laid a wreath, paying homage to the more than 20 million Soviet soldiers and civilians who died in World War II. Before returning to the Kremlin, Nixon's motorcade stopped in front of the Museum of History and he stepped out of his limousine to walk over to greet several hundred spectators. There were shouts of "Peace, Peace," "Come back again," and "We don't want another war."

The summit's morning session was held at the Kremlin's St. Catherine's Hall, "an ornate room about 25 yards long and 15 yards wide," the pool reported. While it was going on, I went with Mark to the Gum Department Store; he wanted to buy a swimsuit to take to Yalta, the next stop. The visit to the imposing old bazaar-like building, with its three tiers of shopping stalls and stone steps grooved through the years by millions of footsteps, provided a grim slice of Moscow life. The sight of unsmiling Moscow citizens standing in long lines was depressing. Making a purchase

there was nothing to smile about. After finding our way to the
counter with bathing suits, we stood in line to select one, went to
the cashier, stood in another to pay for it, then returned to the
counter and waited in line again to pick up Mark's purchase.

That night the Nixons attended a performance at the Bolshoi
Theater, seated in a box with the Brezhnevs, Kosygin and
Podgorny. The American press corps was invited and I filed a
feature story for VOA: "President Nixon applauded enthusiastically
throughout the performance but especially when a costumed chorus
of Russian singers sang an American folksong in both Russian and
English. It was Old Folks At Home. . . a southern Negro spiritual
that starts out with the words, way down upon the Swanee River."
The spectacular show included a solo by the prima ballerina Maya
Plisetskaya, a foot–stomping dance by a Georgian group, and for
the finale, a Russian dance "with twirling, intricately frantic steps
and knee bending, and some sliding about on the knees."

In addition to filing broadcast pieces on summit events, Mark
and I reported on other Soviet developments during the day,
notably plans by Soviet nuclear physicist Andrei Sakharov for a
hunger strike on behalf of political prisoners, and an international
conference in Moscow, attended by representatives of 60 American
firms, on developing trade and technical cooperation.

On Saturday, Nixon and Brezhnev signed a trade agreement and
a White House fact sheet restated his administration's commitment
to seek authority from Congress for non–discriminatory "Most
Favored Nation" trade treatment for the Soviet Union. As we
reported on VOA, U.S. law–makers strongly opposed granting
MFN until the Soviet government relaxed its emigration policies
and allowed Soviet Jews and others to leave.

In early afternoon Nixon and Brezhnev left rainy Moscow
aboard an Ilyushin–62 for a weekend at the Soviet leader's dacha
complex near Yalta. On arrival at the Crimea's main airport at
Simferopol, they were greeted by sunny, breezy weather,
communist party and Ukrainian officials, and a crowd waving small
paper American and Soviet flags. From there, it was an hour and
a half drive to Yalta through beautiful countryside. Brezhnev had

told Nixon that "on the Black Sea shores hundreds of thousands and even millions of our country's workers, farmers and office employees annually spend their vacations at health resorts. I do hope you like it. We love it." I could see why.

Everything about Yalta was pleasing, the stunning setting, the relaxed tempo, the friendly people, the hotel's amenities, the press accommodations. Most of the press were housed in the seafront Oreanda Hotel, a white–columned, white–balconied structure with old world ambience, high ceilings, parqueted floors and oriental rugs, and a sweeping staircase to the floor where the spacious press filing center was located. Our comfortable rooms even had vases of tea roses. What a contrast to our antiseptic cell-like rooms in Moscow. And I didn't go hungry in Yalta. The Oreanda served excellent Ukrainian, Russian and European dishes.

The pace of our work was leisurely and we spent a lot of time waiting for The Ziggy and Zaggy Show. One afternoon I waited with diplomatic correspondents Marvin Kalb, Darius Zhabvala, the AP's Barry Schweid and others at a table on the sun–lit veranda of the hotel. We decided to pass the time away by ordering dishes of ice cream with fresh cherries on top. I thought it was the best ice cream I'd ever eaten. The beverages sold at the Oreanda included something new to the Soviets, tall bottles of Pepsi-Cola, the labels in Cyrillic characters. The Soviet-bottled Pepsis, an example of the increased business contacts between the U.S. and the Soviet Union, tasted just about the same as the Pepsis at home. We also found copies of *The New York Times*. The Sunday edition, as recorded in my expense account, cost $4 U.S.

While Nixon and Brezhnev were conferring in seclusion on Sunday, Mark and I interviewed vacationers at the beach. They said they hoped for peace and a successful summit. Some were VOA listeners; all were friendly. Before the two leaders began their meeting they took a walk along the seaside in what was frankly a photo op that began at the dacha complex on a cliff overlooking the sea. There they exchanged chit–chat through an interpreter and, as the "dacha pool" reported, Brezhnev said: "The only thing that can spoil the air here is a lot of ships passing by, smoke from the ships. But this is a typical summer day. . . . We call it the Velvet Season, soft, mild, like velvet."

In late afternoon Nixon and Brezhnev took a cruise on a yacht of the USSR's Black Sea Naval Fleet, followed by a "boat pool." The poolers reported passing by the site of the Big Three Yalta Conference, Livadiya Palace, which was not far from Brezhnev's dacha. Yalta of course was a familiar name because of the conference Roosevelt, Churchill and Stalin held there in 1945. Now it was a real place to me, one that I loved seeing. I was sorry our Velvet Season visit was coming to an end.

In our last white line feed of the night I gave my office the schedule for the next day as listed in the trip "bible." The offices of other pool members welcomed these advisories and on future presidential trips the pool producer would alert each of them to listen to "Jurey reading the scriptures."

Nixon flew Monday morning to the industrial city of Minsk, the capital of what was then the Byelorussian Republic (Belarus as of 1991). Brezhnev saw him off at Simferopol airport and returned to Moscow, accompanied by Kissinger and Gromyko. Nixon's visit took place as the city of one million people was celebrating the 30th anniversary of its liberation from the Germans in World War II. Crimson banners were stretched across streets, crimson flags and bunting decorated buildings, and there were large signs emblazoned with "1944–74." The city's pride in its recovery from the war's devastation was underlined in packets of literature that local officials distributed to us in the press filing center.

During his brief stay Nixon went to Victory Square in the center of Minsk to lay a wreath at the foot of the monument in memory of the war dead. Such ceremonies are pro forma affairs but I was moved by the sight and sound of a Soviet band playing the U.S. National Anthem. Several thousand people were waiting at the square to see the president and after the ceremony he "walked along the perimeter of the crowd, shaking hands and chatting in American campaign style," I reported. "People applauded and reached out to shake his hand. . . ."

Elsewhere in Minsk, a group of 13 Jews was in the fifth day of a hunger strike to dramatize an appeal they had sent to Nixon for his help in easing emigration of Soviet Jews. They didn't know if their message had reached the president. Mark filed a report for VOA, noting that "all 13 have applied for emigration to Israel, some as long as three years ago, and all have been rejected."

Nixon returned to Moscow that night aboard an Ilyushin–62 that the press dubbed Soviet One. The press corps also flew on Ilyushin–62s within the Soviet Union. These had nothing comparable to the luxury of the White House press planes. We were wedged into rows of narrow seats, our overnight bags stowed at our feet and equipment bags and typewriters on our laps. On one flight my plane had an engine flame–out and made a jolting, sickening drop. I thought we'd had it, but in seconds the plane steadied. No one was hurt; we were packed too tightly to be thrown about. Aeroflot stewards hastily passed around trays with little glasses of vodka, and we gulped down the restorative liquid.

While we waited Tuesday for the summit talks to resume, a press pool escorted by Ziegler toured the Nixons' seven–room Kremlin apartment, and reported word from the president's valet, Manolo Sanchez, that "the Russians kept a doctor in the kitchen" to taste the food prepared for the Nixons by a Russian chef. The pool report also described the various rooms visited, the crystal chandeliers, etc. The most meaningful description was of the bathroom, "as big as your typical Intourist Hotel room."

That night Nixon gave a televised speech to the Soviet people in which he referred to the evolution in U.S.–Soviet relations from confrontation to negotiation and said, "Now we are learning cooperation." Nixon had spoken on Soviet television at the 1972 summit, and Brezhnev on American network TV at the 1973 summit. In toasts at a dinner on the night of Nixon's speech, both he and Brezhnev referred to their plans for a fourth summit, to be held in 1975 in the United States. The dinner was given by the Nixons in honor of the Soviet leadership at Spaso House, the official residence of American ambassadors to Moscow since diplomatic relations were inaugurated in 1933.

At the Intourist press center, radio correspondents were preparing to file stories when the Soviet technicians — Doug Allmond's buddies up to then — "pulled the plug" on the white line, breaking the connection to the U.S. We were told the technicians went on strike because "they didn't like what was being reported." This was an obvious reference to American coverage of Soviet dissidents and we automatically assumed it was not the technicians but the Soviet government that didn't like it. Mark Hopkins and I immediately placed calls to VOA's Washington newsroom on our "unilateral" telephones. While I alerted the editors, he got through to the news operations studio which records correspondent reports, hooked up a tape recorder to the phone, and filed a story. VOA correspondents routinely write the news anchor's introduction to their reports, and Mark's "intro" was eloquently matter of fact: "Soviet authorities imposed a communications censorship on American broadcast correspondents Tuesday night just hours after President Nixon and General Secretary Brezhnev had expressed satisfaction with closer relations resulting from their third summit meeting."

As Mark reported, "U.S. communications technicians were told earlier Tuesday that their Soviet counterparts might strike because of alleged anti-Soviet broadcasts by the American networks — NBC, CBS and ABC." This warning was delivered when the Soviets learned that NBC had a newsfilm on Sakharov and the other networks were planning TV reports on dissidents. When the TV correspondents tried to transmit their material from the Soviet television center, a news blackout was imposed. They tried to report the blackout and were cut off again. Then radio correspondents at the Intourist tried to file and the white line was shut down.

The censorship was curious because VOA and others had had no problem earlier in reporting Sakharov's hunger strike to protest Soviet political repression. The next day, the last day of the summit, a Soviet official said the blackout at the TV center was ordered "by a low-level executive who had no understanding of the political consequences," and a spokesman for the Soviet State Committee for Radio and Television apologized.

There was no further interference and the white line operated without interruption as we filed stories on the summit agreements and communique. "The two leaders," I reported, "agreed to limit anti–ballistic missile systems in each country, to restrict underground nuclear tests and to explore negotiation of a pact to prevent environmental warfare. They did not work out a permanent comprehensive agreement on limiting strategic offensive weapons. That was not expected at this summit."

I always found it difficult to translate arms control agreements into language that would be understandable to radio listeners, and to provide background without being too wordy. I didn't always succeed, particularly when writing the story in a hurry. In reporting the agreement limiting anti–ballistic missile systems, I explained that it was a protocol to the 1972 ABM treaty which allowed the two countries to maintain two sites each for ABM launchers. The U.S. had chosen for its first site the defense of an intercontinental ballistic missile field, and the Soviets had chosen defense of Moscow. At this summit they decided to maintain only one site each, and stuck with their first choices.

In reporting on communiques, correspondents have to read between the lines, and this was the case in the section dealing with the 35–nation Conference on Security and Cooperation in Europe, CSCE. The Soviets were pressing for a European summit meeting as a finale to the Conference's work, but the U.S. and West Europeans were holding out for concrete proposals, especially on the free flow of information, people and ideas. The communique said both the U.S. and Soviet Union assumed that results of the CSCE on political, economic and social relations would justify holding a summit. As Mark pointed out in his VOA report, this was not an absolute American commitment to a summit, and the wording reflected the West's demands for "something more than generalities." The European summit didn't take place until 13 months later.

We were briefed on the Moscow summit documents by Henry Kissinger, and his detailed explanation of MIRVs and other issues was another of his virtuoso performances before the press. He was in a good mood, frequently responding to questions with a joke. Kissinger had many fans in the press who recognized his ego and craftiness but admired his intellect and enjoyed his sense of humor. I wasn't a fan, remembering, perhaps unfairly, how he'd eclipsed Secretary of State Rogers, but I did appreciate the meatiness of his press conferences.

The final summit event was a reception given by the Presidium of the Supreme Soviet in honor of the president. The traveling press was invited, but many of us couldn't go because we were still working on stories, trying to file as much as possible before leaving for the flight home. As I wrote, I glanced up from time to time at the closed circuit television monitor to view the reception in the elegant St. George Hall of the Grand Kremlin Palace and wished I could have gone. Reporters who did attend gave favorable reviews of the affair, and the sturgeon and caviar. Nixon left Moscow in late afternoon for the nine-hour flight to Loring Air Force Base in Caribou, Maine, where he made a televised planeside address on the summit before flying on to Florida for a weekend rest at his home in Key Biscayne. He said both sides had committed themselves to making the process of improving U.S.–Soviet relations irreversible.

During the Air Force One flight, Chief of Staff Haig was asked by pool reporters whether Watergate affected the negotiations. His answer, they said, was in effect that he found U.S. problems are "not viewed the same abroad as they are in the U.S." He was stating the obvious. In both the Soviet Union and Middle East, I could see that people didn't understand Watergate and wondered why Americans should be so concerned about it

The 1974 superpower summit was, I thought, worthwhile in terms of continuing detente. I was pleased with our coverage, which benefited from Hopkins's extensive knowledge of Soviet dissidents and Soviet policies. As a reporter, and personally, I valued the experience of visiting the Soviet Union and being exposed to the dismal texture of Moscow under the communist system.

On the TWA press plane flying home a spontaneous cheer went up when the pilot announced we were crossing the border out of Soviet territory. We'd had enough of the authoritarian ways of the security men who had hassled the press and the White House staffers escorting us. One of the staffers, Eric Rosenberger, was a hero of the press corps for literally forcing his way past guards to get the press to its destination.

Twelve years after the Nixon trip I was reminded of Mike Hoffman's caution about the vulnerability of American reporters, when Nicholas Daniloff, the Moscow correspondent for *U.S. News & World Report*, was entrapped and arrested by the K.G.B. on charges of spying. I knew that Nick, a friend since the time we both covered the State Department, was just a reporter, a good one, not a spy. Nick was jailed for two weeks in Lefortovo Prison, then released to the custody of the American ambassador, and finally allowed to return to the U.S. in an exchange that preceded the 1986 Reagan–Gorbachev summit in Iceland. Entrapment was not just a remote possibility; it was a reality. Yet I continued to wonder if the woman who appeared at my Intourist door came to me because she thought the VOA White House correspondent could help her.

From the mail VOA broadcasters received, I found that our listeners developed an attachment to us. Radio is such an intimate medium that those who hear a familiar voice tend to think of the broadcaster as a friend. One of the most touching letters I received was from the Soviet Union in 1987. It was sent by a family in Sochi and said: "Greetings dear Flamina. Our family invites you for the birthday of our daughter, whom we named in honor of you, Flamina. On the 10th of December she will be 10 years old and we would like you to be present at our celebration. And I think this friendship with you will make still stronger the peace between our countries. For today children of the entire world are a symbol of peace."

The letter was translated by Fred Pope, the audience relations officer for our Russian service, who also translated my reply. I said

I was deeply moved by the invitation and their naming their daughter after me, and explained I couldn't attend the celebration because I had to cover the Reagan–Gorbachev summit in Washington. For a birthday present, I enclosed some notecards with reproductions of paintings by Mary Cassatt. My letter was never delivered. It came back to me in March 1988, with "Return to Sender" and "Retour, Addresse Inexacte" stamped on the envelope. Strange, because Fred Pope had written the address on the envelope exactly as it had been given by the family. I felt terrible that Flamina and her parents never knew how I felt; they must have thought I didn't care.

5
A Basement Seat to History
The Downfall of a President
Reporting the Story to Listeners Overseas

My workspace in the White House was in the basement press room, past an area presided over by The Knights of the Green Ottoman and at the end of a corridor that we called The Avenue of the Rising Sun.

The Knights were correspondents who lounged on green leather couches and chairs, their legs stretched out on a big round green leather ottoman, and ruminated about Nixon while waiting for briefings or for the Press Office to announce "a lid for the day." The lid signaled nothing more to cover and reporters could go home.

The Avenue of the Rising Sun was lined on one side with broadcast booths for radio correspondents and on the other with shoulder-high wooden panels which served as partitions for desk areas used by print correspondents. On these panels were a half-dozen or so wall telephones, leased by correspondents from Japan. VOA's broadcast booth was a cubby-hole bulging with tape recorders, microphones, telephones, a fax machine, shelves with files to the ceiling, a counter that served as desk for my typewriter, and two chairs, for a radio technician and me. It was my basement seat to history. Closeted in the cubby-hole I spent countless hours reporting on the final months of the Nixon administration.

If there was any single story in my time at the Voice that indelibly stamped VOA as a credible source of news, it was Watergate and the downfall of President Nixon. Watergate wasn't an easy story for VOA to cover. It required a good deal of explanation for overseas listeners who couldn't fathom what all the fuss was about. And yes, there were pressures on VOA, efforts to limit its coverage because it was a U.S. government radio. Yet the VOA news staff shook them off and reported the news — and that's what counts. The newsroom went about the business of "telling it like it is" in reporting the scandal spreading from the June 17, 1972, break-in at the Democratic Party's Watergate offices by agents of the Committee to Re-Elect the President (CREEP).

As for coverage restraints that I knew of, I was called to the VOA program manager's office one day while I was temporarily in charge of the newsroom. He beseeched me, "Do we have to say 'scandal'?" He clearly was uncomfortable and I assumed he was under pressure. I argued for a while but figured that by then Watergate was known to be a scandal and agreed to drop the word.

Much more serious was an order from USIA Director James Keogh in June 1973, forbidding the VOA newsroom from carrying Watergate stories based on unidentified sources. Because of this policy a VOA story was killed. The story had carried reports by *The Washington Post* and *The New York Times*, quoting "reliable sources," that ex-White House Counsel John Dean was prepared to testify Nixon knew of the coverup, and it included the White House denial of the reports. The newsroom insisted it couldn't report the denial without carrying what was being denied. A new version of the story was written, leading with the White House statement and then going into the reports about Dean by the two newspapers, and that was okayed. As Keogh was quoted later: "My guidance has been to cover the Watergate story factually, but do not use rumor, speculation, hearsay or anonymous accusation." He also said that "if an accusation is important enough to warrant a denial, it's a different thing."

In reporting American news, it was not uncommon for VOA to carry stories on what major American newspapers were reporting and to attribute the information to the papers. The Keogh order would have foreclosed our picking up much of the newspaper accounts on Watergate, causing a gap in our coverage, but we got around it by seeking White House reaction when Watergate revelations based on anonymous sources were published. Then we would start our stories with the White House comment and follow it with the report, identifying which of the news media had carried it. Or we would start them with "The White House has declined comment on a published report that. . . ." After I began covering the White House, I made repeated treks to Deputy Press Secretary Gerald (Jerry) Warren's office to ask him for reaction to this or that report. Jerry was accessible to reporters; he was in a ground floor office next to the briefing room, and he kept his door open. I always found him to be patient and cordial, even though he had little to say.

In our reporting of Watergate, I think VOA succeeded in conveying to listeners abroad the sense, feel and dynamics of the events. We provided a lot of background and explanatory material, for example, a wrapup I filed May 9 when the House Judiciary Committee began its hearings on whether there were grounds to impeach Nixon:

"For the second time in United States history an examination has begun into whether there is evidence to bring formal accusations against a president for trial by the Senate. This is an impeachment proceeding, as provided for in the Constitution. Under the Constitution, a president shall be removed from office on impeachment for, and conviction of, treason, bribery, or other high crimes and misdemeanors. When the Judiciary Committee completes its work — which will be weeks from now — it will report to the full House of Representatives, which then will decide whether to vote impeachment. If it does, President Nixon would be tried by the Senate. . . ."

The same report noted that as the hearings began "there was an erosion of support for the president among members of his own party," that a Republican congressional leader, John Rhodes, said the president should consider resignation as an option, and that the White House "said again the president does not intend to resign."

Part of telling listeners what was going on at the White House was of course reporting on the defense of the beleaguered president. When Nixon's daughter, Julie, and her husband, David Eisenhower, held a press conference in May to deny speculation that her father planned to resign, I reported her comments that his mood was good and he didn't feel shackled by Watergate. Privately I empathized with her. Any daughter who loved her father would.

A succession of Nixon aides spoke out against criticism that transcripts of tape-recorded White House conversations on Watergate showed a lack of morality. Presidential assistant John McLaughlin, then a Jesuit priest (later a TV talk show host), said the president's morality should be evaluated from the standpoint that he had provided a climate of charity by reducing violence in the international community and at home. Casper Weinberger, then Secretary of Health, Education and Welfare, said the transcripts represented only a very small proportion of the total activity and achievements of the president's first term. He also said he hadn't read them. Nixon speech writer Patrick Buchanan (later a TV commentator and GOP presidential contender), insisted the transcripts did not contain an impeachable offense.

During this period I learned that when the Press Office put on the "lid for the day" it was unwise to pay attention to it and go home, because very often in late afternoon presidential aides trotted out to defend Nixon in interviews on the lawn in front of the White House, where TV network correspondents do their "standups." I duly reported the defense along with the swelling criticism, and reported as well Nixon's activities and statements involving domestic programs and foreign policy. In May, for instance, he announced steps to help the ailing U.S. housing industry, and met with Japan's foreign minister and NATO's secretary general.

While Nixon was on his Mideast and Soviet trips, his lawyers were fighting attempts by the Judiciary Committee and Watergate Special Prosecutor Leon Jaworski to obtain more Watergate tapes from the White House. Jaworski wanted the tapes of 64 White House conversations for the Watergate coverup trial of six former Nixon aides, scheduled for September. Nixon had been named an un-indicted co-conspirator in the grand jury's investigation.

In late July came one reversal after another for Nixon and his lawyers: The Supreme Court ordered him to surrender the 64 tapes, and the House Judiciary Committee, on national television, debated and adopted articles of impeachment against him — for obstruction of justice, abuse of powers, and refusing to comply with Committee subpoenas. On July 28 Nixon returned to Washington from a stay at his San Clemente, California, home, and began reviewing the tapes that were being turned over to Federal Judge John Sirica under the Supreme Court's order. Administration officials continued to insist he was concentrating on the business of government as well. Domestic Counselor Kenneth Cole told reporters he had not noticed any effect of the impeachment proceedings on the government's day to day operations. I reported Cole's remarks; any comments on the functioning of the U.S. government were newsworthy for VOA's listeners. I also reported Jerry Warren's acknowledging pro–impeachment sentiment in the House of Representatives when he said, "If you had to make odds, you'd put the president in the role of underdog." It was equally important to inform VOA's listeners of House sentiment in favor of voting to send Nixon to trial by the Senate.

VOA wasn't operating in a vacuum; the wire services and newspapers around the world were reporting these developments. The Voice would have been distrusted if it had not. And there is this to consider: For listeners in countries with little access to information, the Voice is a major source of news. With its comprehensive newscasts, VOA is their *New York Times*, *Washington Post* and *Wall Street Journal*.

Throughout this period I frequently phoned a White House source from my home in early morning to check on various developments that the papers, particularly *The Washington Post*, were reporting. I regarded this person, who shall be nameless here, as a reliable source. The answers to my questions were guarded but from the tone of our conversations I was able to file reports with confidence that I was on firm ground.

On Monday, August 5, a day after Nixon had summoned a group of his aides and his Watergate lawyer James St. Clair to meet with him at Camp David, the Senate's second–ranking Republican, Robert Griffin, called on the president to resign. In late afternoon the White House Press Office released a presidential statement. It was "the smoking gun." I quickly filed a story but, I blush to say, it did not reflect the enormity of what the statement revealed. It contained the relevant information but the lead wasn't sharp enough and stuck too closely to the statement's wording rather than reporting what Nixon had done: "President Nixon is releasing the transcripts of conversations he had with one of his chief aides six days after the Watergate break-in in 1972 — transcripts of tapes that he says contain portions which are at variance with certain of his previous statements on Watergate. . . ."

A VOA newsroom editor, Nancy Smart, phoned me and pointed out the wire service stories were harder and more to the point than mine. I believe that in writing the story I had been trying to be fair in reporting the president's defense of himself. But Nancy was right, and I quickly did a rewrite: "The president has admitted that he withheld potentially damaging information in White House conversations on Watergate from congressional impeachment investigators and from his own staff and defense lawyers. In other words, he says he did not tell the whole Watergate story — that this was a serious act of omission which he deeply regrets. . . ." I also reported that the transcripts "show that the president authorized his aide (former White House Chief of Staff H. R. Haldeman) to seek limitation of the FBI investigation of the Watergate break-in and that he was aware of the political implications."

The firestorm that greeted Nixon's admission was reported in our broadcasts, as was the dismay of his allies in Congress — for example this passage in one of VOA congressional correspondent Robert Lodge's reports from Capitol Hill: "House Republican leader John Rhodes rose from a sickbed to issue a statement. He called it a tragedy that the president's truthfulness was put in question by the disclosure that he apparently attempted to use a government agency to cover up the depth of the Watergate conspiracy. . . ."

On Tuesday, August 6, Nixon called a meeting of cabinet members on short notice and, they told reporters afterwards, ruled out resignation and said he wanted to go through the impeachment process. For the overseas audience, my report included substantial coverage of what Secretary of State Kissinger said. Maybe this could be considered propagandistic, but I thought his remarks were newsworthy; they amounted to a warning against any attempt to take advantage of the United States at a time of weakened leadership. Kissinger "told newsmen the impeachment proceedings will not affect the conduct of American foreign policy," I reported. "The secretary said that when the questions of peace and war are involved, no foreign government should have any doubts about the way in which United States foreign policy will be conducted."

That events were moving toward a climax was reflected in our broadcasts the next day. They included reports on Senator Robert Dole's assessment that there were not enough Nixon supporters in the Senate to avoid conviction, mounting demands that Nixon step down, and widely circulated press reports that he would. In late afternoon that day, Wednesday, August 7, Nixon met with Senate Minority Leader Hugh Scott, House Minority Leader John Rhodes and conservative Senator Barry Goldwater.

"This capital has been awash with reports since Wednesday afternoon that a presidential resignation is in the offing," I reported in a wrapup. "A White House spokesman said he could not confirm the news reports and repeated that the president's position is unchanged. A short time later Republican congressional leaders met with the president, told him that the impeachment situation in the Congress is gloomy, and then told newsmen that resignation was not discussed. They left the impression that President Nixon is pondering a decision on resignation, however, when they said the uppermost thought in the president's mind is that whatever decision he makes it will be in the best interest of the country."

The meeting was pivotal, informing Nixon that he faced eviction from office. (A few days later, Senator Scott recalled that prior to the meeting Chief of Staff Haig told them the president was almost on the edge of resignation and if they suggested it he might take umbrage and reverse field. And Senator Goldwater said they told Nixon "the honest truth as we saw it, that it was an impossible case.")

Thursday morning, August 8, the White House press area was filled with reporters, the presence of so many creating an air of expectancy, a feeling that the drama was building inexorably to its conclusion. Just before 11 a.m. Jerry Warren announced the president had asked the vice president to come over to the White House at 11 for a private meeting. Wire services soon quoted an unnamed White House aide as saying Nixon called the meeting to tell Ford he had decided to resign. Warren declined comment.

At 12:20 p.m., Ziegler appeared in the packed briefing room and told us: "I am aware of the intense interest of the American people and of you in this room concerning developments today and over the last few days. This has been of course a difficult time. The president of the United States will meet various members of the bipartisan leadership here at the White House early this evening. Tonight at 9 o'clock Eastern Daylight Time the president of the United States will address the nation on radio and television from his Oval Office." At 3 p.m. Kissinger met with Vice President Ford, and after that, Ford cancelled an 11–day trip scheduled to have begun later in the day.

By early evening, hundreds of reporters, more than at any time in the recent past and representing news organizations from around the world, had assembled at the White House. "The anticipation is, and has been for some hours, that President Nixon will announce his decision to resign," I told VOA listeners. My report, describing the atmosphere, ended with: "Meantime, White House routine business goes on. On what may be Mr. Nixon's final full day in office, he has signed two bills, urged approval of his trade reform bill again, made several appointments. . . named the U.S. delegation to the presidential inauguration in the Dominican Republic, and vetoed the appropriations bill for the Agriculture Department and Environmental Protection Agency. . . ."

Between 6:30 and a few minutes after 7 p.m., the door to the press area was locked and we weren't allowed outside. The reason, we were told, was to provide a brief period of privacy for those walking from the White House over to the adjacent Executive Office Building. I am uncertain about the exact time that I looked out a window of the briefing room and caught a glimpse of Nixon walking toward the EOB, but it must have been while the press was locked in. His meeting with congressional leaders was scheduled to take place in his EOB office. I saw him from the back, his shoulders hunched, and I thought he looked like one of those mechanical toy soldiers.

Nixon announced his decision to resign, effective at noon Friday, in a 16-minute address to the American people. It was carried live by VOA. "He is the first president to resign in the nation's history," I reported, "and is ending his presidency because of Watergate — in the face of threatened conviction and removal from office by the Senate. He says that as a private citizen he will continue to work for the causes of peace, prosperity, justice and opportunity for all, and he hopes that will be his legacy."

Late that night, Ron Ziegler gave his final briefing to White House correspondents and I thought his comments about the press were worth reporting: "Whatever our differences have been, I believe that there are no simple answers to the complex questions that this period poses," he said, "but above all, I think I take away from this job a deep sense of respect for the diversity and strength of our country's freedom of expression and for our free press."

On the morning of resignation day, August 9, 1974, Nixon made his emotional farewell to members of his administration gathered in the East Room. I was outside with the bulk of the press waiting to cover his departure and listened through the earphone of my tape recorder plugged into the "mult box" as he spoke — "Only when you've been in the deepest valley do you know how magnificent it is to be on the highest mountain. . . ."

Then the departure: "Richard Nixon stepped aboard the presidential helicopter on the South Lawn of the White House for the last time as president," I reported, "turned around, waved to his cabinet and staff, gave a big smile, and flung his arms open wide and made the V–for–Victory sign that has been such a characteristic of him on his many campaign appearances. It was 10 o'clock in the morning, the skies were overcast."

At noon aboard Air Force One over America's midlands on the way to his home in California, President Nixon became private citizen Richard Nixon. His letter of resignation had been delivered,

Richard Nixon leaving the White House for the last time as president, August 9, 1974. (Courtesy, Nixon Presidential Materials Staff, National Archives)

as provided by law, to the secretary of state 25 minutes earlier. Haig gave it to Kissinger. The Press Office released copies: "Dear Mr. Secretary: I hereby resign the office of President of the United States. Sincerely, Richard Nixon."

As a reporter I was grateful — well, I thanked my lucky stars — to have had the chance to cover one of the biggest stories in my lifetime, an unparalleled chapter in the annals of the American presidency. As a citizen I was relieved that he was out of the White House. I thought he had done some good things as president — the opening to China and other foreign affairs initiatives, and domestic programs like revenue sharing — but he was no longer fit to govern the country. With his complexity, his political ups and downs and comebacks, his dark side, his doing himself in, Richard Milhous Nixon was the most fascinating of the presidents I covered. The late John Lindsay expressed it so well to me a few years ago: "I count it among my many blessings that if the Lord meant for me to be a journalist, He was sensitive enough to my needs to place me on this planet not as a contemporary of the likes of Tyler, Taylor, Pierce, Fillmore and Buchanan, but of Richard Nixon."

Much has been written since Nixon's resignation about the days leading up to it (Nixon praying, and so on) but I've dealt here with VOA's reporting of events based on information available at the time, and I am proud of the straightforward job it did.

One member of our team that covered Watergate felt otherwise about VOA's reporting. In an opinion piece published in *The Washington Star* in 1977 after he'd left VOA and become a freelance writer, Ron Grunberg complained that he'd not been allowed to do original investigative reports. But as News Division chief Bernie Kamenske and I pointed out in our responses to Grunberg, also published by *The Star*, VOA does not do investigative reporting. This is hardly a serious omission. Many other news organizations don't have investigative reporters. Those that do are mainly the major print and broadcast media which have the resources to deploy them. Their stories are then picked up or followed up by the rest of the media.

Grunberg acknowledged that in covering sensitive stories, including Watergate, "almost never was what I wrote censored." But there was, he said, "a more subtle policy of prudence which leads to self–censorship." This is a danger that does exist, but VOA's writers and editors are conscious of it and for the most part have avoided falling victim to it. They believe, I wrote in my response, "that telling things as they are is in the long run the best service we can give."

An independent view of our Watergate coverage came in May 1974 from *The Wall Street Journal*, which called it "straight–arrow reporting." Under the headline: "At Voice of America, There's No Cover–Up On Watergate News," the newspaper reported that VOA had broadcast the voice of Senator Richard Schweiker "reading his get–out–now letter to the head of the American government, and it was the American government that put him on shortwave radio for the whole world to hear. Although the liberal Pennsylvania Republican never has been a big ally of President Nixon in the Senate, his open call for resignation was news, and the Voice of America is in the news business."

The *Journal* article said VOA sought balance in its coverage, but the "flow of events on some days seems to run just one way" — that is, unfavorable to the president. It quoted VOA Director Kenneth Giddens as saying that on such days "we're just going to have to say it that way." Giddens said he "must rely mainly on his professional news staff's seat–of–the–pants editorial judgment." And he did. Although Giddens felt loyal to Nixon for appointing him to head VOA, he was devoted to the Voice and a strong protector of its integrity.

Besides the News Division's reporting of Watergate, two other parts of VOA were involved in the coverage: Worldwide English, which produced the news programs and broadcast "actualities" — the voices of people in the news, and the Current Affairs Division, which produced commentaries, opinion roundups, and surveys of newspaper editorials. Michael Hanu, who became Current Affairs chief in the midst of Watergate, has recalled that some of the letters received from overseas listeners "berated us for what they considered washing our own linens in public, but a large majority sent us the same basic message: If I ever had any doubts about VOA's objectivity, they have been dispelled by your reporting of the Watergate story."

Praise also came from Americans. For example, a member of the Rhode Island House of Representatives wrote VOA that he had tuned in its overseas broadcast on the night that Nixon announced he would resign. "I must congratulate you and your staff," he said, "on the objective and complete manner in which the Nixon resignation and presidency were presented to the world. . . . Your presentation of the facts far excelled the presentation to the American public by the three major television networks. It is a shame that more Americans did not have an opportunity to listen."

And now a new president. At noon August 9 in the East Room Gerald Rudolph Ford was sworn in as the 38th president of the United States and told Americans "our long national nightmare is over." An hour later he appeared in the briefing room to introduce his White House press secretary, Jerry TerHorst, and pledged to reporters an open and candid administration. He was a breath of fresh air. And reporters welcomed his selection of TerHorst, a newspaperman for 31 years and a highly respected member of the Washington press corps.

To report on President Ford I was joined by Bob Leonard, who had covered him as vice president and was known by him. Other news media also moved their vice presidential reporters to the White House; it made sense because they'd built up contacts with the Ford staff. From then on VOA's White House bureau was a two-person bureau, a move that also made sense, given the amount of travel and the long hours spent in covering presidents.

On Ford's first day in office he held a series of meetings as he moved quickly, we reported, to assure an orderly transition and to assure other countries of the continuity of U.S. foreign policy. He began the work of organizing his government and tackling the inflation problem. And uppermost in his mind, TerHorst told us, was his constitutional responsibility to nominate a successor as vice president. As one of our VOA reports explained, under the 25th

Amendment to the Constitution, when there is a vacancy in the office of vice president, the president nominates a candidate for scrutiny and approval by the Congress. Only eight months before, Gerald Ford became the first appointed vice president under the amendment, named by Nixon to fill the vacancy resulting from Spiro T. Agnew's resignation. On August 9 Ford thus became the nation's first non-elected president.

That afternoon, White House Press Office staffers — both Nixon people and Ford people — did a yeoman job in responding to reporters' queries. Oh, there was a bit of confusion, for instance when a reporter asked a secretary if she had a transcript of the president's remarks. "Sure," she replied, then paused, "Which president?"

In succeeding days, Bob Leonard and I broadcast reports to VOA listeners describing the new president, his background (star football player at the University of Michigan, Yale Law School graduate) and state of health (in top physical condition), and quoting from profiles in the American press. One quote was from *The Detroit Free Press*: "Gerald Rudolph Ford is Mr. Middle America, as solid and functional and comfortable as the furniture that used to come out of his home town, Grand Rapids." That was written by Saul Friedman, whom I came to know as an astute observer of presidents and the people around them.

Jerry Ford enjoyed a honeymoon with the press; he seemed to like reporters; we liked him. In describing his relations with the news media, I told VOA listeners that previous presidents had honeymoons with the press at the outset of their administrations, some lasting longer than others. "How long President Ford's will last can't be predicted. But sooner or later there will be that first quarrel, because the relationship between the government and the press of the United States has always been an adversary one. The press probes and it prods. For now, the atmosphere is relaxed. The press is not being shut out." I ended the piece by noting that guests at a dinner given by the Fords for King Hussein included a sizable number of news correspondents and their wives, including the White House correspondent for *The Washington Post*.

The honeymoon ended, or at least lost its lustre, on September 8, a Sunday. Ford granted "a full, free and absolute pardon" to Nixon for all offenses against the United States which he "has committed or may have committed or taken part in" during the period he was president. Ford said he was acting according to his own conscience and his duty as president to insure domestic tranquillity. Nixon issued a statement in San Clemente accepting the pardon and admitting "that I was wrong in not acting more decisively and forthrightly in dealing with Watergate. . . ."

The stunning news prompted many questions from the crush of reporters at a White House briefing by Ford's counsellor, Philip Buchen. He denied the pardon was in any way related to obtaining concessions in return from Nixon, and said Ford granted the pardon as an act of mercy. Also announced that day was an agreement providing for the government's temporary custody of Nixon's presidential documents and tapes. And because of the pardon, Jerry TerHorst resigned as Press Secretary. He was succeeded by former NBC correspondent Ron Nessen.

In the outcry over the pardon, I didn't agree with those who asserted Nixon should have been prosecuted, convicted and sent to prison. It seemed to me that having to resign as president in disgrace was greater punishment. He had fallen from "the highest mountain."

Questions about the pardon persisted and in Congress resolutions of inquiry were introduced seeking answers from Ford. On October 17 he appeared before the House Judiciary Committee's Subcommittee on Criminal Justice to respond. He said he granted the pardon "not for Mr. Nixon but for the purpose of changing the national focus," I reported. "He wanted to move attention from the pursuit of a fallen president to the pursuit of the urgent needs of the nation." I added that Ford did disclose information that had been the subject of unconfirmed reports in the press: "That was that he discussed the question of a possible pardon as part of a series of options with White House Chief of Staff Alexander Haig before President Nixon resigned."

According to Press Secretary Nessen, initial public reaction to Ford's testimony was favorable. The pardon did, however, diminish his standing in the polls.

Gradually Nixon was replaced as the leading topic of the Knights of the Green Ottoman and others of us who covered him; we were concentrating on the new president. Still, he remained a fascinating subject, and through the years we followed his emergence from the seclusion of San Clemente, his foreign travels, his books, and his becoming an elder statesman whose views on foreign policy were respectfully received.

And was he mellowing? A garden party was given in June 1985 by friends and colleagues of John Lindsay, who was retiring from *Newsweek*, at the home of Ben Bradlee and his wife, Sally Quinn, in Washington's Georgetown section. Ben went into the house to take a telephone call and came rushing out, nonplussed, with the news that Nixon was on the phone and wanted to speak to John to wish him well. Who would ever have thought that Nixon would place a call to the home of the executive editor of *The Washington Post*! Lorraine, John's wife, later told me Nixon said he would have gone to the party except that it was at Bradlee's home. John Lindsay was one of the top journalists who had covered Watergate, but Nixon respected him as an objective reporter. When John was ill with cancer, Nixon wrote to him, and sent him a box of Nixon memorabilia and copies of his books, and when John died he sent flowers and phoned Lorraine to offer his condolences.

In the basement press room at the White House, the green ottoman no longer exists; it was removed, along with the green sofas and chairs, to make room for additional work areas for new members of the expanding press corps. The original Knights are gone from the White House, too, except for our basement philosopher, counselor and provider of perspective when it came to presidential rhetorical excesses, Alexander Sullivan of USIA's press service. Al has covered presidents since LBJ and ranks second to Helen Thomas in seniority among the regulars in the White House press corps. Two other Knights, Gil Butler of WTOP and Don

Fulsom of UPI–Radio, joined VOA and became household names to listeners overseas.

The other occupants of the basement press room when I began covering the White House included Fay Wells, my mentor in Bad Axe, and a basement legend for her inventive reporting of a Nixon gold policy announcement. It was of great interest to Japan, and the Japanese correspondents rushed to their White House phones to file bulletins. For her radio report, Fay opened the door to her broadcast booth, thrust her microphone into the Avenue of the Rising Sun, and captured the sound of the babble of Japanese voices to show how Japan was getting the news.

Fay was considered the first woman broadcaster to become a regular on the White House beat. Joining the regulars in 1974 was ABC's Ann Compton, who became the first woman network television correspondent assigned to the White House. The regulars are those who spend the entire day, and many evenings, at the White House and travel with the president around the country and abroad. There are only 40 to 60 among the approximately 2,000 holders of White House press passes. The others are press people who go there just occasionally, and include columnists, technicians and news executives.

Another who welcomed me to the basement was the famous interrogator of presidents, Sarah McClendon, who had been reporting on them since Franklin Roosevelt. Her coverage extended beyond the White House and included Capitol Hill and government agencies. She was called a gadfly, but then gadflies are necessary in reporting the news. I found her to be warm, gracious, and helpful to newcomers, as well as a dedicated journalist.

All the basement folks were helpful, and so was Youngstown friend Sid Davis, who was then running the Washington bureau of Westinghouse News and was a former White House correspondent. Sid gave me much useful advice, such as to get a seat at the front of the press bus so that if a presidential motorcade stopped suddenly I could leap out and be among the first to check on what happened.

As for presidential motorcades, when I finally started serving on White House travel pools, I learned never to wear tight skirts and always to wear comfortable shoes. The travel pool generally rides in vans, and climbing in and out of them quickly is no easy feat when constricted by a tight skirt. The vans are always behind many cars carrying officials, and when the presidential limousine comes to a stop, poolers jump out and race along the line of vehicles to catch up with the president. Hard to do in high heels.

Months went by, however, before I was assigned to any press pools. VOA correspondents weren't allowed to serve on them, or to ask questions at the daily White House briefings. This was the policy of the White House Correspondents Association and it was backed by the White House Press Office. Later I learned that Kennedy Press Secretary Pierre Salinger opposed VOA raising questions in briefings. When I met Pierre on presidential trips abroad, however, he complimented VOA's coverage.

I appealed to the Correspondents Association to drop its policy, citing the VOA Charter and our Watergate coverage, and pointing out that VOA correspondents were allowed to ask questions at State Department briefings, provided they did not initiate a new line of questioning. I suggested that we be permitted to ask questions "so long as there is a binding and unbroken pledge that no question is planted with us and that VOA correspondents are not privy to inside information leading to questions."

The Association was not persuaded. Its president, James Deakin of *The St. Louis Post-Dispatch*, wrote me September 30, 1974, that the officers and executive committee "unanimously agreed it would not be proper to permit representatives of agencies of the United States government to ask questions at press briefings or to be represented in press pools." Jim said he was sorry and added that they felt "the relationship between the government and the news media should be an arms–length one, under all circumstances."

The response was depressing. I could understand, philosophically, the Association's concerns, but felt that VOA should be allowed to report the news without being hobbled, so I didn't give up. Colleagues in the White House press corps assured me that the

Association's stand was nothing personal, and treated me as a fellow reporter, not an outsider. The Association no doubt was worried that the VOA correspondent, as a government employee, would get preferential treatment or would ask questions that would give the White House spokesman an opening to put the administration in a favorable light.

Throughout my years covering presidents, I received no preferential treatment, no inside information, from White House officials, and in fact was at the bottom of the pecking order under which the White House grants interviews, holds special background briefings, leaks stories, and returns phone calls. VOA and USIA reporters were the last names on the White House list of the press to call in case of an emergency briefing or happening.

At the top of the pecking order were the correspondents for the television networks and wire services, followed by those with major newspapers and the news magazines. Clustered at the bottom were the correspondents for "guerrilla radio," the independent radio organizations: AP–Radio, UPI–Radio, Storer, Mutual, RKO (later United Stations), Sheridan, NPR and VOA. At times VOA was even left out of background briefings to which the other radio correspondents were invited. I think this was because White House officials forget or ignore VOA since it broadcasts overseas and not to Americans, i.e., American voters.

I didn't want favored treatment, but I felt that the Voice should have had the same access to information as the other news media. Also, it was shortsighted of the White House to exclude VOA from the special background briefings, since some were held to explain or promote the administration's position on issues of interest overseas. In any case, correspondents who attended them usually gave me a fill on what, if anything, was newsworthy. We were a collegial group.

It was not until the Carter administration that VOA correspondents could ask questions at the daily White House briefings. But, thanks to our participation in the white line, I began serving on White House press pools on Ford's first trip overseas as president.

President Ford drops by the White House briefing room, an informal lounge setting until auditorium-style rows of seats were installed during the Reagan administration. (White House photo)

Jurey's Basement Seat to History: VOA's broadcast booth at the White House.

6
Surprises in Vladivostok
The Vietnam War "Is Finished"
Helsinki. . . and the White Butterfly

Ford's first overseas venture as president — to Japan, South
Korea and the Soviet Far East for a mini-summit with Leonid
Brezhnev at Vladivostok — was a mixture of symbolism, substance,
surprises, and some comic episodes.

He left on the trip 100 days after taking office, despite criticism
that he should stay home and tend to domestic affairs, especially
since the office of vice president was still vacant. Ford contended
he couldn't wait for Congress to act on his nomination of Nelson
Rockefeller: "I can't sit and twiddle my thumbs and not do
something which I think is important for the benefit of the foreign
policy of the United States."

Ford was the first American president in office to pay a state
visit to Japan and the Japanese welcomed his arrival as historic and
a symbol of closer ties with the U.S. He was greeted by Emperor
Hirohito in a nationally televised ceremony at Akasaka Palace, the
official guest residence. Ford's formal attire, morning coat and
striped trousers, got most of the attention. Especially from
American photographers. His striped pants were too short.

After the ceremony Ford rode with the emperor in the imperial
limousine to the Imperial Palace for a courtesy call on the royal
couple. I was in a press pool that waited outside, where palace
guards stood at attention and, in a vignette I couldn't resist
reporting, a palace functionary dusted the already-spotless
motorcade limousines with an imperial-sized feather duster.

Ford's packed schedule of meetings and appearances in Tokyo
included a speech to the Japanese people in which he said the
United States would remain a trustworthy ally and be a reliable
trading partner. He praised Japanese business enterprises in
America, such as a Japanese company assembling musical instruments in his hometown of Grand Rapids, and declared, "We

welcome them." The forum for his address was the Japan National Press Club, whose president presented him a silver fountain pen. Ford said it was beautiful and proceeded to sign the club's guestbook with it. The pen had no ink.

The speech and the joint communique on the president's talks with Prime Minister Kakuei Tanaka and other officials reflected the amity that existed in 1974 in U.S.–Japanese relations. There had been forecasts of massive protest demonstrations and the Japanese had instituted very tight security, remembering demonstrations that forced cancellation of President Eisenhower's visit in 1960. But there weren't any big ones during Ford's stay.

In covering the visit, I joined VOA's knowledgeable Far East correspondents, Tokyo–based John Schulz and Hong Kong–based Edward Conley. We filed our reports on the white line at the Okura Hotel, where the White House press (139 men/7 women) stayed. I remembered the Okura and its superb service fondly; my husband and I had stayed there in 1965. And I remembered our getting lost on the Ginza, wandering helplessly until a kind gentleman who understood a bit of English pointed us to our destination. This time no chance of getting lost; on presidential trips the press is shepherded on buses and vans by White House Transportation Office staffers.

The white line was run by Tony Brunton of CBS, a hard–driving, super–efficient producer who made sure the correspondents of all its participating radio organizations, VOA included, were on every press pool. The Japanese credentials for pools were ribbons of various colors, each for a specific event. We wore them along with the card–like White House pool credentials and our laminated White House press passes on chains dangling from our necks. By the end of the visit my multi–ribboned chain looked almost like a lei.

Ford headed for Kyoto after an exchange of bows with the emperor in a farewell ceremony at Akasaka Palace. As a pool reporter noted, "The arrival bit was duplicated, with exception that everyone wore business suits instead of formal morning dress. Ford's suit was a perfect fit."

In Kyoto, the "city of peace" and onetime imperial capital, the president went sightseeing, touring ancient sites such as the more than three centuries old Nijo Castle. A delightful episode was played out in the garden of the castle, near a teahouse beside a pond. While our "garden pool" was waiting for Ford's arrival, it began to rain. It stopped and a half dozen girl musicians in silk kimonos took their places on the red-carpeted platform built for the occasion and began rehearsing traditional Japanese songs on kotos, a 16th Century stringed instrument. It rained again. They scurried away to shelter. The rain diminished and they came back, this time carrying parasols. They took their places and despite renewed drizzling stayed at their posts with the parasols providing some protection. The rain stopped a minute or two before the president arrived. He stood and listened to the beautiful music, and afterwards sat down with the young ladies and tried his hand at playing the koto, accompanied by their giggles.

There were some scattered demonstrations in Kyoto, a city with many universities and colleges and the locale of some radical groups, and earlier in Osaka, where Ford had transferred from Air Force One to a helicopter on his way to Kyoto. Most of them were protesting not Ford's visit but the rising cost of living and the leadership of Prime Minister Tanaka, who was in the midst of a domestic political crisis. John Schulz interviewed some of Kyoto's residents and reported most felt "President Ford should be shown a sample of traditional Japanese hospitality."

A sample came at a Kyoto restaurant, where the president's hosts arranged a dinner for him and his aides with a group of geisha girls. The American party and the delicately painted porcelain-faced women dined at a low table on legless padded chairs and, as reported by pooler Margaret Mayer (*Dallas Times-Herald*), young geishas performed a classical Japanese dance to the accompaniment of stringed instruments played by older geishas wearing dark kimonos. At a nearby restaurant a group of us reporters dined on tempura. The deep-fried vegetables, coated with the lightest of batters, included what were said to be chrysanthemum leaves. Whatever they were, the tempura was heavenly.

The next morning we left for South Korea, where opposition to the Park Chung Hee government had increased in the past year. In the weeks before Ford's visit, anti–government demonstrations by students spread from Seoul to other cities, journalists protested press restrictions and accused the police of harassment, and Roman Catholic protest rallies were held. Park's opponents charged that the American president's visit would strengthen the repressive actions of the Korean government.

Ford's purpose in making the visit was to symbolize the U.S. commitment to South Korea and emphasize the importance of maintaining stability in the region. Kissinger told pool reporters aboard Air Force One on the flight to Seoul that "if there is chaos on the Korean Peninsula it has consequences in Japan and many other countries." He said the advantages of going there outweighed "some negatives."

Huge, exuberant crowds turned out to greet Ford as the presidential motorcade drove from Kimpo International Airport to the center of the capital. A police official estimated the total lining the streets at over two million, about a third of Seoul's population then, but the figure didn't seem to be inflated. Some of the welcoming signs said "We Love Ford," "We Like Ford," and (I was taken with this one) "We Really Like Ford." The welcome was climaxed by a snowstorm of confetti showering the motorcade as it approached the Chosun Hotel, where the president and press were staying. At the filing center there I joined VOA's Ed Conley, who had flown in earlier from Tokyo. Ed knew the domestic political situation well; he'd covered the turbulence in South Korea on previous trips.

Before his talks with Park, Ford visited American troops serving under the United Nations Command, at Camp Casey near the demilitarized zone separating South and North Korea. He went through a chow line, had lunch with servicemen in a field mess, attended a game of combat football, watched a grunting martial arts match, and told the cheering troops, "I'm proud of you, as commander–in–chief." The servicemen gave him a plaque, which he said he would take home to his wife, Betty, and "it will touch her heart." Mrs. Ford was convalescing from her surgery for breast cancer.

Ed and I spent the rest of the day filing reports on Ford's talks with Park, a joint communique, a briefing, a reception and a banquet. In sum, Ford reaffirmed U.S. support for South Korea and said there were no plans to reduce the American 38,000–troop level in Korea. Park discussed efforts to maintain a dialogue with North Korea and accused the North of hostile acts. In the briefing, Philip Habib, the assistant secretary of state for East Asian and Pacific Affairs and a former ambassador to Seoul, was pressed by reporters on whether Ford discussed South Korea's domestic political situation with Park. He said only "the subject did come up."

The fears felt by opponents of the Park regime were dramatized for me that night when my hotel room became a refuge for Washington–based Julie Moon of U.S. Asian News. Julie was convinced the South Korean security forces knew her room number and was afraid of possible retaliation for pieces she had written about the government, so she asked to stay with me. My room also was a refuge earlier in the day for Ed Conley, who napped there while I was at Camp Casey. Ed had been bumped from his room by a roomless White House aide.

Julie and I slept peacefully while Ed, as he recalled later, spent the dark night "sitting in the Chosun lobby watching ice form on the hotel windows." It was very cold in Seoul but the hotel management, aware of Ford's fondness for swimming, opened its outdoor pool "in commemoration of his visit" and named it "The Gerald Ford Swimming Pool." The visit lasted only 24 hours, and there wasn't time to grasp what Seoul was like, except to recognize that it was big and bustling and that its people, though under repression, were vigorous and ambitious.

Next stop, Vladivostok. But only about half the White House press went with Ford. The Soviets had limited the number allowed in to 70. I was lucky to be among them. The rest of our colleagues were deposited in Tokyo to wait for us to rejoin them for the trip home.

The site for Ford's meeting with Brezhnev was in an isolated area more than 10 miles northeast of Vladivostok, at a health resort named Oceanside Sanatorium. Our press contingent was quartered about a mile from that in a large resthouse, and we shared the press center with an equal number from the Soviet media. Fresh snow had fallen and the setting was like an old picturebook drawing or a movie set of a winter scene, minus sleighs. May as well enjoy the view, I thought, we're going to be stuck here.

We didn't expect to see Vladivostok. It was a closed city; no foreigners allowed. According to notes in the White House "trip book," this port city, headquarters for the Soviet Pacific Fleet, had been closed to non-communist foreign visitors for 26 years. And I'd read in a pre-summit dispatch by *Washington Post* Moscow correspondent Peter Osnos that the restrictions had not been lifted for the Ford-Brezhnev meeting. So it was a surprise when a spokesman for the Soviet Foreign Ministry told us at a briefing that a guided tour of Vladivostok and its harbor was being arranged for us the next morning. Remarkable.

The excursion took place after only a couple of hours sleep for the press, because Kissinger had had a post-midnight briefing on the talks. "The president and the general secretary appear to be developing new guidelines for the Geneva negotiators on limiting strategic arms," I reported in a wrapup for VOA.

About 30 of us toured the city by bus, with a young woman Intourist guide proudly pointing out numerous institutes, for marine studies, science of the sea, and so on. We saw memorials to Soviet sailors, no churches, memorials saluting the October Revolution and Lenin, and here and there new buildings, apparently put up recently. Our guide told us the city's population had grown to half a million. The new buildings didn't overwhelm the charm of the baroque architecture of the older ones, like the richly curlicued railroad station, painted a soft green. Color was a striking feature as we drove into the closed city, with houses and summer cottages in greens, blues, and golden yellows. And then there was the clear pure blue of the harbor and Amur Bay.

We were told we wouldn't be allowed to take pictures, but some of our group got out their cameras and snapped away. Our escorts were't happy about it but did nothing more than frown.

The bus tour was followed by a two-hour cruise aboard a passenger ship of the state-owned Far East Shipping Company that accommodated more than 300 and normally sailed between Japan and the Soviet commercial port of Nakhodka, near Vladivostok. Our hosts had a sumptuous buffet waiting for us, plus vodka, cognac and soft drinks. Vodka toasts so early in the morning? It wouldn't have been courteous to refuse. From the warmth of the salon (and the vodka) I went for a bracing walk around the deck with a broadcast colleague, Walter Rodgers. The weather was brilliantly sunny but cold; chill winds from the Arctic made me thankful for the long underwear a foresighted friend, Dina Modianot, had given me for the trip. Walter risked another Soviet frown when he took my picture standing windswept against the railing, with a Soviet Navy ship in the background. The naval vessels we saw included two destroyers, a communications ship loaded with equipment, and a cruiser.

The excursion was fun and made a good story: The first foreigners allowed into Vladivostok in a quarter century. The first American journalists admitted, we were told, since 1922. At the press center I immediately filed stories for VOA, reporting the "extraordinary gesture" by Soviet authorities in opening the closed city to us, and describing what I'd seen, with a quote from an official of the shipping company: Detente "would be good for business."

Everything transmitted on the white line is heard by the home offices of the news organizations participating in the U.S. Radio Pool, and soon the reporters who had chosen to sleep in received calls from their news desks asking when they were going to file. We shared our information with the slugabeds and they were able to file matching stories.

Ford, meanwhile, extended his visit by several hours to continue talks with Brezhnev. In late afternoon a "breakthrough" in the negotiations on limiting offensive nuclear weapons was announced.

The two leaders had agreed to ceilings on the number of U.S. and Soviet strategic delivery vehicles (missiles and bombers) and on the number of MIRV–equipped intercontinental and sea–launched ballistic missiles. Kissinger said this produced "a very strong possibility" of a new SALT agreement in 1975. An exultant Ron Nessen, in remarks relayed by a pool reporter, said he thought the press corps was "dazzled" by the agreement and predicted that "the president will be returning home in triumph."

The agreement was page one, top of the broadcast news, but dazzled? Frazzled might be a better word, for we had only an hour or so to wrap up the story before leaving for the airport and the flight to Washington. While we rushed to finish our work, Ford became another foreigner to see the closed city, with Brezhnev the guide for his tour.

President Ford and Soviet leader Brezhnev reach agreement on ceilings in the negotiations on limiting offensive nuclear weapons, at their Vladivostok summit, November 24, 1974. (Courtesy, Gerald R. Ford Library)

Vladivostok remained a closed city but change was afoot in 1990, as I learned in reading Strobe Talbott's column in *Time* magazine. He reported from Vladivostok that the city government and private sector, and the leader of what was then the Russian Federation, Boris Yeltsin, were pressing for removal of the restrictions. In March 1991, a USIA cultural exhibition, "Design USA," was in Vladivostok at the end of an eight-city tour of what was then the Soviet Union. And by May 1993, I read in *The New York Times*, the "forbidden city" had become "wide open." According to the dispatch by Serge Schmemann, Vladivostok was opened in January 1992, American and other consulates had been established, foreigners were touring the harbor, and freighters of the Far East Shipping Company were doing a "lively business."

Reaction to Ford's 1974 agreement with Brezhnev was generally favorable, although there was some criticism that the ceilings were too high and actually would result in more spending on arms. The Geneva SALT negotiations dragged on and Ford was disappointed in his hopes for a new treaty.

President Ford faced a range of difficult issues in 1975, reporting to Congress in January that "the State of the Union is not good." He grappled with recession and inflation, fought for his energy proposals, and faced an uphill battle in his requests for additional aid for South Vietnam and Cambodia. He warned that the odds were in favor of disaster if South Vietnam didn't get ammunition and other military equipment to counter North Vietnamese attacks. Through February and March I reported the White House appeals for the aid, and also reported that the president's requests were in trouble in Congress.

In late March, Ford left Washington for the desert sunshine of Palm Springs, California, to spend Easter week combining golf and work. The Vietnam problem accompanied him. On the flight to Palm Springs he was notified that Da Nang had fallen. Ford did play golf, and made side trips to a naval petroleum reserve and to San Diego and San Francisco for speaking engagements, but the deteriorating situation in South Vietnam dominated his public comments and our briefings.

On April 10, Ford made a foreign policy address to a joint session of Congress and asked for emergency military and humanitarian aid for South Vietnam, a hefty increase over his earlier request. He also asked Congress, I reported, "to clarify immediately its restrictions on the use of U.S. military forces in Southeast Asia" so they could be used "for the limited purposes of protecting American lives by protecting their evacuation if this should become necessary."

And now we come to the sorry business of censorship. Working at home on the Sunday after Ford's speech, I covered Senator Henry Jackson's appearance on ABC–TV's "Issues and Answers." My report included his comments supporting evacuation of Americans from Vietnam and a review of what the president had asked Congress. Soon after filing it by telephone to VOA, I received a call from the newsroom's coverage desk and was advised that there were "strictures on the subject of evacuation and we weren't supposed to mention it." I refused to rewrite the story, refused again when I received another call, and said I would rather not do the story at all if an important part of it would be left out. In spite of my protests, the portion of my report dealing with evacuation was deleted from the text and excised from the tape, and the censored text was issued on the VOA house wire.

I was incensed, and thought it mind–boggling that even President Ford's request, which I'd previously reported on VOA, was being censored as well as the views of a senator of the stature of Henry Jackson. There was no deletion, by the way, on Monday, when I reported after the White House briefing that "President Ford is described as optimistic that he will receive the authority he requested from Congress to carry out a humanitarian evacuation in South Vietnam if it should become necessary."

Word of the censorship of my Jackson piece leaked out, and on Tuesday The Washington Post reported: "The Voice of America has been ordered not to make any mention of possible American evacuations from South Vietnam except official government statements or official actions by the administration or Congress. This policy led to the deletion from a broadcast of at least one report this past weekend in which Sen. Henry M. Jackson (D–Wash.) mentioned the evacuation issue. . . ."

The story quoted a USIA spokesman, Andrew Falkievicz: "We've got a fluid situation, a situation where we have to be very conscious at all times about adding to the complications already existing — even to the extent of placing American lives in jeopardy." Andy (my rescuer at the Moscow airport in 1974) explained that "normally the news coverage of VOA is not limited to congressional actions or official expressions. But," he said, "the situation in Saigon is not normal."

The Baltimore Sun carried a story as well, reporting that "Voice of America broadcasts about the national debate over Vietnam are being censored out of concern for the lives of Americans still there, United States officials said yesterday."

At the White House, Ron Nessen ended his briefing Tuesday by referring to the *Post* story and said: "The question of reports on possible evacuation and so forth is a sensitive and difficult subject. It seems to me it doesn't have anything to do with censorship but it has to do with responsibility. The Voice of America is trying to be responsible in a very difficult situation. It's the official voice of the United States government overseas and so its broadcasts carry special weight with the people who listen to it. And so it must operate I think with some constraints on occasion. Reports that are involved with speculation about evacuation could very well substantially add to the problem. I don't think anybody, either reporters or officials of the government, would want to endanger lives. . . ."

Certainly nobody wants to endanger lives, but the possibility of evacuation was raised, after all, when the president asked Congress about the use of American military forces. Shouldn't VOA's listeners be aware of the thinking in Washington — not merely at the White House but on Capitol Hill as well? How could VOA not report what other international news organizations were reporting? Censoring VOA was a disservice to its listeners and violated the newsroom's responsibility to report accurately, objectively and comprehensively. It was a sad episode.

Ford was unable to persuade Congress to go along with the emergency military aid and by April 22 the White House was describing the Vietnam military situation as "very fluid." On April 23, a Wednesday, Ford made his Tulane University speech declaring that the Vietnam war "is finished, as far as America is concerned." Bob Leonard covered the Tulane trip and when the embargoed advance text of the speech was distributed to the press Bob, of course, put the statement in the lead of his story. But it was deleted, on the grounds that VOA should wait to report it until Ford actually uttered the words. When Ford spoke — and delivered the sentence as it had appeared in the advance text — VOA did carry it. The editor who had made the deletion may have been stricken with super-caution, given the restraints under which the newsroom was operating, but this was a departure from the normal practice of reporting what is in presidential advance texts.

In a report after the Tulane speech I wrote: "Even though President Ford says the Vietnam war is finished as far as America is concerned, he has not abandoned his belief that additional military aid would help stabilize the situation, and would help bring about a ceasefire or negotiated settlement." My report also said Ford was described by his spokesman as gratified that both houses of Congress had acted favorably on his request for humanitarian aid "and on the clarification of his authority to deploy American troops if necessary for an evacuation."

On the evening of Monday, April 28, Ford convened the National Security Council after dispatches from Saigon reported that Tan Son Nhut Airport had been attacked. I filed stories from VOA's broadcast booth into the night, and at 3:40 Tuesday morning (afternoon in Saigon) the announcement came that the president had ordered the evacuation of the remaining Americans in Vietnam. In late afternoon, just past 5 p.m., Ford announced completion of the evacuation. Kissinger told us in a briefing that 6,500 people (upgraded later to more than 7,000), including about 1,000 Americans, were flown out, and that in the past two weeks the U.S. had evacuated some 56,000 South Vietnamese whose lives were in jeopardy, in addition to all the Americans. There had been about 6,000. The next day, April 30, 1975, communist forces captured Saigon, and South Vietnam surrendered.

The VOA newsroom followed the airlift of the last Americans from Saigon closely, not only in reporting the news but out of concern for our Saigon correspondent, Steven Thompson. Steve's "last view of Saigon was from the rear bay of an American Marine helicopter racing away from a city bracing for the final North Vietnamese assault," he has recalled, and his "last remembrances of the airport" were of "panic, fires and exploding rockets." VOA also had been concerned about its two South Vietnamese employees in the Saigon bureau; they were evacuated to the U.S. and became valued members of the newsroom staff in Washington. In 1981, Steve, then our Bangkok correspondent, revisited Saigon, its name changed to Ho Chi Minh City, and reported that when people learned he was an American, their faces "would break into a broad smile."

As for the restraints on our coverage, there was fallout on Capitol Hill. Senator Charles Percy called them a violation of the VOA Charter and said, "If VOA is to be believed, it must be left free to tell the truth." Percy, as previously noted, co-sponsored writing the Charter into law, Public Law 94–350, in 1976.

With American involvement in Vietnam ended, other foreign policy issues moved to center stage in 1975. In late July, Ford left Washington for visits to four European countries and talks with Brezhnev in Helsinki, Finland, where they would be attending the 35-nation European summit conference. This was the summit Brezhnev had lobbied for, a gathering of leaders to sign the Final Act of the Conference on Security and Cooperation in Europe (CSCE). Nobody then even ventured a guess that the event would be of enormous consequence, spurring the democratic reforms that were to sweep Eastern Europe within a scant decade and a half.

In fact, Ford came under fire for agreeing to attend the summit, with critics denouncing the Final Act, known as the Helsinki Accords, on the grounds that it would freeze borders and give legitimacy to communist domination in Eastern Europe and the Baltic states. Exiled Soviet novelist Alexandr Solzhenitsyn charged in a statement published in *The New York Times* that Ford would be taking part in "the betrayal of Eastern Europe" by signing the accords.

Ford's aides responded that the document was not a legally binding treaty and that the U.S., the western allies, and neutral countries, had insisted on language providing for peaceful changes of borders. Kissinger also made the point that the summit was part of the general pattern of reducing tensions, i.e., detente. Ford himself met with a group of Americans of East European background to reassure them, and his departure statement on July 26 contained further reassurance: There would be no change in the longstanding U.S. policy of not recognizing the Soviet incorporation of the Baltic states of Lithuania, Latvia and Estonia. In delivering the statement Ford omitted that passage, but his spokesman said the White House stood by the text.

Ford's trip included visits to West Germany and three countries then under communist rule that were, I reported, becoming increasingly friendly with the U.S.: Poland, Romania and Yugoslavia. His first stop was Bonn, where he underscored cooperation with the western allies. At Kirchgoens, near Frankfurt, he attended a picnic of U.S. and German soldiers and their families and told them he stood "solid as a rock behind America's commitment to the freedom of Berlin."

In Warsaw, an estimated 250,000 people turned out to see him, and he emphasized the friendly ties between the United States and Poland in his talks with Communist Party chief Edward Gierek. He traveled to southern Poland to lay a wreath at Auschwitz and give a speech at Krakow (which I spelled "Crock-Off" in my copy so I'd pronounce it correctly). VOA European correspondent Larry Freund covered the Polish visit with me and I was relieved that I didn't have to go to Auschwitz; I shivered at the thought of seeing the former Nazi concentration camp. Instead, I went on to Krakow to check out the filing arrangements in a building on the edge of the ancient and pretty town square, where throngs of Poles — many with relatives in America — were waiting to see the president.

Ford's first meeting with Brezhnev in Helsinki was on July 30 and was one of a series of individual meetings he held with other leaders attending the summit. Mark Hopkins was covering the Helsinki stop with me and he reported on the summit proceedings while I concentrated on Ford's activities. As learned on previous White House trips abroad, problems accompany a president. On this one the problem was Ford's dispute with Congress over aid to Turkey, which was linked to the negotiations for a settlement of the conflict in Cyprus between the Greek Cypriots and Turkish Cypriots. Ford was trying to get the House of Representatives to reverse its vote against resuming U.S. military sales to Turkey. After the House vote, the Turkish government moved to close U.S. bases in Turkey. Ford met with the Greek and Turkish leaders in Helsinki but nothing came out of the meetings. Kissinger said in a briefing that the whole complex of issues was taking on the aspect of a Greek tragedy. In reporting his comment, I nodded in agreement, remembering the ethnic divide of Cyprus that I had seen five years earlier. The Middle East also was an issue that went along on the trip; Kissinger was trying to work out a Sinai settlement between Egypt and Israel.

On the final day of the summit, August 1, Ford was scheduled to address the assemblage in the morning. Before the session we reporters seized on a freshly distributed pool report in case it contained some news. In the annals of White House pool reports it was unrivaled. The three–and–a–half-page document dealt in staggering detail with Mrs. Ford's activities the previous day, and included this excerpt from a description of her visit to a farm complex:

"Inside the courtyard are lilac bushes and dainty white birch trees. The roof of each of these houses is made of wooden shingles. Suddenly, a white butterfly floated by in the bushes."

The pool report was authored by Naomi Nover, the widow of a respected *Denver Post* correspondent, who ran a news service after his death and was legendary in her determination not to let anyone get in her way as she stoutly went about her pursuits. Naomi went on almost all of the overseas trips. We never saw any of her dispatches, nor did we know where they were published, but her pool report was widely circulated and prized as a memento. The Helsinki summit was the culmination of two years of negotiations to draft what VOA news analyst William W. Wade called a "30,000-word East-West code of conduct." But it sticks ridiculously in memory as "the white butterfly" summit.

Ford said in his speech to the conference that the U.S. intended to participate fully in turning the results of the summit into a living reality. And, as I reported on VOA: "To the countries of Eastern Europe, President Ford said it is important that they recognize the deep devotion of the American people and government to human rights and fundamental freedoms — and thus to the pledges that this conference has made regarding the freer movement of peoples, ideas and information." He ended the speech with: "History will judge this conference not by what we say here today, but what we do tomorrow; not by the promises we make but by the promises we keep."

In the afternoon, 35 leaders ceremonially signed the Final Act, a volume bound in green leather and containing copies in the six conference languages: English, French, German, Italian, Russian and Spanish. Ford left Helsinki the next day after a meeting with Brezhnev in which they discussed the SALT negotiations. When the two leaders came out the door of their meeting place, they told the travel pool they had made progress. The correspondents on the pool, Henry Bradsher, John Mashek and Henry Trewhitt, tucked into their report an inspired line: "Suddenly, an English sparrow flew across the entrance."

Ford's next stop was Bucharest for talks with Romania's communist leader Nicolae Ceausescu (always worried about pronunciation, I spelled it Chow–SHESS–coo in my copy). In a banquet toast Ceausescu noted that Nixon's visit to Romania six years earlier was regarded as "somewhat exceptional" and said "changes of particular importance have occurred in the world since." The changes he referred to were his growing independence from the Soviet Union and improving relations with the U.S. In 1975, Ceausescu was regarded favorably in Washington and a week before Ford's visit, Congress approved Most Favored Nation trade treatment for Romanian products.

Relations were rosy then, and in a festive episode Ford and his wife Betty joined a costumed group of young people in a Romanian circle dance, then Ceausescu and his wife Elena joined them, along with Kissinger. Later, at the train station in the old resort of Sinaia, Ford and Ceausescu ate bread dipped in salt and drank wine from a leather flask in a ceremony of friendship.

Neither Larry Freund, who covered the Romanian visit with me, nor I, nor anyone else for that matter, could foresee that there would be more "changes of particular importance" in Romania, where Ceausescu became a hated despot, was overthrown in 1989 and, along with his wife, put to death.

In Belgrade, our final stop, where I teamed up again with Mark Hopkins, President Tito was at the airport to greet the president, a rare gesture on the part of the Yugoslav leader. Ford praised Yugoslavia for its "fierce pride in its independence." Tito pursued a foreign policy independent of the Soviet Union and was a leader of the non–aligned countries. Under his policies Yugoslavia was a respected player on the world scene.

In summing up the 10–day trip, I reported from Belgrade that the president was "returning home from what is regarded as a successful visit to Europe — during which he demonstrated closeness to the western allies and reinforced the U.S. policy of developing closer ties with the countries of Eastern Europe." I regret that my lead sentence didn't even mention the Helsinki summit. Its significance wasn't apparent then, and indeed it continued to draw flak, with critics saying that the Soviets were the winners in Helsinki.

History's judgment came 15 years later, more quickly than anyone could have anticipated, when leaders of the countries represented in Helsinki gathered for a summit in Paris, and the Helsinki Accords were credited with laying the foundations for the stunning changes in Eastern Europe. The November 1990 Paris summit took place, as a *New York Times* dispatch put it, "to ratify a redrawing of the map that nobody expected so soon." This time there were 34 countries instead of 35; the two Germanies, East and West, now were one.

Ford returned to Europe in November 1975 for another summit, the first economic summit of the major industrialized democracies, held at Rambouillet, France, which was covered by Bob Leonard. We took turns on trips, and it was my good fortune to go on the next one overseas — to China.

7
China and the VOA
The Peking of 1975, with Ford
The Beijing of 1984, with Reagan

"Responsible persons" at the airport. Mandarin oranges and Jasmine tea on the dresser table in my hotel room. I was in China! I thought about the tale told to American children in the 1930s when I was a kid in New Castle: If you dig a hole deep enough, you'll reach all the way to China. I warmed my nightgown with a chemical heatpad that had kept a television camera warm in Alaska, and climbed into bed.

The White House press corps arrived in Peking on the night of November 30, 1975, while President Ford overnighted in Anchorage before flying to the Chinese capital. Exhausted after more than 30 hours of travel, including coverage of Ford viewing the Alaska pipeline, we were met by a receiving line of escorts–interpreters provided by the Chinese government. Called "responsible persons," they gave us our hotel room numbers, and a soft–sell pitch on the thoughts of Chairman Mao. Some of them asked Bob Schieffer of CBS and other colleagues to point me out.

We were quartered at the Min Zu Hotel, and on my dresser table, along with the oranges and tea, was a thermos jug which was constantly replenished with hot water. The Min Zu was our workplace as well as lodging, with the press filing center on the 10th floor in a large briefing room containing banks of tables, the work areas for the television and radio pools on the 9th, the White House press office on the 7th, and, just below, the Chinese Foreign Ministry's information office. The radio pool was efficiently organized by ABC's Joe Keating, who supervised a crew of technicians, including Chinese techs who listened to everything we filed on the white line. Each floor had a lounge area, and the moment we sat down in the comfortable chairs (with antimacassars like the doilies my mother crocheted for the parlor furniture in

New Castle), a waiter materialized to offer soda pop, beer, coffee or tea.

In that chill winter, a child with a coloring book would have colored Peking blue and gray. Blue from the uniformity of clothing worn by the bicycle riders who jammed the streets and those on foot who jammed the sidewalks; gray from the smog — emissions from charcoal burners and factories fueled by soft coal and dust particles carried by winds from the north. (I had a raspy throat but the hot tea took care of that.) There was no greenery. Trees were mere infants; a tree–planting program had recently been instituted.

The Chinese quickly provided hospitality for the press, disciplined hospitality, with an exhaustively detailed briefing followed by a spectacular lunch. We were given credentials and an array of identification tags, and were assigned to mini–buses (mine was number 136) and "responsible persons" who would look after us, and keep us from straying. Mine was a likeable young woman from the Foreign Ministry who spoke English well and proved to be a savvy source.

The lunch, at the Peking Duck Restaurant, was a 10–course meal that of course featured Peking duck, with crackly crisp skin and plum sauce divine, and was hosted by the director of the New China News Agency. His toast was the first of countless toasts to "Chinese–American Friendship!" that we would drink during the visit. Responding for the American journalists was, appropriately, a rotund lover of fine food, Richard Growald of UPI. The top American diplomat–toaster was George Bush, then the head of the U.S. Liaison Office which was opened in Peking after President Nixon's ice-breaking visit in 1972. He was seated at a table with some of the media luminaries. The traveling press (158 men/6 women) included network anchors Walter Cronkite, John Chancellor and Harry Reasoner; Barbara Walters, then with NBC's "Today" show, and Helen Thomas, who was not at the luncheon because she was on the pool traveling with Ford on Air Force One. Other women in the press contingent were ABC's Ann Compton, Clare Hollingworth of *The London Daily Telegraph*, and Naomi Nover.

I was at a table in a far corner of the restaurant doing some toast-exchanging when Bill Greener, the affable deputy White House press secretary, came over with someone he said wanted to meet me — Ambassador Bush. Bush told me VOA was listened to in China. "You are," he said, "our link to the outside world." And later, my basement radio colleagues Roger Gittines and Walter Rodgers said, "The Chinese don't know Walter Cronkite but know Philomena."

Our first big story came at the welcoming banquet the first night of Ford's visit. He had flown in at 3 in the afternoon with his wife Betty, 18-year-old daughter Susan, and a large official party, to an airport welcome by Vice Premier Deng Xiaoping, then spelled Teng Hsiao Ping. Thanks to my "responsible person," I'd reported earlier that he would greet the president. This small figure of a man, who would become China's paramount leader after Mao, was the top Chinese government official in the absence of the ailing Premier Chou en-Lai.

Deng delivered a banquet toast that John Osborne of *The New Republic* later wrote was "what many reporters regarded as a whizzer of a story" and "a shocker." Deng said the country "which most zealously preaches peace. . . is the most dangerous source of war." He was clearly echoing Chinese concerns about the Soviet Union, so his toast wasn't quite as astonishing as some reporters thought, but it was a good story, and after the banquet I rushed along with the others to file. I led my report with Deng's "attack on the Soviet Union" and after using his quotes, added a sentence putting them in perspective: "His remarks were the latest by China's officialdom expressing reservations about the U.S. policy of relaxing tension with the Soviet Union." I also quoted Ford's response, "The United States will strive both to reduce the dangers and explore new opportunities for peace without illusion."

In updating the story for succeeding newscasts, I reported White House reaction that "the United States considers the Vice Premier's remarks frank, but non-provocative." All my stories on this subject contained the U.S. position that it was sticking to its policy of detente. Did this mean I was being an "official spokesman"? No, I was simply reporting the news.

Before the banquet, the American guests, including the press corps, posed for a huge group photo with Chinese leaders (except for Chou and the reclusive Mao but including Madame Mao, Chiang Ching) on the landing of a vast staircase in the Great Hall of the People. In the background was a large landscape painting with an inscription from Mao's poem, "Snow." The Chinese government gave us copies of the photo. I am peeking out from behind Walter Cronkite.

During the nearly three–hour banquet we listened to Chinese musicians play their distinctively high–pitched versions of "Home on the Range" and other American songs. It was a replay of what I'd seen on television when Nixon visited China, true, but to be there was electrifying. The Chinese at my table were confirmed cigarette smokers, and we exchanged my Camels for their Pandas, along with toasts with Chinese wine (not as good as Chinese beer) and then the rice brandy Mao Tai (potent stuff, which one learned to sip slowly). By the end of the evening, I was stuffed. Counting the luncheon and the banquet, which included a silver sharkfin casserole and steamed Wuchang fish, I had consumed 19 courses of marvelous food.

Jurey and "responsible person" at the Great Wall of China.

For this Chinese government photo, a memento of President Ford's December 1975 visit, the American entourage posed with Deng Xiaoping (front row) and other Chinese officials at the Great Hall of the People. Jurey is peeking out from behind Walter Cronkite (front row, left).

President Ford and his daughter, Susan, look on while Chairman Mao greets Henry Kissinger, during the president's visit to China in December 1975. When the aging Mao saw Susan, Mrs. Ford reported, his eyes "lighted up brightly." (Courtesy, Gerald R. Ford Library)

Apart from the festivities, little information was given about Ford's schedule, and press coverage was limited. Susan Ford was the one to provide a story. We accompanied her on a visit to the Great Wall. The climb to the top was steep; we ran out of breath and welcomed rest stops while Susan took pictures, photographers took pictures of Susan taking pictures, and we all took pictures of each other. The cold was piercing, even though I was layered with clothes, including the same long underwear I'd worn in Vladivostok. Gertrude Tai of VOA's China service had advised me to take "warm pants and warm underwear." But covering the president's comely daughter was an enjoyable outing. We followed Susan to the Ming Tombs, where a buffet lunch awaited us. On her arrival she received word to return immediately to the Guest House where her parents were staying. Forget the lunch, we reporters insisted on leaving too. We suspected the Fords had been invited to meet with Chairman Mao.

Yes, they had. For upcoming newscasts we radio correspondents filed "quick and dirty" reports, stories with not much meat, and then waited for a "read-out." Hours later, the Chinese news agency, Hsinhua (now Xinhua), carried some information: Ford and the 82–year–old Mao had "earnest and significant discussions on wide–ranging issues in a friendly atmosphere. " But no details were given. Still later Press Secretary Ron Nessen told us the Hsinhua report appeared to be "a fair description," but refused to say more. We agonized for details, not wanting to sound like Peking Radio, which carried a recitation of the list of participants in the meeting. It took Mrs. Ford finally to give us a morsel: Mao's "eyes lighted up brightly when he saw Susan." Of course I reported that. Later Susan was asked by a pool reporter if Mao "really had a glint in his eye" when he shook her hand. "Yes," she said, "he was nice. I don't think he expected (pause) me."

Hard news was sparse, and Chinese officials, not wanting to see idle reporters unleashed to explore on their own, tried to keep the American press occupied by laying on daily excursions. One was to the Evergreen People's Commune, where our group saw a "barefoot doctor," something like a paramedic, treating patients in a clinic, and elementary school children, dressed in bright clothing, singing and reciting their lessons in English, and dancing in front of a portrait of Mao. We visited a "model home," a tiny and spare apartment, drab except for a small aquarium with darting goldfish and a windowsill with potted plants. On the wall, a picture of Mao. We also were shown a greenhouse, where our kindly host gave each of us a cucumber.

My color story on the commune pleased VOA's China service, as did the "wild sound" that I recorded and then fed on the white line. VOA's language services are always eager for language "actualities," and my tape included narration in Mandarin by the commune hosts. For Worldwide English, which was pleased to get feature material for its 20-minute news programs, I had the luxury of filing "long" reports of two and a half minutes, an unthinkable length for U.S. domestic broadcasting, where radio correspondents are limited to 40 seconds or less. My radio colleagues chafed at having to abbreviate their stories, bringing to mind a former Mutual Radio correspondent who called his reports "duck farts."

Another feature was on a visit to a ballet school, where Betty Ford kicked off her shoes and joined in an "impromptu" dance with girls dressed in blue leotards (royal blue). This got wide play in the U.S. media. Garry Trudeau of "Doonesbury" fame, covering the trip for Universal Press Syndicate, described the "joyful pas de deux" as "those few moments of magic." But the magic nearly didn't happen. My "responsible person," Duh-yen (phonetic), had told me Mrs. Ford was going to dance in Classroom Number 4, where Peter Lisagor, Hugh Sidey and I were waiting, but someone slipped up and forgot the scenario. Duh-yen saved the day. She and a puzzled Sheila Weidenfeld, Mrs. Ford's press secretary, did some quick whispering to the appropriate persons, and the dance finally took place.

In between excursions and filing stories, Helen Thomas and I seized some moments to go shopping. We made a quick trip to the Chinese government store for foreign tourists, the Friendship Store, where I bought a useful souvenir — a Chinese-made "Panda" shortwave radio. But my main shopping mission was to find dictionaries. Gertrude Tai had asked me to try to get copies of the new English–Chinese dictionary published in Shanghai, four if possible, for the China service. The dictionary would be invaluable in updating VOA's Chinese broadcasters.

Where to find it? Repeated requests for information were unsuccessful, or, a suspicious thought, stonewalled. What about such-and-such bookstore, I asked. "No, they wouldn't have it," I was told, "we don't think you can get it anywhere." But on the day before we were to leave, I made a final try, at the Foreign Ministry's information office where the staffers said vaguely they'd see what they could do. I was skeptical. Then in late afternoon, while waiting in the Min Zu lobby to change remaining Chinese yuan back into dollars, I felt a tap on my shoulder. The tapper was a young woman from the ministry who asked if I were the one looking for a dictionary.

With my "yes, yes," she directed me to the lobby counter where picture postcards and little red books of Chairman Mao's Thoughts were sold. An unlikely place for selling a dictionary, but the counter attendant smiled affirmatively. Obviously Chinese officials had concluded it was okay to let the VOA correspondent buy it. "How many copies do you have?" "Three." "I'll take them!" I hand-carried the heavy volumes home as if they were headed for the rare-book section of the Library of Congress.

Although I didn't have time to buy presents for relatives and friends, Connie Gerrard of the White House Press Office did some Christmas shopping for me, and thanks to her, I took home some beautiful, and inexpensive, cashmere sweaters. Some correspondents did well in their shopping. The most imaginative purchase was made by Dick Dudman of *The St. Louis Post Dispatch*, who bought two Chinese bicycles, for his wife Helen and himself.

The final event of the visit was a reciprocal banquet that the president and Mrs. Ford gave in honor of Deng and other Chinese officials. Five hundred guests, including the White House press, were invited to the affair in the Great Hall of the People, where our toasts were exchanged with California champagne. Ford and Deng, I reported, used very similar language in their toasts. They reaffirmed that the U.S. and China shared common interests in the world despite their differences, and that they would keep working toward the goal of normalizing relations. After a Kissinger briefing, I finished filing stories at 2:30 a.m., then packed my suitcase for our baggage pickup two hours later. I purposely did not pack a book about China by Ross Terrill that I'd taken along on the trip.

We had been advised that we shouldn't give presents to the Chinese, as they might be offended. But I wanted to give Duh-yen something tangible to show how much I appreciated her help, and so when we said goodbye at the airport, I said I didn't have room for the book and asked her if she'd do me the favor of taking it off my hands. She understood.

Ford's visit got good play in the Chinese media, but was generally kissed off in the American press as not having accomplished anything tangible, as merely a media event. A *Time* magazine article concluded, "The diplomatic emptiness of the trip suggested Ford might have accomplished more by staying in Washington than by taking a showboat to China." I thought the trip was necessary, at what was a toddler stage in U.S.–Chinese relations, and told a VOA staff meeting if Ford hadn't made it, "that would have been a story." He was carrying on the policy of developing normal relations between the U.S. and China, spelled out in the 1972 Shanghai communique on Nixon's visit — a policy in which the U.S. acknowledged the position that "there is but one China and that Taiwan is a part of China" and said the Taiwan question should be settled peacefully "by the Chinese themselves."

Throughout the Ford visit, our "responsible persons" delicately probed American reporters for not only our views on detente but also on American politics. They specifically wanted to know about the conservative, pro-Taiwan Ronald Reagan, then preparing to challenge Ford for the Republican presidential nomination.

Nine years later the Chinese were welcoming Ronald Reagan as president. By the time of his trip — dubbed by reporters as a "slow boat to China" because it took nearly a week to get there, what with rest stops in Hawaii and Guam — formal diplomatic relations had been established under Carter and diplomatic ties with Taiwan were severed, replaced by non–governmental relations. And Deng Xiaoping and Premier Zhao Ziyang had made visits to Washington.

The Peking of 1984, its name changed to the more musical Beijing, was no longer the gray and blue of the Peking of 1975. It was Spring and the late April sun brightened evidence of progress. The gray smog was gone, and because of the tree–planting program, graceful young trees flowered near new buildings and construction sites for apartment houses. The streets still were full of bicycle riders, but there were more cars, buses and trucks. People wore clothing of bright colors instead of the glum blue. Billboard advertising, mostly of manufactured goods, had come to Beijing since the Ford visit, and there seemed to be fewer outdoor signs bearing government exhortations. Of the visible official signs, the ones that struck me and my colleagues riding to event sites on White House–chartered press buses were pictures of a little girl and the words, translated for us, "Mommy, Daddy, and me." In the one–child–per–family campaign to control population growth, this was an anti–infanticide admonition: Do not do away with your little girl in hopes of having a boy.

The traveling press had no "responsible persons" to look after us and talk with us, no excursions arranged by Chinese officials to a People's Commune. We were left to our own devices, but as it turned out, there was less exposure to the Chinese than in 1975. Reporters didn't have as much free time because press coverage was extensive. Although there were more of us, since major news organizations, including VOA, now had resident correspondents in China, we were kept busy serving on pools and covering Reagan speeches and other presidential events.

Wayne Corey, VOA's first correspondent in Beijing, covered the Chinese briefings, obtained what were rare English language copies of Chinese banquet toasts and tracked their nuances, and stood duty in the filing center while I served on press pools. For this trip, VOA also sent a reporter from the China Service, Sinclair Ke, and a radio technician, Danny Kawaguchi, on the White House press plane, so I didn't have to worry about getting language "actualities" or fixing recalcitrant tape recorders. Having Danny on the trip meant I didn't have to carry the extra tape recorders, cassettes and cables that I had taken with me on the Ford visit to China. I still had a lot of gear, including the White House and State Department–compiled trip book with its leather cover, in yellow. Red also had been eschewed for Ford's visit; the trip book's cover then was green.

The traveling press corps (137 men/21 women on the White House manifest) was quartered away from the heart of the city, in the new and aggressively Western–style 22–story Great Wall Hotel (with glassed elevators), one of the Chinese–American business ventures resulting from improved relations and efforts to modernize China. We might as well have been staying in a Hyatt or Hilton in Dallas or Detroit. Our rooms had good showers, but no Jasmine tea and Mandarin oranges. The press filing center was cramped and there were no lounge areas where we could chat with waiters. In the lobby we passed through a filter of American–accented conversations among business–suited men seated on plush lounge chairs, not a doily in sight. The hotel's Chinese restaurant had not yet opened, so many of us ate in its Western–style restaurant. The limited offerings included a feeble version of hamburgers.

With the avowed anti–communist Reagan in China, making his first official visit to a communist country, and with Chinese leaders who had once viewed him with apprehension and scorn now giving him a fulsome welcome, reporters did have a "whizzer" of a story, and some choice soundbites. One that we all broadcast or quoted came at the welcoming banquet, when Reagan said in his toast that Americans want to be good neighbors to the Chinese people, and "neighbors can be dear and trusted friends."

The banquet itself, to which the traveling press had been invited, was a repeat of the one given for Ford, but being there was as stirring as before. The meal was again a multi–course affair; it was the best of our stay in Beijing. Security on the American side was very much in evidence, with Secret Service agents checking the press at every whip–stitch. The Chinese security was much more subtle, and reporters even were allowed to wander around the banquet tables beforehand and peer at the main table where the

Reagans would dine. The centerpiece was a large pagoda–like construction with tiny electric lights, flanked by several large swans made out of spun sugar.

The banquet was the start of a re–visit to celebrity status for me. To my left was a young man from the Foreign Ministry who said he and his colleagues listened to VOA every day. Across the table a Chinese official told Gene Gibbons of UPI–Radio (later Reuters) that he recognized my voice. This and similar incidents were enough of a curiosity that Gene broadcast a report to listeners back home: "Some of the biggest names in American journalism are covering this presidential trip, people like Ted Koppel, Sam Donaldson, Chris Wallace and Lesley Stahl. But the Chinese don't know any of them from Adam. The most famous broadcaster with the president, as far as the Chinese are concerned, is a woman most Americans never heard of. . . ." Et cetera. Donnie Radcliffe of *The Washington Post* also wrote an item, including "Jurey was the one media celebrity Chinese officials wanted to meet."

Being singled out is heady stuff, but actually other VOA broadcasters were household names in China, especially Wayne Corey and his successors as Beijing correspondent. Surveys have shown that many Chinese listen to VOA's programs in English to learn the language. This had been brought home to me when Youngstown friends, Vera and Fred Friedman, visited China and met a university professor who impressed them with his fluency in English. They asked Chen how he'd learned the language; he said it was by listening to VOA. They asked if he'd ever heard their friend Philomena Jurey; he said that hearing me reporting from the White House was the reason he spoke English so well.

The Friedmans kept up a correspondence with Chen and in 1982 alerted me and June and Bill Loch, also friends from our *Youngstown Vindicator* circle, that he was coming to the U.S. to teach at a Washington area university. We met at the Lochs' home in suburban Washington. Chen wrote the Friedmans that he had met "what would be considered as two legendary figures in China — a correspondent covering the White House and the manager of a Las Vegas club, her brother." My brother Joe, a retired school teacher, was visiting me from Las Vegas, where he was then managing a poker room in a casino.

Chen said that as he listened to our talk, he "began to realize how dull and limited my life had been — a life that had been spent in the classroom and in the library." His life was hardly dull; we learned later that during the disastrous Cultural Revolution, he had been dispatched to the country to tend pigs on a farm. Chen helped me with Chinese pronunciations when I was preparing for Reagan's China trip. From him I learned how to say Beijing with just the right intonation.

On the second day of Reagan's visit, he made a speech to 500 Chinese community leaders that was to be shown in full on Chinese television after the evening news. But the Chinese deleted portions of it, and reporters had a good story. Edited out were mention of Soviet "troops massed on China's borders," a comment that "America and China both condemn military expansionism, the brutal occupation of Afghanistan and the crushing of Kampuchea," and references to God and the American Revolution. I was thankful my initial report, written from the advance text distributed to the press, contained all that material, since it was broadcast back to China, and worldwide, including the Soviet Union, and anyone listening to VOA would hear it. In reporting on the deletions, I carried the material again, adding that long–time foreign correspondents in Beijing "say it's customary for the Chinese press to delete anti–Soviet comments from visitors, and also references to God."

The next day, the Chinese cut out a portion of a recorded Reagan interview with Chinese TV that was similar to the remarks deleted from his speech. My broadcast piece reported that a Chinese government spokesman "when asked why the speech was censored said it is the practice not to carry comments by visitors to third countries." And, "A White House spokesman said the decision to drop passages was a Chinese internal matter, but expressed regret." A dispatch in *The New York Times* had some additional material which, looking back, I wish I'd mentioned. It pointed out that

"Peking has entered into talks with Moscow aimed at normalizing relations."

The extensive press coverage gave us exceptional chances to see Chinese leaders up close. At an impromptu news conference with our press pool, Premier Zhao fielded hard–ball questions from Sam Donaldson with self–assurance and pragmatic answers. One of his responses was that relations between countries shouldn't be based on ideology.

Deng Xiaoping reminded me of shrewd old Italian gentlemen discoursing amiably on the sides of a bocce court, and not letting a single thing escape their eyes. He was jovial, had a grandfatherly look, and I thought China was lucky he was leading it into the modern world. If one were trying to make a hit with Reagan, one couldn't have done it more adroitly than Deng — he was very warm to Nancy Reagan. During a photo opportunity, he praised her for helping the campaign to provide food for China's giant pandas, then suffering from a shortage of their normal diet of bamboo, and he invited her to visit China again, even suggesting that she should do so without her husband. This chit–chat took place in a reception room at the Great Hall of the People. Deng was in an overstuffed armchair, complete with antimacassars; next to him was a tea–table with a translator behind it; in the center sat Reagan in a similar armchair, and Nancy was in another at the right.

Our press pool was then ushered out, to wait in the spacious corridors while Reagan and Deng held talks and had lunch. Norm Sandler of UPI and I staved off hunger by sharing a bag of peanuts that one of us had saved from the press plane. After lunch Nancy Reagan rejoined the president for a drive through the countryside to see the Great Wall of China, accompanied by our pool. During the more than one–hour drive each way, crowds of Chinese watched the presidential motorcade speed by. The visit amounted to a brief photo op, nothing like our breathless excursion with Susan Ford. No steep climb this time for a great view of the Great Wall. What was impressive, though, was to see the press corps

Deng Xiaoping exchanges pleasantries with President Reagan and his wife Nancy in April 1984, and invites her to visit China again. (Courtesy, Ronald Reagan Library)

descend on the souvenir shop there. I thought the American press did its share in improving commerce between the two countries.

In the picture–taking session at the wall, the TV camera folks included a crew that was doing a documentary on the trip for the Republican Party, for use in the president's re–election campaign. In one of my broadcast pieces, I noted that "Mr. Reagan's visit to China is obviously regarded by his campaign aides as a political plus. He is receiving publicity in the news media in his role as a world leader, while the opposition Democratic presidential contenders are engaged in fractious battle for their party's nomination."

That evening the Reagans gave a reciprocal banquet in honor of Premier Zhao. It was held at the Great Wall Hotel and, unlike the scenario of the Ford visit, the whole press corps wasn't invited, just a few of the media stars. Robert (Bob) Sims, the White House spokesman on foreign policy matters, told me later that some of the Chinese guests asked my whereabouts. I was being "held hostage," along with other members of the press, in the filing center. Its exits had been blocked off because of tight security during the banquet. Sam Donaldson took up our cause in a disputatious encounter with the Secret Service, and eventually we were liberated.

At the banquet, Reagan and Zhao emphasized the positive in Sino–American relations during their exchange of toasts. Reagan had been using quotes from Chinese poet–philosophers in his speeches in Beijing, and Zhao reciprocated by quoting an American poet, Emerson: "The way to make a friend is to treat others like friends."

A photo op that lasted all day was the Reagans' visit to the great archeological find at Xian, the tomb of the emperor who unified China in 221 B.C. They flew there on a U.S. Air Force plane (substituting for the regular Air Force One), the first time a foreign leader had been allowed to use his own government aircraft within Chinese airspace. The press corps made the flight aboard two Chinese Airline planes, coddled by smartly uniformed pretty young women who gave gracious speeches in English about

Chinese-American friendship. A long ride aboard press buses in the presidential motorcade took us from the airport through fertile farmland to the ancient dust of the excavation. I was mesmerized by the rows of life-size terra cotta warriors and horses unearthed from their underground vigil.

The press was kept on a platform while the Reagans posed for TV and photos alongside the clay figures below. Suddenly, we saw Naomi Nover, our Helsinki "white butterfly" pool reporter, at the other end of the pit. A wag in the press corps had shown one of the Chinese functionaries a dollar bill with its picture of George Washington and had pointed out Naomi's resemblance to Washington. Obviously she was a VIP, and was allowed into the pit.

Before leaving Beijing, Reagan recorded his Saturday radio broadcast to the American people, describing China's efforts to modernize, foster the spirit of enterprise and open its doors to the West. Throughout his visit he preached the gospel of free enterprise. He also gave something of a travelogue, and in one of his typical homey touches, told Americans, "All of you who like bike riding would love Beijing." In a farewell ceremony in Beijing, President Li Xiannian described the president's visit as very successful.

The visit ended in Shanghai, where crowds estimated by local police at over one million turned out to see Reagan as his motorcade drove by. During appearances at Fudan University, he called on China's students to understand America and said Chinese and American students and scholars have a great role to play in their countries' futures. On the lovely campus I spied a tall statue of Mao, almost hidden by shrubs and trees, and, it seemed to me, neglected. Mao was seldom mentioned during the whole stay in China and the little red books of his thoughts were unseen.

The press was quartered at the Jin Jiang Hotel in the former French concession, one of the settlements established by Western colonists after Shanghai opened as a trading port in the mid-1800s. The hotel had an agreeable old world charm and a dining room that served, thank heavens, no hamburgers. I ventured forth with a companionable colleague of many White House trips, Candy Crowley of AP-Radio (later CNN), to investigate a department store nearby. But we soon gave up, unnerved by the crush of wall-to-wall people out enjoying the sunny May Day holiday.

On the way home Reagan said during a stop in Alaska, where he met with the traveling Pope, that he was impressed with the "injection of free market spirit" in China's economy — and, startling reporters, referred to "this so-called Communist China." He was making the point that the Chinese weren't "expansionist" communists, but it was a quote that all of us zestfully quoted. In comparing my stories with those of other reporters, I found, as I had on the Ford trip, that while some of them had more "hype" than mine, we covered the same ground. The newspaper stories were more detailed; as an ex-newspaper reporter, I envied the fact that print reporters have more space than broadcasters do.

As for my admittedly surface look at the changes in China, I did wonder how modernization would fare in the face of the problems of running a country with a population of one billion and of a system with twin government and communist party bureaucracies in control, the party more equal than the government. But I failed to recognize something *The Washington Post*'s Michael Weisskopf wrote in a dispatch from Beijing at the time: ". . . beneath this patina of progress lies a conservative political undertow that pulls China back whenever the forces of change challenge Communist Party authority." What I saw in 1984 was that things were getting better for the Chinese people. I wasn't smart enough to predict the pro-democracy movement and the violent crackdown in 1989. Nor were others aboard the returning 747. Yet I don't think we were lacking in acuity. We were reporters; we did not see ourselves as prophets. I happen to believe that being a reporter — in VOA's case, a reporter to the world — is a high calling. So I am content to have had that role, and grateful it took me, twice, to see the country which years ago mystified a little girl in New Castle, Pennsylvania.

8
Jerry and Ronnie, Jerry and Jimmy
Debates and Whistlestops
A Party in Vail, Christmas in Plains

Every seat in the auditorium of the Shrine Mosque in Springfield, Missouri, was filled and people were standing in the aisles. Republicans were holding a state convention and were waiting for a speech by Ronald Reagan, a day after President Ford had appealed for their support in his struggle with Reagan for the party's presidential nomination. I perched on a step, sweating like everyone else. On this humid June Saturday it was steaming hot in the hall.

I had covered Ford's convention-eve visit to Springfield the day before and then stayed over to cover his rival. This was the opening round of a new phase in the 1976 campaign for the Republican nomination, I explained to VOA listeners. With the string of state primary elections over, neither Ford nor Reagan had accumulated enough delegate support to win the nomination on the first ballot at the party's national convention in August. Now both were focusing on the state party conventions that would be selecting delegates to the national one. The president and his challenger, I reported, were facing a situation where every delegate counts.

In Springfield, 19 national delegates were at stake. Thirty others already had been chosen — 15 for Ford, 12 for Reagan and 3 uncommitted. During his visit, Ford courted the Missouri Republicans in a series of meetings and at a reception, and told them he was more electable than Reagan. His supporters pointed to a statewide public opinion poll that showed he could do better than Reagan against the likely Democratic presidential nominee, Jimmy Carter. (The poll had Carter winning against both, with Ford 12 percentage points higher than Reagan.)

But a banner in the Shrine Mosque proclaimed "This Is Reagan Country." And that's what it was. For nearly an hour the former California governor had the rapt attention of the 1,439 state

delegates and their alternates. He wowed them with his conservative message and some of his moralistic stories, including the one
about the dope hidden in a baby's diaper, and, as I reported to
VOA's listeners, displayed his masterful timing and skill as a
speaker. This was the first time I'd seen him and the chemistry he
had with an audience. He is, I thought, a formidable politician.

"That's a tough act to follow," said Senator Robert Dole, who
spoke next on behalf of Ford. The Missourians applauded his
remarks, but their hearts were with Reagan and his philosophy. He
collected all but one of the 19 delegates. Ford, despite the setback,
was still ahead of Reagan in the national total of delegates, although
by a small margin.

National political campaigns had everything: Drama, comedy,
high stakes, the unexpected, the crowds, the hoopla, the rhetoric.
I loved covering them. Besides, I thought, a presidential election
campaign is VOA's best story to report to the world. It spotlights
America's democratic processes. It also reflects the nation's rich
diversity as seen along the campaign trail. The story is a challenging
one to tell overseas listeners. It involves explaining the mysteries of
convention delegate counts and electoral college votes, giving the
background of campaign issues, and making sure that campaign
rhetoric on foreign policy issues, whether from the president or his
opposition, is put in the context of the election battle.

I had been an on–scene observer of the national conventions in
1964 and 1968, when I went on leave and accompanied my
husband, and in 1972, when I took vacation time again and served
as an extra hand for Sid Davis's Westinghouse broadcasting team.
So I was delighted, and well–backgrounded, when I was assigned to
the VOA teams covering the 1976 conventions. At the Democratic
convention in July in New York City, I had an extra advantage.
My stepdaughter, then living in Tallahassee, was a Carter delegate
from Florida. Diane took me to a convention–eve party hosted by
Jimmy Carter for delegates, alternates and their guests at a Hudson
River pier, and I wrote a feature about it for VOA. The
party–goers were served 10,000 pieces of fried chicken, gallons of
cole slaw and potato salad, and plenty of beer and soda pop.

Delegates stood in a long line waiting to congratulate the former Georgia governor on his pre-convention victory in the primaries. The Jimmy Carter smile was very much in evidence. Bands played and delegates sang the Democratic theme song, "Happy Days Are Here Again."

My first night in New York wasn't so happy. I was having a drink with Diane in a bar at the headquarters hotel, reached down to get my purse on the floor beneath my chair, and discovered it had been stolen. I was more worried about my convention credentials than anything else in the purse, concerned that the thief would use them to get into the convention on some possibly mischievous or harmful mission, and immediately notified the Convention Office, the Secret Service, and so on, and received new passes by the time the convention opened. I never put my purse under my chair again.

My assignments included covering the keynote speech by Barbara Jordan (with her magnificent oratory, the 46-year-old black Congresswoman from Texas captured the audience), interviewing Senator Daniel Patrick Moynihan on the platform's foreign policy plank, and writing profiles of leading figures at the convention; among them, the "Happy Warrior," Hubert Humphrey, whom I greatly admired. I was raised in a Republican household; my father, a devout Republican, had a picture of Richard Nixon in the living room, until Watergate. But I became a Democrat because of the principles which the Democratic party stood for and which Humphrey ardently represented. As a reporter, however, I couldn't and didn't let my personal views affect my work.

Carter brought down the house in beginning his acceptance speech with the line he used when he was an unknown starting his campaign: "My name is Jimmy Carter and I'm running for president." His speech was reported by Ed Conley, who had covered him during the primaries. I was satisfied just to be there. A White House correspondent should be, needs to be, exposed to what the president's opposition is saying.

After the convention I resumed covering the president and his contest with Reagan. A White House event I relished witnessing was the swearing-in of the first woman to be the U.S. chief of protocol, the curly headed child movie star of my childhood, Shirley Temple. Now she was a sleekly groomed 48-year-old diplomat, Shirley Temple Black, leaving her post as the U.S. ambassador to Ghana. I filed a feature for VOA's broadcasts to Africa that included an anecdote she told Ford. A Ghanaian chief in Cape Coast had named her his honorary deputy, and before she left for Washington she received his permission to remain an honorary African chief while serving as protocol chief.

Her protocol debut was at a White House reception and concert for Washington's diplomatic corps. It was a bicentennial event, one of many Ford presided over during the national celebration that coincided with the toughest fight of his political career. Ford also entertained a series of bicentennial visitors from abroad.

The visitor who most interested me, and just about everyone in Washington, was Queen Elizabeth. She was dressed simply, a coatdress of pale blue with matching hat, when she arrived on July 7 for the ceremonial welcome on the White House South Lawn, but in her body language she was the very definition of regal. My stories about the queen's visit of course noted that she represented the colonial power from which the United States had won its independence. At a White House state dinner, Queen Elizabeth noted that, after the Revolutionary War, "Hostilities soon broke out between us, and even burst into this house." She was indulging in a royal bit of understatement, given the fact that the Brits burned the White House during the War of 1812.

Ford increased his visibility as the incumbent president in his meetings with visiting world leaders, in his travels to the shrines of American independence, and in hosting the second economic summit, in Puerto Rico, just a few weeks before the Republican convention. None of that helped much in his campaign.

One week before the convention I reported on VOA, "No one can say absolutely whom the Republicans will pick as their presidential nominee. President Ford is viewed as the likely winner of the nomination, but Ronald Reagan, as *The New York Times* put it, has kept his candidacy alive and also has increased the possibility, though still not a probability, that he can defeat Mr. Ford on the floor of the convention."

The Reagan threat ended in the roll call vote on the night of August 18 at the convention center in Kansas City, when the West Virginia delegation cast 20 of its 28 votes for the president, putting him over the number needed for the nomination. The next night, to the cheers of the delegates, Ford declared in his acceptance speech: "I am ready, I am eager to go before the American people and debate the real issues face–to–face with Jimmy Carter."

Within minutes Carter issued a statement taking Ford up on his challenge. Ford's offer to debate was an unconventional thing for him to do. An incumbent president is hardly expected to give his opponent the nationwide publicity that comes with such events. But he was the underdog, far behind Carter in the opinion polls, and his aides thought he'd do well in debating the Democratic nominee.

First he had to pull his minority party together. He called on Reagan, in Reagan's hotel room, and then they appeared together in a display of unity. Reagan had a farewell meeting with his supporters and campaign staff and told them he and his wife "aren't going to go back and sit on a rocking chair on the front porch and say well, that's all for us." VOA's Sean Kelly covered the session and ended his report by quoting a Reagan supporter: "We'll be back to fight another day."

Ford and Carter had the first of their nationally televised debates on the evening of September 23 in the historic Walnut Theater in Philadelphia. It was the first such encounter since Kennedy and Nixon had faced each other in 1960, and the League of Women Voters, sponsor of the debates, called it a unique event. It was unique in more than one way. The sound went out. I was in the audience, and after wrapping up the debate, wrote a color story about the 28–minute debate gap. Ford and Carter were models of patience, serene islands at their separate lecterns, while electronic technicians scurried to and fro trying to locate the trouble. Neither spoke to the other as they waited under the hot television lights. At one point they were told they were off–camera and in that brief moment both whipped out their handkerchiefs, almost simultaneously, and mopped their brows.

VOA carried the debate live, and I sympathized with the anchor and others in Worldwide English who had to fill the time until the sound was restored. Being in the theater audience that night was useful, but it was not the way to cover a campaign debate. More important than seeing the candidates in the flesh was seeing how they came over on the television screen to the vast viewing public. So in future debates, I decided, I would watch the tube. Even then, it's not always easy to determine the winner immediately.

The next debate, on foreign policy and defense issues, was scheduled for October 6 in San Francisco. A few days before that, Carter made a speech at the 4–H Club headquarters in Bethesda, Maryland, and there I switched places with Ed Conley to cover the Democratic candidate for a while. Carter went on to Plains to spend the weekend in his hometown, and I flew on "Peanut Two," the press plane that accompanied "Peanut One," the names inspired by Carter's background as a Georgia peanut farmer. Peanuts are not known as peanuts in many other countries, so just about every time a VOA story mentioned them we'd say something like, "or groundnuts as they're called elsewhere."

The press flew to Albany, Georgia, which I learned to pronounce "awl–benny," and from there drove to the press motel in Americus, about 10 miles from Plains via a two–lane road bordered by farmland and the rapacious kudzu vine.

A campaign fundraising dinner in Plains, unlike any other I'd covered, was held at the country home of Carter's mother, known simply as Miz Lillian, who was of interest to overseas listeners because she served as a Peace Corps volunteer in India in the late 1960s. Democratic Party faithful from around the country journeyed to Plains, then down a dirt road to Miz Lillian's Pond House to dine on "down home" food at tables set up among tall pine trees near a pond. The ladies of Plains had spent three days preparing for the party, each cooking enough for 12 persons: Fried chicken, country ham, creamed squash and creamed sweet potatoes, potato salad, corn on the cob, and of course, black–eyed peas. The feast was consumed to the sounds of "down home" music, country fiddling. I taped the fiddling and used part of the sound in the color piece I filed, noting that the event raised over $1 million.

The San Francisco debate took place at the Palace of Fine Arts, where CBS, the network serving as the television pool, had three back–up systems to guard against any repetition of the electronic problem at the first debate. There was a problem of another sort at this one, and it was Ford's.

One of the three panelists, Max Frankel of *The New York Times*, asked the president a question about several aspects of the U.S. relationship with the Soviet Union and said, "We virtually signed in Helsinki an agreement that the Russians have dominance in Eastern Europe." Ford pointed out that 35 nations, including the Vatican, had signed the agreement, and then declared: "There is no Soviet domination of Eastern Europe, and there never will be under the Ford administration."

Frankel followed up: "Do I understand you to say, sir, that the Russians are not using Eastern Europe as their own sphere of influence and occupying most of the countries there, and making sure with their troops that it is a communist zone, whereas on our side of the line the Italians and French are still flirting with communism?"

Ford replied: "I don't believe, Mr. Frankel, that the Yugoslavians consider themselves dominated by the Soviet Union. I don't believe the Romanians consider themselves dominated by the Soviet Union. I don't believe that the Poles consider themselves dominated by the Soviet Union. Each of those countries is independent, autonomous. It has its own territorial integrity and the United States does not concede that those countries are under the domination of the Soviet Union. As a matter of fact, I visited Poland, Yugoslavia and Romania to make certain that the president of the United States and the people of the United States are dedicated to their independence, their autonomy and their freedom."

Other foreign policy issues were debated but this was the one that made news, and the Carter camp, I reported, intended to make

Ford's "no Soviet domination" a campaign issue. Carter kept up the attack, pointing to 300,000 Soviet troops in Eastern Europe, in campaign stops at various cities, including two with large populations of Eastern European origin, Cleveland and Chicago, where leaders of ethnic groups expressed dismay over the president's remarks. Ford eventually acknowledged he'd misspoken. The public opinion pollsters awarded the debate to Carter. He needed the boost, for his lead in the polls had been substantially reduced in September.

By mid–October I had resumed covering the White House and the Ford campaign, and off we were on an old–fashioned whistlestop tour in Illinois. The nine–hour excursion aboard a train named after Abraham Lincoln, the "Honest Abe," took us to seven towns, starting with Joliet on a clear, shining, brisk morning. Ford delivered essentially the same speech at every stop and clearly enjoyed saying things about Carter like: "He wanders, he wavers, he waffles and he wiggles." It was a phrase that lived on. In 1992 Senator Bill Bradley led the Democratic convention in a chant accusing Republican President George Bush of waffling, wiggling and wavering, and Bush used it against his Democratic challenger, Bill Clinton.

Ford had another oft–repeated phrase on the whistlestop. He charged that Carter wanted to cut the defense budget by $15 billion, recalled President Theodore Roosevelt's advice, "Speak softly and carry a big stick," and adapted it to assert that "What Jimmy Carter says is speak loudly and carry a flyswatter!" In Alton, Illinois, the final stop, the phrase didn't trip so readily off the tongue: "What Jimmy Carter says is speak loudly and carry a flyspotter, a fly spot. . ." and finally he got it out, "a flyswatter." Ford laughed at himself and said, "It has been a long day." In a speech that night in St. Louis he did the flyswatter bit again, only this time he got it right.

The whistlestop through prairie lands, cornfields and historic communities was a natural for a campaign feature. The entourage included members of Congress, local candidates, pretty girls distributing campaign buttons, movie and TV stars, several hundred press people, and a Dixieland band, which paraded through the aisles.

Apart from reporting on the issues and key states and their electoral votes, I broadcast features to convey the flavor of traveling with the presidential candidates, and used tape of the sounds of the campaign, like a Polish–American group serenading each candidate with *Stolat*, a song wishing that he may live a hundred years.

Ford and his political aides made the most of the trappings of his office as he swept about the country. Air Force One performed fly–bys over countless community airports, and the presidential limousine was put on display. At many of these stops Ford declared, "A government that's big enough to give you everything you want is big enough to take away everything you have." He said it so often that the press took to chanting the last part of the sentence with him.

Reporters traveling with a president have an easier time doing their jobs than those traveling with the opposing candidate. The White House makes available transcripts of the president's speeches and remarks to press pools and feeds the sound through the mult box. With an opposition candidate, there are few if any transcripts. On the Carter campaign we were indebted many times to veteran reporter Don Irwin (*Los Angeles Times*), who typed out transcripts of key sections of speeches and gave them to those who wanted precise quotes. Radio reporters serving on pools dubbed their tapes of the candidate's remarks for fellow broadcasters through a "daisy chain" of tape recorders. The cord from the pooler's recorder was plugged into another, and the cord from that into another, and so on. In my first pool duty on the Carter campaign, I was worried that I wouldn't be able to muscle past camera crews to get close enough to him, that my microphone wouldn't pick up clear sound, and that my tape recorder would fail. But I managed. What a relief when my colleagues looked up from the daisy chain and said the tape quality was good.

On election day November 2 Ford voted in Grand Rapids and returned to the White House to follow the returns on television with his family and friends. He watched far into the night as projections put Carter in the lead. About 3:15 a.m. he went to bed, Nessen told us waiting reporters, still believing he would win. Soon Jimmy Carter was declared the winner in network projections and made his victory statement. The White House briefing room was packed when Ford appeared shortly before noon with his family to deliver his statement on the election. His voice was hoarse; he had strained his vocal cords, we were told, in the final intense days of campaigning; and he asked his wife to read the statement and his telegram to Carter. Betty Ford did it gallantly, this very human First Lady, admired for her candor and courage in dealing with breast cancer and for her outspokenness on issues. In the telegram, Ford assured Carter "that you will have my complete and wholehearted support as you take the oath of office this January." When Mrs. Ford finished reading, the president stepped down from the podium to mingle with the press. Reporters shook his hand and said, "Good luck, Mr. President," and he told us: "It's been real nice to see you all. It's been a lot of fun."

Yes, it was a lot of fun covering Ford. On one of his vacations in Vail, the press decided to give a party for Jerry and Betty. Don Irwin and *New York Times* correspondent James Naughton wrote a skit, entitled "My Fair Jerry," with lyrics to the music from *My Fair Lady.* I collected the money for the tickets, then had to check off each member of the press entering the party site under the watchful eyes of Secret Service agents. After the cocktail–buffet, the show went on. Helen Thomas, a superb mistress of ceremonies, declared that the press had gained a rich new understanding of the working vacation, finding presidential coverage invigorating indeed on the tennis courts, on the golf course, and at a favorite nightspot in Vail. This was a reference to Sheika's, where the Fords had danced cheek–to–cheek one night when some of us went there to see the Ink Spots.

Among the reporter/soloists was Pete Kumpa, who did a rendition of "The Rain in Spain" poking fun at the midwestern president's way of pronouncing words: "My judg–a–ment is GAR–en–teed to puzzle/ Phoneticists who think I need a muzzle." Pete couldn't carry a tune, and Ford, who guffawed throughout the whole show, said he was going to ask the mayor of Vail to give Kumpa the "off-key to the city."

Kissinger was the target of another solo, sung by Jim Naughton: "Henry is shrewd and so appealing. He said so just the other day." For the finale the press corps raggedly joined in lyrics dealing with Ford's promise to Congress to conciliate, cooperate and compromise: "Send me a bill. I get my thrill Screwing the Hill. Veto!"

In responding, Ford got in some licks of his own. He resented, he said, the inferences that he spent too much time on the golf course. "As a matter of fact, it tees me off." Undaunted by our groans, he went on: "It's a pretty brassy approach, if you ask me. I've been driving hard every day and yet you people chip away at me. No matter what, I won't be trapped. I want to be treated in a fair way."

The accomplished pianist for "My Fair Jerry" was Connie Gerrard, a valued assistant to a string of White House press secretaries going back to 1964. As Helen put it that night in Vail, "she knows the score." Connie remained the right hand to presidential press secretaries up to the end of the Reagan administration. As for Ford's golf, on a vacation in Palm Springs I was in a foursome behind his and can report he was no bumbler on the links. In fact he was graceful, and had an enviable swing.

The day after Ford's election defeat my office told me to get down to Plains as soon as possible. On Thursday I flew to Georgia and began covering the president-elect, reporting on the congratulatory telegrams sent to him, including one from the Kremlin signed by Nikolai Podgorny, and on "the warm and cordial tone" established by Ford and Carter since the election. This was reflected in Ford's making an Air Force jet available Saturday to fly Carter and his family to a vacation on St. Simon's Island off the coast of Georgia. The 707 was no ordinary jet. As Carter told the travel pool, "President Johnson was sworn in on this plane and it was used for Nixon's trip to China."

The five-day vacation was a good opportunity to get to know Carter's closest aides better, press secretary Jody Powell and campaign director Hamilton Jordan. We reporters had relaxed, informal sessions with them, with a good deal of joshing and give–and–take. I came away from them liking the Georgians.

In describing Plains for VOA's listeners, I did the same thing many other observers did, comparing it to a Hollywood set of a hamlet with a block–long main street of weatherbeaten storefronts. At one end was the old, no longer in use, wooden–planked railroad depot, at the other the Carter peanut warehouse. Plains had a population of 683, increased when Carter's brother Billy's wife, Sybil, gave birth to a boy. Among the most prominent citizens, I reported, was Carter's mother, "who sits in a rocking chair at the railroad depot and busily signs autographs and willingly poses for pictures with tourists." Miz Lillian clearly enjoyed talking with the male reporters and merely tolerated the female ones, though she seemed to take a liking to Ann Compton. Billy Carter held court too, at his gasoline station in "downtown" Plains. Billy had an easy–going relationship with the press, and often confided in Helen Thomas.

Plains was growing as a tourist attraction, with motorists detouring from superhighways out of curiosity to see Carter's hometown. An enterprising physics professor from Georgia Southwestern College in Americus, David Ewing, had begun operating a sight–seeing business, "Carter Country Tours," which included a look at young Jimmy's treehouse. The driver of the 14–seat tour bus, Joyce Jordan (pronounced JER–den, just like Hamilton's last name) said she averaged more than 100 tourists a day, including people, she said, "from everywhere all over the world." I interviewed some tourists from other countries for VOA, including a young doctor from India who was specializing in pediatrics at a hospital in Ohio and planned to return to India on completion of his studies. "Oh, I like it," he said of Plains, "I'm surprised that such a small town can produce such a thing, such a great man."

The number of tourists swelled to an estimated 5,000 a day during the Christmas holidays. Souvenir shops proliferated. By the summer of 1977, the manager of one, the Peanut Patch, reported between 2,400 and 2,500 visitors to the shop in a single day. On the road between Americus and Plains the kudzu was joined by billboards, a new service station, new campgrounds and later, a fancy French restaurant in the shape of a stone castle.

The press corps ballooned too. Most of us stayed at the Best Western Inn in Americus, in standard-drab motel rooms equipped with two double beds, two chairs, a dark green and turquoise color scheme for bedspreads and draperies, an oak chest of drawers, television set, and 60-watt light bulbs. In the room booked by VOA, Ed Conley had had a telephone with a coupler installed, for transmitting reports to our news operations studio, a glassed-in studio that we called "the bubble," which recorded feeds from VOA correspondents around the world. I fed most of my reports from the motel room because the press filing center in Plains was a makeshift affair, a storefront office with haphazardly arranged tables, a high noise level, and a few phones that didn't always work. When television arrived in full force, the networks had their own facility, a complex of trailers near the peanut warehouse.

Covering Carter involved trailing him around Plains and running up the mileage on our rental cars as we rushed out to the airfield to stake out personages coming to see him, drove to the Southwest Georgia Agricultural Station for his press conferences, and shuttled between Americus and Plains numerous times a day.

Our stakeouts included Sunday mornings spent standing outside the Plains Baptist Church. The church had drawn national attention, I explained to VOA's listeners, because its congregation was embroiled in a dispute over racial integration, and it was the church where the president-elect worshipped. The controversy began when a preacher, who operated a non-denominational mission in Albany, tried to enter the church. The deacons refused to admit him by enforcing a 1965 resolution barring what they called Negroes and other civil rights agitators from entering. Carter's position was clear; in 1965 he was one of five members of the church — the four others were his relatives — who had voted against the resolution.

On a cold mid-November Sunday, scores of press people and tourists waited on the church grounds for nearly three hours in intermittent rain as the congregation voted on the issue. The outcome was 120 in favor of opening the church to everyone who wanted to worship there, 66 against. The following Sunday at least four blacks, including the Albany mission preacher, attended the service. The church grounds were crowded with tourists and members of the American and foreign press, including the New York–based representative of Moscow's *Literary Digest*. As the service was getting under way, a young father carrying two of his children came out of the church and said he could not worship because of the presence of the news media. While cameramen were photographing him, he cried out to the press, "Please leave us alone," and he walked across the street to the Lutheran church.

In reporting all this, I told VOA's listeners: The presence of the news media on the once quiet grounds of the small Plains Baptist Church is likely to continue, although not likely in such numbers as last Sunday and this. It is a dilemma not only for the church members but also for the press, which is uncomfortable over the impression that it contributes to a circus–like atmosphere. There is constant coverage of a president, and in this case a president–elect. One television producer commented, "We have to be here because he is here. Jimmy Carter is not a private citizen."

The producer was right, but that didn't lessen the sadness I felt for the young father, nor the distaste over invading the privacy of others while covering a public person. The stakeouts at the church dwindled, but some reporters were always there Sunday mornings in case they could extract a comment from Carter on one issue or another after the service.

The personages who met with Carter in Plains included Walter Mondale, the vice president–elect; George Bush, who had been named CIA director the year before and gave Carter and Mondale a briefing on intelligence matters, and Henry Kissinger, who briefed them on international issues. After his nearly five–hour briefing at Carter's home, another stakeout location, the president–elect took the secretary of state on a tour of downtown Plains. They mingled with a crowd of delighted tourists and townfolk, and shook hands with those who were able to get close to them in the crush of people.

The briefings were part of what apparently was a smooth transition, underscored when Carter flew to Washington and met with Ford on November 22. The meeting between the president and the man who defeated him attracted the largest press gathering at the White House since Nixon's resignation. The two men and their wives greeted each other warmly, and while Ford and Carter talked in the Oval Office, Betty Ford had tea with Rosalynn Carter in the family quarters and showed her around the White House. In remarks to reporters, Ford again promised 100 per cent cooperation in the transition, and Carter said there could not have been a better demonstration of unity, friendship and good will than had been shown to him by President Ford.

On December 20 I flew to Georgia to begin a long stint covering the president-elect. He completed selection of his cabinet three days later, and I wrote a profile of the group, noting that "Mr. Carter campaigned against the Washington establishment but ended up choosing a cabinet that is just about evenly divided between people who have served in government before and people who are new to government service." His official family was "a mixture of political liberals, moderates and conservatives and of diverse backgrounds," and it included two women, one of them the first black woman named to a cabinet (Patricia Roberts Harris).

With Carter's latest appointments announced, the press faced a quiet Christmas. Many of our colleagues left for home to spend the holiday with their families. For those of us who had to stay in Plains/Americus the prospect was dreary. No turkey dinner, no festive occasion. Our choices for meals were limited: The Best Western, where we had eggs and the morning newspapers for breakfast, cheeseburgers and gossip for lunch, and an occasional dinner. Faye's Barbecue Villa in Americus, the "in" spot for the press, where we ate fat-rich steaks at crowded cloth-less tables, drank cheap "Hearty Burgundy" wine bought at the liquor store on the highway, and nibbled over the day's news. A Pizza Hut. A

Kentucky Fried Chicken outlet. Or ribs from a take–out place. The French restaurant hadn't yet been conceived.

For many years, I had carried on a tradition, started by my husband, of inviting acquaintances who were alone to Thanksgiving and Christmas dinner, and I always roasted a turkey. So why not do a turkey this Christmas for the waifs of the press? I talked it over with visiting friend Carol Woodard, and two days before Christmas I arranged to rent an apartment and we posted a sign–up sheet: "Some of us are going to fix our own Christmas dinner with turkey and so on. Time: about 6 p.m. Christmas Day. Place: Apt. 805A at Parkview Apts. down the road on Rt. 19 across from Kentucky Fried Chicken. If you'd like to join in the festivities, please sign below so we'll know how much food to prepare. All you have to do is come (and maybe bring your own bottle), but if you'd like to help cook, or contribute anything, or grocery shop, please tell phil jurey."

Twenty–seven signed up for the party, but others came too, and many volunteered to contribute food or beverages, shop, and help cook. We had bought two turkeys at the Big Star Supermarket, plus foil roasting pans and other supplies. Saul Friedman made a gourmet stuffing with garlic for one of the turkeys and a less potent one, without garlic, for the other. He also made a sweet potato dish, the hard way. We didn't have a potato masher, so he made do with a fork. Merilee Cox, then with UPI–Radio, and her AP–Radio competitor and future husband, Bob Berkowitz, concocted a vegetable dish and the salad. Helen Thomas brought pies; Julie Moon, cranberry sauce; Peter Maer of Mutual brought fruit; Howard Young of USIA's press service and his wife Hallie provided lemons, butter, various staples, and soap powder. My job was to baste the turkeys every half hour with lemon butter.

The small apartment, with kitchen open to the living room, was full of people, on the sofa, every available chair, the coffee table, and the floor. We toasted one another with champagne and wine, and after consuming the meal listened contentedly to a tape of a piano recital Saul's wife Evelyn had given back home. We sang, many of us misty–eyed, "Joy to the World," "Oh Little Town of

Bethlehem" and other Christmas carols. It was a family–style Christmas. And we had presents to unwrap. On the sign–up sheet someone had added a P.S.: "Bring a small gift for our grab bag." Everyone did. I still have the gift that fell to me, a 45 rpm record of a hit song in Georgia that year, "Drop Kick Me, Jesus, Through the Goal Posts of Life."

New Year's Eve was festive, too, with a sentimental touch. I spent it with a group of other White House correspondents at Faye's, where we clustered around the phone in the kitchen as Ann Compton placed a call to Vail so we could give President Ford our fond regards and wish him a Happy New Year. Those who talked with him included Helen Thomas, her respected AP competitor Frank Cormier, Bob Pierpoint, and Faye West, the restaurant's gregarious owner.

For the final days of the Ford administration I was back in Washington, while VOA's David Gollust, a highly competent young reporter who would be joining me on the White House beat, covered Carter in Plains. In a retrospective on Ford's stewardship, I wrote that "he gave the nation something it sorely needed; he restored a sense of decency to the White House." Mending the broken trust of Americans in their government "was perhaps the chief legacy of the two and a half years of the Ford presidency."

Ford himself felt this was his greatest achievement. In discussing his record with reporters, he also said his greatest disappointment was that he wasn't able to turn the economy around as effectively as he'd hoped. When he took office, the inflation rate was 12 per cent; when he left, it had been cut in half, but unemployment had risen and was hovering around eight per cent.

During his presidency Ford had a near–frenetic travel schedule, and I was grateful that Bob Leonard and I alternated trips. Bob was in California with Ford in September 1975 when there were two assassination attempts against him, the first in Sacramento by a young woman and the other 17 days later in San Francisco by a woman in her mid–40s. Reporters don't like to miss stories, but I was glad not to be present for either. Ford vowed not to let the attempts keep him from getting out into the country, and praised the Secret Service for doing a "super" job. I wrote a feature on the Secret Service for VOA, explaining that "it is actually not so secret; it has been in existence since 1865 and is the U.S. federal government's oldest general law enforcement agency." Under the Treasury Department, it was established to suppress counterfeiting of U.S. currency and began protecting presidents in 1901, after President William McKinley was assassinated.

The most back–breaking Ford trip overseas that I covered was in 1975 when he went to China and then on to Indonesia, the Philippines and Hawaii. His purpose was worthy, to proclaim that the U.S. was and intended to remain a Pacific power. But the trip was an example of how a president can be overscheduled when traveling abroad. Cramming so much into a trip is, I think, a form of insanity, even though the bulk of the work is done in advance. Most speeches and statements are already written and the agenda for discussions already established. The unexpected could happen, however. A tired president could be taken off–guard. And a tired press corps covering a multitude of events could miss an important element or nuance. I was grateful that VOA had sent regional correspondents Wayne Corey to Jakarta and Jim Miller to Manila to cover the visits with me.

Although the Fords were clearly tired, and the press too, there were some light moments to lessen the fatigue. In Jakarta the presidential entourage relaxed at a performance of Indonesian regional dances by pretty young ladies from Bali, Java and West Sumatra in stunning costumes and headdresses. Indonesian musicians played "Home on the Range" on a wooden xylophone, what a sweet sound. In the Philippines the Fords relaxed at a party given by President Ferdinand Marcos and his wife, Ymelda, aboard a yacht on their way back to Manila after a wreath–laying ceremony on Corregidor. They danced to songs from the Fifties and Sixties, and made a try at the traditional Tinikling dance. Pierre Salinger was the pool reporter and said Ford was the winner, while "the booby prize goes to Secretary Kissinger, whose Tinikling footwork is not in a league with his diplomatic footwork."

There were no time-outs, however, on the last day of the trip, December 7. We left Manila in the afternoon and flew to Honolulu where, because of time zones, it was still morning. Ford observed the anniversary of the 1941 Japanese attack on Pearl Harbor in a speech at the sobering U.S.S. *Arizona* Memorial. In a second speech, at the East-West Center, he spelled out his Pacific Doctrine, declaring that America has "a vital stake in Asia."

On January 20, 1977, Jimmy Carter took the oath of office as the 39th president of the United States and began his inaugural address: "For myself and our nation, I want to thank my predecessor for all he has done to heal our land."

Carter also was grateful to Ford for being, as he put it, "extraordinarily nice to me" in the transition, which laid the foundation for what would evolve into a friendship between the two men that was pleasing to track. In 1978 Jerry and Betty Ford were at the White House for a ceremony unveiling their official portraits, and Carter said of Ford: "He's a man who is beloved and appreciated, and no one appreciates him more than I do."

Their relationship grew in 1981 when President Reagan asked the three living ex-presidents to represent the United States at President Sadat's funeral in Cairo, and gave them a ceremonial sendoff on the White House South Lawn. The former presidents, Nixon, Ford and Carter, lined up beside the incumbent president, television lights shining on them in the evening darkness. I felt lucky to be a witness; seeing four American presidents together was then, as I reported, unprecedented in modern American history. Reagan thanked his predecessors for undertaking the mission and ended with a nice touch, the Irish saying, "Until we meet again, may God hold you in the hollow of His hand." Before boarding the helicopter taking them to Andrews Air Force Base, Carter walked over to shake hands with reporters who had covered him in the White House, another nice touch.

The warmth between Ford and Carter was in evidence at a public policy conference they co-hosted in February 1983 at the University of Michigan. My office decided at the last minute to send me to Ann Arbor to cover it. I arrived in time for the opening session, but too late to get into the conference hotel, and found a room at a Red Roof Inn with a "Sleep Cheap" sign in the lobby. The Jerry and Jimmy show went on for two days, to the enjoyment of conference participants, the press, and an overflow audience of students. In between discussing issues like federal budget deficits, they praised each other.

Ford: "I campaigned hard against you, President Carter, in 1976 and again in 1980, but in between those years when the national interest was at stake I found it fitting and right to support you on such issues as the ratification of the Panama Canal Treaty, the normalization of relations with the PRC, and the Camp David Agreement. . . and I now know that were our roles reversed, you would have done the same for a Ford administration." Carter: "The first words that I ever spoke as president of the United States were to and about Jerry Ford, on behalf of the 220 or more million Americans, to express my appreciation for what he did for our country in some very troubled times. And I haven't changed my mind. . . I still feel the same way."

The two defeated presidents also bantered and laughed at themselves. Carter: "Presidents come and go. Sometimes all too frequently." Ford: "I agree."

Their joint appearance at the university coincided with the publication, in *The Reader's Digest*, of an article they co-wrote on the Middle East, urging negotiations by the United States, Israel and moderate Arab nations. The article and conference were the first of endeavors that Ford and Carter, once political foes, now friends, would undertake together.

They campaigned against each other but became friends. Ex-Presidents Jimmy Carter and Jerry Ford at the University of Michigan in February 1983. (Courtesy, Gerald R. Ford Library)

Presidents Ford, Reagan, Carter and Nixon share a lighthearted moment at the White House, October 1981. (Courtesy, Ronald Reagan Library)

9
Travels with Carter
A Gaffe in Warsaw and Other Tales
VOA's Overseas Correspondents

With Jimmy Carter occupying the White House the press had to
be on alert, for he invariably answered questions in impromptu
encounters with reporters, and frequently made news. And in a
public forum, he might go beyond previously stated U.S. positions,
as I found in a small milltown in Massachusetts when his
presidency was barely two months old.

Carter was taking part in a town meeting in Clinton, near
Boston, on his first official trip out into the country since taking
office. More than 800 citizens crowded into the town hall, their
names drawn in a lottery, and for nearly an hour and a half he
answered questions from the audience on subjects ranging from the
Middle East to whether the town could receive federal help to
revitalize its downtown area.

This was a great feature story, but wait a minute. I did hear him
support a "homeland" for the Palestinian refugees, didn't I?
Previous U.S. references to the Palestinians said merely that their
legitimate interests should be taken into account. I checked my
notes and his Middle East remarks on my tape. He listed, as he had
before, three requirements for peace: Recognition of Israel,
establishment of permanent borders, and dealing with the
Palestinian problem. "The Palestinians claim," he said, "that Israel
has no right to be there; that the land belongs to the Palestinians.
And they've never yet given up their publicly professed commitment to destroy Israel. That has to be overcome." And then he
said: "There has to be a homeland provided for the Palestinian
refugees, who have suffered for many, many years. . . ."

In reporting on the town meeting, I focused on that, inserting
the tape so VOA listeners could hear the president's words in his
own voice. Carter's position on a homeland was refined two
months later, suggesting the "possibility of some arrangement for

a Palestinian homeland or entity, preferably in association with Jordan," if the Palestinians recognized Israel's right to exist in peace.

Another issue Carter discussed in Clinton, to applause from the audience, was human rights, and I filed a separate piece on that. "I feel very deeply," he said, "that when people are put in prison without trials, and tortured, and deprived of basic human rights, that the president of the United States ought to have a right to express displeasure and to do something about it." The next evening the president talked about human rights again, this time at the United Nations. He called for strengthened international machinery to advance the cause of human rights, and said, "No member of the United Nations can claim that mistreatment of its citizens is solely its own business."

Carter had said a number of times that his remarks on human rights weren't directed at any particular country, but the Soviet Union suspected otherwise. It had bristled when he wrote to Andrei Sakharov in February in response to a letter from the Soviet dissident. Carter's letter, which said human rights was a central concern of his administration, was distributed to western newsmen in Moscow, then confirmed by White House Press Secretary Jody Powell, who told reporters the president wasn't attempting to challenge the Soviet government.

Jody went on to say, I reported, that it was worth noting the Soviet Union has in the past exercised its right to comment on domestic differences within the United States, such as *Pravda's* expression of support for black activist Angela Davis. He also cited Moscow Radio's frequent comments on American domestic events.

On another meet–the–people trip in 1977, this one in July to a small community in Mississippi, Yazoo City, Carter told applauding citizens he would keep on speaking out on human rights even though, he said, "I've been criticized a good bit for being so outspoken about it, because it might make some leaders of other nations angry. . . I'm not trying to bring back the cold war." He also reminded his fellow Southerners that the South was guilty for many years "of the deprivation of human rights of a large portion of its citizens," and declared the Civil Rights Act was "the greatest thing that ever happened in the South" in his lifetime.

The session was held in the Yazoo City High School gymnasium on a hot, humid evening, and provided some wonderful Americana for a feature: There was a constant fluttering throughout the gymnasium as some 1,500 perspiring men, women and children made use of cardboard fans, provided by local funeral directors, to try to work up a breeze. Brigades of little Boy Scouts carried cups of water to people at their seats.

Carter's town meetings were part of the brisk pace he set in office from the time that he and his wife and daughter began their surprise walk at the head of his inaugural parade. On his first full day in office, he granted a blanket pardon to those who had evaded the military draft during the Vietnam war. In his first 100 days, he released a flood of policy pronouncements and proposals, notably an economic stimulus package and a comprehensive national energy plan; sought to diminish the trappings of the imperial presidency; and made new arms reduction proposals to the Soviet Union, which Moscow didn't like.

In early May Carter left Washington on his first mission abroad as president. He traveled to London for his initiation into international summitry, at the annual seven-nation economic conference and at a NATO summit. And he went to Geneva for talks with Syria's President Assad. Before the official portion of his six-day trip began, he visited a town in northeastern England that I was eager to see.

Escorted by Prime Minister James Callaghan, he went to Newcastle Upon Tyne, the place that my hometown was named after. The region once was a major coal-producing area, the origin of the saying that one doesn't carry coals to Newcastle, a saying that I heard often as a child. The area around the town's new Civic Center was packed with people and they gave Carter what the local newspaper, *The Evening Chronicle*, called an "incredible welcome." In Newcastle and other stops on their tour of the region, the president and prime minister did a lot of campaign-style handshaking. Callaghan's Labor Party was being pressed by the opposition

Conservatives, headed by Margaret Thatcher, whom the president met during his stay in London.

That night the prime minister gave a dinner at Number 10 Downing Street for the leaders who would be attending the economic summit. The press had a free evening and I went to dinner at the home of Mimi and Pete Kumpa, who was then *The Baltimore Sun*'s London correspondent. Royally wined and dined and talked out, I was drowsy on the cab ride back to the Churchill, the hotel for most of those on the White House press list (172 men/11 women). But I became fully awake on learning that Carter had talked to the pool reporters after the dinner, and whipped out a report for VOA. He said he and his summit colleagues were determined to address extremely controversial issues, including, as I reported, "preventing the spread of the capability to make nuclear weapons." Some of VOA's language services don't have a way of translating non–proliferation and that's why we used phrases like "preventing the spread of."

These annual gatherings of leaders from Europe, Japan, Canada and the United States may be called economic summits, but they also are used for talks on international political developments, and often the summit statements on non–economic issues capture the headlines. The world press descends on the summit sites in extravagant numbers; at the 1992 gathering in Munich, according to *The Washington Post*, the press totaled 4,234, including 444 Americans.

At economic summits, VOA covered not just the U.S. delegation but the others as well. For the 1977 summit, and the NATO summit two days later, I was glad to have the company and the expertise of VOA's Brussels–based correspondent, Edith Smith Apple, who knew all the background of European and Common Market issues, and VOA's diplomatic correspondent, Mark Willen, who was traveling with Secretary of State Cyrus Vance.

The first day of the summit went well, by all accounts, and in the evening the leaders were guests of Queen Elizabeth at dinner in Buckingham Palace. Carter, who had seen the palace several years before as a tourist, through the fence, sat next to the queen and said he had a good time. The summit ended Sunday with a declaration, plus individual statements by each of the leaders, a practice eventually discontinued and replaced by a single statement by the summit host, making life easier for everyone including the press. Among other things the leaders agreed that their most urgent task was to create more jobs while continuing to reduce inflation.

The next day, Monday, Carter flew to Geneva to meet with Assad. They first made statements to the press assembled at the Intercontinental Hotel, and I described the atmosphere as one of extreme cordiality. Assad repeated Syria's position on Middle East peace efforts, and Carter, who had had a series of meetings in Washington with most other Mideast leaders, said the U.S. role was to act as an intermediary. They exchanged warm words at dinner, with Carter indulging in a bit of humor. He said he'd discovered that the Syrian president "reads the finest American literature. He is about halfway through reading *Why Not The Best?*" This was the 1975 Carter autobiography, which I took with me on trips when he was president, just as I did Reagan's 1965 book *Where's The Rest of Me?* when he was president, in case I wanted to look up a pertinent quote.

The NATO summit on Tuesday opened with a trumpet fanfare from Her Majesty's Royal Marines and calls for maintaining the military strength of the Alliance. Carter warned that the communist military buildup in Europe was continuing and urged development of a long–term program to keep NATO strong. His suggestion was well–received by the allies. When Carter returned to Washington that night, he had reason to be pleased with his first venture in international summitry. The press, at home and abroad, referred to the two summits as a personal success for the new American president.

By the time Carter took a vacation in early August, White House reporters were ready for one too, brief as it was. He spent it in Plains, visiting his mother and brother, going fishing, and playing softball. In those games, played on the field beyond Billy Carter's gas station, the president was the captain and pitcher of a team of White House staffers and Billy was captain and pitcher of

the opposing team of reporters. Billy's team won the first two
competitions, and the press began joking that we were destined to
stay in Plains until the president won a game. In the third contest,
Billy's team was leading 11–5, but Jimmy's team, bolstered by four
Secret Service agents brought in as substitutes, rallied and the game
was tied, 16–16. The public address announcer, NBC White House
correspondent David Rush, told what happened next: "Now, 17–16,
White House staff. And guess who put that run across — who?
Jimmy Who! That's who." The president's team won, final score
19–17.

Not a natural athlete, I didn't play on the press team but was a
faithful spectator, cheering my colleagues on while developing the
art of fighting off swarms of gnats. Slapping at them wasn't enough.
The thing to do, I learned, was to purse your lips as though to
whistle but then work the lips sideways and blow a jet of air at the
gnats coming in for a landing. It always worked.

A few days after our return to Washington, Carter announced
the details of one of the most controversial issues of his presidency,
the treaty with Panama to relinquish U.S. control of the Panama
Canal by the end of 1999. Unveiled with it was a companion treaty
giving the U.S. the permanent right to defend the neutrality of the
canal. The negotiations on the waterway had faced opposition for
some time and had been a campaign issue in Ford's primary
election fight with Reagan, who repeatedly declaimed that the U.S.
bought it, paid for it, owns it, and should not give it up.

Carter and Panama's leader, Brigadier General Omar Torrijos,
signed the new treaties September 7 in a ceremony at the graceful
Pan American Union in Washington, the headquarters of the
Organization of American States. The audience was an
inter–American summit gathering, an impressive show of support
for the treaty package. Attending were high–ranking officials from
26 other Western Hemisphere nations, 20 of them heads of
government or state. Carter and Torrijos emphasized the fairness
of the treaties but acknowledged there was opposition in both their
countries. (After a tough fight, the treaties were ratified by the U.S.
Senate in 1978. Carter has credited Ford with helping convert

doubtful senators.) At a White House state dinner that evening for the visiting leaders, Carter said one difference between the new treaties and the old one was that this time the Panamanians had a chance to read the document before signing.

The president also met individually with the hemisphere officials who ranged, I reported, "from civilian democratic leaders to long-entrenched military strongmen, and include leaders of countries, such as Chile, which he has criticized in the past on human rights and other issues." Although most of these meetings received little attention in the U.S. domestic news media, they were important stories for VOA, particularly his discussions with the presidents of Chile, Argentina, Paraguay and Uruguay on human rights abuses in those countries, and his tribute to Costa Rica as an example for other nations in preserving human freedoms.

By late October Carter was coming under increasing criticism, with what I described as "complaints in the American press and in Congress that he has too many programs and initiatives under way at one time, and that he cannot cope with them." His response was that he couldn't delay tackling problems important to the U.S. simply to avoid controversy. One of the problems he listed was the Middle East, and in November came a riveting event in that part of the world, the visit to Jerusalem by Anwar Sadat.

"For ordinary Israelis the visit cut through three decades of suspicion and hate," VOA's Charles Weiss reported from Jerusalem, "and what came across was a fervent desire that there be no more wars. Wherever President Sadat went, wherever people could get a glimpse of him, he was applauded and cheered. . . . Here was the president of Israel's most powerful enemy checking into the King David Hotel. . . ." At the White House, Carter watched coverage of the visit on television. For him, I reported, it was of particular significance; he'd probably spent more time on the Middle East than any other issue.

Carter continued his Mideast peace efforts during a trip that began at the tail end of 1977. At first look it was a mish-mash of a trip, with no rhyme or reason. He was going to Poland, Iran, India, Saudi Arabia, France and Belgium. As it turned out, he added another stop midway to meet with Sadat, and we visited seven countries in nine days. Carter called it a journey reflecting "the diversity of the world we live in." The aim was to show that the U.S. wanted to play a responsible leadership role in a changing world.

In Warsaw, our first stop, his purpose was to demonstrate U.S. interests in Eastern Europe while continuing a policy of accommodation with the Soviet Union. I was working in the filing center at the Victoria Intercontinental Hotel when some of the reporters came back from a reception given by the Poles. Laughing, almost gleeful, they had a story: Carter's interpreter, they'd been told at the reception, had made embarrassing, lewd, mistakes at the arrival ceremony. Word of the gaffes spread, and nearly everybody started writing the story. One newspaper reporter wearily pulled out his typewriter and announced, "I'd better protect my ass." I was reluctant to do a story based on second-hand information, and I certainly didn't want to file a report that would be broadcast back to Poland unless I was certain it was true.

Here was a case dealing with one of the languages in which VOA broadcasts. So I phoned our newsroom in Washington and asked that the Polish service give me a reading on the translation — was it really that bad? While waiting for my call to go through, I spied Jerry Schecter, the White House spokesman on foreign affairs. He wouldn't comment on the interpreter's performance but in answer to my questions, did say that "according to officials" the interpreter was being replaced. The verdict from VOA's Polish service came in the early morning hours, and I filed a report confident of the facts.

My lead was on the replacement of the president's interpreter "because of what was described as an incredibly poor translation." The story went on to say that "those familiar with the Polish language say the translator, a State Department official, Steven Seymour, used Polish as it was spoken 100 years ago by uneducated people," and that "U.S. officials obviously were embarrassed by the incident." Seymour's mistakes included interpreting Carter's "when I left the United States" as "when I abandoned the United States," and using a low form of Polish for the word "desire" so that it came out as lust. I felt sorry for the Carter folks, and sorry for Seymour when I read later in a *New York Times* front page story that he was a part–time interpreter hired by the State Department's short–staffed translators' section, and the last time he'd interpreted in Polish was two years earlier during trade talks in Washington.

While in Warsaw, Carter held a press conference, the first ever by an American president in a communist country. He opened it by noting that a few who wanted to attend were not permitted to, and that he would answer their questions in writing. It was believed they were representatives of Polish underground newspapers, I reported, and that some of the questions they wanted to ask dealt with human rights.

His press conference, on a range of subjects that included human rights and the Mideast, was transmitted live on the white line to the home offices of the U.S. radio pool members, and simultaneously the Polish translation was fed on another line to VOA, so our Polish service could broadcast the entire session or big chunks of it. Poland's state radio and television carried it later, and the official party newspaper printed the transcript. For this trip, the U.S. radio pool had seven members, with Mutual, UPI–Radio and AP–Radio joining the three networks and VOA on the white line. And for the first time I was accompanied on a presidential trip by a VOA radio engineer, Earl Allen Brown, and didn't have to worry about technical matters. In reporting the Warsaw events, I joined forces again with Munich–based Mark Hopkins and we divided up the coverage, with Zora Safir of VOA's USSR Division broadcasting reports in Russian.

Secretary of State Cyrus Vance and the president's assistant for national security affairs, Warsaw–born Zbigniew Brzezinski, accompanied Carter and held extensive briefings both on the record and on background throughout the trip. Many were in–flight briefings to the Air Force One pool reporters, whose laboriously typed transcripts provided fodder for our stories.

From Warsaw we flew to Tehran, where I was immediately struck by the air pollution. It masked the mountains nearby and scratched at the throat. The pollution, and construction projects seen everywhere, marked the tremendous growth of the city. Security was extremely tight. At the Tehran Hilton where we stayed there were four armed guards near the elevators on every floor. I didn't feel comfortable with the thought that their presence was necessary. I also felt uncomfortable on learning that the Iranian government was intending to pay the hotel bills of the American press; we were all greeted by letters saying we were guests of the Shah. This would not do, so I went to Jack Shellenberger, the U.S. public affairs officer in Tehran who had served a stint as a VOA official, and asked if he could solve the problem. He arranged to have a notice posted advising the press that those who didn't want to be the Shah's guests (most of us) should sign up at the USIS desk in the hotel, and USIS would see to it that we would be billed.

USIS did a first-rate support job for the press entourage in Tehran and all the other stops on the trip. On presidential travels abroad USIS posts distribute "ready reference" booklets, about the size of a travel agency's "trip-tik," with easy flips of graduated pages containing information on schedules and event sites, biographical sketches, telephone numbers, lists of restaurants, and so on.

In the filing center I joined Charlie Weiss, who had arrived earlier from Jerusalem to file advancers on the visit, and we churned out one report after another. There was plenty to cover: the welcome for the president, the talks between Carter and the Shah, and the lavish state dinner, given in honor of the Carters, where they were joined by King Hussein. Then, after the dinner, Carter confirmed that he was adding a stop to his trip, to confer with Sadat at Aswan.

This was New Year's Eve and the Iranians laid on a big party for the press at the Hilton. When midnight came some of us were still at work in the filing center. Missing the party wasn't too disappointing. As Al Brown said later, Iran is a dry country. We did welcome in 1978 with champagne at midnight Washington time on the zoo plane flying to our next stop, New Delhi. Aboard the writers' plane, Al Sullivan said, there was a ragged cheer at 39,000 feet over the vast wasteland of southeastern Iran.

At the New Delhi airport I was welcomed by VOA's resident correspondent, Fred Brown, brandishing a copy of *The Times of India*. He pointed to a front page story with the headline, "Capital dolls up to welcome Carters," and said I had to read it. The sixth paragraph I read twice (at least). It said guests at the Ashoka Hotel would include correspondents "from major networks like CBS, ABC, NBC, VOA, UPI and AP," and, "Of the major personalities staying at the Ashoka would be Barbara Walters of ABC, Jody Powell of the White House staff, Miss Philomena Jurei of VOA and Mr. Robert Pierpoint of CBS." With mention like that, who cares about spelling. The newspaper story was a high for me, and so was the Ashoka bill when I checked out. It bore the notation V.V.I.P.

Carter's visit to New Delhi symbolized friendlier relations between the United States and India after a period of strain when Prime Minister Indira Gandhi leaned toward the Soviet Union. Under the new prime minister, Morarji Desai, India's non–alignment policy was re–instituted. Hundreds of thousands turned out to welcome the president, and a vast throng assembled that afternoon in a big field between New and Old Delhi, the Ram Lila meeting ground, to hear him extend New Year greetings from the American people and tell of his "deep interest" in India because of his mother's Peace Corps service.

The next day Carter announced the United States would send India another shipment of enriched uranium fuel for its Tarapur nuclear power plant and would make available supplies of heavy water, an important ingredient in producing nuclear power. He inserted the announcement in a speech to the Indian parliament. "This is a cold technological subject," he said, "but Prime Minister Desai and I have had warm and productive discussions about this field." The insertion was made, and its wording was deliberate, because of an episode a few hours earlier that pointed up differences between the U.S. and India over nuclear energy. In a private chat with Vance during a photo session, Carter, unaware of an open microphone nearby, said Desai was being "pretty adamant," and that on their return to Washington they should write Desai "another letter, just cold and very blunt."

The remarks were taped by the NBC technician on the pool and written up in a pool report, by Vernon Guidry of *The Washington Star*, that was routinely mimeographed and distributed by the White House Press Office — and snatched up by American and Indian reporters. Fred Brown, who quickly filed a story for VOA, was extremely helpful not only to me but to Vern and other members of the traveling press, providing us with details on the dispute. The U.S. had been insisting that India agree to nuclear safeguards preventing the spread of weapons–making capability. India, which had renounced the development of nuclear weapons, contended that such safeguard standards discriminated against non–nuclear nations.

White House officials acted quickly to minimize the "cold and blunt" remark, and Jody Powell said the president meant there should be a written communication setting forth the facts in a straightforward and frank manner. This included the fact that the U.S. Congress would be enacting legislation, supported by Carter, with restrictions on shipments of nuclear fuel. In his joint briefing with Indian Foreign Secretary Jagat Mehta, Jody also said, "Perhaps this incident will confirm that our publicly stated belief in the freedom of the press has some substantive component to it."

Indian officials did not appear concerned about the affair, and the talks continued in an atmosphere characterized by both sides as warm and friendly. Carter's address to the parliament was built on the theme that democracy is the best path to social and economic progress for developing countries. India (the world's most populous democracy) and the United States (the second largest) have shown, he said, that "freedom is the engine of progress." The speech was interrupted 20 times by applause and the pounding of desks.

The seat of parliament was decorated with floral displays, and I noticed flowers everywhere in New Delhi, flowers, and poverty. On a drive to Fred and Sally Brown's home, the sight of people living on street corners couldn't be escaped. A wing of their house served as the VOA office and newly built studios, where I filed some of my reports. The house was the former North Korean Embassy. Fred told me he had found bugs, the listening device kind, in the fireplaces. He got rid of them.

On our last day in India, Carter visited a poor village a half hour's drive from New Delhi. It was a good story for VOA, but only pool coverage was allowed and the White House Press Office turned down my requests to be added to the pool. I waited impatiently in the filing center for the pool report, hoping to file a story before having to leave for the airport. Finally word was relayed from the village by a network producer. When Carter inspected a villager's Gobar gas operation, a process transforming cow dung into methane gas through fermentation, Sam Donaldson asked him if it was too late to get the Gobar into his energy program. That was it, just the cow dung exchange between Sam and the president. What about the village itself? What else happened?

The complete pool report wasn't issued before we left for the airport, and I was fuming when I boarded the press bus, angry at the Press Office because I'd learned it had added others to the pool, and angry at myself for not being pushy enough. Barry Jagoda, the presidential assistant for media and public affairs, sat next to me and pleasantly asked how things were going. I wrathfully replied, telling him the Carter White House was just as bad as the Nixon and Ford White Houses, that all it cared about was getting coverage on American television and in American newspapers. This was the case at the White House under all four presidents that I covered, with the television networks in ascendance as lords of the media.

The village, Daulatpur–Nasirabad, was renamed Carter–poori (Carter Place) in honor of the president's visit, as described in a detailed pool report that was written by Jim Wooten of *The New York Times* (later ABC) and was distributed at our next stop, Riyadh. There, Jim generously agreed to my interviewing him for VOA, even though he'd had next to no sleep in the past 40 hours. His eyewitness account was far better than any I could have filed.

Al Brown recorded the interview and transmitted it to Washington while I met up again with Ibrahim Abdin, VOA's Cairo-based Arabic language reporter who had also been in Tehran for the Carter visit. We compared notes on Saudi and regional matters and again he was helpful with background and with my constant concern, pronunciations.

The president's stay in Riyadh was short, a little over 15 hours in which he reviewed the Mideast situation with King Khalid and Crown Prince Fahd and was guest at a state dinner. The dinner pool reported this exchange: One of the Saudis asked Judy Woodruff (then with NBC), "Are you Barbara Walters?" When told no, he asked, "Is it true she makes a million dollars a month?" When told a million dollars a year, he said, somewhat incredulously, "Just a year?"

The next day took us from Riyadh to Aswan to Paris. At the Aswan airport, the Egyptian and American presidents met in the terminal building while the press shivered outside in unexpected cold weather, with winds that bit through the wool lining of my trench coat. VOA's Mideast correspondent, Doug Roberts, was at the airport when the press planes arrived and gave me a quote from the Egyptian foreign minister that I used to flesh out my story as the talks got under way.

Sadat had been concerned that there was a change in the U.S. position on Palestinian self-determination, but during the meeting he apparently was reassured that there wasn't. When the two leaders came outside Sadat told the press, "I am very happy to say our views were identical, and we have agreed upon certain steps to keep the momentum of the peace process." I filed a quick report before the press planes left for Paris, and Doug covered Carter's departure and wrapped up the story. Aboard Air Force One, the president phoned Israeli Prime Minister Menachem Begin to give him a summary of his talks with the Arab leaders. Israel and Egypt were to begin talks in Jerusalem in mid-January, with Vance joining the discussions.

Paris crowds shouting "Jimmy, Jimmy" gave Carter an enthusiastic reception as he and President Valery Giscard d'Estaing took a 10–minute walk down the Champs Elysee after he laid a wreath at the Arc de Triomphe. The two presidents then held talks at the Elysee Palace and Carter ended the day with the second major speech of his trip. Like the first one, in New Delhi, it was on democracy.

The White House made the advance text available, and VOA's Paris correspondent John Bue performed the impressive feat of translating it into French and then broadcasting it to Washington for airing on VOA's French to Africa service. I enjoyed working again with John, the dean of radio correspondents in Paris, and he was a big help in giving me and others in the traveling press a fill on French politics. Elections were coming up in March, and Giscard d'Estaing was facing a strong challenge from the left.

The American and French presidents made a symbolic visit to Normandy the next morning to pay tribute to allied forces who lost their lives in the invasion that began the liberation of Europe from the Nazis. They looked out at Omaha Beach, where American troops landed on D–Day, June 6, 1944, and walked through the Normandy American cemetery, where 9,386 Americans are buried on a cliff overlooking the beach, their graves marked by marble crosses. The sounding of taps never seemed so poignant to me as it was during the ceremony when the two leaders laid wreaths at the memorial to the Americans. Giscard d'Estaing recalled that news of the allied landings had spread like wildfire through Paris and said the troops had come "to give us back hope and freedom." Carter said "We are determined, with our noble allies here, that Europe's freedom will never again be endangered."

The two presidents proceeded to Bayeux, the first French town liberated from the Nazis, where virtually the whole populace of 12,000 turned out to greet them — and where we had a mishap with the white line. One of the network technicians ended his transmission of some recorded material and said, "That's a good night." Those of us waiting to file were horror–stricken, for "good night" on the white line meant we had nothing more to feed. The receiving end in New York followed procedures and shut the white line down. We hurriedly recorded our reports and left the tape cassettes with the pool tech in hopes he could restore communication, which to our relief he eventually did.

Carter's next stop was Brussels, where he reaffirmed American support for a strengthened Atlantic Alliance. In a speech at NATO headquarters, he said he would propose increases in U.S. defense spending and planned to boost by 8,000 the American troop level in Europe, then about 200,000. During the six-hour stay, Carter also visited the European Common Market commission headquarters, held talks and lunched with King Baudouin, and met Belgian officials. Edie Apple covered all those while I filed a wrapup of the entire trip, including themes Carter emphasized: Political liberties, basic human rights, the need to resolve conflict without violence.

On the way back to Washington he answered questions from the Air Force One pool. Of particular interest was his response to a pooler who described the press as "completely exhausted" and asked if he thought the trip was too hectic. The president replied that while he could go to bed, "you all have to file your stories and get up and be ready for me to emerge the following morning" and added, "I think that factor is one we would consider in the future." The press had had only two to four hours of sleep per night, and we were still catching up the following week. Helen Thomas told me she found herself so drowsy at a dinner party that she was agreeing with everything everybody said.

Despite exhaustion, there is, to use Al Sullivan's words, a fatal fascination in following a president abroad. Before long we were readily writing our names and passport numbers on the White House sign-up sheet for a trip to Latin America and Africa. In late March Carter flew to Caracas, first stop on a one-week, 14,000-mile journey to Venezuela, Brazil, Nigeria and Liberia. He was accompanied by his wife and 10-year-old daughter Amy, an official party headed by Vance and Brzezinski, whom we referred to as Zbig, and a press party of more than 150, including a nucleus that went on the entire trip (132 men/7 women).

The trip was a journey in contrasts and a first-hand look at the problems faced by Third World countries, including those that have rapidly growing cities. In Venezuela, the hillsides around Caracas were covered with shanties, the city's streets were clogged with traffic, and a two-hour power outage darkened the press filing center in the Holiday Inn. We wrote our stories by candlelight, reporting on the president's arrival and his laying a wreath at the tomb of the liberator Simon Bolivar (Carter spoke in Spanish on both occasions), and the concern expressed by Venezuela's president, Carlos Andres Perez, about reservations the U.S. Senate had added to the Panama Canal treaties. When the lights came back on, cheers went up, but at the same time the water was turned off for a while. We made do by drinking beer.

Sharing candlelight and coverage with me was VOA's Latin American correspondent Al Ortiz (later CBS's foreign news editor and London bureau chief), while Miguel Bomar-Rosenberg of VOA's Spanish service did language broadcasts. As expected, a major subject of Carter's talks with Perez and speech to the Venezuelan Congress was the North-South dialogue on relations between rich and poor countries and how to improve the economies of developing nations. Another was the commitment of the two presidents to human rights.

In Brasilia, the next stop, human rights was a subject on which Carter and President Ernesto Geisel frankly disagreed. Carter saw human rights as an international problem, with world pressure used to correct violations; Geisel didn't. They also differed on Brazil's plans to buy a nuclear reprocessing plant from West Germany to meet its energy needs. The U.S. objected because the plant would produce weapons-grade plutonium. Brazil said its nuclear program was peaceful. Neither president changed his mind during the visit, but both accented the positive by stressing the longstanding friendship between their countries.

From the starkly modern Brasilia, the U.S. party flew to Rio, with the press looking forward to some free time sunning on the beach. But Zbig had another of those background briefings on Air Force One, and reporters instead spent the afternoon working in the press center at the Hotel Intercontinental. That evening, though, I did get a sampling of one of Rio's famous attractions, thanks to the Carters. The president and Rosalynn, accompanied by Vance and Brzezinski, made an unannounced visit to a nightclub featuring the Brazilian Follies. Bystanders recognized them as they entered, and soon reporters found out and converged on the scene. Several of us got into the club through a backdoor entrance, enjoyed the Follies too, and wrote features about the Carters' night on the town, seeing performers ranging from showgirls to dancers doing the samba.

Before leaving for Nigeria the next morning, Carter discussed human rights concerns with a small group representing various sectors of Brazilian society, including Dom Paulo Avaristo Arns, the Roman Catholic archbishop of Sao Paulo and, as Al Ortiz reported, "one of the most vocal critics of the Brazilian government's record on human rights." The press planes had already left Rio, but the meeting was covered by Al, who was not going on to Africa. In reviewing the Latin American visit, Al noted that Venezuela's news media warmly praised it while Brazil's news media were skeptical, with a newspaper cartoon suggesting that the only thing the U.S. and Brazil agreed on was soccer.

In Lagos, VOA's regional correspondent John Roberts was reporting on preparations for Carter's visit, including a new coat of paint on the Baptist Church where he would worship Sunday. John was at the airport when the press planes landed and gave me a fill on what the Nigerians expected to discuss with Carter. Together we watched as the first American president to pay a state visit to black Africa was welcomed by Nigeria's head of state, Lieutenant–General Olusegun Obasanjo.

On the long bus ride into town from the airport, an American official stationed in Lagos told me, "If you give Nigerians a smile, you will always get a smile in return." He was right. There were smiles from onlookers as the U.S. party traveled about Lagos, smiles from workers at the Eko Holiday Inn where the press was lodged, beaming smiles from dancers giving a performance for the American party, and sympathetic smiles when our White House press buses got stuck in a "go–slow," the Nigerian expression for a traffic jam.

Carter spelled out his policy on Africa in a major speech in Lagos. He appealed for accommodation in efforts to reach peaceful solutions on Rhodesia (now Zimbabwe) and Southwest Africa (now Namibia), and said relations with South Africa would depend on progress toward full political participation by all its people and an end to racial or ethnic discrimination. He again decried foreign military intervention in Africa, in an obvious reference to Soviet and Cuban involvement in the Horn of Africa. These issues were covered in his talks with Obasanjo, along with North–South relations, human rights, and oil prices. Carter said Obasanjo was interested in how his energy proposal would affect Nigeria, the second largest source of American oil imports.

VOA has a large audience in Nigeria, one of the largest in the world. That was probably the reason I was a guest of the Nigerians at the state dinner for the Carters. I'd never been to a state dinner before, either at the White House or abroad. I had a good conversation about VOA with a Nigerian official while dining on Nigerian dishes for the first time. After smashing entertainment by folk dancers, Carter and Obasanjo signed a joint communique, and I went back to work. Besides reporting on the dinner, I filed a feature on the president's visit earlier in the day to Tin Can Island.

Once a dumpheap for boxes of empty tin cans, the island had been reclaimed and now was Nigeria's new $325 million port facility, reducing the huge backlog of ships waiting to unload at Lagos, the busiest port in West Africa. Carter, Rosalynn and Amy went on a tour of Lagos Harbor. The press was to follow in smaller boats, but there weren't any designated for us. So Paul Costello, a young press advance officer on Mrs. Carter's staff, commandeered a motor launch, the "Mekling V," and we piled in — AP's Jim Gerstenzang, ABC mini–cam crew Doug Allmond and Eric Speights, Helen Thomas, Paul and I — and off we went in hot pursuit. Nobody complained about our appropriating the launch and we got our story: "Huge cargo ships and freighters tooted foghorn salutes to President Carter as he went by in a cabin cruiser."

President Carter confers with Nigerian leader Obasanjo in Lagos, April 1978. (Courtesy, Jimmy Carter Library)

Doug Allmond focuses his mini–cam as a press group follows a launch taking the Carters on a tour of Lagos Harbor. Left to right: Eric Speights, Jim Gerstenzang, Helen Thomas and Jurey. (White House photo)

Our Third World tour ended with a visit to Monrovia, Liberia, where the president was greeted by thousands of cheering men, women and children. Liberia was one of America's closest friends in Africa. Founded with the help of American colonization societies for repatriating freed American slaves, it became a republic in 1847, with the U.S. Constitution the model for its own. Monrovia was the site of an important VOA transmitter relay station, which I regretfully did not get to see because the visit was so brief, only four hours.

Carter's talks with President William Tolbert included investment opportunities in Liberia and U.S. economic aid. Liberia was struggling to become self-sufficient in agriculture, and, as I reported, this was underscored in signs along the road from the airport into Monrovia. "This is no joke," they said. "No more imported rice by 1980."

Two years after Carter's visit, Tolbert was killed in an army coup, and then in late 1989 civil war erupted in Liberia. American employees at the VOA transmitter station were evacuated in 1990. Liberian staffers kept the station operating until it was over-run by rebel forces, ransacked, and shut down later that year. VOA made up the loss by beaming broadcasts to Africa from its relay station in North Carolina, and via a transmitter site in Botswana.

Carter went to Europe again in 1978, making a symbolic journey to West Berlin and attending the economic summit in Bonn. In a visit to the Berlin Wall, he viewed a section that had been freshly whitewashed by the East German regime. At a town meeting with West Berliners, he said the paint could not cover up the limitation of human rights behind the wall. This was my first long look at the Berlin Wall; the whitewash was incredible, did the East Germans really think they could make indecency look decent?

These travels with Carter reinforced my appreciation of the professionalism of VOA's overseas correspondents and their contribution to our newscasts. In 1977 many of us at the Voice were worried about the future of our correspondent corps. Carter had proposed a reorganization plan under which the State Department's Bureau of Educational and Cultural Affairs would be merged into USIA, with the new entity, the U.S. International Communication Agency (USICA), under the secretary of state's direction. He told Congress VOA would be solely responsible for the content of its news broadcasts, for "there is no more valued coin than candor in the international marketplace of ideas." At VOA, we were concerned the State Department would be strengthened in attempts to control our news coverage. In November 1977 a dispute between VOA and State over a correspondent's role was made public by *The Washington Post*. Doug Roberts wanted to interview all parties involved in the conflict over the Western Sahara, including the Polisario guerrillas. The State Department said he couldn't talk with the Polisarios. VOA Director R. Peter Straus and USIA Director John Reinhardt challenged the restriction, without success.

Straus named a panel of outside experts to study the role of VOA's overseas correspondents, and this added to fears of a move to abolish the correspondent corps. There was a school of thought that VOA could use broadcast reports filed by network correspondents stationed abroad instead of its own correspondents. We need not have worried. The panel was very good. Its chairman was Chalmers Roberts, the retired diplomatic correspondent of *The Washington Post*, and the other members were Pauline Frederick, the former NBC United Nations correspondent and then NPR's international affairs analyst; E.W. (Ned) Kenworthy, retired *New York Times* correspondent; S. William Scott, Westinghouse's vice president for radio news operations, and Franklin H. Williams, former ambassador to Ghana. They began their work in mid–January 1978, interviewing VOA correspondents and others. In meeting with them I said our overseas correspondents are vital to VOA news, in checking reports, filling in gaps in wire service dispatches or American network reports, and reporting developments which might not be covered by the U.S. domestic media. Broadcasts by the network foreign correspondents are aimed at the American audience while VOA's audience is worldwide. I also told them there needed to be a clear statement that a VOA correspondent should be free to carry out the duties of a responsible professional journalist.

The panel asked why I used a regular passport instead of an official one. I acknowledged my resistance to being categorized as a government official, pointed out that I wasn't concealing my employment since my credentials identified me as a VOA employee, and said there was a distinction between me, a correspondent, and, for example, an official of the White House Press Office.

In its report March 9, the panel said "VOA journalists are inescapably government employees," but added: "At the same time there can be room enough for them to perform with a high degree of professionalism." It said its recommendations were designed "to mitigate these inherent difficulties in order to increase and improve VOA's acceptance around the world as a purveyor of 'accurate, objective, and comprehensive' news." The panel recommended that "VOA should continue to assign some news correspondents abroad" because they can check on reports from other sources and "provide access to areas which commercial journalists seldom cover for their American audiences." Other major recommendations were:

"The VOA must have the right, free of diplomatic restrictions, to gather and send news to Washington headquarters."

"The status of VOA correspondents should be as close as possible to that of correspondents of commercial American press and broadcasting organizations. These correspondents should be news persons and not interchangeable with diplomatic personnel." In connection with this, the panel said that VOA correspondents "should not have access to classified material" and that ambassadors and other American government personnel abroad should give them "the same courtesy, consideration and assistance extended to any other American correspondent — no more, no less."

I thought the panel's report was great. And it was unique because it was short and to the point, only seven pages, and it didn't sit on a shelf gathering dust. The newly reorganized agency, USICA, came into being April 3, 1978, and on June 30 issued a new circular, "Guidelines and Operating Procedures for VOA's Foreign Correspondents," containing recommendations of the panel, some in almost the same wording.

It freed our correspondents from embassy attempts to control their work, said they were directly under the VOA news chief in Washington, and said embassy public affairs officers "will not supervise the work of a VOA correspondent, and the correspondent has no obligation to clear copy with anyone before transmitting it to VOA Washington." If an embassy wanted to see a correspondent's story, the correspondent would provide a copy "after it has been filed." The circular instructed our correspondents — 15 then, many more now — to inform embassies of their travel plans and the nature of their assignments, and said if the embassies objected the matter was to be referred to VOA Washington for resolution. Missions abroad, it said, "bear no responsibility for the content of material broadcast by the Voice of America."

The new guidelines didn't stop ambassadorial reservations or complaints about VOA's coverage, nor did they prevent future cases of friction between the Voice and the State Department. But they made it much easier for VOA correspondents overseas to do their jobs as reporters, and for the Voice to fight to protect the credibility of its news.

VOA's newscasts received a boost in a March 1978 column by James ("Scotty") Reston of *The New York Times*. Writing from Damascus, he said that in the past three months he had "listened carefully to its English language broadcasts in such diverse places as Japan, Australia, Tahiti, West Germany, Yugoslavia, Italy, Egypt, Jordan, and here in Syria," and he went on to say: "For detailed accounts of the world's news, I believe there is nothing that equals its performance." It is, he said, "very cool. It says here is the news, and even Walter Cronkite wouldn't be ashamed to read it. . . . It is an honest service, reporting our national failures as well as our virtues, which also troubles those who want it to produce nothing but propaganda. But heard over here, a long way from home, it seems worth the money and even makes you proud."

The white line in operation overseas in 1977: Pool producer Tony Brunton of CBS holds the microphone for Jurey while Vic Ratner of ABC waits his turn and CBS technician Dale Kelsey monitors the sound. The mult box is in the left foreground. (Photo by E. Allen Brown, VOA)

10
The Camp David Mideast Summit
Linus, Sebastian, and Walter Cronkite
A Peace Treaty Signed

In September 1978, reporters from around the world descended on Thurmont, Maryland, a friendly little town near the presidential retreat in the Catoctin Mountains. We were there to cover President Carter's Middle East Summit at Camp David with the president of Egypt and the prime minister of Israel.

In announcing that Anwar Sadat and Menachem Begin had accepted Carter's invitation to meet with him, the White House said the purpose of the summit was "to seek a framework for peace in the Middle East." It would begin September 5; it would have no time limit.

I made a dry run to check out Camp David's location and accommodations in Thurmont. Down the street from a block of stores, I found the American Legion Hall, where the press filing center would be set up and Jody Powell would hold his briefings. Through town and up a two-lane road I drove into the wooded mountains, absorbing the serenity of the setting. There it was, the fenced reservation used as a retreat by presidents since Franklin Roosevelt began going there in 1942. He called it Shangri-La but President Eisenhower renamed it Camp David, after his grandson. Eisenhower's talks there with Nikita Khrushchev in 1959 led to the phrase, "Spirit of Camp David," describing improvement in U.S.-Soviet relations.

At the Rambler Motel, next to a large field of grass near the edge of Thurmont, I confirmed my reservation and confirmed that I could bring my two dachshunds with me, as long as they were quiet. Normally when I was traveling, I could count on one of my regular sitters to stay with the dogs in my home. The sitters were young career women, Rosemary Cullen, who had been in high school with my stepdaughter, and her sister Kathleen. But I thought neither would be available for an indefinite period and, frankly, I wanted to take the dogs with me for company.

On Monday, September 4, Carter flew by helicopter to Camp David after delivering a sober statement at the White House, warning that the issues were very complicated and the disagreements were deep. I drove to Thurmont, Linus and Sebastian in the back seat, their bed, comforter, food and dishes in the trunk. At the American Legion Hall, telephone crews were completing installation of 150 phones for use by the international press. The number of news people accredited was in the high hundreds, counting those with White House and State Department press passes.

Long rows of tables were set up in a large multi–purpose room transformed into our filing center. I chose a workspace in the last row, next to the exit, and VOA tech Al Brown fashioned a three–sided cubicle at the end of the table to serve as a "broadcast booth," shielding the microphone, and my talking head, from room noise. From there I filed reports, with Linus and Sebastian curled up at my feet.

Sebastian and Linus attending a briefing at the Camp David Middle East Summit in September 1978.

Members of the press were allowed inside Camp David Tuesday afternoon to witness the arrivals of the Egyptian and Israeli leaders. It was a rare, though limited, look at the presidential retreat. We were confined to the vicinity of the helicopter landing pad, set in the midst of manicured lawns surrounded by trees. It was a perfect day for the beginning of the summit, I reported, with the sun shining brilliantly as President and Mrs. Carter emerged from a path through the trees to walk slowly toward the helipad. "The first to arrive was President Sadat, aboard the U.S. presidential helicopter, Marine One, exactly on time at 2:30 in the afternoon. The two presidents embraced, shook hands, and the Egyptian leader had a kiss for Mrs. Carter. A little over two hours later, Prime Minister Begin arrived, also aboard Marine One. The president and the prime minister embraced, and Mr. Begin kissed Mrs. Carter."

No statements were made. There had been remarks earlier at Andrews Air Force Base where the two leaders were welcomed by Vice President Mondale. Sadat said, "This is no time for maneuvers and worn-out ideas. It is time for magnanimity and reason." Begin expressed hope that the summit would produce "a day when the nations of the world will say *Habemus pacem* (We have peace)."

The Carters escorted their guests to their cottages, one-story wood structures painted gray, with redwood patios and stone foundations and steps. We didn't get to see the buildings, but the White House press was given photos of them. All the lodges at Camp David are named after trees. Sadat was in Dogwood; Begin in Birch; Carter, Aspen, and the main conference center was Laurel.

Carter met with Begin that evening, with Sadat Wednesday morning, and the three leaders held their first meeting together Wednesday afternoon after issuing a statement calling on people of all faiths to pray that their talks would result in peace. They conferred in isolation after a photo session on the patio of Aspen Lodge. What did they talk about? What was the atmosphere? Reporters tried to find out, but secrecy was imposed. We'd been told in advance of the summit that there would be no comment on the discussions because the three leaders felt their job would be easier if different points of view were not aired in the press while the talks were under way. So Jody Powell, who served as spokesman for all three summit delegations, limited himself to giving out snippets of information, such as the meeting lasted an hour and 40 minutes.

Among the morsels: Before the three leaders met, Begin and Sadat had a chance encounter while they were taking noontime walks through the woods, their first encounter since their December meeting at Ismailia, Egypt. They chatted for two or three minutes, exchanging pleasantries, and Israeli Defense Minister Ezer Weizman rode up on his bicycle and warmly greeted the Egyptian president. In late afternoon the prime minister and Mrs. Begin went for a walk with the Carters, and Sadat went for a drive around the countryside bordering Camp David.

In addition to filing reports on Wednesday's proceedings, I wrote a color piece reporting that Thurmont, population 3,000, was taking the summit in stride. As the local paper put it, the residents were nonchalant about the whole thing. They were accustomed to the comings and goings of presidents and their families, and had seen world leaders before, like Winston Churchill, who held wartime talks with Roosevelt at Camp David. Several presidents had worshipped at churches in Thurmont. Eisenhower and British Prime Minister Harold Macmillan, who were holding a summit conference on the Berlin crisis in 1959, attended a Sunday service at Trinity United Church of Christ. The sermon topic then was fitting for summit deliberations: "Perseverance."

Throughout the Mideast summit, the snippets of information came in postings of notices to the press as well as in Jody's daily briefings. He may not have realized it, but the assemblage included not only many famous journalists but also Linus and Sebastian. They soon became celebrities; reporters stopped by to give them a pat and praise for their behavior, and even took pictures of them. The dogs barked only once, embarrassingly one late afternoon when Walter Cronkite was recording his narration, the "track," for his evening television report. I was mortified, but Cronkite didn't make anything of it. Apart from that incident, Linus and Sebastian slept through all of Jody's briefings.

The dribs and drabs of information he gave us were dull enough to induce slumber, despite the best efforts of nuance–alert reporters. They were mostly announcements of meetings. For example on Thursday, September 7: The Egyptian, Israeli and American leaders met alone for three hours in the morning and two hours in the afternoon. Carter and his top advisors started the day by conferring with Begin and his top advisors, and held a late–night meeting with Sadat and his advisors. There also were two U.S.–Israeli meetings at the ministerial level, and a meeting by Mondale and Vance with the Egyptian foreign minister. "The secrecy lid clamped on the summit is still holding tight," I told our listeners, "but presumably the talks have covered such thorny issues as the occupied West Bank and Gaza Strip."

Thursday wasn't all talk, however. That night Carter had arranged special entertainment for his guests: U.S. marines from the Marine Barracks in Washington performed their traditional evening parade on the Camp David helipad. Seating for the news media was limited, with preference given to the Egyptian and Israeli reporters, so I was delighted to be among the 124 members of the press attending. The marines put on quite a show, but the most impressive show, I reported, was the extraordinary sight of the three men, President Carter flanked by President Sadat and Prime Minister Begin, standing at attention on a platform, bathed in floodlights, watching the marines pass in review.

On Friday the talking continued, but there was no three–way meeting by the leaders. In early evening, we had a bit of news, that progress had been made in some areas. I reported this came from "informed sources" who had no details on what the remaining problems were or where the progress was made. Jody Powell confirmed the progress Saturday morning, but cautioned that "substantial differences" remained "on other important issues."

After his on–the–record briefing, Jody held a "for guidance only" briefing and told us that on Sunday, Day 6 of the summit, the three leaders would tour the nearby Gettysburg battlefield. For security reasons, this was not to be reported until 10 a.m. Sunday, when the excursion would begin. The advance word gave us time to make coverage arrangements. VOA assigned correspondent Debra Weinstein, Arabic language correspondent Muhamed Ghuneim, and radio engineer Hubert Katz to join Al Brown and me. Thus we would be able to spread out and cover all the points the leaders would visit. Debi would file the story afterwards while I would do another piece on the summit talks.

I knew the battlefield pretty well, its peaceful farmland, hills, monuments to the fallen, for my husband was a Civil War buff. We were married in the Methodist Church in Gettysburg, toured the battlefield then, made another pilgrimage with Youngstown friends, and I gave him Bruce Catton's books on the Civil War for birthday presents.

In my "hold for release" story I quoted Catton. The July 1863 battle at Gettysburg was, he wrote, "A three–day explosion of storm and flame and terror, unplanned and uncontrollable, coming inevitably (as the war itself had come) out of the things that hard–pressed men had done in the light of imperfect knowledge." I cannot remember how I happened to use that quote; did I take one of Catton's books to Thurmont with me? I frequently took books along on extended trips. Or was it in a long–lost press release?

One of the points on the tour was the place where Lincoln spoke for two minutes at the dedication of the battlefield's cemetery on November 19, 1863. Jody Powell told us Begin was a great admirer of Lincoln and wanted to visit the site of his famous address. "Emotions continue to be stirred by quotations from Lincoln's Gettysburg address," I told VOA listeners, and of course recited his closing words: "That we here highly resolve that these dead shall not have died in vain — that this nation, under God, shall have a new birth of freedom — and that government of the people, by the people, for the people, shall not perish from the earth." I knew that by heart, having memorized the address in grade school.

When the talks resumed after the tour, there was again no three–way session. I had started making a chart of all the meetings, and my table-mates, Pierre LeSourd and Jean-Pierre Altier of Agence France Presse (AFP), took notice and joined me, agreeing there was a pattern. As I reported, "A pattern of shuttle diplomacy within the confines of Camp David has emerged in the summit discussions as the leaders of Egypt, Israel and the United States wrestle with the complicated problems of the Middle East. President Carter has met with Prime Minister Menachem Begin, then with President Anwar Sadat, then again with the Israeli leader and again with the Egyptian leader, and so on. Sunday afternoon, Mr. Carter had his fourth session with Mr. Begin, and if the pattern holds, this would be followed by his fourth session with Mr. Sadat."

Monday, Day 7, still no three-way meeting of the leaders. At the mid-day briefing, Jody Powell was asked, "Doesn't that show the conference is stalemated?" "No," he said, "I don't think it would be appropriate to draw that conclusion. . . ." In summary, he told us there had been a cycle of bi-lateral meetings followed by tri-lateral discussions, then a pause for assessment, and now a new cycle had begun with Sunday's Carter-Begin meeting.

VOA's 20-minute news programs and half-hour breakfast shows always needed material, so I also supplied a feature on the American Legion post. Founded in 1945, it was named after Edwin C. Kreeger Jr., the first local boy to die in World War II. By 1978 the post had 650 members — veterans of both World Wars, the Korean conflict and the Vietnam war. Its many activities included projects to look after needy children and the underprivileged, and it made its hall available for community activities and as a shelter for storm victims. Now it was sheltering reporters spending days waiting for news.

Members of the post and the women's auxiliary went out of their way to make the press feel welcome. They always had sandwiches, snacks, beverages, and cheery words for us. As a way of saying thank you, some of us took up a collection to contribute to its projects. I don't remember how much money we gave, except that it was a respectable amount. While we waited for news, how did we spend our time? We re-read briefing transcripts in search of nuances that might have escaped us, decided where to go for dinner (the restaurant on the highway again, or to the Cozy downtown, or to that good French restaurant in Gettysburg?), and tried to track down rumors.

The hot rumors on Day 8 were that (1) new Israeli proposals had been conveyed to the Egyptians, (2) Sadat had phoned King Hussein the day before, and (3) Hussein would be joining the Camp David talks. Questioned about them, Jody Powell said (1) ideas had been expressed by all the participants, and he couldn't assess how new they were, (2) yes, Sadat had phoned Hussein, and (3) no, the Jordanian monarch wouldn't be joining the talks. On Day 9 the rumor was that an American plan had been put forward to the Egyptian and Israeli leaders. Jody sidestepped that. He did say the "intensity and specificity" of the discussions had increased, and "we are obviously approaching the final stages" of the conference. On Day 10, Thursday, he said the summit participants had not yet drafted a framework for peace but intense efforts were continuing.

VOA's diplomatic correspondent Mark Willen came up to Thurmont to join me in filing for our hourly newscasts, and I finished a sketch of the three leaders. Sadat, 59, under pressure from other Arab countries to win concessions, "has become known for his bold and dramatic steps and broad visionary statements. He is a man of many moods, among them impatience with detail. . . . He is a man of humble origins, who once wanted to be an actor but entered the military. He was little known outside of Egypt until he succeeded President Nasser on his death in September of 1970. . . . (He) is a devout Moslem, a religious man like the two other summit leaders."

Begin, 65, was influenced by "both the past and his Jewish faith" in his insistence on "a secure peace for Israel." His style "is that of a Talmudic scholar, relishing legalisms and detail. . . . A mild–looking man, almost always formally attired, he is a former guerrilla leader who fought against the British first and then the Arabs. He made his way to Palestine after being held prisoner by Soviet forces. In his early years in Poland, he was leader of a Zionist youth group.

Members of his immediate family were killed by the Nazis in World War II. . . . Mr. Begin was elected Israeli prime minister in 1977 in a surprise victory. . . ."

Carter, 53, "is a softspoken man who made the climb to the White House through dogged persistence. . . . A Christian — he is a Southern Baptist — he has espoused morality in public office. He has brought morality and persistence into play in this extraordinary gathering of extraordinary men at Camp David."

In writing the sketch, I used bio material about Begin and Sadat collected from newspaper and magazine articles. White House and State Department correspondents habitually save clippings for future reference, and my files were thick with articles torn from various publications. It's a habit I haven't yet shorn.

On Friday, Day 11, there was an intriguing exchange in Jody Powell's mid–day briefing. Question: "Was there a point last night at which it appeared as if the talks were about to break down and President Sadat leave and go home, or back to Washington?" Answer: "No, there was not." Question: "Was there a crisis last night?" Answer: "No, not that I am aware of." The questions were well–founded, we learned later.

As for Jody's answers, he wrote in his 1984 book, *The Other Side of the Story,* that the rumor of Sadat's threat to break off the talks "was true, although I didn't know it at the time." He explained: "By that afternoon I had checked with the President and he confirmed the rumor. Although my statement at the briefing had not been intentionally deceptive, it was, nevertheless, completely false."

According to Carter's 1982 memoir, *Keeping Faith*, Sadat had objected to a new draft on the Sinai issue and Carter concluded that there appeared to be "no answer that would satisfy both sides." On that Friday, he sent Sadat and Begin a handwritten proposal to adjourn on Sunday, and both accepted it. Secretary Vance was summoned by Sadat, and on his return told Carter: "Sadat is leaving. He and his aides are already packed. He asked me to order him a helicopter!" Carter went to see Sadat and persuaded him to stay.

In the American Legion Hall that day, most of the press, if not all, knew none of this. I did not make much of the Q-and-A on Sadat because the summit was still going on and Sadat obviously was still at Camp David. Postings later in the day said merely that Carter met with Sadat, and that Mondale met with Sadat and then with Begin. I reported that "a framework for peace has so far eluded the leaders of Egypt, Israel and the United States."

Saturday, Day 12, began as another monotonous day, but at 11:35 a.m. Jody Powell began his briefing with an announcement: "After consultation involving all three delegations, it has been agreed that tomorrow, Sunday, will be the final day of the summit." That was greeted with a burst of applause; our long stay was coming to an end. Jody told us there were still "outstanding differences in important areas" and that "serious efforts" to resolve them continued.

After filing several reports for hourly newscasts on the "last-ditch" effort, I got out my chart and chronology of the meetings and wrote a sidebar on the summit, one of the longest in recent world history. (It was exceeded by the World War II Potsdam summit, in 1945.) There were at least three dozen meetings, not counting informal exchanges, chance encounters, social hours, or the many sessions held by each individual delegation. Carter was involved in at least 21 of the meetings that were announced up to Saturday, but, I added, "it's understood he also took part in some of the long hours of talks held by the legal experts of the Egyptian and Israeli delegations." They were Egypt's Osama El-Baz, a Harvard Law School graduate and undersecretary of state in the Foreign Ministry, and Israel's Aharon Barak, former attorney general who had been named to the Israeli Supreme Court.

And now the 13th and final day of the summit, Sunday, September 17. As we waited for announcements I filed holding spots, for instance: "President Carter has stepped up efforts to win agreement. . . . (He) met for two and one-half hours with President Sadat Saturday afternoon and then for four and a half hours with Prime Minister Begin in a session that stretched beyond midnight . . . ." Mark Willen and I alternated writing broadcast pieces as the day dragged on. Carter met with Sadat from 10:30 to

11:15 a.m., with Begin from 3:27 to 3:33 p.m., then began another meeting with Sadat at 3:40 p.m. The outcome of the summit, I reported, was "still uncertain as evening approached."

Then, about 7 p.m., this Notice to the Press: "There will be an announcement at 10:30 p.m. in the East Room of the White House involving all three principals. There will be a background briefing at 9:00 p.m. in Room 450 of the Old Executive Office Building." I hurriedly packed my gear, gathered up the dogs, piled into the car, raced to the Rambler to check out, sped to Washington in a pouring-down rain and record time, deposited bewildered Linus and Sebastian at home and got to the Old EOB, where Neil Strawser of CBS had saved a seat for me, in time for the briefing. Once briefed, a large contingent of the press crowded into the East Room to see the three leaders announce the Camp David Accords. I felt so lucky to be a witness.

"Ladies and gentlemen, the President of the United States, the President of the Arab Republic of Egypt, the Prime Minister of Israel." With that announcement, so began the White House ceremony as the three leaders entered to a standing ovation from the audience of Egyptian, Israeli and American officialdom. It was the first of many during the 32-minute nationally televised ceremony, which VOA broadcast live.

Sadat's words rolled forth melodiously. "Dear friend," he told Carter, "we came to Camp David with all the good will and faith we possessed, and we left Camp David a few minutes ago with a renewed sense of hope and inspiration." Begin spoke at length, a torrent of words, and declared: "Ultimately, ladies and gentlemen, the President of the United States won the day. . . ." He said the Camp David Conference should be re-named; it was, he said, "The Jimmy Carter Conference." Carter called the accords "a significant achievement in the cause of peace, an achievement none thought possible a year ago — or even a month ago, an achievement that reflects the courage and wisdom of these two leaders."

The documents signed by Begin and Sadat, with Carter as witness, were a general framework for "a comprehensive peace" and a framework for an Egyptian-Israeli peace treaty that was to be

President Sadat and Prime Minister Begin embrace, with President Carter
looking on, after the announcement of the Camp David Accords, September
1978. (Courtesy, Jimmy Carter Library)

concluded within three months. I filed a straight write–through for VOA's language services first, then a version with soundbites from the three leaders, then sidebars. A color spot reported: "The sight of the Egyptian and Israeli leaders hugging each other brought another standing ovation and cheers from the audience." One of the sidebars was based on the background briefing and included word that a U.S. negotiating proposal aimed at breaking the impasse was the first of 23 major draft texts discussed.

That Sunday night in the East Room all three leaders cautioned that hard issues remained and difficulties lay ahead, but for now they were ebullient. Carter won praise from Congress and from political pundits, who said he had shown he was a competent leader. The cover of *Newsweek* had a drawing of a grinning, big–toothed Jimmy Carter with a headline that said, "Born Again."

By the end of 1978, however, the euphoria was gone. Negotiations had stalled, and the December 17 target date for conclusion of the Egyptian–Israeli treaty had slipped by. The first two months of 1979 were marked by deadlock, frustration and pessimism. Carter invited Begin to Washington, and after four days of talks a White House handout on March 4 said the president had "put forward suggestions designed to help resolve some of the outstanding differences between Egypt and Israel." The next day, a Monday, came word of a positive response from the Israeli cabinet, and then the announcement that Carter would visit Egypt and Israel — and would leave Wednesday!

In filing scenesetters on his bid to salvage the treaty, I reported that "his spokesman says the president believes the prospects for peace, which seemed so bright last September, must not be allowed to continue to dim and perhaps vanish." The journey was crucial for Carter himself. "The trip comes at a time when his standing in the public opinion polls has declined again, from the high approval rating he received following the Camp David Summit," I reported. "And it comes at a time when his critics have charged that he has been ineffective and not forceful enough in his conduct of foreign policy." On the day of Carter's departure, a *New York Times* editorial said, "The failure of the Camp David accords would be a costly personal defeat at a time of doubt about his leadership."

The White House Transportation Office did a remarkable job making arrangements for the traveling press corps (163 men/12 women), and on Wednesday afternoon the Pan Am and TWA charters were on their way to Cairo, preceding Air Force One. And NBC, which was in charge of the U.S. Radio Pool for the trip, did a remarkable job in setting up the white line, considering the logistical problems.

As I read in a dispatch by *Washington Post* Cairo correspondent Thomas W. Lippman: "In an overcrowded and chaotic city like Cairo, long on history, but short on facilities, a short–notice visit by the president of the United States is not just a historic event, it's a logistical nightmare. Egyptian and American officials were scrambling around the capital this morning (Tuesday), cursing the antiquated and overburdened telephone system, in a frantic rush to arrange hotel rooms, security and communications for the president, his entourage and the press." The traveling press didn't have to worry about where to sleep; we stayed at the Nile Hilton, which had been taken over by the Egyptian government for use by the presidential party.

Carter arrived in Cairo Thursday afternoon, and the scenario was almost a repetition of the welcome given Nixon in 1974, with hundreds of thousands of cheering Egyptians lining the route of the motorcade from the airport into town. To those of us who had been on the Nixon trip, the turnout didn't seem as large, but was just as enthusiastic. At various points along the route of the 50–minute ride to Qubba Palace, doves were turned loose, flowers were thrown and laurel branches were waved; people chanted "Carter, Carter," and so on. After the welcoming ceremony at the palace, where Carter began his remarks with the Arabic wish Salaam alaikum (Peace be upon you), the two leaders began their talks on the new U.S. proposals and Egypt's reaction to them.

I was pleased to be working again with the VOA Mideast contingent, Doug Roberts, Ibrahim Abdin and Fawzi Tadros, plus our radio tech, Don Barth. Our team effort paid off Friday when Carter and Sadat went by train to Alexandria. I was on the 23–member press pool aboard the presidential train, so Doug went by car a portion of the way to cover the reaction of crowds as the train went by and then returned to Cairo to file reports to VOA. Don Barth flew to Alexandria on one of the Egyptian C–130s that had been laid on for the rest of the press party, and we met at the press center in the Palestine Hotel. Filing out of Alexandria was difficult, as we'd expected, and Don recorded my reports as a back–up and transmitted them to VOA when the C–130s returned to Cairo.

During the four–hour train ride, Sadat and Carter stood much of the time in the open Victorian era car waving to the crowds at rail stations, to clusters of men, women and children in small settlements, and to farmhands pausing in their work in the Nile Delta to wave back at them. The Egyptian Railways gave us a handsome brochure in English and Arabic listing the towns along the route, but, like many hastily printed documents, it had a typo. The cover read: "Itinerary of The Special Train of Mr. G. Carter, the President of the United States of America, 9th March 1979." As the train crossed into the fertile Delta, Sadat told Carter, "This is my Georgia." It was his home province.

We reporters were escorted in mini–groups to the presidents' car for brief interviews. Helen Thomas and I were with them a few minutes, and though I was preoccupied with recording what was said, I marveled that I was really standing there next to Sadat and seeing that wonderful face of his up close. Helen asked Carter if the talks were going "as bad as they look," and he said, "There are still some problems as you know." In a later interview on the train with Walter Cronkite, John Chancellor and Peter Jennings, Carter said he obviously would be going on to Israel with some differences remaining.

Sadat's assessment, however, set off a flurry of press activity. "With President Carter still being cautious about his Middle East peace mission," I wrote, "President Sadat startled reporters by saying he thinks Egypt is on the verge of a peace agreement with Israel. The Egyptian leader did say there were some words here and there holding up a treaty. He maintained there are no obstacles in the way, only a misunderstanding about the main issues. He did not elaborate."

The train ride to Alexandria was smooth, just as it was in 1974. Carter got a tremendous reception there, exceeding the one given Nixon, I thought; and the two presidents returned to Cairo the next day by helicopter. In a speech to parliament, the People's Assembly, Carter appealed to Egyptians, Palestinians and other Arab countries to support the treaty, said it was "within grasp," and urged, "Let us seize this opportunity." But he and Sadat emerged from their final round of talks to tell reporters that while they had resolved some difficult issues, other difficult issues remained. Sadat then took the Carters to see the Pyramids before they left for Jerusalem, and I hastily filed a report for Worldwide English's recorded weekend shows that there was "no certainty" the president's mission would be successful.

These weekend programs included roundups of the week's events and were re–broadcast at various times on Saturday. With Cairo and Jerusalem seven hours ahead of EST, I was able to update them with the latest information. For instance, after Carter's arrival in Israel Saturday night, local time, the roundup spot was updated with a sentence on his remarks at Ben Gurion Airport that he was looking forward to completing the urgent business at hand.

In Jerusalem, after a warm reunion with Charlie and Harriet Weiss, we got down to the business at hand. Charlie worked mainly at the international press center set up by the Israelis; I worked at the White House filing center at the Jerusalem Hilton, and we consulted constantly to be sure VOA didn't miss anything. On Sunday he shuttled between both while the Carter–Begin talks were going on, as I was the pool reporter for Rosalynn Carter's visit to a residential and teaching complex for new immigrants.

This turned out to be a good story for VOA's broadcasts to the Soviet Union. Recent Soviet immigrants at the Mevasseret Absorption Center made appeals to her, and through her to her husband, on behalf of Soviet Jews. They asked specifically for help to obtain the release of Anatoly Scharansky, Vladimir Slepak and Ida Nudel. Mrs. Carter's visit included a tree–planting ceremony at which she gave the center a cypress. When she plants a tree, it is not just a ceremonial turning of a bit of earth; she really shoveled the dirt into the hole.

After more than five hours of talks Sunday, Carter said there were still unresolved issues, and Begin announced he was calling his cabinet into a night–time session and would give Israel's replies to the president the next morning. The cabinet met through the night. Charlie Weiss maintained a vigil and reported: "As dawn was breaking, a very tired Mr. Begin came out" and said the cabinet's decisions would be given to the president at a meeting rescheduled for 10 a.m. so its members could get a few hours sleep.

At mid–day Carter addressed the Israeli parliament, the Knesset, and reported that efforts to reach agreement on a peace treaty had fallen short. "We have not yet fully met our challenge," he said, and, in a passionate appeal, "We must not lose this moment."

After Carter's address, Begin spoke, despite repeated shouting and heckling by parliament members from both ends of the political spectrum. Among other things, he repeated Israel's insistence on an exchange of ambassadors with Egypt as projected in the Camp David Accords.

Consultations continued. The Israeli cabinet went into another session. Carter had lunch with the foreign affairs committee of the Knesset. Vance met with Begin and members of the cabinet's defense committee. Then Begin emerged to say "great progress" had been made in solving outstanding problems. Several problems that remained would be negotiated constantly until a solution was found, he said, adding that he believed it would be found.

Later we were told that Carter had decided to extend his stay in Jerusalem to have more talks with Begin Tuesday morning, after which he would fly to Cairo for an airport meeting with Sadat on his way back to Washington. We learned that Secretary Vance was meeting with Foreign Minister Moshe Dayan, and that Carter had a long telephone conversation with Begin.

Now we come to the atmosphere on that Monday night, March 12. The Israelis told reporters that real progress had been made. After their briefing, Jody Powell held his on–the–record briefing and said that compared to the distance which had been traveled, the distance separating Egypt and Israel was very small but it might be a very difficult final distance to travel. Then Jody held two late–night background briefings for the White House press in a room at the Jerusalem Hilton. I was in the group for the second one, which started at 11:30 p.m. The room was stuffy, jammed with reporters anxious to know what was really going on. There were three unresolved issues, we were told, negotiations on self-rule in Gaza, oil supplies for Israel, and the exchange of ambassadors. The atmosphere was gloomy. When a reporter asked Jody how he would report the story, he replied that he would give an assessment of the situation as it stood, but "you've got to leave the door open a crack." He told us: "You'd better protect your ass."

I compared notes with correspondents who had been at the earlier background briefing and confirmed that Jody had said essentially the same things at both. A good many reporters concluded, and reported, that the president's mission apparently had failed. Some said it flatly. I conferred with Charlie Weiss; we couldn't ignore the Begin comment about "great progress." We knew Vance and Dayan were in contact. And the trip wasn't over yet. How could we report failure when Carter was going to see Begin again and then meet with Sadat? So I hedged, and reported continuing efforts to reach agreement.

For a holding spot Tuesday morning Jerusalem time, filed for broadcast on VOA while the Carter–Begin meeting was in progress, I took into account the fact that some of the American media had already reported failure, but I was still hedging: "President Carter went into his final talks with Israeli Prime Minister Menachem Begin with no agreement on an Egyptian–Israeli peace treaty in sight. The prospects before the meeting were that his Middle East peace mission would end in failure or at best, limited success — but efforts continued to resolve the remaining differences."

As the White House press headed for Cairo, Charlie waited out the two-and-a-half-hour Carter–Begin meeting. As he reported (the traveling press of course did not know this), one of the Israeli participants in the final half hour said the talks were successful, and Begin's spokesman, Dan Patir, described as "totally unjustified" the pessimism which had appeared in the American media. Then, in a farewell statement at Ben Gurion airport, Begin told Carter he had succeeded in his peace mission!

At the Cairo airport, about five hours later, Carter came out of his meeting with Sadat and made the stunning announcement that both the Israeli prime minister and Egyptian president had accepted U.S. proposals for resolving issues blocking the treaty. With Sadat at his side, he said, "I am convinced that now we have defined all the main ingredients of a peace treaty between Egypt and Israel. . . ."

Pandemonium ensued in the press corps. Correspondents who had reported failure were furious with Jody Powell, some of them suggesting that they had been manipulated, either to make the breakthrough more dramatic or to put a form of negotiating pressure on the Israelis, by being led to report the mission had failed. I did not feel manipulated, and I thought the impression conveyed to reporters Monday night was an accurate portrayal of the American perception at the time. I didn't have any inside information, but had the gut feeling that reporters develop. Besides, we had been cautioned to protect our rears. Correspondent Jeffrey Antevil of *The New York Daily News* wrote afterwards that "it was not Powell's backgrounder" that had persuaded him to file a story "all but writing off the trip as a failure," but rather Carter's speech to the Knesset and the announcement that he was planning to go home with difficult issues unresolved. Jeff added, "I believed at the time, and I still believe, that the pessimism that Carter and Powell were expressing on Monday was genuine."

So do I. The trip was hard to cover, "a journalist's nightmare," as one reporter put it. I wouldn't have missed it for anything.

On March 26, 1979, Menachem Begin and Anwar Sadat signed the peace treaty, with Jimmy Carter as witness, in an afternoon ceremony on the Pennsylvania Avenue side of the White House grounds, the North Lawn. Rarely used for formal events, the North Lawn was jammed with 1,600 invited guests and an abundance of press. Across the street, Lafayette Park was crowded with spectators, who heard the proceedings on loudspeakers. The ceremony was televised live in the U.S. and to the Middle East, and broadcast live on VOA.

The sun shone brilliantly, highlighting the Egyptian, Israeli and American flags fluttering from their staffs to the left of the signing table. The three leaders in turn signed the treaty documents and then with eloquence addressed the gathering. Carter: "So let us now lay aside war. Let us now reward the children of Abraham who hunger for a comprehensive peace in the Middle East." Sadat: "Let there be no more wars or bloodshed between Arabs and Israelis. Let there be no more suffering or denial of rights." Begin: "No more war. No more bloodshed. Peace unto you. No more bereavement. Shalom. Salaam. Forever."

In a sunlit ceremony on the White House North Lawn, President Sadat, President Carter and Prime Minister Begin celebrate their achievement, the signing of the Egyptian–Israeli Peace Treaty, March 26, 1979. (Courtesy, Jimmy Carter Library)

11
More Summitry
Carter and Brezhnev in Vienna
Meow and Malaise

The Egyptian–Israeli peace treaty was a shining achievement for
Carter and he had some other successes in 1979. But he also was
plagued by problems, notably the American economy and his energy
proposals.

The year, however, got off to a pleasant start. On January 4 the
president left wintry Washington for the tropical climate of
Guadaloupe to attend an informal summit with three other leaders:
French President Valery Giscard d'Estaing, the host, British Prime
Minister James Callaghan and West German Chancellor Helmut
Schmidt. In the relaxed surroundings of a seafront resort on the
French island, called "the emerald of the Caribbean," they reviewed
world developments.

One of the places they were watching closely was Iran, where
violent anti–Shah demonstrations had mounted in 1978 and the
Baktiar government was trying to restore order. All four leaders were
concerned about stability in the Persian Gulf; their countries were
major importers of Iranian oil.

The main topics discussed were relations with the People's
Republic of China and the Soviet Union. The United States had
established formal diplomatic ties with the PRC on January 1, and
the four leaders made clear in their closing statements that improvement in relations between China and the West did not diminish their
pursuit of detente with Moscow. And Carter's summit partners
endorsed the U.S. negotiations with the Soviet Union on limiting
offensive nuclear weapons.

When the summit was over, Carter and his wife and daughter
stayed on for two more days, which suited the traveling White
House press (94 men/12 women). We explored the lush island, sat
around the swimming pool at the press hotel, the Holiday Inn, and
dined on French and Creole food. One evening at a Creole

restaurant, the woman owner encouraged us to dance. A nimble Brzezinski joined in.

The new chapter in Sino–American relations was celebrated in late January 1979, when Deng Xiaoping, then China's senior vice premier, became the first leader of the PRC to visit the United States. Carter was criticized for inviting Richard Nixon to the White House state dinner in Deng's honor, and in defending the invitation, cited the opening to China as one of Nixon's major achievements. "I have no apology to make," he said, "it was a proper thing to do." At the dinner, Nixon got a warm handshake from Deng. An even warmer handshake went to Shirley MacLaine, who had done a television documentary on China and was told by Deng that she would be welcomed back on another visit.

During his stay in America, Deng was publicly critical of the Soviet Union, which was not surprising, given China's anti–Soviet attitude at the time. Carter pointed out the United States and China had differing views, and at a press conference in February said that the U.S. wanted sound relationships with the Soviet Union and that both were negotiating in good faith on a new SALT agreement.

On the afternoon of April 27, Jody Powell announced that five Soviet dissidents had been released to the U.S. in exchange for the release of two convicted Soviet spies. His announcement was followed by a background briefing, by a high–ranking White House official, which came perilously close to the deadline for VOA's English broadcast heard late at night in the Soviet Union. As the briefing dragged on, I kept looking at my watch, agonizing over whether it would end in time for me to get the story on the air. It ended with moments to spare and I dashed to my basement cubby–hole and made the deadline with a bare–bones story:

"Five Soviet dissidents, including Alexander Ginsburg, have arrived in New York following their release by the Soviet Union, and two convicted Soviet spies are on their way to Moscow following the commutation of their prison sentences by President Carter. . . . The five dissidents, described by U.S. officials as prisoners of conscience, are all reported to be well." I was told later that Mrs. Ginsburg was listening to the English newscast and that's how she learned of her husband's release.

In early May it was announced that American and Soviet negotiators in Geneva had reached agreement on a SALT II Treaty, and that Carter and Brezhnev would sign it in June in Vienna. Before their summit Carter launched a campaign for Senate ratification, trying to reassure critics that the treaty would be enforceable and verifiable. He also made public his decision to build a full-scale MX long-range missile. The announcement, I reported, was aimed at two audiences, the Kremlin and the U.S. Congress; he was in effect making clear to both that he intended to maintain the strategic balance between the two superpowers. One of the treaty's strongest critics was the influential Senator Henry Jackson, from Carter's own party, who accused the Carter administration, and the Nixon and Ford administrations, of following a policy of appeasement toward the Soviet Union, a charge that Secretary Vance labeled misguided and simply wrong.

The Vienna meeting was the first U.S.–Soviet summit in over four years and attracted an international press corps of 2,000, including about 200 in the White House contingent. I teamed with our Vienna correspondent, Ron Pemstein, and Bill Marsh of our Munich bureau in covering it, and in eyeing Brezhnev. The 72-year-old Soviet leader had recently been ill, and the press was curious about his condition. It became obvious he wasn't in great shape. During talks at the Soviet embassy Brezhnev slipped on a step as he was escorting Carter out for the lunch break. Carter and Soviet security agents helped steady him.

In the summit sessions the two leaders and their advisors discussed world troublespots, arms control, and U.S.–Soviet issues before getting to the main event, the signing of the SALT II Treaty and related documents on June 18, 1979, in the ornate and historic Hofburg Palace. At the ceremony, Brezhnev spoke first. "In signing this treaty," he said, "we are helping to defend the most sacred right of every individual — the right to live." Carter said he and Brezhnev "both have children and grandchildren and we want them to live, and live in peace." They signed all the documents and then, I reported, "the American president initiated an exchange of kisses with the aging and ailing Soviet leader."

SALT II, to be in effect until the end of 1985, set ceilings on strategic nuclear delivery vehicles and included sub–limits dealing with warheads. It faced intense scrutiny in the U.S. Senate and a debate which, as my colleague Ron Pemstein forecast, "seems destined to go on for months."

Carter also was having continuing problems with Congress on his various energy proposals. He had been urging energy conservation since April 1977 when he told the American people that this was the "moral equivalent of war," a phrase that was seized on by pundits who labeled his energy plan MEOW. By May 1979, when Carter's gasoline conservation measure was pending in Congress, Jody Powell had a memorable White House briefing. He was trying to

An embrace and exchange of kisses after Jimmy Carter and Leonid Brezhnev sign the Salt II Treaty in Vienna, June 18, 1979. (Courtesy, Jimmy Carter Library)

make the point that it would be unwise to push up production of gasoline supplies to meet shortages during warm weather, because crude oil stockpiles were needed for heating homes in cold weather. He turned story–teller and rendered his version of Aesop's tale of the grasshopper and the ant.

Leaving out asides, laughter and wisecracks from the press, it went this way: The ant worked hard and spent all his time trying to stockpile food for the winter because he knew there were bad times ahead. The grasshopper, on the other hand, spent Spring and Summer fiddling, chirping and generally poking fun and making irresponsible statements about what the ant was trying to do. Then came the first frost, and food became scarce. The ant of course had food stocked away. The grasshopper began to think less about fiddling and more about food, and by and by there was no food available and the ground was covered with snow. Finally, out of desperation, the grasshopper comes to the ant and says, "Mr. Ant, I made a serious mistake here. I didn't lay anything by for the wintertime. I know I made a lot of fun of you when you were working hard. . . but wouldn't you be willing to share a little food with me?" And the ant said, "Kiss off," and the grasshopper died. After a burst of applause, Jody returned to a less colorful discussion of the energy problem. And I wrote a feature for VOA about his fabled briefing.

By early July long lines of motorists were waiting to buy short supplies of gasoline, and striking independent truckers were protesting diesel fuel prices and shortages. The Organization of Petroleum Exporting Countries, OPEC, had announced a new price increase, and Carter had just returned from the annual economic summit, held in Tokyo, where the leaders had agreed on a common effort to restrain energy consumption. The energy problem, I reported, was also a political problem for him. His job performance rating in the ABC–Lou Harris poll had dropped to 73 per cent negative.

Carter conferred with his advisors and scheduled a speech to the nation on the energy crisis for Thursday night, July 5. But on Wednesday afternoon, while he was spending the Independence Day holiday at Camp David, he abruptly cancelled the speech, without explanation. A terse White House announcement Thursday said he was remaining at Camp David, was assessing major domestic issues, and would be consulting with people both in and outside of government. Thus began the Camp David Domestic Summit.

In the week that followed helicopters shuttled in and out of the presidential retreat carrying a wide variety of visitors to confer with him in privacy. The total was estimated at more than 150 and included members of Congress, state and local officials, energy experts, economists, civil rights and religious leaders, and employment specialists. Only scraps of information were given out at the White House, but some of the summit participants talked after meeting with the president, and it was clear, I told VOA listeners, that the conversations were a philosophical exercise as well as an analysis of specific issues, primarily energy and the economy.

Toward the end of his stay at Camp David, Carter slipped away for a surprise visit to a steelworker's family in Carnegie, a Pittsburgh suburb. VOA's Paula Wolfson happened to be visiting her family in Pittsburgh and filed a story. She reported the meeting centered on inflation and energy, and that the steelworker, 29-year-old William Fisher, and a group of his neighbors "did most of the talking. Mr. Fisher says he told the president that he thinks the country is on a downhill spiral right now, and that Jimmy Carter agrees."

By the time of the Domestic Summit, VOA had a two-woman bureau at the White House. Jane Berger had succeeded Dave Gollust, who had become VOA's diplomatic correspondent. Again I was working with a fine reporter. And we had plenty to cover. Carter went on television and radio Sunday night, July 15, and in a remarkable speech said there was a crisis of the American spirit, a crisis of confidence in the United States. He urged citizens to rally in a war on the energy problem and outlined a program to cut U.S. dependence on foreign oil. The country, he said, was at a turning point in its history.

His speech, I reported, could also be a turning point in his presidency. "At a time when public opinion polls show little confidence in his ability to handle the energy and economic problems, the president has embarked on a campaign to re–establish his leadership." Carter's address came to be known as his "malaise" speech, even though the word "malaise" was not in the text. It was, as I recall, in a *Washington Post* story previewing the speech, based on comments by Clark Clifford, advisor to Democratic presidents.

On the Tuesday after the address, Jody Powell called reporters to his office and announced: "All members of the senior staff and cabinet officers have offered their resignations to the president during this period of evaluation." A background briefing produced little information. The idea was that the resignations would give Carter a freer hand in restructuring his administration. Were foreign policy officials involved? Everyone, we were told. When we left Jody's office I placed phone calls to try to find out whether Vance and Brzezinski were affected, something that naturally would be of interest to listeners overseas. Nobody returned my calls. I went ahead and reported, "Presumably, since the Camp David discussions were devoted exclusively to domestic problems, the president's shakeup will involve advisors concerned with domestic affairs."

Then I learned that almost immediately after the briefing Jody Powell, Jerry Schecter and others in the Press Office phoned or went around to the wire service and network booths to pass the word that foreign, defense and national security advisors were not affected. No official had thought of passing it on to VOA. Friends in the press corps informed me, and I filed a quick update. "Reporters have been told," I reported, that Vance, Brzezinski and Defense Secretary Harold Brown "are safe." (Cabinet members replaced in the shakeup included Treasury's Michael Blumenthal and Energy's James Schlesinger.)

Another outcome of the Domestic Summit was that Carter and his advisors decided they needed to do a better job of communicating with the public. He stepped up informal interviews with reporters and syndicated newspaper columnists. I was among 25 reporters invited to share his thoughts over hamburgers and French fries on July 21. The briefing rules were that we couldn't quote Carter directly but could convey his views through such devices as, "The president is known to feel. . . ." On the cabinet changes, for instance, I reported that "his intention was to have a loyal harmonious team in place to deal with the challenges facing the nation."

During the lunch in the State Dining Room I sneaked a look at the underside of my dinner plate to see if it might be Castleton China, made for the White House in the Eisenhower and Johnson administrations by the Shenango China Company in my hometown. I did the same when traveling abroad because china from New Castle was then exported extensively and used in places like luxury hotels around the world. The lunch china wasn't Castleton (and Shenango China no longer exists).

Carter also answered questions from citizens from around the country in a two-hour call-in program broadcast by National Public Radio in mid-October. Inflation and energy were the main topics, with the SALT II Treaty and U.S.-Soviet relations next. One question, from a doctor concerned about radiation, dealt with nuclear power. The Three Mile Island nuclear power plant accident had occurred in March. Carter restated his position that nuclear power must be part of the nation's energy industry, but promised continued efforts to make sure it was safe. The doctor, I reported, told Carter: "I'm not completely satisfied with your answer."

Apart from domestic problems, there was Iran, where the exiled religious leader Ayatollah Ruhollah Khomeini had returned at the end of January 1979 to begin his revolution. The Shah had left Iran on January 16, going first to Egypt. Two days later Carter spoke at the annual national prayer breakfast in Washington and predicted that religious fervor in the Persian Gulf would produce one of the year's major news stories. The fervor of militant Khomeini supporters did do that, although it was not the kind of story Carter had in mind. He was referring to the "inclination" of devout religious leaders to cling to the past in a "modern, rapidly changing technological world."

In the early morning hours of November 4, 1979, in Washington, Carter was notified that the American embassy in Tehran had been overrun by militants and its staff seized. The Iranian hostage crisis had begun.

12
The Iranian Hostage Crisis
The Soviet Invasion of Afghanistan
The 1980 Campaign

In writing stories about the Iranian hostage crisis, I kept hoping that maybe the hostages were being allowed to listen to our newscasts and would know about the efforts to get them released. I realized this was very probably not the case. They were being held incommunicado. I assumed the authorities in Tehran were monitoring VOA, however, so perhaps the news we reported would filter through to the captives.

Apart from any diplomatic contacts, international radio was one of the fastest ways, if not the fastest, to inform the Iranians of reaction in Washington. From the outset of the crisis, VOA reported American statements emphasizing that the most important concern was the safety of the hostages, and day after day Jane Berger and I filed stories from our White House broadcast booth on steps taken by Carter. His initial actions included cutting off oil imports from Iran and freezing Iranian assets in American banks, and he refused Iranian demands for extradition of the Shah, who was in the U.S. for medical treatment.

A month after the embassy takeover, he declared his candidacy for re-election but announced on the same day, December 4, that he was postponing campaign travel to devote efforts to resolving the crisis. He called the hostage-takers "a mob and a government that have become one and the same."

A few days later I reported that Carter was "known to be considering the possibility of additional economic pressure against Iran." And that "it's been learned" he had been studying the Moslem religion and the Koran, and material on the Ayatollah Khomeini and various Iranian officials. These reports stemmed from a breakfast session the president had with a handful of correspondents in the small family dining room off the White House state floor, which I attended. Under briefing rules, we couldn't quote him directly. In filing the stories, I knew VOA's expanded Persian service would welcome them.

VOA routinely reported news of regional interest in broadcasts beamed to different regions of the world, and I filed reports for specific language services when there was something of special interest to them. The Persian service broadcasts had been re-instituted in April 1979 because of the Iranian revolution and were increased after the embassy takeover in November. Under VOA's then acting director, the highly respected Hans N. (Tom) Tuch, broadcasts in Farsi went to two hours a day by the end of the year, with further increases planned. Language programs to the Islamic world would be expanded even more in the months to come because of another crisis, next door to Iran.

Soviet troops had invaded Afghanistan in late December, and the Afghan government was ousted in a Soviet-backed coup. From then on Carter was preoccupied with both Iran and Afghanistan, and the stories of the hostage crisis and the Soviet invasion unfolded virtually in tandem, along with the 1980 election campaign and other troubles the president had.

In reaction to the Soviet invasion, Carter shelved the Salt II Treaty, which was still in difficulty in the Senate, and embargoed grain shipments to the Soviet Union except for deliveries required under a five-year agreement. The Soviets had intended to buy millions of tons more than the agreement provided. Carter pressed for United Nations action to condemn the invasion and call for the withdrawal of Soviet troops, but the Soviet Union vetoed the U.N. Security Council resolution. It also used its veto in the hostage crisis, killing a resolution that had called for sanctions on exports to Iran.

Carter announced on January 20 that the U.S. would boycott the Moscow Summer Olympics if Soviet troops were not pulled out of Afghanistan in a month. And in his State of the Union address to Congress on January 23, he delivered a warning. It was the enunciation of a Persian Gulf doctrine in words stronger than previously heard: "An attempt by any outside force to gain control of the Persian Gulf region will be regarded as an assault on the vital interests of the United States of America — and such an assault will be repelled by any means necessary, including military force." In February, Carter met with American scholars in Islamic studies and told them U.S. policy toward Islamic nations was unchanged despite the crisis in Iran. The White House released his statement to them, and I reported it in detail. VOA thus was a vehicle for the message he was trying to send to the Islamic world, but at the same time the message was newsworthy. In the statement Carter said he was determined to strengthen "the longstanding bonds of friendship and cooperation between the U.S. and many Muslim nations," and, "We will lend our support to any nation working for peace and justice and to resist external domination."

What appeared to be a major development in the hostage crisis came on April 1, when Carter summoned reporters to the Oval Office shortly after 7 a.m. and welcomed Iranian President Bani–Sadr's statement that control of the hostages would be transferred from the militants to the Iranian government. As we reported, Carter called it "a positive step" and deferred additional sanctions against Iran for the time being. April 1 was the date of the Wisconsin primary election, and Carter's opponents charged he was politically motivated in making his televised remarks that morning.

Before the day was over, there was word that Bani–Sadr was dissatisfied with Carter's response. The transfer fell through when the Ayatollah Khomeini refused to give his approval. On April 7 the president announced the U.S. was breaking relations with the Iranian government, and banned all American exports to Iran, except food and medicine. The militant captors threatened to put the hostages on trial and to kill them if the U.S. took the slightest military action against Iran. Carter said the U.S. would pursue every legal use of its power to bring the hostages home and pressed the European allies and Japan to join in the sanctions. On April 17 he barred all U.S. imports from Iran, travel by Americans to Iran, and all financial payments by Americans to any Iranian entity, and said Iranian authorities should realize that "the availability of peaceful measures, like the patience of the American people, is running out."

A few days later *The Los Angeles Times* reported that some Carter aides had expressed concern in a White House staff meeting about possible military action. It quoted speechwriter Henrik Hertzberg as saying he had "an uneasy feeling that we're slipping down a slippery slope toward military confrontation." Jody Powell was asked about it at his briefing but said he didn't consider it responsible to comment on such matters. The April 23 story was written by the paper's Washington bureau chief, Jack Nelson, who had good sources at the White House; other news organizations quickly followed with their own stories, and I filed one for VOA the next day, a Thursday. It noted that Carter's chief of staff, Hamilton Jordan, "was quoted by *The Los Angeles Times* as saying that some of the staff members had the erroneous impression that the president had already made a decision to exercise a military option, such as mining Iranian harbors or imposing a naval blockade. Mr. Jordan told *The Times* he stated unequivocally that the president has made no such decision. . . ."

Late that night — it was shortly before 1 a.m. Friday, April 25, the White House phoned me at home and Rex Granum, the deputy press secretary, came on the line in a conference call with me and the BBC correspondent. Simultaneously, Jody Powell was making a conference call to the wire services and networks. They dictated a statement, for release at 1 a.m., disclosing the aborted attempt to rescue the hostages: "The President has ordered the cancellation of an operation in Iran which was underway to prepare for a rescue of our hostages. The mission was terminated because of equipment failure. During the subsequent withdrawal of American personnel there was a collision between our aircraft on the ground at a remote desert location in Iran. There were no military hostilities, but the President deeply regrets that eight American crew members of the two aircraft were killed and others were injured in the accident. . . ."

I took down the 11–sentence statement as fast as I could, thanked Rex, phoned the VOA newsroom, and dictated it to one of the writers. I was grateful the White House phoned me at the same time as the other correspondents, for VOA thus had the full statement while the wire services were still moving bulletins with fragmented quotes, and was able to get a detailed story quickly on the air. After informing the newsroom, I wrote a broadcast piece which noted that the White House statement also said the mission "was not motivated by hostility toward Iran or the Iranian people and there were no Iranian casualties."

The following Monday, the resignation of Secretary of State Vance was announced. He had resigned before the rescue mission began because he could not support it, but did not make his decision public and stayed in his post while it was in progress. In a handwritten letter accepting the resignation, Carter told Vance, "I know this is a matter of principle with you," and said he looked forward to his continuing advice on matters of importance "to our country, which you have served so well." The 63-year-old Vance had a distinguished career in public service dating back to 1957 and continuing into the early 1990s, serving, at the age of 75, as a United Nations special envoy in the effort to mediate conflicts in the former Yugoslavia.

As Vance's successor, Carter chose Senator Edmund Muskie, a key member of Congress and Hubert Humphrey's running-mate in the 1968 presidential election campaign. The nomination was speedily confirmed and Muskie was sworn into office May 8. The next day Carter went to Philadelphia to speak at a town meeting, and in answer to a question from the audience, described the role he saw for his new secretary of state: "I see Ed Muskie as being a much stronger and more statesmanlike senior-citizen figure who will be a more evocative spokesman for our nation's policy — not nearly so bogged down in the details of protocol like meeting with, and handling, the visits of constant streams of diplomats who come to Washington."

I didn't focus on that in my story on the town meeting, but just about every other reporter in the press filing center interpreted Carter's remarks as an attack on Vance, and led their stories with it. I wasn't so sure they were right. However, this was going to get big play in the media, so I caved in to pack journalism and wrote a story, but I think I reported it objectively:

"Mr. Carter's remarks were seen as indirect criticism of former Secretary Vance, who resigned as a matter of principle. . . But White

House spokesman Jody Powell quickly quoted the president as saying he was not being critical of Mr. Vance." I noted that Carter made his remarks when asked if Vance resigned because of differences with Brzezinski and that Carter denied such differences. As for Brzezinski, I also noted, the president described him as "kind of feisty; he's aggressive, he's innovative, and he puts forth bright ideas, some of which have to be discarded."

Carter's appearance in Philadelphia marked the end of his self-imposed travel ban. It was his first trip in six months, except for a flight to Texas to see the five hospitalized servicemen injured in the aborted rescue mission.

In addition to Iran and Afghanistan, inflation and recession, efforts to keep the Mideast peace process going, and the challenge from Senator Edward Kennedy for the Democratic presidential nomination, Carter was facing another problem — the influx of Cuban refugees. They were arriving in Florida daily aboard small boats in what the administration branded as an illegal and unsafe operation encouraged by Cuban President Fidel Castro. The numbers of Cuban refugees swelled to more than 125,000 in the operation, known as the Mariel boatlift, creating burdens for Florida, and a political problem for Carter in his re-election campaign.

A problem of a different sort presented itself on May 18, the eruption of the Mount St. Helens volcano in Washington State. With appeals for federal aid flowing into the White House from state and local officials in Washington and Oregon, Carter flew to the Pacific Northwest to survey the disaster from a helicopter flying low over the volcanic area. I was on one of the three press helicopters that followed, and told VOA listeners, "what once were forests of tall green trees now are scenes of cratered land covered with ash and mud and littered with fallen trees strewn about like matchsticks or layers of straw." Carter told a press conference in Portland after his tour that the cost of the recovery effort would be of such magnitude that he'd have to make a special request to Congress for funds, which he did.

In June the president traveled to Europe to take part in the 1980 economic summit, in Venice, and pay visits to Rome, Belgrade, Madrid and Lisbon. It was a good trip in terms of news — Carter turned it into a campaign against the Soviet invasion of Afghanistan — and the cities we visited weren't exactly hardships. Who can complain about being in Rome or taking a boat through the waterways of Venice to cover a summit? Certainly not the large press corps (183 men/12 women) that traveled with the president for most of the tour.

In Rome, our first stop, Carter conferred with Italian government leaders, met with Pope John Paul II at the Vatican, and took some time out to go sightseeing with his wife and daughter. Escorted by an expert in Roman history and trailed by a company of gladiators from the press, the Carters visited the Colosseum and had a magnificent uncluttered view of the vast amphitheater. It had been emptied of other tourists, sealed off for security reasons, and only a few kittens were scampering about in the stadium where centuries ago Christian martyrs were thrown to lions. "In modern day," said Carter, "it would be politicians."

Serving on a press pool covering a president does have its advantages; I was able to see much more of the Colosseum than I had in past visits to Rome. One was with my father, who at the age of 75 was making his first trip back to his native Italy in 60 years. Papa cut short our stay in Rome because he was eager to go on to Altomonte, his birthplace, for a reunion with his sister. He also cut short our visit to Altomonte and other stops in Europe. He'd satisfied his wish to see "the old country," but it was America he loved, and he just wanted to go home to New Castle.

Carter's trip to Europe was noteworthy because of the expanding role of television coverage. More than half the members of the traveling press were from the American TV networks, including correspondents, producers and mini–cam crews. For the first time on a presidential trip abroad the entourage included a small team from Ted Turner's Cable News Network, CNN, which had just made its debut on June 1. The traditional networks looked down their noses at CNN in 1980. They don't do that any more. The trip marked the emergence of a television network that would gain in stature and become a powerful force in international communication.

TV's presence was very much in evidence in Venice, where the waterways swirled with ferry boats and launches taking the press to and from the economic summit site. ABC, CBS and NBC hired their own boats, which sped about with flags bearing their names flapping vaingloriously in the breeze and spray. The print media wasn't unrepresented; *The New York Times* also hired a boat. Covering the summit with me were Edie Smith Apple, then VOA's Paris correspondent, economics correspondent Barry Wood, and our radio tech, Rick McLeaf. The logistics were complicated, since there were two press centers and they were on separate islands. But we arranged our schedules with an eye to the schedules of the boat shuttles, so that we wouldn't miss anything at either the White House filing center at the Excelsior Hotel on the Lido or the international press center on San Georgio Maggiore, adjacent to the summit conference site.

Carter's first event in Venice was a meeting with Helmut Schmidt on the eve of the economic summit. The president and the West German chancellor were involved in an apparent dispute over plans for deployment of American nuclear missiles in western Europe. These were intermediate range missiles, then referred to as TNF, for Theater Nuclear Force. NATO had decided in December 1979 on a two–track policy: To proceed with TNF to counter Soviet missile deployment, and at the same time to pursue negotiations to limit the number of missiles deployed by the Soviet Union and NATO. The Carter administration was concerned that Schmidt was going back on the NATO decision, since he had suggested a three–year moratorium on missile deployments. And just before the Venice summit there were reports that the president had sent him a harshly worded letter.

The two men were smiling when they appeared before reporters after their meeting. Carter said he'd assured the chancellor that he had "absolutely no doubt" about West Germany's commitment to the NATO TNF agreement. He also said they "agreed completely" that the Soviets must withdraw all their troops from Afghanistan. Schmidt, who was planning to visit Moscow for talks with Brezhnev, said he "would like to underline any single sentence that the president just spoke."

A few nights later Schmidt figured in a little episode that I witnessed. Edie and I had had dinner at a restaurant near the Piazza San Marco and were sauntering toward the boat dock when we encountered her ex–husband, R.W. (Johnny) Apple of *The New York Times* and Jody Powell. They invited us to join them and we went in search of a place to chat over drinks. We tried the Danieli, one of the hotels lodging summit delegations. As Johnny subsequently wrote, someone had told Jody he could get a late–night meal at the Danieli because the chancellor was having a party there and the kitchen was staying open later than usual. "Mr. Powell misunderstood and thought the host was John Chancellor of NBC News, instead of Helmut Schmidt of West Germany. Bristling with credentials, Mr. Powell presented himself at the hotel and was turned away." Johnny is a fine reporter whom I respect but I have a different version of the ending. When we entered the hotel, we spotted Schmidt inside. Jody turned around, said something like "let's get out of here," and we left and went somewhere else. It was obvious he would rather not have to exchange pleasantries with the chancellor who had been a problem for his boss.

The situation in Afghanistan dominated the first day of the summit, Sunday, June 22. The Soviet Union, in an announcement apparently timed to coincide with the summit's opening, said it was withdrawing some of its army units. The seven leaders in Venice responded by calling for a complete withdrawal and declaring that "the Soviet military occupation of Afghanistan is unacceptable."

The summit ended Monday with agreement on steps to produce more alternatives to oil, including plans to double coal production by 1990. The leaders were concerned about the impact of the price and supply of oil on inflation. Reducing inflation, they said, was their immediate top priority. In a display of unity, they made individual statements expressing satisfaction with their talks. Among those I quoted was the Japanese foreign minister, Saburo Okita, who said, "We are all riding in the same gondola." The occupants of the gondola had their differences, however. Although they condemned the holding of the American hostages, their summit statement did not mention sanctions against Iran, which the U.S. wanted. Nor did it mention specific measures in response to the Soviet invasion.

In Belgrade, our next stop, Carter again hit hard at the Soviet presence in Afghanistan, calling it "an unjustifiable act of armed aggression" against a small country that, like Yugoslavia, was a founding member of the non-aligned movement. He also praised the Yugoslav transition following the death of President Tito. Covering the visit with me was Ron Pemstein, who earlier had been VOA's Belgrade correspondent. Because he knew Yugoslavia so well, I left the "hard news" stories to him and wrote features for Worldwide English and the Serbian, Croatian and Slovene language services. One was about Mrs. Carter's and Amy's visit to the small town of Leskovac, an hour's drive from Belgrade, to see an internationally known wood-carver and sculptor, Bogosav Zivkovic (written in my copy as Zhivkovich, so I could pronounce it). A lovely young Yugoslav woman employed by USIS, Rajka Nisovic, served as interpreter in my interview with him and in other interviews with citizens in Belgrade's Kalemegdan Park.

In this park, on a bluff overlooking the juncture of the Danube and Sava Rivers, the Carters watched young costumed folkdancers performing regional dances, Macedonian, Slovenian, Albanian, Serbian, Croatian and Dalmatian, and then joined them in the Serbian kolo. President Carter may have been a bit awkward on his toes, I reported, but he appeared to be enjoying the dance. A dozen years later the memory of those joyful young ethnic folkdancers made the ethnic hatreds and killings in dismembered Yugoslavia seem all the more senseless.

The last two stops on the eight-day trip were Madrid, where Carter called the growth of Spanish democracy a tonic for the western world and expressed appreciation for Spain's support in the hostage crisis, and Lisbon, where he hailed Portugal's restoration of democracy. Portugal was an early and staunch supporter of the U.S. stand on both Afghanistan and Iran, and that was reflected in a joint statement issued after his talks with President Ramalho Eanes (in my copy I wrote it Rumalyoo YAWN–oosh) and other Portuguese leaders. It called for concrete measures to put pressure on the Soviet Union, and it said economic sanctions on Iran were needed to convince the Iranian authorities to release the American hostages.

Carter returned to Washington June 26 facing another decline in public opinion polls. The economy was the major reason, but there was increasing dissatisfaction with his conduct of foreign policy. Carter also had been bruised in his primary election battle with Ted Kennedy, although he did emerge from the primaries with more than the number of delegates needed to be renominated at the August Democratic convention.

In the Republican primaries, conservative Ronald Reagan had steadily amassed delegate votes, and by the time of the GOP convention in July in Detroit, there was no doubt that the presidential nomination was his. I was covering Carter in Georgia and watched television coverage of the Republicans nominating Reagan and George Bush as his running–mate, exceedingly annoyed with my office for not having assigned me to the VOA reporting team in Detroit. For the first time since 1964, I was missing a national political convention.

Carter faced more trouble in July when a furor developed over his brother's dealings with the Libyan government. A Justice Department investigation of Billy Carter led to his registering as an agent of the Libyan government and his acknowledging that he received $220,000 from the Libyans. Congress began inquiries to look into whether there was any White House connection.

This was not the first controversy involving Billy. About a year and a half earlier he had made remarks widely interpreted as anti–Semitic, while escorting a Libyan delegation visiting Georgia. In a profile of him then, I told VOA listeners, "Billy Carter has been described as a buffoon, a hard–drinking good old boy, outrageous, jolly, a shrewd and serious businessman, charming, and an embarrassment to his brother the president. He is probably all of those things. He is a complex, independent person whose life has been overshadowed and affected by that of his older brother. Billy

Carter says he is not a political person. 'I'm blunt,' he says, 'and sometimes folks don't like it.' "

On August 4 the president had an extraordinary one-hour press conference in which he said "categorically" that Billy had no influence or effect on his decisions on any U.S. government policy or actions concerning Libya. In my report I said he was "effective in putting distance between himself and his younger brother, while at the same time making some rather poignant remarks about their affection for each other and about Billy's independence."

Carter also described Billy's role in seeking Libya's help in the efforts to gain release of the American hostages in Iran. As Jody Powell had told reporters earlier, Billy arranged, at the request of national security advisor Brzezinski, a meeting with a Libyan diplomat and Brzezinski at the White House in late November, and later Brzezinski was informed that Libyan leader Muammar Qaddafi had sent a message to the Ayatollah Khomeini urging release of the hostages. The press conference removed the Billy affair as a convention issue, but the president still faced a "dump Carter" movement and a convention struggle with Kennedy as the Democrats began assembling in New York City. On the opening night, Monday August 11, Kennedy withdrew from contention, after Carter supporters won a vote on a convention rule that guaranteed the president's renomination. This rule bound the delegates to vote for the candidate to whom they were pledged as a result of the primaries.

In his 51-minute acceptance speech, Carter said a new economic renewal program his administration was developing would meet the nation's immediate need for jobs by attacking long-term problems which caused unemployment and inflation. He accused the Republicans of proposing a tax cut that would benefit the rich and not the poor, of abandoning arms control, and of offering a make-believe world. Reagan had charged in his speech accepting the Republican nomination that the Carter administration lived in the world of make-believe.

After the Democratic convention I spent a week covering Reagan and heard him enunciate some of the themes he had sounded in his acceptance speech. He addressed the Veterans of Foreign Wars convention in Chicago and, as I reported, "accused President Carter of responding to the Soviet military buildup and Soviet expansionism with weakness, inconsistency, vacillation and bluff." Reagan rebutted Democratic charges that his policies would lead to an arms race and said Republicans wanted to restore the "margin of safety" in American military power. He also told the VFW that U.S. participation in the Vietnam war was "a noble cause."

During the trip, which included speeches in Philadelphia and Boston on the theme of "peace through strength," press access to Reagan was limited. But in Los Angeles he had a brief exchange with reporters, as I recall at the airport, during which he sought to alleviate Chinese concern about his position on China and Taiwan. The next day, at a press conference in Dallas, he stood by his previous statement supporting an official governmental relationship with Taiwan but said again that he was not talking about a two-China policy.

That night in Dallas, Reagan spoke at a national affairs briefing sponsored by the Religious Roundtable, a conservative group that said it was non-partisan and advocated support for what its leaders called God-honoring candidates for public office. He endorsed their movement, and they made clear he had their approval. "Ronald Reagan received standing ovations from an estimated 15,000 evangelical Christians," I reported, "as he called for a restoration of traditional moral values in public policy."

After my return to Washington, I wrote a longer piece on the Religious Roundtable event, reporting to our overseas listeners that it "could turn out to be a significant development in American political life." The estimated number of evangelicals in the U.S. was then at least 30 million, and some projections put it at more than twice that. One of the speakers preceding Reagan was a fiery television preacher, James Robison, who exhorted the evangelicals to abandon their previous apathy. I used a soundbite of Robison that included audience reaction: "I'm sick and tired of hearing about all of the radicals and the perverts and the liberals and the communists coming out of the closets. It's time for God's people to come out of the closets (applause), out of the churches (applause and cheers) and change America (more applause)."

Carter began his general election campaign at a Labor Day rally in the South — in Tuscumbia, Alabama, a region known as "yellow dog Democrat country." People there said they would vote for a yellow dog before voting for a Republican. But, as I told VOA's audience, the president couldn't take the South for granted. Reagan had substantial appeal among conservatives and evangelical Christians in the South.

The Carter campaign also was concerned about the Anderson factor. Longtime Republican Congressman John Anderson of Illinois was running for president as an independent candidate, attracting the interest of moderate and liberal voters. When public opinion polls showed support for him ranging from 13 to 18 percent, the sponsor of the presidential debates, the League of Women Voters, invited him to take part. Carter's campaign chairman, Robert Strauss, said "no" to the invitation. Including Anderson in the debates would give him more national exposure and enhance his candidacy at the president's expense.

Reagan accepted, and on September 21 he and Anderson confronted each other before an audience of several thousand in Baltimore's Convention Center and a television audience estimated at more than 50 million. Besides clashing with Reagan, Anderson criticized Carter for absenting himself from the debate. After covering the event, I followed Anderson on the campaign trail for a few days. He was heartened by a lunch–time crowd of some 2,000 in Chicago but drew a devastatingly low turnout in Philadelphia, where only a few hundred of the auditorium's 4,500 seats were occupied. His campaign fizzled, but he said he would stay in the race, and the Anderson factor remained.

On the day after the Reagan–Anderson debate, Carter was presented with another foreign policy problem: War between Iran and Iraq. Saddam Hussein's planes attacked Iranian airfields in a dispute over the Shatt–al–Arab waterway. As the fighting escalated, Carter supported international efforts to bring the conflict to an end, said the U.S. was not and would not be involved in the dispute, and emphasized the importance to oil–consuming nations of keeping the Persian Gulf open for shipping. He also stressed that the U.S. continued to hold the government of Iran responsible for the safety and well–being of the American hostages.

Carter and Reagan meantime continued to hurl long–distance charges at each other as they traveled about the country, from rural to urban areas and including the suburbs. Both camps were giving increasing attention to suburban voters. Reagan, who was ahead in the public opinion polls, hit hard on the issue on which Carter was most vulnerable, the economy. Carter accused Reagan of proposing a massive nuclear arms race with his plan to scrap the SALT II treaty and build up America's nuclear strength so as to induce the Soviets to engage in new arms control negotiations. Finally agreement was reached on a face–to–face encounter. Their debate would be held October 28 in Cleveland.

In a scenesetter for VOA's listeners, I wrote: "The stakes are always high in a presidential debate, but they are especially so in the debate between President Jimmy Carter and his challenger Ronald Reagan because it comes just one week before the election, with the race very close and with a large bloc of still–undecided voters." Carter was going into the debate, I noted, with public opinion polls showing that he had pulled even with Reagan in voter sentiment, but that Reagan retained a lead "in the projections of electoral college votes which will determine the election outcome."

VOA carried the Tuesday night debate live and scheduled a live report from me as soon as it was over, so I had to stop monitoring it in the final minutes in order to write a summary. My lead was that Carter and Reagan "crossed swords on arms control, defense, the American hostage situation in Iran and the economy as they held a free–swinging debate." I missed what was later generally agreed to be the key moment in the encounter. It came near the end, when Reagan advised voters to ask themselves: "Are you better off than you were four years ago?" The debate at first was seen to be something of a draw, but within a few days it was clear Reagan had scored.

The morning after the debate Carter headed for stops in the North, East, Midwest, and South as he tried to galvanize traditional Democratic Party constituencies. On Friday came an acknowledgment that his campaign had stalled. "Opinion polls taken for the Carter campaign have shown what a White House official called 'a pause in the momentum' of the president's drive for a second term," I reported. "One of the reasons cited was the American hostage situation in Iran. The official, who declined to let his name be used, said the president appears to have been hurt by the fact that expectations about the release of the hostages were raised so high, and then were dashed on Thursday."

A public debate on the hostage issue was to have been held Thursday by the Iranian parliament, the Majlis, which had seemed to be moving toward some decision on conditions for releasing the hostages. The debate was blocked, however, by Islamic fundamentalist members who boycotted the session.

The "pause in the momentum" comment by the unnamed White House official was made to the Air Force One press pool on a flight from Lakeland, Florida, to Memphis, Tennessee. As pooler Eleanor Randolph (then with *The Los Angeles Times*) reported, the official also said Reagan "probably got a little help out of the (Cleveland) debate. . . ."

During the long days of Carter's final campaign swing, the press plane served as our filing center. It was equipped with telephones that were plugged in at every stop; we quickly filed our stories, scrambled off the plane to hear Carter's speeches, and then scrambled back on to fly to the next destination. The White House Transportation Office arranged the seating in clusters, so that newspaper correspondents sat together, radio correspondents were in another group, and so on. Between stops we radio reporters dubbed tapes in daisy chains. It was crowded, with our typewriters, recorders and files spread out over our pull–down tables, the arms of our seats, and our laps. My seatmate was UPI–Radio's Roger Gittines, a thoughtful reporter who could say much in just a few words, and we wrote our stories in companionable calm.

Carter spent Saturday campaigning in closely contested Texas — from Houston to Brownsville, San Antonio (a rally at the Alamo), Abilene, and Fort Worth. He stopped in Milwaukee for another rally, and flew to Chicago late Saturday night. Early Sunday morning the press was awakened at the Hyatt–Regency with the news that Carter was cancelling his campaign appearances and returning to Washington to confer with his advisors "on the action of the Iranian parliament."

We had no details; Jody Powell issued a statement which said: "The precise meaning of that action is unclear. Until it has been clarified, there is no basis for assuming a successful resolution of the hostage crisis." The president left Chicago before dawn; we filed bare–bones stories and left for Washington soon after.

Aboard Air Force One, as recounted by pool reporter Terence Smith (then of *The New York Times*), Jody Powell read a prepared statement to the travel pool. In brief, it said that the Majlis "stated that their decision is compatible with the four points previously announced by the Ayatollah Khomeini." On Carter's return to the White House, Jane Berger filed reports on VOA on his meeting with his advisors and on the Iranian conditions that had been set by the Ayatollah Khomeini in September. These were: Release of Iranian assets frozen by Carter after the embassy seizure, non–interference in Iranian affairs, cancellation of financial claims against Iran, and return of the Shah's wealth. (The Shah had left the U.S. for Panama in December, then went to Egypt in March, and died in July.)

Carter met again with his advisors at 2 p.m., and Jody told reporters they were assessing information from a variety of sources but still had not received an official text of the Iranian conditions. He continued to caution against expectations that a resolution of the hostage crisis was near. We also were told Carter would resume campaigning Monday, "if the situation permits."

The White House was still waiting for an official translation of the Iranian demands when Carter appeared in the briefing room at 6:23 p.m. and made a brief statement. "As we understand the parliament's proposals," he said, "they appear to offer a positive basis for achieving" the two fundamental U.S. objectives in the crisis:

Protecting America's honor and vital interest, and working to insure the earliest possible safe release of the hostages. Carter also took note that the election would take place in two days and said his decisions "will not be affected by the calendar."

A notice advised the traveling press to be at Andrews Air Force Base at 8:15 a.m. Monday for the flight to the first stop, Akron, Ohio, but to phone the number for the White House press information tape recording early in the morning to learn if the trip was still on. The recording, instituted when Ron Nessen was Ford's press secretary, gave schedule and pool information and was warmly welcomed for reducing calls to, and busy signals on, the regular Press Office number.

The next morning, the recording confirmed the trip, and off we were to Akron, then westward to campaign stops in the St. Louis area and airport rallies in Springfield (Missouri), Detroit, Portland, and, the last one, at 11 p.m. PST, Seattle, where he was given one of his most enthusiastic receptions. And then we flew on to Georgia in the early morning hours of Election Day, November 4, the anniversary of the embassy takeover in Tehran. Jimmy and Rosalynn Carter would vote in Plains before returning to Washington.

Filing time was limited in Seattle, so I had phoned a wrapup to VOA from Portland on Carter's marathon campaign day and last-ditch effort to persuade wavering Democrats to vote for him. As I reported, "Pre-election opinion polls, taken before the new developments in Iran, showed the Carter-Reagan contest to be very close, with Mr. Carter still slightly behind in popular vote sentiment, and substantially behind in projections of the state-by-state electoral college votes which will decide the election."

The piece ended with: "On election eve, the president said 'yes' when asked if he expected to win. Reporters covering his campaign did not share that view. They and a handful of White House staffers on the press plane were polled on who they thought would be elected. The result was Reagan, by a sizable nine point margin."

In Plains shortly before 8 a.m. Carter voted at the rundown building where he had attended high school, and addressed a crowd gathered at the depot. "The president, his voice choked with emotion and with tears in his eyes at one point, told his neighbors and friends in Plains that he believes he will be re-elected. But in the face of opinion polls pointing to defeat, Mr. Carter was serious and, to some, almost fatalistic in his demeanor," I reported. He spoke of the difficult decisions he and Congress had made, some of them, he said, politically costly. A member of the travel pool, Curtis Wilkie of *The Boston Globe*, a first-rate reporter and a native of the South who had covered Carter from the start of his climb to the White House, wrote: "After five years of observation, the president appeared to be very dispirited, as if the end, indeed, is near."

The end came quickly. At 9:30 p.m. Carter left the White House for the Sheraton Washington Hotel to deliver his concession statement. The White House press was alerted beforehand and I was in place at a VOA microphone in the hotel ballroom for our live coverage of his remarks. "I promised you four years ago that I would never lie to you," he told his supporters, "so I can't stand here tonight and say it doesn't hurt. The people of the United States have made their choice. . . ." He delivered the statement, I reported, "with grace, a touch of humor, and a promise to work closely with Mr. Reagan to insure an orderly transition — the best in history, he said." In a separate piece, I told our listeners that Carter had been "prepared for defeat. It's been learned that the outcome was anticipated in the final days on his long, hard-fought battle for re-election, when public opinion samplings taken by his campaign pollster reflected the downturn for him."

Not long after the election I received a letter from a VOA listener in West Africa, a 26-year-old school teacher in Yengema, Sierra Leone, Mr. Sahr K. Mafinda, who said he had followed the campaign: "You traveled a lot with President Carter. I listened to the Cleveland, Ohio, debate. . . I enjoyed and liked the summary you made. . . I was up when the election results were coming in on Nov. 5th. . . Philo, did you sleep that night? Oh! I enjoyed and like the way the Americans do their thing."

I loved that letter because it expressed a sentiment that was reflected in much of the mail I received from overseas. They did like the way we Americans do our thing. It was always gratifying to get letters confirming that the Voice had faithful listeners. Our audience in 1980 was estimated at 80 million, a conservative figure, as VOA Director Mary Bitterman noted during a session with reporters. "We don't have Nielsens or Arbitron," she said, pointing out the difficulty of measuring listenership in many countries. VOA's audience in China, for example, was not included in the estimate.

Mary Bitterman took office as VOA director in March of 1980 at the age of 36. Named by Carter, she had been executive director and general manager of the Hawaii Public Broadcasting Corporation and chairman of the Board of Governors of the East–West Center in Honolulu. She was the first woman to head the Voice, the only one as of 1995, and was one of our best directors. She reached out to employees, immersed herself in every aspect of VOA operations and was absolutely committed to the VOA Charter.

Armed with Mary's support, I again brought up the issue of VOA correspondents asking questions at the daily White House briefings. Press Secretary Jody Powell had no objections, and neither did "Sir Ralph," the veteran Reuters correspondent Ralph Harris, who was then president of the White House Correspondents Association. Under guidelines I drafted for all VOA correspondents attending the briefings, including those who were infrequent visitors to the White House, we could ask questions on any subject in the public domain. The guidelines had only two restrictions: Under no circumstances may a VOA correspondent pose a question based on privileged information. And under no circumstances may a VOA correspondent be used by the White House as a vehicle for offering its views on any subject — in other words, questions may not be planted with VOA correspondents. So we began asking questions in the briefings, and nobody objected.

On the day after Reagan's landslide victory (489 electoral votes to 49 for Carter, and a popular vote margin of 10 per cent), Carter called a group of us into the Oval Office for an informal talk that ranged over the election to his plans for the future. Among the factors in his defeat that he discussed were the capture of the hostages, oil price increases, negative reaction to the Panama Canal treaties, and the influx of Cuban refugees. He was relaxed, said he felt "good," and said that in his remaining time in office he would pursue negotiations for release of the hostages, would do the best he could to continue the Mideast peace talks on Palestinian autonomy, and would keep his successor informed.

Reagan held a press conference in Los Angeles the next day and said he was not going to intrude in the hostage crisis and that "foreign leaders must be aware" that Carter "is still the president." Negotiations to free the hostages were continuing through Algerian intermediaries, and Deputy Secretary of State Warren Christopher traveled to Algiers on November 10 to relay the U.S. response to Iran on its conditions for their release.

The president–elect's transition team opened a Washington office on November 12, and eight days later Reagan met with Carter at the White House. While they conferred in the Oval Office, Nancy Reagan met with Rosalynn Carter in the residence and received a briefing on the executive mansion. Reagan told reporters afterwards that Carter "has been most gracious and most cooperative, he and his people, with regard to this transition, and has certainly made it a much easier time than it could otherwise have been, and we're deeply grateful."

The meeting came near the end of Reagan's first pre–inaugural visit to the capital. Although he had campaigned as an outsider, he moved quickly, and adroitly, to woo the Washington establishment. He not only met with the leaders of Congress and promised them cooperation, he also invited more than 50 powers in political, business, civic, cultural, academic, sports and publishing circles to dine with him and Nancy at the fashionable F Street Club.

In December I covered Reagan in Los Angeles for a week. This involved staking out his home in the Pacific Palisades and using our "tree phone" to file reports. There was no place nearby for filing facilities, so VOA's L.A. bureau chief, Ray Kabaker, had arranged for a phone cable to be extended to a tree down the street from the Reagan residence, and we connected a telephone to the cable, concealing the phone in the tree. There wasn't much news to report, for Reagan had no public appointments on his schedule, except for going out to dinner with friends and visits to his barber and tailor. But on Tuesday, December 16, he announced Alexander Haig as his choice for secretary of state. The nomination of the former NATO commander and White House chief of staff during the decline of the Nixon administration "is a controversial one," I reported, "but Mr. Reagan has expressed confidence that General Haig will be confirmed by the Senate and says one of the reasons he chose him is his integrity."

In early January, there was another step in the negotiations for resolving the hostage crisis. The Iranians had asked more questions about the U.S. position; the U.S. reply was dispatched to the Algerian intermediaries on January 7, and Carter sent Warren Christopher to Algiers again that night. The next day Carter flew to Plains to spend a few days. On his arrival in Plains he told reporters he had received an initial report from Christopher during the Air Force One flight to Georgia, but there was no Iranian reaction yet. The American proposals were "reasonable and a foundation for resolving differences," the president said, "but I can't predict success. I think that would be a mistake."

This was Carter's last visit to Plains as president, and we reporters gave a dinner party for him and Rosalynn at the French restaurant on the road between Plains and Americus, Le Normandie. Again, as it had been at the party for the Fords in Vail, it was my assignment to collect the money for the dinner tickets. Phil Gailey and I shared the task of making arrangements, and we checked off attendees at the door, under the watchful eyes of the Secret Service. Nearly all of the 56-member traveling contingent came to the party. Carter bantered with reporters at the head table, while the rest of us strained to hear what they were laughing about. With dessert, he rose and, speaking softly and without rancor, made off-the-record remarks. Carter himself broke the ground rules later when he recalled that he had been asked whom he would rank as number one among all the public servants that worked with him, and he unhesitatingly said Warren Christopher. Other remarks he made at the dinner were humorous, such as: If he had one wish for his successor, it would be to wish on him Sam Donaldson. He also named a foreign leader, but I won't break the ground rules on that.

I sat at a table next to Rosalynn Carter and correspondent Don Irwin. She was clearly hurt over comments in the press that style and sophistication would be returning to the White House after a lapse of four years. For instance, *Time* magazine columnist Hugh Sidey wrote: "This time around let's have a little class." The Carters were criticized for entertaining White House guests with country music. Actually, they had featured a wide variety of performing artists, like Vladimir Horowitz, Andres Segovia, Leontyne Price and Mikhail Baryshnikov. We told Rosalynn we thought she had class.

The purpose of Carter's visit was to set up an office in Miz Lillian's "in town" house for use on his retirement. He had no formal schedule, so the routine we followed was for a small pool to stand by at the Best Western Motel, where most of us stayed, to be ready to move whenever he traveled about town. White House staffers alerted the pool by hanging a red "flag," which looked like a blanket, over the balcony above the press office. Ten minutes after it appeared, the pool was to leave for Plains.

After a four–year excursion into the limelight, Plains was returning to normal. There were some tourists, but gone were the hordes of visitors who once made Main Street impassable. Some of the shopkeepers said they would try to stay in business. One was preparing to display, alongside souvenir dishes with pictures of the Carters, new dishes showing the likeness of Ronald Reagan.

Returning to Washington, Carter remained preoccupied with the hostage negotiations as he completed his duties. On January 16 the White House reported arrival of a "positive" message from the Iranians. The U.S. and Iran appeared to be moving closer to an agreement resolving the crisis. The cliff–hanging final days of Carter's presidency lay ahead.

13
A Joyous "Tag Line" on Inauguration Day
"Honey, I Forgot to Duck"
Travels with RR

Tuesday morning, January 20, 1981: Jimmy and Rosalynn Carter left the White House with Ronald and Nancy Reagan for Capitol Hill and the ceremony installing Reagan as the nation's 40th president. I was stationed at the North Portico to do a live broadcast describing the scene to VOA listeners: The two couples walking down the steps and getting into limousines, a ritual, one of the symbols of the peaceful transfer of power. In less than a minute of air time, I also summarized the suspense of the past few hours. The agreement to release the 52 American hostages had at last been nailed down. But they hadn't left Iran yet. And now Jimmy Carter was leaving office — without being able to announce they had been freed on his watch.

Carter had spent two sleepless nights consumed with concluding the agreement and then overcoming last–minute hitches, working with his top aides at the White House and in communication with Warren Christopher in Algiers. In a round–the–clock vigil, I had been on duty all night Sunday and Jane Berger all night Monday, filing reports and updates for hourly newscasts. The agreement was first reported early Sunday by the Iranian news agency, but it was not confirmed at the White House until 4:56 a.m. Monday when Carter came into the briefing room and announced he had received word that the necessary documents had been signed in Iran and then in Algiers by Christopher.

Carter had hoped to fly to Wiesbaden to greet the hostages and return to the White House in time for Reagan's inauguration. But their release was delayed and those plans were cancelled. The hitches involved the transfer of frozen Iranian assets to an escrow account in preparation for transferring them to Iran after the hostages were freed. With fewer than four hours remaining in the Carter administration, Jody Powell announced completion of the final step placing the assets in escrow, and declared, "We now have every right to expect, and do expect, the expeditious release of the hostages."

The announcement that the hostages' 444–day ordeal was over came from the newly inaugurated President Reagan as he was concluding a nationally televised toast at a luncheon with congressional leaders: "With thanks to Almighty God, I have been given a tag line, the get–off line that everyone wants for the end of a toast or a speech or anything else. Some 30 minutes ago the planes bearing our prisoners left Iranian air space and are now free of Iran."

Carter learned of their release as he was on his way to Plains, and the next day flew to Wiesbaden to greet the hostages on behalf of his successor. In a handwritten report to Reagan, he said the U.S. should abide by the agreement on their release, "but never do any favors for the hoodlums who persecuted innocent American heroes."

In summing up Carter's presidency, I reported to VOA listeners that he left office "with substantial achievements to his credit, but submerged by perceptions that he was an indecisive and impotent president. He tackled difficult, controversial, issues and in some cases registered historic successes like the Panama Canal treaties and the Camp David–engendered Egyptian–Israeli peace treaty. He was tested by extraordinary external events, the most frustrating of them the taking of the American hostages in Iran. He made the enhancement of human rights a major element of American foreign policy. He tried to solve the nation's chief domestic problems, making some progress with energy but failing to prevent inflation from worsening. And he told the American people time and again that there were no easy answers. In the end, all those things, including his successes, were politically costly to him."

And now the new president. In a pre–inaugural report, I told VOA listeners the former California governor and former Hollywood actor, radio broadcaster and television personality "is a gifted communicator, and is certain to use his communicating skills to advantage in presenting his programs to the American people." Unlike Carter, who immersed himself in detail, "Mr. Reagan is expected to delegate authority to trusted aides after setting guidelines and making policy decisions."

The first big event over which Reagan presided was the White House homecoming for the hostages, one week after their Inauguration Day release. Six thousand guests were invited to the celebration on the South Lawn. Yellow ribbons, the symbol that they had not been forgotten during their captivity, were everywhere, including a giant yellow bow on the balcony above the White House diplomatic entrance, and Nancy Reagan wore a yellow dress. "We're all very happy to have you back where you belong," Reagan told the freed hostages. Bruce Laingen, the highest ranking diplomat of those held captive, spoke for them: "Mr. President, in very simple words that come from the hearts of all of us, it is good to be back. Thank you, America, and God bless all of you." In reporting the event, I included Reagan's warning: "Let terrorists be aware that when the rules of international behavior are violated, our policy will be one of swift and effective retribution."

In his first presidential press conference, on January 29, Reagan made news by asserting that the Soviets seek a "one-world socialist state" and reserve the right "to commit any crime, to lie and to cheat." At the same time, he said he had put the grain embargo, imposed by Carter against the Soviet Union after the invasion of Afghanistan, on the agenda for a cabinet meeting. He later lifted the embargo, as he'd promised to do in his campaign against Carter, on the grounds that it hurt American farmers. Reagan opened the press conference with a statement expressing his determination to reduce the federal budget deficit, "this inflationary monster."

The oldest American ever elected president, Reagan celebrated his 70th birthday on February 6. Because of his age, his health was a subject examined in the press. "He appears physically fit and trim," I reported to overseas listeners, and noted that since becoming president he "has pursued a busy schedule." By the end of his first month in office Reagan unveiled a far-reaching set of economic proposals that included tax cuts and sweeping reductions in spending. He told Congress, "The taxing power of government must be used to provide revenues for legitimate government purposes. It must not be used to regulate the economy or bring about social change."

On March 30, his 70th day in office, Reagan took his campaign for his economic program to a national conference of the AFL–CIO Building and Construction Trades Department, held at the Washington Hilton Hotel. This was a Monday, my regular day off, and I was at work as a volunteer tutoring second graders in reading and arithmetic at a public school in a low income neighborhood. My White House colleague, Jane Berger, was on assignment in Mexico City, substituting for VOA's correspondent there, so a competent 25–year–old woman on our newsroom staff, Mallory Saleson, was covering the president that day. When I finished tutoring, I deposited the textbooks in the school principal's office and saw that an old black and white television set was on, showing a flickering image of a scuffle. The staffers told me, "Someone tried to kill the president! But he's all right, he wasn't hurt!" I phoned my office, said I was on my way to the White House, and listened to bulletins on my car radio as I sped to downtown on the Suitland Parkway in pouring rain. The reports were confusing. Was the president really okay? Or was the initial report wrong, and had he been shot? Now I was hearing that the president was believed to have been wounded.

At 3:37 p.m. it was confirmed at the White House that Reagan "was shot once in the left side." David Gergen, the communications director, told reporters his condition was "stable," and a decision was being made on whether to operate to remove the bullet. In the basement press room, Mallory had been joined by David Gollust in filing reports.

Mallory had witnessed the assassination attempt. Once Reagan finished his speech, she had rushed outside to cover his departure from the hotel. The president emerged from a side door and smiled and waved to a crowd of onlookers who had gathered along with the press. "The shots rang out at 2:25 in the afternoon," she recounted in a broadcast report. "There were six of them. I heard the shots, and was able to see the flash of the gunfire. . . ." Mallory dropped to her knees at the sounds, as Reagan was being pushed into the limousine by the Secret Service officer guarding him. She saw people lying on the ground. "Police started shouting to the crowd to get down, and get back." Mallory ran back into the hotel, found a phone, and called the newsroom. It was 2:30 p.m.

Travel pool correspondents Sara Fritz (then with *U.S. News & World Report*) and Gilbert Lewthwaite (*Baltimore Sun*), who were closer to the scene of the shooting, reported seeing three bodies on the ground. They recognized White House Press Secretary Jim Brady, who was lying face down, with "blood pouring from a wound in his right temple." They watched as "a police car backed into the service alley and the suspect, looking to be a fair-haired white male in his late 20s or 30s, with his hands cuffed behind his back, was bundled in."

Although VOA normally does not require two sources when its own correspondent is on the scene, the newsroom held off running a bulletin until other news organizations began reporting the shooting. At 2:39 p.m. the Voice carried its first bulletin: "Shots rang out near a Washington hotel a few moments ago, as President Reagan was leaving the hotel to return to the White House. . . ." As News Division chief Bernie Kamenske later explained, "When someone is shooting at a president, you do some hard, quick thinking. I remembered that when Kennedy was assassinated, the BBC did not go with his death until they heard it confirmed on VOA. They said they knew we could not afford to be wrong on that story." Columnist Tom Dowling wrote in *The Washington Star* that "VOA had a possible world scoop on the Reagan assassination attempt" but that its "caution paid dividends in credibility." VOA was cautious throughout in reporting the story as one rumor after another was circulated, and Dowling said it "did a measurably better reporting job than the commercial networks — if, that is, the relative absence of misinformation is the standard by which news should be judged."

Secretary of State Haig appeared in the White House briefing room at 4:14 p.m. and said the president was undergoing surgery, that Vice President Bush was returning to Washington from Texas where he was to have made a speech, and, his voice quavering with emotion, told reporters there were "absolutely no alert measures" necessary at this time. When asked who was making decisions for the government "right now," Haig made the comment for which he was later criticized: "As of now, I am in control here, in the White House, pending return of the vice president and in close touch with him."

I viewed Haig's comment as well-intentioned, made in an effort to reassure countries around the world that the U.S. government was functioning. That evening, as David Gollust reported, Bush made a point of stressing the continuity of government operations by reassuring "this nation and the watching world that the American government is functioning fully and effectively."

From the White House I had rushed to George Washington University Hospital, where presidential assistant Lyn Nofziger told the mass of reporters at 5:10 p.m. that Reagan had gone into surgery "roughly an hour ago," and that a preliminary report from doctors was that his condition was "good" and "stable." Nofziger also said the president had told Nancy, "Honey, I forgot to duck." Of course I reported his quip. It lost something in translation, as I learned some days later. Jane Berger sent me a postcard from Mexico City with a message that the newscaster for a Mexican TV station quoted Reagan as saying, "Honey, I forgot the duck."

The president "sailed through" the operation. Dr. Dennis O'Leary, the dean for clinical affairs at the hospital, summed it up in that quote during an extensive briefing that began at 7:30 p.m. Reagan was in the operating room for approximately two hours, during which a single bullet was removed from his lung. O'Leary told us the president "is physiologically very young," his vital signs "were absolutely rock stable throughout this whole thing," and "at no time" was he in any serious danger.

I found a phone in a nearby building housing the hospital's radiology department and did a live broadcast, relaying to overseas listeners O'Leary's "sailed through" quote and reporting that the outlook for the president's recovery was described as excellent. Later, at the White House, I wrapped up the story. Jim Brady remained in critical condition following surgery; a bullet had passed through his brain. Two others wounded were a Secret Service agent, Timothy McCarthy, and a Washington policeman, Thomas

Delahanty. A 25-year-old white man from Evergreen, Colorado, John Hinckley, Jr., had been formally charged with attempted assassination of the president and assault with intent to kill a police officer. "The suspect is the son of an oil company executive and is said to have had psychiatric problems," I reported. "According to authorities, only a single gunman apparently was involved in the shooting. There has been no word on the suspect's motive."

One of my broadcast pieces that night ended with: "Mr. Reagan was joking both before and after he underwent surgery. When he was in the recovery room, receiving normal post-operative care for surgery of this kind involving the lung, he had tubes in his mouth. So he gave his doctors a handwritten note. As quoted by a presidential aide, it was an old show business one-line joke: All in all, I'd rather be in Philadelphia."

The next morning, the president met in his hospital room with his three top White House aides, Chief of Staff James Baker, Counselor Edwin Meese and Deputy Chief of Staff Michael Deaver, and signed a dairy price support bill, photocopies of which were distributed to the press. Through the day, doctors and White House officials sought to clear up some of the confusion from initial reports following the shooting. Dr. O'Leary said the president himself did not know he had been shot until he entered the emergency room. "Mr. Reagan walked into the hospital on his own," I reported, "but it's now been disclosed that when he got to the emergency room he collapsed. He was given blood transfusions and then successfully underwent surgery."

Baker acknowledged that there was a difference of opinion between Haig and Defense Secretary Casper Weinberger after the assassination attempt, and said White House officials had agreed the secretary of state should be in control in the White House situation room, pending Bush's return to Washington.

Twelve days after the attempt on his life, on Saturday, April 11, Reagan left the hospital, saying that he felt great. On his arrival at the White House, I told listeners, "A healthy-looking President Reagan was given a cheering welcome home by members of the cabinet and his White House staff."

Meantime, there were reports that his condition after the shooting was more serious than the public had been told. Was the public misled? Dr. O'Leary stood by his initial comments, and said he was being as upbeat as possible without damaging his credibility. After the president's operation, he'd been asked how far the bullet was from the heart and said "probably several inches." It should be noted he also said he "wasn't specifically there in the operating room." On April 16, *The Washington Post* carried a story quoting the primary surgeon who operated on Reagan, Dr. Benjamin Aaron, as saying that the bullet was no more than one inch from his heart.

I had saved the transcripts of all the doctors' briefings, compared what Dr. Aaron said earlier with the *Post* account, and wrote a story noting that "doctors have been consistent in saying that Mr. Reagan's life was not ever in danger prior to and during the surgery." In an April 3 briefing and in the newspaper story, Dr. Aaron said he could not find the bullet until after another x–ray was taken. "The reason why he couldn't locate the bullet in the first place, he said, was that it had been flattened almost as thin as a coin." Dr. Aaron actually said "dime," but for overseas listeners I thought it was clearer to say "coin." At the April 3 briefing, he did not say that the bullet was an inch from the heart, but showed pictures of its location, explaining that it was behind the heart and pointing out its "proximity" to "the major structures in the chest."

Jim Brady continued to make what his doctors called "remarkable" progress. The good–humored Brady was popular with the White House press corps because he was fair and up–front. At Reagan's first formal televised press conference, Brady instituted new procedures, changing the way reporters were recognized to ask their questions. Reporters now were to raise their hands instead of shouting out for recognition as they had in the past. Brady called the change an effort to restore dignity and decorum to presidential press conferences.

Before Reagan's inauguration, Brady wrote letters to the press corps asking for suggestions on the operations of the White House Press Office. In reply, I said that if he had background briefings in his office, I hoped an effort would be made to alert the occupants of the basement press room, who sometimes were forgotten. And VOA didn't want any special favors; "just remember we are here, and treat us like everyone else in the press corps."

Many of us in the White House press corps complained about the briefing room, a cluttered lounge furnished with sofas, leather chairs, some round tables, and TV cameras on tripods here and there. The tables often were littered with paper cups and plastic dishes, the debris from meals sent in for network television crews. Brady had already decided to move the TV cameras to a platform in the rear of the briefing room, and Deputy Press Secretary Larry Speakes followed through on having the room changed into an auditorium style arrangement, with most of the seats assigned to the regulars. Each seat has a brass plate bearing the name of a news organization. VOA's is about midway in the rows of seats, in the sixth row between *The Chicago Tribune* and *The Boston Globe*.

Brady made his first visit back to the White House on November 9 to take part in the opening of the renovated briefing room, an event marked by misty-eyed levity and an outpouring of affection for him. "Hello, good friends," he said. He was in a wheelchair, his mobility limited but his humor and zest for jousting with the press undiminished. When he left to return to the hospital, reporters called out, "Come back soon, we miss you." Brady was discharged from the hospital November 23, still partially paralyzed, with arduous therapy ahead of him. In triumph, he walked out. Wearing leg braces and using a cane-crutch, he stood with his wife Sarah at his side and waved to cheering, applauding friends.

In Reagan's first year in office, he established himself as a leader who set about doing what he said he was going to do. He focused his energies, and his communication skills, on his economic proposals, and won almost all he wanted from Congress in spending cuts and a three-year tax reduction program. There was a consistency about him. He emphasized national defense, took a tougher line toward the Soviet Union, and a softer line toward regimes which, while authoritarian, were America's friends. Despite controversy over some of his policies, he remained popular. He came over to the public as a very human person, engaging, disarming. This was underscored in a photo op with Mother Teresa, then 70, who had lunch with the Reagans in late Spring. As they posed with this tiny woman, who devoted her life to helping the poor in Calcutta, Reagan was asked what they talked about with her. He paused, held out his hands, and said simply: "We listened."

Reagan's first trip out of the country after the assassination attempt was in July, to Canada for the 1981 economic summit, held at a resort near Ottawa. It was his debut in international diplomacy and a sizable press corps (156 men/17 women) accompanied him. The talks were held at the Chateau Montebello, which had the distinction of being the world's largest log building and, with the tips of the logs painted red, looked like a structure made of giant lipsticks. The discussions on economic matters, including trade and relations with developing countries, were overshadowed by events in the Middle East. The president's Mideast envoy, Philip Habib, had been trying to defuse the Lebanese crisis between Syria and Israel. Also, Reagan had suspended delivery of four F–16 planes to Israel in June, following Israel's use of American–supplied aircraft in its attack on an Iraqi nuclear reactor. At Montebello, the seven leaders called for restraint in the Lebanese crisis, and later Haig announced that the president was deferring shipment of six more F–16s to Israel because of the escalating cycle of violence in the region. Haig told reporters at the press filing center in Ottawa that this was not linked to the efforts of Habib, then in Israel, to seek a ceasefire. The next day Haig welcomed what he called Israel's concurrence in a visit by Habib to Lebanon to try to calm the situation. A ceasefire was achieved.

Reagan's first year in office was a time of angst for many VOA staffers, who feared the administration would try to make our news broadcasts propagandistic, and thus damage VOA's credibility. In March, *The Washington Post* reported that the administration, "as part of its campaign to counter the spread of Soviet influence, plans to increase U.S. radio propaganda activities overseas." The story, by John M. Goshko, went on to say that funding boosts were budgeted for Radio Free Europe/Radio Liberty and VOA.

In the months that followed, there appeared to be an increase in complaints from administration officials and ambassadors about VOA's output. These included criticisms that the Voice had referred to the resistance against the Soviet–supported regime in Afghanistan as "anti–government guerrillas," and that it had called a transport helicopter sent to El Salvador a "gunship." The U.S. embassy in Moscow protested that VOA had given a substantial amount of air time to Soviet spokesman Georgi Arbatov. VOA's new director, James Conkling, a former broadcasting executive, asked Claude (Cliff) Groce, the acting program manager, for the names of those who had prepared the broadcast. Cliff, a VOA employee for more than 30 years, demurred. To him it sounded "very much like the McCarthy era." Conkling withdrew his request. Cliff later was transferred out of VOA to another part of the parent agency.

The Arbatov tape aired by VOA, as Deputy Director M. William Haratunian reported, was a 23–second excerpt from an American television interview in which he assailed U.S. plans for the neutron weapon. Bill Haratunian noted that VOA had also broadcast a four–minute report by National Public Radio on the same subject, which "began with a statement by President Reagan forcefully giving his reasons for producing the neutron weapon," and then contained a Q–and–A with the Soviet press attache in Washington by an NPR correspondent.

The VOA news staff's in–house publication, *News/Room* reported in early September that the complaints had "created a difficult psychological atmosphere which increases the danger of self–censorship," and that there was a "growing debate about the purpose and methods of VOA." It published an interview by its editor, Mark Willen, with Conkling, in which the VOA director denied the complaints were "a concerted effort" to limit the newsroom's output. Portions of the interview were picked up by *The Baltimore Sun* in a story by Ernest B. Furgurson on the "furor" at VOA, which said Conkling "conceded that he did not yet have a clear statement of VOA's purpose." Conkling said "We have to keep it a voice of truth," and added, "We're going to have problems once in a while."

Because I spent almost all my time at the White House, I was only peripherally aware of what was going on at VOA. Ambassadors had made complaints in the past, particularly those who were overly concerned with the sensibilities of their host countries when VOA aired news they thought was unfavorable to those countries. So I advised my colleagues in the newsroom not to panic and also told them, "Sometimes ambassadors' complaints have merit," and "if we're sloppy, if we're not accurate, comprehensive and objective, then we deserve to be criticized."

Morale in the newsroom worsened when *The Washington Post* carried a front–page story on November 10 by Murray Marder: "A highly combative U.S. information policy overseas to challenge the Soviet Union, Cuba and 'Marxist societies' in general is evolving inside the Reagan administration." Marder reported the "core of this burgeoning campaign" was Project Truth, which included plans for creation of a broadcast service to Cuba. He also quoted Charles Z. Wick, a close Reagan friend and head of USICA (later changed back to USIA), as saying the agency would be "more aggressive" in responding to the Soviet Union, but would not engage in propaganda. "Whatever we do will in no way change or skirt the Charter of the Voice of America," he said.

But three days later, a memo recommending that VOA should function as a propaganda agency was revealed in another Marder front–page story in the *Post*. The memo had been written by a newly named VOA official in charge of coordinating commentary and news analysis, Philip Nicolaides. Among excerpts quoted in the story were: VOA should abandon the contention that it is "a journalistic enterprise of some sort" and should portray the Soviet Union as "the last great predatory empire on earth."

After the story broke, a petition calling for Nicolaides's ouster was circulated at the Voice. Conkling said that he wouldn't fire him and that the memo was only "private reflections" and had "definitely not" been adopted as VOA policy. Nicolaides was "a former Houston conservative activist," according to *The Houston Post*, which said he had been "a regular contributor in the past to right–wing magazines and journals."

The story received considerable play in the press. An account in *Newsweek* said, "Many VOA staffers fear that Wick will politicize the news broadcasts," and, "Some VOA staffers suspect that Wick also aims to purge the radio network of many veteran officials. Last week deputy director and longtime staffer M. William Haratunian was removed." And then came this sentence: "Wick denies that a purge is beginning, but close associates say he suspects not only that some VOA staffers are 'communist dupes,' but that VOA itself 'may have been penetrated.'"

I was enraged. Curtis Wilkie phoned me at home after the *Newsweek* story appeared, for a piece he was writing for *The Boston Globe* on the turmoil at VOA. He said my remarks could be on background but I said I would talk on the record and Curtis quoted me: "Things have come to such a pass where we have to speak up." And, "I really resent Wick's impugning our integrity. I've worked for the U.S. government for 20 years and I deeply resent being called a communist dupe. He's besmirching our newsroom."

The quotes were picked up by other publications. Wick was furious, I learned, and a succession of VOA officials told me he was demanding that I apologize to him. I refused. It was then arranged that I meet with Wick. The session in his office, with VOA Director Conkling and a USIA official attending, lasted 45 minutes or so; it seemed forever. Wick chewed me out royally. I didn't apologize, but I did say that as a reporter who always tried to be accurate, I regretted that I had attributed to him the quotes by what *Newsweek* called his "close associates." I explained that I — and others at VOA — believed that those were his views.

After he simmered down, we talked about the integrity of VOA news, and he told me about all the things he was doing for the agency and the Voice. I suggested that he should let people at VOA know his views and his plans, doing so on a regular basis, and told him that because of his friendship with the president, there was a real chance to increase VOA's budget and improve its operations. And I promised him that in the future I would tell him whenever I was upset with the agency, before speaking publicly. I survived the confrontation, and stayed on the White House beat. Wick instituted a regular report to agency employees, which ran in the USIA house organ (years later, I ghost-wrote one of them). I told only a few friends about the episode, and kept my promise to Wick.

As 1981 drew to a close, VOA's news staff was stunned when Bernie Kamenske announced that he was leaving to take a job as senior news editor in CNN's Washington bureau. For 27 years, the past eight of them as news chief, he had fought for the integrity of VOA news. His departure notice drew wide coverage in the domestic media. A *Washington Post* story quoted "a veteran Senate staff member" as saying, "He more than anyone else has kept the sanctity of VOA news. He sleeps with the First Amendment every night."

A *New York Times* editorial said that "over the decades the Voice has won an enormous audience around the world. It has earned trust because it is rarely strident or tendentious. Yet today, sad to say, that hard-won trust is being put in jeopardy by over-eager idealogues. For months, Voice editors have been pressed to give a more polemical edge to their commentaries. Against the advice of VOA professionals, the administration is starting a new station, Radio Marti, to mount a propaganda counterattack against Fidel Castro. It is this background static that makes all the more damaging the resignation this week of Bernard Kamenske, director of the Voice's news division." The editorial noted that there had been no basic changes in VOA's news format "as yet," and concluded: "To change the Voice's approach and heighten the ideological pitch will not make it an antidote to Radio Moscow. Only an echo."

At a farewell party given by the newsroom, Bernie didn't spell out differences with Conkling, but told the staff: "I ask you to remember that every time you approach a typewriter, every time you edit a piece of copy, every time you write a report, remember one thing: You all represent the American people and its free press." Bernie's departure was a great loss for the Voice, but his influence was lasting. And many of us shared what he said about VOA in an interview with *News/Room*: "This is a place that gets in your system. It becomes a passion. It becomes a love."

Within a few months Nicolaides left VOA, and Conkling resigned as VOA director. His successor was John Hughes, the Pulitzer Prize–winning columnist for *The Christian Science Monitor*, who served only a few months in 1982 before becoming the State Department's chief spokesman.

Reagan visited VOA's studios and newsroom on its 40th anniversary in February 1982 and in a speech to staffers, made remarks that were in part reassuring, in part disconcerting. I filed a report: "President Reagan told VOA employees that by giving an objective account of world events and by communicating a clear picture of America and its policies at home and abroad, the Voice serves the interests not only of the United States but of the world. The president also declared that truth remains the ultimate weapon in the arsenal of democracy. At the same time, he said that truth can be attractively packaged. He did so in recounting his early days as a radio sports announcer when he broadcast play–by–play descriptions and had to rely on terse teletype messages which did not give him much information except for the outcome of the play.

"If the game was dull, said the president, one could report that the shortstop went after a hard–hit ball, picked it up, and got the opposing player out just in time. It wasn't known, he said, whether instead the player just took the ball when it came to him. Mr. Reagan added: But the truth got there, and, in other words, it can be attractively packaged. In another anecdote, the president told of a sound effects man in radio who tried to duplicate the sound of water falling on a board. He tried all kinds of devices but nothing worked. Finally, said Mr. Reagan, one day he tried water on a board — and it sounded just like water on a board."

More than a few of us at the Voice were uneasy at the thought of attractively packaging the news. Was Reagan giving us a message? Or was he just telling stories?

In his remarks at VOA, Reagan also referred to an address he had delivered earlier that day to the Organization of American States, unveiling CBI, his Caribbean Basin Initiative (VOA broadcast it live in English and, with voice–over translation, in eight other languages). The aim, he said, was to promote "peaceful economic and political development in Central America and the Caribbean Basin," and to encourage "the democratic process in the region." The centerpiece of the initiative was a free-trade arrangement for Caribbean Basin products exported to the U.S.

Reagan discussed the new program with Caribbean leaders in April of 1982, when he and Nancy went to Barbados to spend Easter vacation visiting with their long-time friend, actress Claudette Colbert, who had a beachside home on the island. The presidential party and press corps (83 men/22 women) flew first to Kingston, Jamaica, arriving on April 7 to sunny skies and a warm welcome, including costumed Jamaican dancers and a calypso band at the airport. Secretary of State Haig was to have accompanied the president on the trip, but because of the Falkland Islands crisis between Britain and Argentina, Reagan had dispatched him to London and Buenos Aires to seek a peaceful solution. Britain had possession of the islands as a dependency; the small population was mostly of British origin. But the Argentine government asserted a claim to the islands, which it called the Malvinas, and invaded them.

Reagan's theme in his talks with Jamaican leaders was that the free enterprise system would produce economic progress for the Caribbean countries in contrast to the economic failure and loss of political freedom in Castro's Cuba. Prime Minister Edward Seaga, a free enterpriser like Reagan, hailed the CBI as a window of opportunity for the hard-pressed Caribbean countries.

In Barbados the next day, the president had a luncheon meeting with the leaders of five small Eastern Caribbean island nations: St. Vincent and the Grenadines, Antigua and Barbuda, Dominica, St. Kitts-Nevis, and Barbados. He condemned Cuba for trying to "shut the door on democracy" in El Salvador and warned: "El Salvador isn't the only country that's being threatened with Marxism, and I think all of us are concerned with the overturn of Westminster parliamentary democracy in Grenada. That country now bears the Soviet and Cuban trademark, which means that it will attempt to spread the virus among its neighbors." The leaders told Reagan that before their countries could take advantage of the CBI program to spur trade and investment, they needed direct aid for road-building and similar infrastructure projects. They spelled out their views at a press conference, which was largely ignored by reporters for the U.S. domestic media but was a good story for VOA. We had a large audience in the region. In addition to our regular English newscasts and language service broadcasts, we had a "Report to the Caribbean" each weeknight and a Sunday evening program called "Spotlight to the Americas," and the Latam division's placement service, headed by Lillian Tagle, provided VOA news material to Caribbean radio stations for rebroadcast. In both Jamaica and Barbados, local broadcasters told me they used my reports in their newscasts.

I was impressed with the Caribbean leaders, particularly Prime Minister Eugenia Charles of Dominica, who was eloquent and frank: "We made it quite clear that we appreciated the Caribbean Basin Initiative. We were glad that there was an initiative at all. It means that at last the U.S. realized the Caribbean existed. . . But we wanted to make it quite clear that we thought the amount of aid for the small islands was insufficient." The leaders did not seem worried about immediate threats from Cuba and Grenada, I reported, although Premier Kennedy Simmonds of St. Kitts–Nevis noted that the island nations were "very vulnerable to violent overthrow; our defenses are limited, in some cases non–existent."

The president spent much of the rest of his stay in Barbados relaxing at the Colbert residence, swimming and enjoying the sun. The press corps relaxed too, swimming, shopping, and enjoying the Barbadian hospitality and rhythmic lifestyle, reflected in a local singing group's recording of "Uncle Sam Goes Calypso."

Reagan stepped up his travel at home and abroad in 1982 and devoted more time to foreign policy issues than he had in his first year in office. In May he returned to his alma mater, Eureka College in Illinois, to deliver a commencement address on the 50th anniversary of his graduation. At Eureka, he was introduced simply with his college nickname, "Dutch Reagan, Class of 1932," to a standing ovation in the packed 2,000–seat auditorium. Reagan used his speech to announce his proposals for deep cuts in U.S. and Soviet nuclear arsenals. Instead of SALT talks on strategic arms limitation, the negotiations would become START, for talks on a strategic arms reduction treaty. His plan called for phased reductions, with the first phase to include a one-third cut in ballistic missile warheads.

In the speech, I reported, Reagan also "offered to build a new understanding with the Soviet Union" and "repeated his condemnation of the Soviet Union for aggression against Afghanistan, the martial law crackdown in Poland, support of Vietnam in its occupation of Kampuchea and military presence in Laos, and instability in Africa and Central America brought on by Soviet proxy forces."

Reagan's bags, and mine, were packed again in June, when he made his first trip to Europe as president, for visits to four countries and participation in the 1982 economic summit at Versailles and a NATO summit in Bonn. In scenesetters, I reported that the trip was designed, among other things, to show he was committed to arms reductions and was "not the hawk many believed he was." The president and press corps (a nucleus of 214 men/18 women, with others joining for specific stops) flew first to Paris, where Reagan held talks with President Francois Mitterrand in a pre-economic summit visit. He also met with Prime Minister Margaret Thatcher and they discussed the crisis in the Falklands, where British troops had landed in May.

In covering the Versailles summit, I teamed up again with correspondents Edie Smith Apple, John Bue and Barry Wood, and engineer Rick McLeaf. There were, as usual, endless briefings by the various delegations, but the setting was grand, and so was the food provided by the French for the press at buffet tables set up on the lawn — paté, hors' d'oeuvres, and other temptations.

The economic issues discussed at the summit were overshadowed by the Falklands story, and then by news from the Middle East: Israel had invaded Lebanon. The summit conferees expressed shock and backed a U.N. call for an immediate ceasefire, and Reagan sent Ambassador Habib to Israel. The president, his aides, and the press, were occupied with the fighting in Lebanon as the trip progressed.

In Rome, the next stop, there was a story of another sort. While Reagan was at the Vatican meeting with the Pope, the traveling press, except for press pools, was installed in a filing center in a

Rome hotel and watched a slightly out–of–focus television transmission of the proceedings in the papal library. The camera panned to Reagan, who appeared to be nodding off while the Pope was making remarks to the guests. Confirmation came from the on–scene pool correspondents, Lou Cannon of *The Washington Post* and Jim Gerstenzang of AP, who reported, "At times his eyes were opened no wider than slits and his head slipped down." Along with everyone else, I reported the story, and noted the extra meetings Reagan had had with his advisors about Lebanon, and that he had been up late the night before at a post–summit dinner and opera performance.

From Rome we flew to London, where Reagan addressed members of Parliament and launched what he called a crusade for freedom, a campaign to promote democratic institutions. In one of the soundbites I inserted in a report, he said the objective was "to foster the infrastructure of democracy, the system of a free press, unions, political parties, universities, which allows a people to choose their own way to develop their own culture, to reconcile their own differences through peaceful means." Reagan said he was describing "a plan and a hope for the long term — the march of freedom and democracy which will leave Marxism–Leninism on the ash heap of history. . . ."

The Reagans were Queen Elizabeth's guests at Windsor Castle, and one of our photo ops there took place on a sunny morning when the president and the queen posed on horseback before going off on a ride. Pretty pictures.

Next stop, Bonn, where the allies at the NATO summit endorsed the president's START proposals. There were, as expected, large anti–nuclear demonstrations. Reagan's reaction was cleverly worded: "To those who march for peace, my heart is with you." On Friday, June 11, he flew to Berlin and went to see the Berlin Wall at Checkpoint Charlie. In a speech before leaving for home, he unveiled a Berlin initiative, proposing "confidence–building" measures between the U.S. and the Soviet Union. In summing up the trip, I reported the president had reassured the Europeans he was not a war–monger.

The Falklands conflict ended June 14 when Argentina surrendered. But the situation in Lebanon remained serious. Reagan also had a continuing problem, dissension among his top aides. On June 25, he replaced Haig with George Shultz, a long-time close advisor who had been treasury secretary under Nixon. Haig, who liked to be regarded as the vicar of foreign policy, had had turf battles with White House officials since early on in the administration. White House aides, my report noted, "pointedly commented that Secretary Shultz would be a team player."

In August Reagan announced he was sending Marines to Lebanon, to serve in a Multi-National Force with troops from Italy and France to monitor the departure of Palestine Liberation Organization leaders and fighters from Beirut. On September 1, with the PLO evacuation from Beirut completed, he announced a Mideast peace initiative, calling for a fresh start in negotiations, based on U.N. Security Council resolutions and the Camp David accords.

Lebanon was still a problem when Reagan left Washington on November 30 for another arduous trip abroad, this one a five-day, nearly 12,000 mile journey to four nations in South and Central America: Brazil, Colombia, Costa Rica and Honduras. Before leaving Andrews Air Force Base, the traveling press (137 men/15 women were accredited by the White House) passed through magnetometers, screening us as a security precaution. Security was tightened by the Secret Service following the assassination attempt, and included the use of police dogs to sniff our luggage and carry-on equipment. The dogs always stopped in their tracks when they got to my portable typewriter in the rows of bags, and I had to explain that my dachshunds had wet on its cover. This embarrassment was removed on future trips, after I bought an electronic typewriter to replace my Olivetti, and later when VOA finally responded to pleas to furnish its correspondents with laptop computers.

On the way to our first stop, Brasilia, I wrote a hold-for-release report based in part on the advance text of Reagan's arrival remarks, noting that "the president intends to underscore his support for democratic institutions throughout his four-nation trip." I fed the spot on the white line at Brasilia's International Airport, in rotation with other members of the U.S. Radio Pool. The routine for airport arrivals was that each participant in the white line filed live reports describing the president stepping down from Air Force One. VOA, however, needed material that could stand up for broadcast for several hours, keeping in mind the requirements for translation, so I filed reports with non–perishable material.

The white line had a full complement of members on this trip, ABC, CBS, NBC, AP–Radio, Mutual, NPR, UPI–Radio, and VOA, and was run by CBS. The CBS radio tech at the airport was Glenn Bowman, who had given me a high–quality microphone on an earlier presidential trip. (Network techs who had known my husband were always lending me a hand.) I used that microphone the entire time I traveled with presidents, instead of a VOA mike.

Reagan began his talks with Brazilian President Joao Baptista Figuereido the next morning, but soon we were writing stories about Lebanon as well. The Lebanese government had requested more troops for the Multi–National Force, to help in the goal of removing Syrian, PLO and Israeli forces from Lebanon. Shultz said the president was willing to consider additions to the U.S.–French–Italian MNF, but before making a commitment wanted to see a specific plan to achieve that goal.

The press had a story of a different sort that night. Reagan mis–spoke at a dinner given by the Brazilian president. I was on the pool covering the dinner, while VOA's regional correspondent, Gary Tredway, stayed in the hotel press center to listen to the toasts piped in and file an immediate report. As Reagan was concluding his remarks, he said: "And now, would you join me in a toast to President Figuereido, to the people of Bolivia (pause) — that is where I am going — to the people of Brazil, and to the dream of democracy and peace here in the Western Hemisphere." When I returned to the filing center, Gary was upset, frustrated; everyone in the traveling press was reporting the gaffe, but VOA wouldn't let him report it. I phoned the newsroom and said I would write an overnighter that would contain the toast and it would be acceptable.

My lead looked ahead to a speech on trade that Reagan would make the next day in Sao Paulo, after which I backed into the state dinner, where he had saluted Brazil for its successful free elections, and inserted a tape from his toast — "What we strive for is a hemisphere where the future is determined not by bullets, but by ballots. . . ." The dinner toasts, I reported, "capped an intensive series of meetings between the two presidents, and Mr. Reagan had one of those slips of the tongue which come at the end of a long day." Then I inserted the tape of Reagan's gaffe, and concluded with: "A White House transcript of the toast amended Bolivia to read Bogota, on the grounds that the president will be going on to Bogota for a working visit to Colombia after his talks here in Brazil, talks which by all accounts have gone extremely well."

I suppose one could say I had "attractively packaged" the truth. In any case, VOA could not be accused of ducking a story that received wide play. As for the White House transcript, it was clear that the stenotypists had written "Bolivia" and that it was then whited out, with "Bogota" typed in its place. The Brazilians weren't bothered by Reagan's mis-speaking. An American reporter based in Brazil said it did not cause as much fuss among the Brazilians as did a *New York Times* map of Brazil, printed before the visit, which showed Brasilia and Sao Paulo in the wrong places.

The big news of the visit was an announcement that the U.S. was extending a short-term loan of $1.2 billion to Brazil to tide it over its current shortage of cash. Reagan and Figuereido got along well, despite some differences, such as Brazilian export subsidies and Figuereido's view that the sovereignty of nations in Central America should be respected "without external interference or pressure."

In Bogota, we had another toast story. This one was really newsworthy. At a luncheon for the president, Colombian President Belisario Betancur scolded the U.S. for its policy in Central America and for not paying enough attention to Latin America. Betancur said Central America and the Caribbean appear to be dueling grounds of "foreign invaders," and referred particularly to the loss of life in El Salvador. And he suggested implicitly that opposition to Cuba's returning to the Organization of American States (OAS) be dropped. I led my stories on the Bogota visit with Betancur's criticism and reported that Reagan was conciliatory in his response, quoting him:

"I came here to listen and to learn — to ask how we could be of greater help in promoting peace and progress in the Americas."

The White House press corps listened with near-astonishment to Betancur's blunt talk as the toasts were piped into the noisy and cramped filing center. We were closeted in a small room of the congressional building — CBS's Lesley Stahl and I practically sat on each other's laps, it was so crowded — and it was hard to hear. We compared notes and replayed the tape to be sure we had heard what we thought we'd heard. I was thankful to have a VOA engineer on the trip, the reliable Hubert Katz, who recorded the toasts, and speedily taped and filed my reports on the white line in the limited time we had; the visit was only five and a half hours.

On the Air Force One flight from Bogota to San Jose, Costa Rica, Shultz told the pool that Reagan agreed in principle with Betancur's view that the OAS should have "universal membership," but added this condition: "Only if Cuba breaks its ties and ceases being a satellite of the Soviet Union." Shultz said Reagan and Betancur agreed on hopes that Nicaragua "move in a more pluralistic" direction, but disagreed on how to handle the situation.

The highlight of our stay in Costa Rica, Latin America's oldest democracy, was an incident at the National Theater, where Reagan was about to deliver a speech but was interrupted by a heckler. Members of the audience reacted with loud shushes, admonishing the heckler to be quiet. When Reagan was able to begin, he said: "I of course could not understand without interpretation, but I was informed that he was expressing the communist viewpoint. And I think, again, a tribute to democracy he was allowed to do so here in this democracy. We wouldn't be allowed to do so in a communist country." Reagan received a standing ovation. The communist deputy, Sergio Eric Ardon, settled in his seat and listened to Reagan's speech. My report of course included the tape of his remarks on the heckler.

This was on the last and most intensive day of the trip. From Costa Rica we went to Honduras, not to its capital but to the airport at San Pedro Sula. While in San Jose, he had conferred with Salvadoran President Alvaro Mangana, as well as Costa Rican

President Luis Alberto Monge. At San Pedro Sula, he had meetings with Honduran President Roberto Suazo and Guatemalan President Efrain Rios Montt. Reagan appeared with the Honduran leader first, then the Guatemalan, to make brief statements to the perspiring press in the hot, noisy, and incongruous setting of our briefing room. This was an airport hangar, transformed into a pathetic auditorium with a makeshift stage against a backdrop of limply hanging blue draperies. In summary, Reagan promised continued cooperation with the democratic countries of the region in protecting against those seeking to "impose totalitarianism on free people."

On the tarmac of that little airport at San Pedro Sula I met our regional stringer, Laurie Kassman, who was about to join the Voice as a full-time staff member and would become one of our valued correspondents. I welcomed her aboard and answered her questions about what it was like working for VOA. At the time, December 1982, Kenneth Tomlinson, a senior editor at *Reader's Digest* and a conservative, was taking office as VOA's third director in less than two years. We would be watching to see what happened under his leadership. I told Laurie we continued to report the news objectively, and the best advice I could give her was to do the same.

14
The Marine Barracks and the Spice Island
Souring Relations with Moscow
A Necklace. . . and "Jesus Loves Me"

The postcard was from the Ivory Coast capital, Abidjan. "Dear Ms. Joury" (sic), it said, "Did you believe that stuff you read about Ronald Reagan's achievements in 1983? Good grief!" I assumed the writer, a woman, was referring to my yearend piece summing up the "foreign policy challenges" faced by the president that year and what the administration regarded as successes. Or possibly she was referring to another report on Reagan's optimistic comments about arms control talks with the Soviet Union and the situation in Lebanon, despite problems in both cases.

Whether I believed "the stuff" is beside the point. Columnists and commentators can say what they think, but reporters aren't supposed to let their personal views creep into their copy. They do, however, have a responsibility to provide relevant information, the background that is essential to a comprehensive, objective story. I was describing the president's position on various issues in my job as a reporter, not because I agreed with him or because I was employed by the government.

In filing reports on speeches, press conferences and interviews by the president or high-ranking officials, in carrying them live or broadcasting excerpts, VOA is legitimately reporting the news, just as other news organizations do. A White House correspondent for VOA should and does try to put what the president says in context, and to report when his policies are under fire. Yet an administration's spin or tone does come through, without any deliberate attempt to make the news propagandistic.

During Ronald Reagan's administration, I received many letters from VOA listeners praising his anti-communist stance, while during Jimmy Carter's administration, I received many letters praising his stand on human rights. That's because Reagan talked about communism so often and Carter talked about human rights so often, and we reported what each said. It was news.

In covering the White House, correspondents always face the risk that an administration will use the press in its efforts to mold public perceptions. The Reagan White House was particularly adept at this when, on October 23, 1983, a terrorist truck–bombing in Beirut killed 241 American servicemen at the U.S. Marine Barracks, and, two days later, U.S. troops landed in Grenada, a tiny Caribbean "spice island" that exported nutmeg, cocoa and cloves. The president and his aides, with their statements conveyed by the news media, VOA included, called the invasion of Grenada a "rescue mission" and focused on its success. In doing so, they diverted attention from the attack on the marines and the administration's disastrous entanglement in Lebanon.

The marines were serving in the Multi–National Force sent to Lebanon to support the effort to get Syrian, PLO and Israeli forces to leave Lebanese territory. The effort was getting nowhere. In the months preceding the barracks bombing, terrorist acts had increased in Beirut, sniper attacks had killed American marines, and Lebanese factional fighting had erupted. Despite reservations in Congress, including calls to bring the marines home, Reagan insisted that the U.S. stay in the Multi–National Force. His rationale was that resolving the Lebanese situation would lead to Arab–Israeli peace negotiations. He put it this way on October 17, when he was asked by a reporter why the U.S. was in Lebanon: "I think it is vitally important to the security of the United States and the western world that we do everything we can to further the peace process in the Middle East."

Reagan was awakened with the news from Beirut on that Sunday morning, October 23, while spending a golfing weekend with Shultz at the Augusta National Golf Club in Georgia. Not known publicly then — reporters were told later — he had received on Saturday a request for help from the Organization of East Caribbean States, whose members felt events in Grenada posed a threat to their security. A violent leftist coup had taken place in Grenada in mid–October, and the deposed prime minister had been killed a few days later.

The president returned to the White House Sunday, and on Tuesday morning, with Dominica's Prime Minister Eugenia Charles at his side, announced that U.S. forces had landed in Grenada, along with troops from the East Caribbean island nations. He said the purpose was to protect innocent lives, including those of up to 1,000 Americans, to forestall further chaos, and to assist in restoring law and order and democratic institutions in Grenada. Along with his remarks, I reported those of Eugenia Charles, who said there was information the Soviets and Cubans had been behind the coup. In subsequent statements, Reagan repeatedly referred to the intervention as a rescue mission, although at one point he had called it an invasion. VOA's management initially wouldn't let us use the word invasion and we had to resort to euphemisms, even though it must have been clear to our listeners that that's what it was. What else could they think in hearing our first reports Tuesday that more than 1,000 U.S. marines and paratroopers and 300 troops from six Caribbean nations had landed in Grenada and taken control of its two airports. One of my reports filed that day did contain the word: "White House spokesman Larry Speakes says congressional leaders of both parties raised no objections when President Reagan briefed them on the undertaking in Grenada. Some lawmakers, however, have charged that the landings were an invasion and illegal."

The early criticism was quickly overridden by praise from the Grenadians and American evacuees. Many of the first arrivals home were students who had been attending medical school in Grenada and said things like, "I don't think there's any more beautiful sight than the United States and the rangers who saved us." Public support grew after television showed scenes like the dramatic shot of a student kissing the ground on his return to the U.S. — and after Reagan addressed the nation on Thursday. He said U.S. forces had found a Cuban base with weapons and equipment in Grenada, and, in a soundbite I used in my report, declared that the island "was a Soviet Cuban colony being readied as a major military bastion to export terrorism and undermine democracy. We got there just in time." In the speech, Reagan linked the events in Lebanon and Grenada, asserting that the Soviet Union assisted and encouraged violence in both through a network of surrogates and terrorists.

Nine days after the troops landed, Reagan told the press that U.S. objectives in Grenada had been achieved. The American servicemen, he said, "not only rescued our own citizens, but they saved the people of Grenada from repression and laid aside a potential threat to all the people of the Caribbean." U.S. casualties in the hostilities were 19 dead and 116 wounded; Grenadian, 45 dead and more than 300 wounded, and Cuban losses were 25 dead, 59 wounded, and more than 600 taken prisoner.

The next day, November 4, the president and Mrs. Reagan attended a memorial service at Camp Lejeune, North Carolina, for those who died in Beirut and Grenada. A steady rain fell on the 5,000 gathered in the amphitheatre. Raindrops mingled with tears. In my report, I quoted a Marine chaplain: "The Lord has given us a day to match our mood of anguish and grief; the men who died invested their life's blood in the future of America." In remarks afterwards, Reagan said those who lost their lives in Lebanon and Grenada believed in defending freedom.

A few days later the White House staged a "welcome home" celebration for the medical students evacuated from Grenada and the servicemen who, the students said, "came to our rescue."

The news media duly reported the White House statements and events, while at the same time protesting to the Pentagon and White House for deciding against press coverage of the invasion and conducting it in secrecy. White House veracity also was called into question. One of my reports, on October 31, included the news that Les Janka, then the White House spokesman on foreign affairs, had resigned. According to *The Washington Times*, Janka was fired by Larry Speakes, the chief spokesman, because he had leaked (to *The Washington Post*) the contents of a letter in which Speakes had protested to a top White House official that the secrecy had damaged the credibility of the White House. Speakes declined comment on his reported letter. Janka, in submitting his resignation, wrote the president that personal credibility is a "precious asset" and that circumstances surrounding the events in the Caribbean had "damaged, perhaps irreparably, that credibility."

Janka gave no details, but in a December article in *The Armed Forces Journal* he wrote: "With no knowledge of the impending operation, press officers unwittingly passed to the press false and misleading information. Withholding and protecting sensitive information is something experienced press officers know how to do, but lying to the media, even unwittingly, is a cardinal sin against credibility."

As many of us in the White House press corps came to know by word of mouth, Bill Plante of CBS had asked Larry Speakes, on the day before the troops landed, if an invasion of Grenada was imminent. Larry checked on it and told Bill this was "preposterous." The source of the "preposterous" quote was the newly named deputy assistant for national security affairs, John Poindexter. Speakes unwittingly was the conveyor of Poindexter's lie. I did not report this, since Speakes was officially mum. He wasn't faulted by the press corps, while Poindexter's credibility was from then on subject to suspicion.

When the Pentagon did allow reporters to go to Grenada, Don Fulsom, who was then covering the White House with me, was a member of a press group that toured the island and was shown evidence of the Cuban presence. Don discovered he was a celebrity in Grenada. Local citizens who had listened to him on VOA recognized his voice and exclaimed, "That's Don Fulsom!"

U.S. combat troops were withdrawn from Grenada by mid–December, leaving behind a small force of servicemen, including military police, to help with security for an extended period. What bothered me about the whole episode was that the White House had effectively capitalized on the intervention to relegate the sacrifice of the marines in Beirut to a remote corner of public consciousness.

Reagan made a brief visit to Grenada on February 20, 1986, and was given a hero's welcome. People held signs with messages like "Thanks for Saving Our Lives," and Prime Minister Herbert Blaize called him "Grenada's national hero." During his stay in the capital,

St. George's, he went to the medical school, where American students had resumed attending classes, laid a wreath at the memorial to the 19 American servicemen, met with Grenadian leaders and with nine Caribbean prime ministers, and delivered a speech at Queen's Park. VOA's Miami correspondent, George Meek, who covered the Caribbean, was in Grenada and filed reports on Reagan's meetings via the white line at the press center, while I went to Queen's Park, a large field used for cricket and soccer games, to be in place for the president's speech.

The park was jammed with people, and costumed performers were singing and dancing to the irresistible beat of Caribbean music. I had been asked to do a special feature for VOA's English to Africa broadcasts, and I filed it with the help of an NBC colleague in the press corps, who lent me his phone. VOA did not send a radio tech on the trip, for budget reasons. It would have cost under $800. A steel band and a calypso singer praising "Uncle Reagan" greeted the president and the crowd roared approvingly when he said Grenada was once again safely in the ranks of free nations. As I reported, he denounced "communist tyranny" in Cuba and Nicaragua and noted that U.S. aid to Grenada included completion of the airport that the Cubans had been building, so that it now could be used for tourists and businessmen. The traveling press also gave an assist to Grenada's economy, by making purchases of its products. I took home jars of ground saffron and nutmeg from the spice island.

That the tone of VOA newscasts can be affected by presidential rhetoric was demonstrated by Reagan's strong criticism of the Soviet Union in 1983, a year of souring relations between Washington and Moscow. On March 8, in a speech to a convention of the National Association of Evangelicals, he characterized the Soviet Union as an "evil empire." On March 23 in a Washington speech on his defense policy, he disclosed his proposal for a Strategic Defense Initiative, SDI, "to counter the awesome Soviet missile threat." The proposal was tucked into a passage that called on the American scientific community to come up with the means to make offensive nuclear weapons obsolete. I have to admit that I glossed over it, focusing instead on Reagan's defense of his increased military budget. I recalled that passage many times in writing subsequent stories about his idea for a space–based missile defense system, nicknamed "Star Wars."

Contributing to the strains between Washington and Moscow were NATO's plans to install new American medium–range nuclear missiles in Western Europe. In May, a few days before the annual economic summit got under way in Colonial Williamsburg with Reagan as host, the Soviet Union threatened to deploy missiles in Eastern Europe if NATO went ahead with its plans. The seven leaders gathered in Williamsburg responded with a statement serving notice that if Moscow did not join in a balanced agreement on reducing medium–range missiles in Europe, the American missiles would be deployed. On economic issues, the summit conferees had some differences, including European concern over high U.S. interest rates and budget deficits.

Reagan stepped up his condemnation of the Soviet Union in a daily barrage of statements and speeches after the September 1 shooting down of a Korean Air Lines passenger plane that had strayed into Soviet airspace, killing all 269 persons aboard. He called the downing of the South Korean 747 "a barbaric act," "a massacre," and "a crime against humanity." He did not break off arms reduction negotiations with the Soviets, however. In a speech to the nation September 5, Reagan made public a segment of Soviet pilot radio transmissions recorded when the airliner was hit, and announced a series of steps in response to the Soviet action. Among them, suspension of consulate and cultural negotiations and cancellation of a transportation cooperation agreement with Moscow. As noted in my reports, conservative groups urged stronger action, including cancellation of a long–term grain sales agreement. He retained that agreement.

Reagan referred to the airliner again, although in a broader context, in his Saturday radio speech September 24. This time he spoke not only to Americans but to a worldwide audience. He delivered it from a broadcast studio at VOA, where, he said, "I am speaking directly to people everywhere, from Los Angeles to New

Delhi, Cairo, and Bangkok, and I'm attempting to speak directly to the people of the Soviet Union."

The speech was another example of his skillful use of the intimacy of radio. In talking about the South Korean airliner, he said, "We have no quarrel with you, the Soviet people. But please understand, the world believes no government has a right to shoot civilian airliners out of the sky. Your airline, Aeroflot, has violated sensitive U.S. airspace scores of times, yet we would never fire on your planes and risk killing one of your friends or your loved ones." Reagan then went on to the main point of his remarks, to portray the U.S. as the good guy, and the Soviet Union the bad guy, in negotiations on arms reductions.

VOA officials reported the speech was broadcast live to three continents, with simultaneous translation in Russian, Ukrainian, Romanian, Lithuanian, Urdu, Bengali, and Hausa, and translated by 34 other language services for their later broadcasts. In Moscow, the speech was heard in evening prime time; the Soviet Union routinely jammed VOA's ethnic language programs but not English. While at the Voice, Reagan posed for a photo holding a picture of President Eisenhower making a speech from the same studio on February 25, 1957. Broadcasting presidential speeches on VOA is both a function of news and an appropriate way to use VOA as, and it's tough for me to say this, a vehicle for propaganda — rather than putting pressures on the newsroom.

When the Korean airliner strayed over Soviet territory, it was bound for Tokyo and then Seoul. It had left Anchorage on a normal flight path, called R-20. A little over two months later, a similar established route from Anchorage to Tokyo was taken by Air Force One, with the president bound for state visits in Japan and South Korea after a stopover in Alaska. Traveling the same route was a chartered Pan Am 747 wide-body jet, used for the press corps accompanying the president (183 men/20 women) instead of two smaller press planes. The zoo plane had passed into legend.

Reagan had originally planned to include visits to the Philippines, Indonesia and Thailand on this trip. But after Philippine opposition leader Benigno Aquino was assassinated in August and violent demonstrations followed in Manila, members of Congress called for cancellation of the Philippine visit. He "postponed" it, and the visits to Indonesia and Thailand too, saying that he was shortening the trip because Congress would still be in session.

The presidential party arrived in Tokyo November 9, greeted by Emperor Hirohito in an outdoor ceremony at Akasaka Palace, and the next night the Reagans were his guests at a white tie dinner at the Imperial Palace. I was on the small pool of American and Japanese press assigned to cover the dinner. We were escorted to a spot just inside the entrance to the palace to wait for the Reagans' arrival and witness Hirohito greeting them. The 82–year–old emperor descended a long staircase, grand in its simplicity, and walked slowly to the glass–fronted entrance, to stand rigidly alone awaiting his guests. As I watched him from a distance of only a few steps, this slight and scholarly elderly gentleman shifted his weight in almost imperceptible movements, the way a child standing at attention might fidget while trying hard not to.

The Reagans swept up in their limousine, television cameramen and still photographers captured the warm greeting, and in a matter of moments the scene was over. No memorable quotes, nothing newsy to report, just a lasting picture for me of the emperor, a hated symbol of our World War II enemy when I was in high school, now so fragile, almost like a figurine. After the emperor and the Reagans retired to a reception room, the Japanese correspondents crowded around me, the only woman in the pool. What, they wanted to know, were the stones in Nancy Reagan's necklace? It was a brilliant necklace of large stones. I don't know much about jewelry and was at a loss. Some of the American still photographers, a laconic group, suggested, "Oh, just say emeralds. Who's to know?" I felt sure they weren't that, and told my eager questioners I thought they were crystals. A few weeks later, I read somewhere that necklaces of crystals were high fashion. Maybe I didn't steer the Japanese reporters wrong.

Emperor Hirohito welcomes President and Mrs. Reagan to the Imperial Palace for a state dinner, November 10, 1983, with pool reporters in the background. (Courtesy Ronald Reagan Library)

The pool was escorted from the entrance to a holding room somewhere in the bowels of the palace, to wait until it was time to take us to witness the exchange of toasts. There was no translation of the emperor's toast, but we were supplied with the English text, in which he said the relations between Japan and the United States "have come through various phases" and that he was "highly pleased to note that our two countries have now become closest neighbors bound by strong bands of friendship."

The major event of the visit was on Friday, when Reagan became the first American president to address the Japanese Diet. He was applauded repeatedly by the parliament members, especially when he declared: "A nuclear war can never be won and must never be fought." And, "I know I speak for people everywhere when I say our dream is to see the day when nuclear weapons will be banished from the face of the earth." As I reported to VOA listeners, "The declaration by the president, as the leader now of the nation which in World War II used the atom bomb against Japan, was of particular significance to his audience." Reagan also assured the Japanese that the U.S. would not accept any agreement in the negotiations with the Soviet Union on missiles in Europe "which transfers the threat of longer–range nuclear missiles from Europe to Asia." And on economic matters, he referred to U.S. objections to some of Japan's trade practices and noted protectionist sentiment in the U.S. Congress.

In filing stories, I again had the benefit of a regional correspondent's expertise. This time it was provided by Steve Thompson. As VOA's Far East correspondent based in Tokyo, Steve also covered South Korean developments, and we divided up coverage duties in both Tokyo and Seoul. On arrival in Seoul, Reagan was welcomed by cheering crowds along the eight–mile route of his motorcade. The turnout, estimated by a South Korean official at more than one million, didn't seem to me to be as large as the one Ford had received, but the people were just as enthusiastic. The signs they held up included one that said, "Ron is a jolly good fellow."

Security was extremely tight in Seoul. North Korea had broadcast threats against Reagan in advance of the visit. And tensions between South and North Korea had heightened since 17 South Korean officials visiting Burma had been killed in a bombing in Rangoon October 9. The Burmese government said it had evidence that North Korea was responsible. In a speech to the National Assembly, Reagan accused the North Koreans of waging a campaign of intimidation, and told the South Koreans, "You are not alone. America is your friend and we are with you." As expected, he denounced the shooting down of the Korean airliner and the bombing in Rangoon.

In wrapping up the day's events, I reported that the purpose of the president's visit was "to show support for South Korea, but the impact of his message has been somewhat diluted by the issue of human rights on his first day in Seoul." According to press reports, the Chun Doo Hwan government had detained or placed under house arrest dozens of dissidents, as part of its security precautions. At a reception for community leaders, where Reagan made a brief appearance, one of the guests was a dissident who had been jailed

five times under the previous government, the Reverend Park
Hyung Kyu, who headed the human rights committee of the Korean
Council of Churches. After Reagan left, the press pool asked the
reverend if he was satisfied with human rights under the Chun
government. "No, I am not," he replied, and said that many young
people had been detained on the eve of the president's visit under
the excuse of security. I also reported that he said he thought the
Reagan administration was "doing some good, at least for Korea,
with quiet diplomacy."

The wrapup also included a tape from Reagan's remarks at a state
dinner, which I led into by saying he had gently suggested more
should be done for human rights in South Korea. His words were:
"Democracy and freedom of opinion are virtues the free world must
cherish and defend. They distinguish us from totalitarian states."
Maybe I was the one being gentle. The *Newsweek* account of the
Seoul visit said that Reagan "made only tepid references to human
rights" in his speeches. The magazine noted that when Jimmy Carter
visited Seoul in 1979 (a trip covered by another VOA correspondent), he "had gone out of his way to meet with opponents of the
South Korean government."

The next day, a Sunday, Reagan helicoptered to the Demilitarized
Zone, where he joined American troops in a morning worship
service outdoors at Camp Liberty Bell, on the southern edge of the
DMZ. "A canopy of camouflaged netting extended over the altar,"
I reported. "There was a tank in the background. During the service
a choir of 16 Korean orphans sang." And here I inserted tape of their
singing, in Korean and English, "Jesus Loves Me" — which I had
sung so often as a child at Methodist Sunday School in New Castle.
("Jesus loves me, this I know. For the Bible tells me so. Little ones
to Him belong. They are weak but He is strong.") The little boys
and girls were from one of the orphanages supported by American
troops. The service ended with the troops and the president singing
"America the Beautiful." The event was so obviously staged for TV,
but the sweet voices of the orphans made the blatancy almost
palatable.

Reagan's visit to the DMZ took him closer to the military demarcation line separating North and South Korea than any previous American president. At the U.S. Army's small Guardpost Collier, 1,000 meters from the line, pool TV cameras recorded his looking through binoculars at the communist North, where he saw a village built by the North Koreans. It was dubbed "propaganda village" because nobody lived there, and Reagan pronounced it "just like a Hollywood back lot." I was on a different press pool, less newsworthy in terms of American domestic consumption, at the South Korean Army's I Corps headquarters, waiting to cover Reagan's arrival there from the DMZ. I didn't mind that assignment, for I saw, along with the president, an exhibition of Tae Kwan Do, the martial art developed over 2,000 years ago by the Koreans. I tried to remember every move so I could describe them to my stepdaughter, who was then enrolled in a similar self-defense course back home. The demonstration ended with some of the Korean soldiers, wearing traditional white pajamas, and black belts signifying their skill, breaking stacks of 15 tiles by striking them with their bodies; one did it with his elbow, several with their hands — and one with his head.

During our stay in Seoul, my exposure to local citizens was limited, but those I saw were friendly, enterprising, and apparently benefiting from South Korea's fast-growing economy. The city was even more bustling than it had been during Ford's visit, and it was a shopper's mecca for members of the press looking for bargains in leather goods and Korean-made products, like footwear and jackets, that bore brand names familiar to Americans.

Much of Reagan's travel in 1983 was domestic, including trips to his California ranch. Don Fulsom and I alternated covering those vacations, and it was my turn when Queen Elizabeth and Prince Philip were scheduled to visit the ranch for lunch with the Reagans on March 1. It was a foggy, rainy, chilly, miserable day, and I was amazed when we were told in the press filing center that the visit was still on and that the royals would drive up the mountain to the ranch. I had been on that road once, and once was enough. On an early visit to Santa Barbara, Norm Hannen of CBS had taken me on a drive so I could see where the ranch was located. The road was narrow, crossing several small creeks, and perilous, with numerous switchbacks, miniscule negotiating room, and, alarmingly, no guardrails to deter a plunge into deep ravines. I took in the scenery, but looked up instead of down. That drive was on a sunny summer day, but now, on March 1, the road was even more perilous, with the creekbeds flooded.

The Reagans had to ride in a four-wheel drive utility vehicle when they came down the mountain to greet their guests at the Santa Barbara airport. That done, they made the trip back up the mountain, with the queen and her husband to follow about an hour later. Pool reporters Frank Clines (*New York Times*) and Larry Barrett (*Time*) said "it seemed to us that the ride was dangerous because of deep, fast-running water intersecting the road at a half dozen places." The royal couple arrived safely, fording the creeks in the same utility vehicle the Reagans had used. According to Mike Deaver, the British had been less concerned about the weather than the White House. "They're used to this kind of weather," he said, adding that Queen Elizabeth had insisted on staying on schedule.

Normally, the weather in Santa Barbara was without flaw when I covered Reagan's trips to his ranch. Curtis Wilkie summed up what it was like covering the president's summer vacations (in the *Washington Journalism Review*): "For those of us who suffered the sweatbees, gnats and sweltering heat of Plains, Georgia, it is like graduating from purgatory to heaven." Most of the press stayed at the Sheraton Santa Barbara, across the street from the ocean, and early morning walks on the beach were divine. We had plenty of free time, and many of the White House press used it to play tennis or go sailing. We had the pick of excellent restaurants, and there were tourist attractions to investigate, such as the superb Botanic Garden. But heaven became boring, at least for me, with nothing to report some days but the president's horseback riding and clearing brush. It was frustrating, too, because high-ranking officials who accompanied the president often leaked information "on background" over dinner with favored correspondents.

In February 1984, however, we did have news to report in Santa Barbara. It was about the marines in Lebanon. There had been growing calls to bring the marines home since December, when a congressional report on the barracks bombing had criticized the military chain of command for inadequate security for the marines. A Pentagon–commissioned study also was critical. Reagan had resisted the calls, and in his Saturday radio speech February 4 had urged bipartisan unity on the issue, declaring there was no reason "to turn our backs on friends and cut and run."

The Lebanon story began breaking when Reagan was visiting his boyhood hometown of Dixon, Illinois, on Monday, February 6 for a celebration of his 73rd birthday, before going on to Las Vegas for speaking engagements and then to California to spend the rest of the week at the ranch. Just about the whole town of Dixon, population around 16,000, turned out for the parade despite freezing weather. The press watched the parade, led by Reagan in his limousine, from a roped–off area, but it was so cold, colder than December at the Great Wall of China, that I made frequent visits to the filing center to ward off hypothermia. The parade was long, 10 marching bands and approximately 30 other units. While it was going on, we were waiting for a promised presidential statement on Lebanon, where there was renewed violence and President Amin Gemayel's government was reported to have collapsed.

Just before we left Dixon, the statement was handed out, and I wrote a quick story quoting from it. Reagan deplored "the continued shelling of innocent civilians" from Syrian–occupied Lebanese territory, called on Syria "to cease this activity," and urged Lebanese political leaders to support President Gemayel's effort to form a new government. From Illinois we flew to Las Vegas to cover the president's appearances Tuesday at a school principals' convention and, with his candidacy for re–election announced several days earlier, a Republican fund–raiser. Those stories were pushed aside when Speakes told us the president had directed Bush to delay his departure for a trip to Europe in order to coordinate Washington activities in the Lebanese situation; had ordered stepped–up diplomatic efforts, and had consulted with America's partners in the Multi-National Force.

We remained in Las Vegas to file our stories after the president left, and soon we were reporting another instalment: Reagan announced the "redeployment" of the marines from Beirut airport to ships offshore and said it would begin shortly and proceed in stages. He also disclosed new rules of engagement, authorizing U.S. naval forces to provide gunfire and air support against any units firing into Greater Beirut from parts of Lebanon controlled by Syria.

In Santa Barbara the next day, the announcement dominated Larry Speakes's press briefing. As I reported, he said the president "decided on the phased redeployment of marines from Beirut in order to make the U.S. presence in the Multi-National Force more effective." Speakes "rejected suggestions that the decision amounted to withdrawing the marines," "warned the Syrians against any misimpression that there is any lessening of U.S. determination to support the government of Lebanon," and "disputed an interpretation that the new rules of engagement amounted to undeclared war."

In reviewing what I reported, I think my postcard writer from the Ivory Coast could well have asked again if I believed that "stuff." Again, that was beside the point. However, the point that is to be made here is that in quoting Speakes I was reflecting questions which had been raised about the rules of engagement and whether the U.S. was pulling out of Lebanon. On Friday, February 10, Reagan received a plan he'd requested from Casper Weinberger on redeployment, which I, like everyone in the press corps, described as the defense secretary's "withdrawal plan." In another report that weekend I noted criticism in Congress that the broadened rules of engagement went beyond a 1983 bipartisan resolution to continue participation in the MNF.

On return to Washington, Reagan had talks with Jordan's King Hussein, who was in the U.S. for medical treatment, and Egypt's President Hosni Mubarak, who was making an official visit. At a White House briefing "a senior American official" said they told Reagan "the Lebanon dilemma" should not sidetrack the Middle East peace process. On February 17 the White House announced Reagan's approval of the withdrawal plan, with all the marines to be moved to ships offshore within 30 days, except for those left to guard the U.S. embassy and other servicemen to provide training for the Lebanese armed forces. On March 30, Reagan informed Congress that he was ending U.S. participation in the MNF. As I reported, "he asserted the United States has not abandoned Lebanon," and said participation was "no longer a necessary or appropriate means" of achieving American goals there.

The fighting in Lebanon raged on. Television footage showed Beirut apartment buildings destroyed. When you hear or read about cities which are news stories, there is a certain detachment. Like Beirut, they're place names, battlegrounds viewed from a distance, remote moments of bloodshed on the picture tube. But they are places where people live, ordinary human beings. I kept thinking of the visit Diane and I had made 14 years earlier to Beirut, when it was alive and well. I recalled our excursion to see the ancient ruins at Baalbek. Now there were new ruins at Baalbek, with Lebanon mired in conflict among factions, including the Druze. In Beirut, we met a Druze, a courtly judge who was the uncle of a Washington friend. He invited us to dinner in the apartment he shared with his sister, and in conversation at table he explained his religious faith. I was afraid the judge and his sister might have been among the many casualties in the shelling of Beirut, and phoned my friend, Nadine Silman, to find out. "They survived all the bombing," she said, and had moved to a small town in Brazil to wait "until things settle down" in Lebanon. It wasn't until late 1993 that they began preparing to return to Beirut.

Reagan was bowing to public opinion in an election year when he reversed his stand on keeping the marines in Beirut. The 1984 polls showed a good majority of Americans wanted them pulled out, and Democratic presidential contenders were criticizing his foreign policy on Lebanon, Central America, and relations with the Soviet Union. On that February 10 in Santa Barbara, when we were reporting Reagan had received Weinberger's withdrawal plan, we had other news to report as well: Reagan's reaction to the death of

Yuri Andropov, the leader of the Soviet Union since Brezhnev's death in November 1982. He sent a message of condolences to the acting Soviet chief of state and later in the day named Bush to represent him at the funeral. A White House handout said the president asked the vice president to "convey to the new Soviet leadership our hope for an improved dialogue and cooperation which can lead to a more constructive relationship between our two countries." The next day, in his Saturday radio speech delivered from the ranch, Reagan repeated his call for constructive cooperation.

This new, softened tone first appeared in a January 16 speech on relations with Moscow, in which he called on the Soviets to return to the arms reduction negotiations. The START talks and the talks on medium–range missiles in Europe, known as INF for Intermediate Nuclear Forces, had ended in 1983 without the Soviets agreeing to a date for their resumption.

After Reagan's April 1984 visit to China, the Soviet Union announced it would boycott the Summer Olympics in Los Angeles, on the grounds of inadequate security. The head of the L.A. Olympics organizing committee, Peter Ueberoth, met with Reagan May 8, and in remarks to reporters afterwards suggested the Soviets were retaliating for Carter's boycott of the Moscow Olympics four years earlier: "It appears we're paying the price for 1980." In reporting his comment, I noted many American Olympic athletes had opposed the boycott of the Moscow games, but complied with it, and that Reagan also had opposed it.

At a press conference May 22 the president heatedly rejected suggestions that his hard–line policies were responsible for the break–off of arms control talks and the Soviet boycott, and that relations between Washington and Moscow were at their lowest level in 20 years. He blamed "political dialogue" for charges that "I somehow have an itchy finger and am going to blow up the world."

In the same press conference, Reagan made another appeal for congressional approval of his military and economic aid program for Central America. Democrats in Congress were insisting that military aid to El Salvador should be conditioned on that government's observance of human rights standards, and they were objecting to covert aid for the Contra forces opposing the Sandinista government in Nicaragua. Many Democratic members of Congress, joined by some Republican lawmakers, also had been expressing concern for several years that the U.S. might become involved in a Vietnam–type conflict in Central America. The president was insisting that the U.S. effort in Central America was to promote democracy and well–being in the face of "Cuban and Nicaraguan aggression, aided and abetted by the Soviet Union."

Reagan made another high–visibility election–year trip abroad in early June, to Ireland, the land of his ancestors; to Normandy, to mark the 40th anniversary of the D–Day landings, and to London, for the annual economic summit. It was Don Fulsom's turn to accompany the president, so I followed the events from home, especially the television coverage in Normandy, where I had covered Jimmy Carter's visit in 1978. That had produced some striking pictures, but nothing to match those of the president and Mrs. Reagan standing in the cemetery where the American servicemen were buried. The Reagan White House, i.e., Mike Deaver, was much more accomplished than the Carter White House in staging events and in working with television producers to position TV crews and still photographers where they would have the best view. The TV folks and still photographers naturally were willing allies; their business was to get good pictures.

While Reagan was in Europe, the final primary elections were held, with former Vice President Walter Mondale claiming victory in his fight for the Democratic presidential nomination. On July 12 Mondale made the stunning announcement of his choice for running–mate, Congresswoman Geraldine Ferraro, the first woman ever to be named as a candidate for vice president on the ticket of a major political party. The very next day, Reagan moved to head off any loss of women's votes in the campaign for the November election. He spoke to a gathering of Republican women who were elected officials and candidates and, as I reported, "had some implicit criticism of the choice of Geraldine Ferraro when he asserted that women advancing through the ranks of his Republican Party are doing so by merit." Reagan also said Britain's Conservative Party chose Margaret Thatcher as its leader "not because she was a woman but because she was the best person for the job. There was no tokenism or cynical symbolism in what they did." And he noted his own choice of Sandra Day O'Connor, the first woman named to the Supreme Court.

While the Democrats were assembled in San Francisco for their national convention, Reagan continued his calls for support of the Contras, whom he called freedom fighters. Because I was reporting on radio, I was always careful to make sure the listener knew when I was quoting him, so I used phrases like "those he called" or "in the president's words." Otherwise in reports dealing with Nicaragua I used journalistically neutral terms, like anti–government forces, anti–Sandinista forces, or Contras. In various speeches Reagan denounced the Sandinista government as "a military dictatorship" and cited the presence in Nicaragua "of thousands of Cuban, Soviet–bloc and Arab radicals."

When Mondale gave his speech accepting the Democratic presidential nomination, he attacked Reagan's budget deficits and foreign policy, including his policy in Central America. Besides making his politically risky declaration on taxes ("Let's tell the truth. Mr. Reagan will raise taxes, and so will I. He won't tell you. I just did.") Mondale promised: "I'll press for human rights in Central America and for the removal of all foreign forces from the region. And in my first 100 days, I will stop the illegal war in Nicaragua."

In a later report on Central America as a campaign issue, I noted that "Mr. Mondale's use of the word illegal was seen as a reference to the Reagan administration's request to Congress for funds for covert, or secret, assistance to the anti–Sandinista forces in Nicaragua. The requested aid became not–so–secret during congressional debate, and Congress thus far has refused to vote for the funds."

Reagan labeled the Mondale charges "demagoguery" at his first formal broadcast and televised press conference after the Democratic convention. And he asserted that the Democrats either didn't understand or were ignoring "the communist threat" in Central America. The president continued to respond the next day, July 25, when he began a two–day trip officially launching his campaign for re–election. In Texas and Georgia, Reagan portrayed Mondale and Ferraro as ultra–liberals. In New Jersey, at a rally in Elizabeth aimed at wooing the blue collar vote, he praised the contributions of immigrants to America, citing Italians, Irish, Polish and so on. His campaign schedulers, it was clear, had duly noted that Ferraro was the daughter of an Italian immigrant and a Roman Catholic as well as a liberal.

In Hoboken, Reagan attended a Catholic parish festival and spaghetti dinner held in honor of St. Ann, the patron saint of women, particularly mothers. Before his speech, he went into the church to see a statue of St. Ann and was accompanied by the Reagans' friend and Hoboken native, Frank Sinatra. In recounting these activities to VOA's listeners, I reported the Hoboken visit was widely seen as an attempt to counter any gains the Democrats might make from choosing Geraldine Ferraro as their vice presidential nominee. In his remarks at the spaghetti dinner, Reagan referred to the Pope's having said the Sandinista government was oppressing the Catholic Church.

VOA's reporting of Reagan's rhetoric on subjects like Nicaragua, Cuba, and the Soviet Union inevitably reflected a hard–line tone, simply because we were reporting what he said. We also reported criticism of his policies, just as we had reported criticism of Jimmy Carter's policies and those of previous presidents. And that's where the newsroom felt pressure. It was instructed by VOA's management to be "balanced" in writing news stories — that is, to present the administration's side whenever a story reported criticism of its policies. An example was a note to editors in September 1983 referring to a correspondent's report on Mondale's negative comments about Reagan's policy in Lebanon. The note advised broadcasters to follow it "with a balancing statement to the effect that the Reagan administration says its policy is geared toward achieving peace in the Middle East."

Basically there was nothing wrong with such an advisory, though it may have seemed to be stretching. Fair reporting demands reporting both sides of an issue. Failing to report an administration's position when it is under attack would be journalistically remiss. It should be noted that it isn't always easy to be balanced. A correspondent stationed overseas, say in New Delhi or Beijing, or a correspondent covering a candidate on the campaign trail, may not always have the information needed to report both sides. In any case, the reminders about "balance" were unnecessary, and were greeted with suspicion by many in the newsroom, who saw them as pressure to put the administration in a favorable light, and thus slant the news.

This suspicion was understandable in view of the daily editorials VOA began broadcasting during the Reagan administration, editorials to reflect the U.S. government's opinion. They were written by a "policy office" staff, composed largely of ultra–conservatives — and totally separated from the news operation. I wasn't able to listen to them, but VOA colleagues, distressed by their content, brought some of the texts to my attention. They were dismayingly strident, and a number even exceeded Reagan's rhetoric.

No wonder, then, that an American listener living in Rhodes, Greece, the site of one of VOA's transmitting stations, wrote a scathing criticism of the Voice in an op–ed piece in *The New York Times* March 19, 1984. The writer, Sally G. Greenway, said that "in the last three years the content of its English–language broadcasts has become so blatantly self-serving of Reagan administration policies that in Greece it is no more credible — and perhaps a little less so — than Radio Moscow." She also said, "In the five years since I made its daily acquaintance, the VOA has degenerated from an innocuous, often entertaining mix of news and varied features to an organ for right–wing tirades."

This terrible indictment — comparing VOA to Moscow Radio?! — was unwarranted so far as the news was concerned. The newscasts reported Reagan's statements, yes, and his critics' statements as well. But were the newscasts and the editorials separate in the minds of listeners? All of us in news who cared about VOA's credibility were troubled by the editorials.

VOA Director Ken Tomlinson and other Voice officials, however, said they saw few signs that the editorials were undermining VOA's credibility, according to an August 31 *New York Times* article. The writer, Stephen Engelberg, reported that "in the past two weeks, the editorials have discussed a number of topics near and dear to the president's heart. One told the story of a Cuban teacher who defected after being sent to Nicaragua to help the Sandinistas. Another attacked the sale of drugs to the United States by communist countries. Yet another ridiculed the impending elections in Nicaragua."

Tomlinson told *The Times* the Voice of America Charter requires the broadcasts to present the views of the administration, and was quoted as saying: "Someone complained that 'your editorials sound just like Ronald Reagan,' and I said you're darn right and I'm proud of it. The editorials should reflect the viewpoint of the party in power."

The Charter requirement is that "VOA will present the policies of the United States clearly and effectively." And, "VOA will also present responsible discussion and opinion on these policies."

The article appeared as Tomlinson was finishing two years at VOA; he was returning to *Reader's Digest* as managing editor. The reporter noted, and I agree, that he had campaigned to raise VOA's visibility in Congress and worldwide. Congress appropriated the first instalment of funds requested by the Reagan administration for a modernization program to increase the number of VOA transmitters and thus improve its signal to reach more listeners. Our audience in 1984 was estimated at 110 million people over the age of 15 who tuned in at least once a week. Under Tomlinson, VOA began publishing a magazine, *Voice*, that contained program schedules and articles about VOA and its broadcasters and was distributed to listeners overseas. The magazine then was printed six times a year and its circulation was limited, only 85,000, because of costs. It was much in demand, but budget cuts forced VOA to end publication during the Bush administration.

While it was still being published, though, it prompted a letter from a listener in Lagos that makes me laugh every time I think about it. It was written by a young man who began by saying "Your voice makes many ears tickle with sweet melody." He said he had "ransacked a pile of the *Voice* magazine" to look for my picture and found it in the July/August/September 1984 issue. And then he said: "Your voice is very much younger than your looks. Bravo!"

15
The 1984 Campaign
Bitburg and Bergen–Belsen
Radio Marti

Covering Reagan was never dull. He was hypnotic. It was fascinating to watch him turn adverse situations to his advantage. He was a snake oil salesman who peddled his policies successfully, even those that were prescriptions with a warning label. He was consistent in espousing his ideology, although his performance didn't always match his rhetoric. He got himself into pickles and controversies and managed to get out unscathed. He was, as Representative Patricia Schroeder rightly branded him, the "Teflon president."

Reagan was perplexing. At times he seemed asleep at the switch, bumbling a question about his administration's policy on this or that. Did he not know the answer? Or was he purposely evasive? Did he owe his successes to his advisors, and to luck, or was he astute? In any case, he came through as a leader.

He was humorous, fast on his feet with ad libs, and a challenge to cover, for instance in interpreting his quips to overseas listeners. Try to explain his saying that he'd had it up to his "keister" with something or other. In airing that soundbite, I told VOA listeners he was using an idiom indicating that his frustration and disgust had grown as high as his derriere. One of the pickles he got himself into involved a joke he made while testing the microphone before delivering his Saturday radio speech August 11, 1984. "My fellow Americans," he said, "I'm pleased to tell you today that I've signed legislation that will outlaw Russia forever. We begin bombing in five minutes."

This drew predictably critical commentaries in the Soviet press and then a government statement which called it "unprecedentedly hostile toward the USSR and dangerous to the cause of peace." The State Department responded, accusing Moscow of "blowing this subject way out of proportion for propaganda purposes." The incident and its fallout received wide press coverage, and White House and campaign aides sought to minimize the damage. Among them was the chairman of the Republican National Committee, Frank Fahrenkopf, who appeared on VOA's Press Conference USA, a weekly half–hour interview program similar to the Sunday network TV interview shows. It was recorded in Dallas, where Republicans were preparing to hold their national convention and nominate Reagan for election to a second term. Fahrenkopf downplayed Reagan's remark as simply a jest and said he did not think it would have a long–standing effect.

He was right; the incident had little if any impact. A month after the "jest," public opinion polls showed that Reagan's lead over his Democratic challenger, Walter Mondale, was sizable. And Reagan announced on September 11 that he would meet with Soviet Foreign Minister Andrei Gromyko later that month. As I reported, he rejected suggestions that scheduling the meeting was a political ploy aimed at responding to Mondale, who had criticized him for not having met with a Soviet leader. Reagan also upped the amount of grain the U.S. was willing to sell to the Soviet Union.

Before his meeting with Gromyko, the president addressed the United Nations and proposed high–level U.S.–Soviet talks, including "umbrella talks" on arms control negotiations. In his speech he discussed regional issues and reaffirmed U.S. support for the efforts of U.N. officials to find a diplomatic settlement on Afghanistan. My report noted that "he did not refer specifically to the Soviet occupation, which he has denounced in the past." The Reagan–Gromyko meeting took place September 28 at the White House, and a few days later, while on the campaign trail, the president described it as "very constructive."

Still later in the campaign Reagan said he should not have said what he did in making a joke about bombing the Soviet Union. At the same time, however, he said the news media also share in a responsibility "for national security," and he did not think the media should have "spread" the story. The press was a convenient scapegoat. Anyone with experience in radio, which Reagan certainly had, should know that you never say anything untoward, even a joke, in front of a microphone. It might be live. Reagan's Saturday radio speeches were carried on the White House mult, so we could tape them, and we could always hear his talkup and microphone checks — and his jokes with the technicians.

Reagan's campaign for re-election was a flag-waving extravaganza, accompanied by the relentlessly repeated sound of Lee Greenwood singing "I'm proud to be an American." Pride in America and confidence in its future were themes of the campaign as the president set about pre-empting patriotism for the Republicans. In his acceptance speech in Dallas, he accused the Democrats of offering "pessimism, fear and limits" for the future, and asserted the Republicans offered "a Springtime of hope for America."

The first of two debates by Reagan and Mondale took place October 7 in Louisville, and, as in previous presidential debates I'd covered, it was hard to determine the outcome immediately. My wrapup began: "President Reagan and his opponent Walter Mondale exchanged their differing views on taxes and other domestic issues in a spirited and sometimes barbed debate. Mr. Mondale, as expected, challenged Mr. Reagan on the huge government budget deficit. The president, also as expected, insisted his policies will continue economic growth and that will help bring the deficit down." But later in the wrapup there was a clue as to how the debate would be perceived: "Mr. Mondale, who has acknowledged his performance on television is not a strong suit for him, seemed at ease and comfortable. Mr. Reagan at times did not seem quite so comfortable."

The debate story in *The Washington Post*, by David Hoffman and Milton Coleman, also had a general lead and further down a clue, noting that the president "spent much of the evening defending himself, at times with obvious unease."

Both sides claimed victory, but Reagan campaign aides conceded that Mondale did well. Within a short time, polls found that Mondale was the winner, and questions were raised about Reagan's age.

After reporting on the Sunday night debate, I switched to covering Mondale, joining the press corps accompanying him to

New York. "Walter Mondale took his revived campaign for the White House to New York City's Columbus Day parade," I reported Monday, "and got a tremendous reception," with New York Governor Mario Cuomo proclaiming a turnout estimated at a million and a half. Mondale, Ferraro and Cuomo marched together in the parade behind a mounted unit, producing some of the most memorable photos of the 1984 campaign as they stepped gingerly over droppings from the horses. At a rally in New York, Senator Daniel Patrick Moynihan declared the Mondale campaign was "born again in Louisville." Later that day in Philadelphia, Mondale was welcomed as "the greater debater."

On Tuesday the lead story in *The Wall Street Journal* was headlined, "New Question in Race: Is Oldest U.S. President Now Showing His Age?" and a subhead said, "Reagan Debate Performance Invites Open Speculation On His Ability to Serve." Written by Rich Jaroslovsky and James M. Perry, the story said, "Until Sunday night's debate, age hadn't been much of an issue in the election campaign," and, "The president's rambling responses and occasional apparent confusion injected an unpredictable new element into the race."

Reagan fired back the next day. As Don Fulsom reported from the White House, he charged that the Democrats were engaged in a "desperate reaching" in trying to make his age a campaign issue. House Speaker Thomas "Tip" O'Neill had said the president "looked tired" in the debate. Reagan denied he was tired and said, "with regard to the age issue and everything, if I had as much makeup on as he did, I'd look younger too." Mondale, campaigning in Pittsburgh, countered with: "The problem in the debate was not makeup on the face; it was the makeup of the answers." Senator Paul Laxalt, Reagan's friend and campaign chairman, blamed the president's pre–debate briefings — too many facts and figures — for his performance.

The following week I resumed covering the president's campaign as he prepared for the second debate, to take place October 21 in Kansas City. In a scenesetter, I reported that Reagan would be under pressure to counter the age issue and the subject would be defense and foreign policy, "areas where a president must tread carefully because everything he says is scrutinized." As for his preparations for the final debate, "the president had what in effect were dress rehearsals earlier in the week." These were campaign rally speeches in which he charged that Mondale's record on defense was weak, and questioned Mondale's grasp of foreign affairs.

When the debate took place, Reagan repeated lines from those speeches, while Mondale hit hard at the leadership issue, criticizing Reagan's record on arms control, Lebanon and Central America. The issue that grabbed attention, though, was the president's age, 73. Henry Trewhitt (*Baltimore Sun*) brought it up, asking if there was any doubt in his mind that he would be able to function in a crisis. Reagan replied: "Not at all, Mr. Trewhitt, and I want you to know that also I will not make age an issue of this campaign. I am not going to exploit for political purposes my opponent's youth and inexperience." Mondale was 56. My report included the tape of Reagan's answer, along with sound of the laughter and applause that followed. The president, one of his aides said, clearly had put the age issue to bed.

Nancy Reagan provided a bit of news the next day as the president flew to California for a speech. She was asked by the travel pool on Air Force One if she thought her husband would go to the Soviet Union in a second term. "I think he'd like to," she said, "I'd love to." Her comment was certainly of interest to VOA's listeners in the Soviet Union, and also in view of the campaign issue of U.S.–Soviet relations, and I wrote a sidebar about it.

Reagan's campaign audiences were large and exuberant, especially college students who enthusiastically chorused "USA, USA, USA." At some rallies there were small groups of hecklers, usually protesting his policy in Central America, but they were drowned out by chants of "USA" or "Four more years." Reagan frequently spoke of the "rescue mission" in Grenada, declaring, "We set a nation free." One such occasion was on October 23, the anniversary of the Marine Barracks bombing in Beirut. Predictably, he didn't mention that.

Reporting some of the nonsensical aspects of campaigns to overseas listeners was a challenge, for instance a rally in a giant suburban Chicago sports arena on November 4. The president and the vice president and their wives made an astonishing entrance riding on a bright red fire engine truck. It circled the arena while a band played and Frankie Avalon led the partisan thousands in a frantic rendition of the song, "Today." I couldn't resist describing the scene and inserting a tape of Reagan repeating the usual close of his campaign speeches: "America's best days are yet to come. And I'm going to say something — I know it drives my opponent up the wall, but I enjoy saying it — You ain't seen nothin' yet!"

On his last day of campaigning as a candidate for public office, Reagan returned to his political birthplace for a series of rallies in California. As he had throughout his administration, he criticized the Carter administration in nearly every campaign speech, and he did so again, recalling "the days of torpor, timidity, and taxes." In San Diego, he spoke at the Fashion Valley Shopping Center, where he had ended his 1980 campaign, and now was ending this one, with opinion polls indicating he would win re-election by a landslide. After his pronouncement, "you ain't seen nothin' yet," was a something-to-see finale: Skydivers dressed in patriotic colors sailing down from above, thousands of red, white and blue balloons sailing up into the sky, and fireworks.

On election day the president and Nancy voted in the neat little town of Solvang, near their mountaintop ranch. That night, Reagan supporters gathered in the main ballroom of the Century Plaza Hotel in Los Angeles for their victory celebration. While waiting for the president's arrival, I filed reports for VOA's live coverage of the returns. Fortunately I had some news to impart. Reagan had had a chat with some reporters earlier in the day and expressed a desire for a U.S.-Soviet summit meeting. The crowd in the ballroom was ecstatic when the president finally appeared and declared in his victory statement that America's best days lay ahead.

After his landslide victory — 525 electoral votes to Mondale's 13 (from Minnesota and D.C.), and a popular vote of 59 to 41 percent, — Reagan flew to his ranch the next morning for a few days relaxation. At a mini–press conference before leaving Los Angeles, he said he thought "the people made it very plain that they approved of what we're doing."

Ronald Wilson Reagan embarked on his second term after taking the oath of office on Sunday, January 20, the Constitutionally required date, in a private ceremony at the White House, and again on Monday, in an inaugural ceremony held in the rotunda of the Capitol instead of outdoors because of bitter cold weather. In his inaugural address, Reagan reaffirmed his intention to seek reduction of nuclear weapons in negotiations with the Soviet Union. He commented further on that during an interview the following Saturday — with the independent radio networks. Yes, Reagan had a half–hour interview with the radio correspondents from the White House basement press room!

Seven of us filed into the Roosevelt Room and settled ourselves in dark brown leather armchairs at the rectangular table. We were to ask our questions in alphabetical order, so we were seated that way, with AP–Radio's Candy Crowley on the president's left and so on around the table. Since VOA was last in the order, I ended up seated at the president's right.

Candy asked: "Mr. President, shortly before today's announcement that U.S.–Soviet negotiators would meet in Geneva March 12th, one of your top advisors to those talks, Ambassador (Paul) Nitze, said that he could not say that chances for an agreement are very good. Is that so?" Reagan's answer was that he was optimistic, although not euphoric, about the coming talks. Next was Mutual's Nelson Benton (formerly of CBS), who asked what effect Soviet leader Chernenko's "apparent infirmity" might have on the talks. In brief, Reagan said the fact that the Soviets had set a date, and named their negotiators, led him to believe they intended to go forward.

After questions dealing with the budget deficit, defense spending, criticism of administration policies by black leaders, and Nicaragua, it was finally my turn. And I flubbed it. "Mr. President, are you going to try to revive your Middle East peace initiative when Saudi Arabia's Prince Fahd and Egyptian President Mubarak come to see you in the next two months?" To my chagrin I discovered later when I listened to the tape that I had mis-spoken. Fahd wasn't Prince, he was King. (Fahd had become king in 1982, succeeding King Khalid, who succeeded King Faisal, who was assassinated in 1975.) I don't think anyone in the Roosevelt Room noticed my gaffe, but I fretted over what listeners in the Mideast must have thought. In his answer Reagan said the Fahd and Mubarak visits were unrelated, but that he was "quite sure" his Mideast peace proposal would be part of the discussions with both leaders.

In the round of Q-and-A that followed, Reagan said he would stay over in West Germany for a state visit after the 1985 economic summit, to be held in Bonn, and replied "no" when asked if he would possibly observe the V-E Day anniversary with the Soviets. He said that if there were an observance, it would be with his German hosts, and added that he hoped it would not be "the rejoicing of victory and recalling all of the hatred that went on at the time. I hope we'll recognize it now as the day that democracy and freedom and peace began, and friendship between erstwhile enemies."

At that point, we ran out of time. VOA broadcast the whole interview, and I filed wrapups leading with the arms control answer. The session may not have produced earth-shaking news, but we were happy that the White House had finally granted us long-ignored basement radio correspondents an interview with the president. Mutual's broadcast booth, I should note, was in the upper press room but its correspondents were considered part of our basement group. I should also note that it was of great satisfaction to me that VOA's inclusion in the interview was automatically assumed, by both my fellow correspondents and the White House.

Chernenko died March 10 and Reagan sent Bush, who was in Geneva at the time, to Moscow for the funeral. This was Bush's third trip for the funeral of a Soviet leader, and it brought to mind a story he had told during the campaign. Bush said Ferraro asked him, "Just in case Fritz and I win, just what does the vice president do?" and he replied, "Let me put it this way, Geraldine, buy yourself a black hat with a veil."

President Reagan is interviewed, in a rare session for the basement radio correspondents, January 1985 in the Roosevelt Room of the White House. At Reagan's right are Jurey; Gene Gibbons, UPI–Radio, and Bob Ellison, Sheridan Radio. At Reagan's left (backs to camera), Candy Crowley, AP–Radio; Nelson Benton, Mutual; Jim Angle, NPR, and Joe Ewalt, RKO (United Stations). Seated on sofa in background, Robert Sims of the White House Press Office and Larry Speakes, the president's chief spokesman. (White House photo)

Reagan said he was willing to meet with Chernenko's successor, Mikhail Gorbachev, that Bush would discuss the matter with him while in Moscow, and that he was pleased the arms control negotiations would begin as scheduled. The president flew to Quebec the following week for talks with Canada's Prime Minister Brian Mulroney that included arms control, the new Soviet leadership, and a subject that was an irritant in U.S.-Canadian relations — acid rain. Canadians thought the U.S. wasn't doing enough to solve the problem of pollution from American industries and automobile exhausts that affected the environment on both sides of the border. The two leaders agreed on a joint effort to examine the issue and announced it on the first day of their talks.

This was St. Patrick's Day, so their meeting was dubbed the Shamrock Summit; there was a celebration, and there was wearin' of the green in the French–Canadian city. Members of the traveling press (103 men/20 women) were greeted with an advisory from the White House press advance office which said it was ESSENTIAL to wear our green trip passes at all times. Reagan wore a bright green tie on his arrival in Quebec, and Shultz a green pocket handkerchief. That night Canadian performing artists staged a gala in the Grand Theatre of Quebec in honor of the presidential party. Many of the songs were French, but the finale was a St. Patrick's Day spectacular, featuring folkdancers and folksingers in an Irish pub setting. The president and prime minister and their wives, Nancy Reagan and Yugoslav–born Mila Mulroney both wearing green gowns, left their box and joined the cast on stage in singing "When Irish Eyes Are Smiling." VOA engineer Gary Jaffe and I put together a "color" feature with tape of the singing that closed with Mulroney doing a solo of the last line, "Sure they steal your heart away."

A "color" feature, literally, dealt with Reagan's press conference on March 21. As I explained to VOA listeners: "Reporters seek to get the president's attention by raising their hands, but some have concluded this isn't enough. For some time now, many of the women correspondents have worn bright clothing, particularly in the color red, so they will stand out in the sea of raised hands. Some of the male correspondents have worn red ties. Thus it wasn't any coincidence that at this press conference, eight female reporters were dressed in red." On the day of the press conference, *The Wall Street Journal* carried a story by its White House correspondent, Jane Mayer, on "The Redding of the White House Press Corps," in which she noted that red seemed to be First Lady Nancy Reagan's favorite color, and the president's as well.

After Reagan made his opening statement, he recognized Helen Thomas: "And now, Helen, I know that Nancy upstairs would die — she's watching on television — if I didn't call on you in that pretty red dress." Helen said that's why she wore it. Seated next to Helen was Lesley Stahl, wearing — a red dress. She was called on later. And Jane Mayer, as Reagan noted in recognizing her, also was dressed in red.

At a subsequent press conference, Johanna Neuman (*USA Today*) got Reagan's attention when she raised her hand. She wore a red mitten. Red or no, the president always called on the AP and UPI correspondents by tradition and invariably recognized those from the networks, major newspapers, and newsmagazines. There wasn't much time left for questions from other correspondents. In the March 21 press conference, only 17 reporters were called on.

Many of the questions at Reagan's press conferences in 1985, and at the daily White House briefings, dealt with Nicaragua and his effort to overcome congressional resistance to aid for the anti–Sandinistas. Congress had banned military aid to the Contras the year before. An amendment, named after Congressman Edward Boland and approved in October, prohibited the CIA, Defense Department, or any other entity involved in intelligence activities from "supporting, directly or indirectly, military or paramilitary operations by any nation, group, organization or individual" in Nicaragua.

In trying to make the case for Contra aid, Reagan sharpened his rhetoric. In a speech March 1 to a conservative political action committee, he even declared that the "freedom fighters" in Nicaragua "are the moral equal of our founding fathers and the brave men and women of the French resistance." To avoid a legislative defeat, the president gave up his request for military aid in April and agreed to a compromise proposal for $14 million in humanitarian, or non–lethal, aid to the Contras. It was killed when the House voted against it.

Reagan had bigger troubles on his hands at the time — the storm over his plan, announced April 11, to visit the German military cemetery at Bitburg. Among the approximately 2,000 buried there, it quickly became known, were nearly 50 troopers of Hitler's hated Nazi Waffen SS. Jewish groups and veterans organizations were outraged, I reported, over his decision to visit the cemetery but not to visit a site in memory of the victims of the Nazis. On April 15, Larry Speakes told reporters that Mike Deaver and another aide would be leaving that evening for Germany, at the request of Donald T. Regan, the new White House chief of staff, to look at "other opportunities" for events on the president's schedule, including the possibility of a concentration camp. Regan, treasury secretary in Reagan's first term, had switched jobs with James Baker in January.

The next day, a Tuesday, the president announced to a conference on religious liberty that he would go to a concentration camp as well as the cemetery during the May visit. He explained that his earlier decision (not to go to Dachau) was based on a mistaken impression of the official agenda. In words reminiscent of what he told us radio correspondents in January, Reagan said his purpose was "not to re–emphasize the crimes of the Third Reich" but "to celebrate the tremendous accomplishments of the German people in 40 years of freedom, democracy and peace." He said he and Chancellor Kohl had agreed to lay a wreath at the cemetery "to cement the 40 years of friendship between a free Germany and the United States."

In my broadcast piece on his remarks, I reported that Jewish leaders welcomed his decision to visit a concentration camp but said they still objected to his visiting the cemetery. After a White House meeting with Don Regan, Chairman Kenneth Bialkin of the Conference of Presidents of Major American Jewish Organizations said they had no objection in principle to honoring the German war dead but were unanimously opposed to Bitburg because those buried there included "officers guilty of crimes which cannot be forgiven." One of the Jewish leaders was Elie Wiesel, the chairman of the U.S. Holocaust Memorial Council, who was scheduled to receive the Congressional Gold Medal from the president in a White House ceremony on Friday.

Fifty–three members of the U.S. Senate also urged Reagan to cancel the cemetery visit. But he insisted that cancelling it would hurt U.S.–German relations and would leave him looking as though he had "caved in" to unfavorable attention. The cemetery at Bitburg was chosen, he told a group of editors, because American servicemen were stationed nearby and he would be having lunch with them. My report included a tape excerpt in which he said, "I think there's nothing wrong with visiting that cemetery, where those young men were victims of Nazism also, even though they were fighting in the German uniform, drafted into service to carry out the hateful wishes of the Nazis. They were victims just as surely as were the victims in the concentration camps."

When Friday's ceremony took place, I listened in VOA's basement cubby–hole as the president's words, then Elie Wiesel's, were transmitted from the Roosevelt Room via the White House mult. Wiesel said he was grateful to the president for being a friend of the Jewish people and for trying to help the oppressed Jews in the Soviet Union. He said he was convinced Reagan was not aware of the presence of SS graves in the Bitburg cemetery. "But now we are all aware," he said. "May I, Mr. President, if it's possible at all, implore you to do something else, to find a way — to find another way, another site. That place, Mr. President, is not your place. Your place is with the victims of the SS." There were tears in my eyes when he finished speaking.

After the ceremony, Larry Speakes announced at his noon briefing that Reagan would visit the former concentration camp of Bergen–Belsen. The president and chancellor would honor the victims of the Nazis in a commemorative ceremony there on May 5, and then would go ahead with the visit to the cemetery. In my report for VOA, I led with the Bergen–Belsen announcement, said it came "shortly after one of the survivors of a Nazi concentration camp, Elie Wiesel, made a private and then impassioned public plea to the president not to go to Bitburg," and inserted tape of his remarks quoted above. I wished that I had more airtime, for there was so much eloquence, sadness, passion, in what he said. He recalled the liberation of Buchenwald. "Mr. President, I was there. I was there when American liberators arrived. And they gave us back our lives."

My story included tape of Reagan's remarks: "We who had not suffered the tragedy of the Holocaust directly shared their grief and mourned for their victims." He said that "today there is a spirit of reconciliation," and it "must grow and be strengthened." The pool reporter who was in the Roosevelt Room, David Hoffman, said Reagan listened intently as Wiesel spoke, and appeared most anguished and intent at the close of the speech as Wiesel talked about Bitburg. The president rose and applauded Wiesel at the end and left after shaking hands with him, David said, and Wiesel sank into a chair and mopped the sweat from his brow with a blue handkerchief.

The protests over Bitburg continued; more than 250 members of the House urged Kohl to drop the visit, and later even more urged Reagan to reconsider, and there was criticism from political commentators and newspaper editorials. A *Time* magazine story on the president's troubles, including Bitburg, the congressional rejection of Contra aid, and "worrisome rumbles" developing in the economy, bore the headline, "Scratches in the Teflon." A few days before the trip Chief of Staff Regan met with a group of correspondents and, as Gil Butler reported for VOA, "Mr. Regan said all President Reagan's life he has been known as a supporter of Jewish people, Jewish causes, and the state of Israel. . . . Now, Mr. Regan said, for an inadvertent thing, he gets criticism, so he's anguished." In his 1988 book, *For the Record*, Regan said Deaver told him that when the White House advance team had surveyed the cemetery in February it was covered with snow and the SS tombstones were not visible.

Chancellor Kohl said it was "most regrettable" that the president was having domestic difficulties over "the noble gesture he envisaged," and said he was grateful to him. Kohl also gave the precise number of Waffen SS soldiers buried at the cemetery, 49, and said 32 were under 25 when they died.

The Bitburg controversy clung to Reagan's stay in West Germany, which began with the 1985 economic summit in Bonn. The presidential party arrived in late morning Wednesday, May 1, with nothing on the press schedule for the rest of the day except for a Speakes briefing — and checking into our boats. Yes, boats. Hotel space was limited — Bonn was a relatively small capital, and a sleepy town at that — so the White House Transportation Office arranged lodging for many of the traveling press corps (192 men/22 women) aboard two Rhine River cruise ships. They were berthed at landings that were near the Bundestag and the International Press Center, and a nice walk of about 400 yards from the White House filing center at the Tulpenfeld Hotel. My boat, to my amusement, was the "Italia." Our cabins were tiny, but I found it cozy and comfortable to be lulled to sleep on my small pullout bed with the sounds of water lapping against the boat. My taller colleagues pointed out that of course I was comfortable, the beds were designed for people who were my size, a little over five feet tall, not theirs. Cozy or no, the most important thing about our cabins was that they were temporarily equipped with telephones, which worked. I filed some of my late–night wrapups from my room on the Rhine.

The Speakes briefing produced some news: Reagan imposed economic sanctions against Nicaragua, including a total embargo on trade. Speakes said the president did so "in response to the emergency situation created by the Nicaraguan government's aggressive activities in Central America." He cited "the new ties between Nicaragua and the Soviet Union announced by Tass in connection with Daniel Ortega's current trip to Moscow." The timing of the Nicaraguan leader's visit to Moscow to discuss economic assistance, so soon after the House rejected Contra aid, was an exquisite blunder. It gave the Reagan administration, and Republican allies in Congress, additional artillery in a renewed fight to win funds for the Contras. Partly because of the Ortega trip, the House of Representatives would, on June 12, approve $27 million in humanitarian aid, an amount adopted later as part of the foreign aid bill.

Reagan's economic summit partners didn't approve of his sanctions against Nicaragua, and there were other disagreements during the May conference. Mitterrand declined to join with the other leaders in supporting Reagan's call for a new round of trade negotiations to start in early 1986, and he didn't like Reagan's Star Wars research program either. Reagan's budget deficits also came under criticism. The conferees did, however, endorse his arms control proposals in the negotiations with the Soviet Union.

Covering the summit was an international press corps of 3,500. VOA had a good-sized contingent, including Bonn correspondent David Lent, economics correspondent Barry Wood, and a group of language service reporters who worked out of an office/studio in the International Press Center, along with radio technicians and a producer. VOA tech Bob Cole and I worked mainly at the White House filing center. Reporters were kept busy covering briefings, and anti–U.S. demonstrations too, but in essence we were marking time for the main events — Sunday's visits to Bergen–Belsen and Bitburg.

The logistics for covering them involved travel by plane, helicopter and chartered bus, and the timing was critical. The trip began shortly before 9 Sunday morning when our press plane left Bonn–Cologne Airport for Hannover, northeast of Bergen–Belsen. At the concentration camp, the sky was gray and the mood somber. On the way to the press area, we walked past heather–covered mounds — they were mass graves — and past the Jewish memorial, a tall stone monument to the 30,000 Jews who perished in the camp. More than 50,000 people, including non–Jews, died at Bergen–Belsen. At the press area, the camera platform faced the camp's obelisk, a stone pillar in front of a stone memorial wall with inscriptions in more than 20 languages.

There, Reagan spoke movingly of the victims of the Holocaust. He called his visit "this painful walk into the past." I followed his words on the advance text of his speech, underlining quotes I would use in my report, and penciling in a phrase he added. He said that in seeing "the emerging Springtime" of the German countryside on his flight from Hannover he had reflected that "there must have been a time when the prisoners at Bergen–Belsen, and those of every other camp, must have felt that Springtime was gone forever from their lives." Then he returned to the text: "Surely we can understand that when we see what is around us — all these children of God, under bleak and lifeless mounds, the plainness of which does not even hint at the unspeakable acts that created them. Here they lie. Never to hope. Never to pray. Never to love. Never to heal. Never to laugh. Never to cry."

He finished speaking at about 12:20 p.m. We radio correspondents had only a very short time to file at the white line "drop" at the camera platform, before boarding the press buses somewhere behind the memorial wall. I was last in the rotation this time, and when I finished my report — including the fact that Jewish leaders invited to the ceremony had boycotted it — no familiar face was in sight. And the buses were gone!

One of the fears a reporter has on a presidential trip, especially abroad, is missing a bus or plane and being left behind. And now this was happening to me? I ran to the front of the memorial wall in search of someone who could help me. No one there. I had to do something. I didn't want to miss going to Bitburg, and, dear God, I didn't want to be left alone in the isolation and doleful surroundings of a concentration camp. I heard sounds of helicopters in the distance and decided to run in that direction. I encountered a German camera crew and a few other Germans on the path, and forgot every bit of the German I learned in high school when I tried to ask them the whereabouts of the White House press corps. I was met with blank stares, and panicky, stumbled on. My equipment bag grew heavier, my breath shorter. At last I reached a helicopter landing area.

It was the one for the president's helicopter, and just then the press buses were driving up, on their way to the zone for the press choppers. A young White House press advance officer, Gary Foster, saw me, quickly took me in tow, hailed one of the buses, and helped me climb aboard. On the ride to the helicopters, I stowed my dangling microphone and recorder cables back into my gear bag, composed myself, and looked out the window at small clusters of demonstrators, who seemed angered by the presence of the American press.

Some 20 minutes after Reagan ended his speech at Bergen–Belsen, we were aboard sleekly modern German helicopters on our way to Hannover airport, arriving there a little after 1 p.m. We boarded the press plane and flew to the Bitburg air base, landing at about 2:15 p.m., and from there were bused to the cemetery — its name Kolmeshöhe. We arrived just before President and Mrs. Reagan and Chancellor Kohl and his wife Hannelore.

It was a very pretty little cemetery, just like those in any small town, and every grave was decorated with Spring flowers. The press area was off to the side, and I don't think any of us could discern where the Waffen SS graves were. I stood on the press table, along with a couple of my colleagues, and watched the wreath–laying ceremony. Altogether, the visit lasted eight muted minutes.

We returned to the air base, where Reagan delivered another eloquent speech, addressing American servicemen, their families, and invited German guests. In referring to the emotions stirred by his cemetery visit, he said, "Some old wounds have been reopened, and this I regret very much because this should be a time of healing." His audience was responsive to his theme of reconciliation. The people of Bitburg, population 12,500, and members of the American community, 10,500 counting military people stationed at the base and their dependents, were proud of their tradition of friendly relations, and upset about the Bitburg controversy. In the filing center at the air base, I filed a quick report to VOA, and then, shortly after 4 p.m., boarded the press plane to return to Bonn. David Lent, who had driven to Bitburg from Bonn, stayed on and filed a longer piece for VOA, including Kohl's remarks. Kohl thanked Reagan for visiting the cemetery with him and called it a gesture of reconciliation "which does not dismiss the past but enables us to overcome it by acting together."

In sorting out my thoughts later, I felt that the visits to Bergen–Belsen and the Bitburg cemetery were a sad, almost degrading experience because of our invasion of these two quiet places. We descended on the stillness of the concentration camp and the stillness of the cemetery with our microphones, tape recorders, cameras, lights, tripods, cables, and other equipment, and matter–of–factly went about our business of being observers. Yet this is what we had to do; we were covering the president. We would have protested if coverage wasn't allowed. The press, we argue, must go where the president goes. I agree with that, but being a reporter, not just covering the White House but covering small towns too, sometimes has its distasteful aspects.

I learned this early on, when two young brothers in New Castle were killed in an automobile crash and I was told by my editor at *The Vindicator* to get their pictures. I talked their mother into letting us have the photos (they were beautiful teenagers), and I dispatched them to the Youngstown office by bus (no fax then) in time for the Pennsylvania edition. Afterwards, I thought she took some comfort in having her sons memorialized with their photos printed in the paper. And I thought that maybe other parents who saw the pictures would be affected by the deaths of the two brothers and make sure their own children drove safely. Still, I felt degraded for having invaded the privacy of the mother's grief.

Despite my feelings, Bitburg was a big story; the president chose to go there and we covered it. And though there were protests in the U.S. and elsewhere, Reagan, by speaking so movingly at Bergen–Belsen and then at the air base, extricated himself from the controversy with minimal damage.

A major theme of his trip was that democracy and freedom bring opportunity and hope, and he sounded it in a speech Monday to thousands of applauding West German young people at Hambach Castle, a restored hilltop citadel to the south of Bonn, and during his visits to Spain and Portugal. In Madrid, there were demonstrations in the streets, protesting U.S. bases in Spain and U.S. policy in Central America, but Reagan apparently got along well with Spanish leaders despite differences over Nicaragua. In covering the Madrid events, I joined my former White House colleague, Jane Berger, then based in VOA's London bureau. One of the pleasures of going on presidential trips overseas was to have reunions with friends stationed around the world.

Reagan's next stop was Strasbourg, France, to deliver a speech on the 40th anniversary of the allied victory in Europe to a special session of the European Parliament. The advance text of his address was newsy, with Reagan blasting the Soviet Union while proposing steps to solve problems in U.S.-Soviet relations, and it had some good rhetoric, such as, "It is my fervent wish that in the next century there will be one, free Europe."

The story turned out to be much newsier. Reagan was heckled repeatedly by leftist and communist members of the parliament, who shouted things like, "Hands off Nicaragua," "Nuclear freeze now," and "Star Wars no." Thirty or so of the 434-member body staged a walkout, and others held up signs, many having to do with Nicaragua. Reagan didn't appear perturbed and plowed on. He also had trouble with the teleprompter, we learned later. At the end of his nearly 45-minute speech, he added to his text, and I scribbled furiously as he told the parliament: "I would like to just conclude with one line, if I could, and say we've seen some evidence here of your faith in democracy, in the ability of some to speak up freely, as they preferred to speak. And yet I can't help but remind all of us that some who take advantage of that right of democracy seem unaware that if the government that they would advocate became reality, no one would have that freedom to speak up again."

Reagan got a standing ovation, and enthusiastic table-thumping accompanied the prolonged applause. Once more he had turned a negative situation to his favor. I quickly updated my story, and topped it with the hecklers and the president's response. Despite the interruptions, he drew frequent applause from the parliament, an advisory body for the European Community that was composed of members from parties covering the whole political spectrum. White House aides said the performance of the hecklers was not out of the ordinary and was fully expected.

In Lisbon, our final stop, Mark Weinberg of the White House Press Office staff told pool reporters it was likely that communist members of the Portuguese Assembly would walk out or not show up when Reagan addressed the assembly. A few boycotted the session, and 35 walked out as he was preparing to speak. His speech, on democracy, was well received however, and one of the bursts of applause came when he said that "trust in the individual — the right to speak, to assemble, to publish and to vote, even to walk out — that is the meaning of democracy."

On May 27, Reagan went to Arlington National Cemetery to lay a wreath at the Tomb of the Unknown Soldier in tribute to America's war dead. A young man from Radio Marti, the new Spanish–language broadcast service to Cuba, came up to me and asked if I would tell him about Bitburg so he could write a piece comparing the wreath–laying ceremony at Arlington with the one at the German military cemetery. I was flabbergasted. I told him there was no comparison to be made, and left wondering what in the world he was thinking of. What's to compare, and why?

Radio Marti had been planned, as part of Project Truth, since Reagan's first year in office, and its creation was aided and abetted by Cuban exiles in Florida whose goal was to unseat Castro. Reagan's intent was to place Radio Marti under the Board for International Broadcasting, on the grounds that its mission was "akin to Radio Free Europe and Radio Liberty," the surrogate stations that broadcast to Eastern Europe and the Soviet Union and were overseen by the BIB. But Congress put it under VOA to be sure it would live up to the standards in the VOA Charter.

In signing the Radio Broadcasting to Cuba Act two years earlier, on October 4, 1983, Reagan said it responded to an "important foreign policy initiative" of his administration: "To break Fidel Castro's monopoly on information within Cuba." He recorded a special broadcast to the Cuban people, aired on VOA January 5, 1984, to promote the new service, "named for your great Cuban patriot, Jose Marti." His message was that the Castro government was censoring information and that Radio Marti would correct this "injustice." VOA was already broadcasting in Spanish and English to the region, and reported on developments in Cuba as well as Cuban involvement in other countries. But Radio Marti was a pet project of the administration and allies in Congress, particularly those with large Cuban–American constituencies.

Many of us in VOA news were not happy to have Radio Marti placed under the Voice. It was set up as a separate entity, with its own staff, newsroom, studios and offices located in a different building from the VOA headquarters building. But still it was considered part of VOA. Its White House correspondent, for instance, wore a press pass with identification as a VOA correspondent. And we were skeptical about whether it would adhere to VOA's standards. The plans for Radio Marti prompted my colleagues in the White House press to joke that it would put a "Havana Hannah" on the air to broadcast propaganda.

When Radio Marti began broadcasting May 20, 1985, the Castro government retaliated by declaring suspension of the Mariel Agreement under which more than 2,700 Cuban refugees not acceptable to the U.S. as immigrants were being returned to Cuba. These refugees, many of them criminals, were among the huge influx of Cubans who came to the U.S. in the 1980 Mariel boatlift. At the White House, I reported, Larry Speakes said Radio Marti's purpose was "to provide the people of Cuba with accurate, balanced and objective news," and that its first broadcasts included a news item on the Cuban government's retaliation.

Radio Marti started out broadcasting 14 and a half hours a day every day, using a frequency that previously had been used for VOA broadcasts to the region. To attract listeners, it carried a soap opera serial featuring a heroine named Esmerelda. The Cubans did indeed tune in. Esmerelda was very popular. In any event, creation of a radio service beamed only to Cuba diverted funding that VOA could have used in broadcasting to countries around the world.

VOA broadcasts were not only a source of information for listeners overseas but were also quoted in newspaper stories in some countries. For example, I was given a copy of the June 13, 1985, edition of the Bangladesh daily newspaper, *The New Nation*, which carried two front–page stories with information attributed to VOA, one of them based on a report I'd broadcast. That story said: "President Reagan yesterday welcomed Indian Prime Minister Rajiv

Gandhi to the United States and the two leaders held talks on a wide range of issues. VOA's White House correspondent Philomena Jury (sic) reported last night that the President and the Prime Minister exchanged warm words of greeting at the ceremony of welcome on the White House south lawn." It also reported, as I had, that the two leaders acknowledged differences between the U.S. and India but stressed what the two countries have in common, and that during the ceremony shouts could be heard from Sikh demonstrators protesting the visit and Indian policy.

The other story was: "The hijackers of a Jordanian plane in Beirut yesterday escaped after releasing most of their hostages and blowing up the plane's cockpit, VOA reported last night." That incident was followed within 24 hours by another airliner hijacking that commanded world attention for 17 days. TWA flight 847 with 153 persons aboard, including 104 Americans, was on its way from Athens to Rome on June 14 when it was hijacked and ordered to fly to Beirut. The armed hijackers, identified as Shiite Moslem extremists, demanded the release of more than 700 Shiite Moslems held by Israel. Some of the hostages were let go in Beirut and others in Algiers, where the plane had flown twice under orders from the hijackers, returning to Beirut each time.

The White House called for the prompt and safe release of all the hostages, and urged Lebanese Shiite Amal leader Nabih Berri to use his influence with the hijackers. Don Fulsom and I filed reports every day on the hostage situation. Our stories included word that Israel had said previously it would release the Shiite Moslems, and that if the hostages were freed, the Israelis would go ahead with their plans. At a press conference June 18, Reagan vowed the United States will never give in to terrorists and called on those holding the American passengers to release them without condition. He urged Lebanese political and religious leaders to "end this crime now" and called on other governments to use their influence. Several days later, Larry Speakes said the U.S. had been in "close touch" with Syria and noted that President Assad had expressed a desire to be helpful and was in a position to do so. The crisis ended June 30 when a Red Cross convoy transported the 39 American hostages across the Lebanese–Syrian border to Damascus. In an address to the nation that evening, Reagan declared: "The United States gives terrorists no rewards and no guarantees. We make no concessions; we make no deals."

During the hostage ordeal one American was killed. Navy diver Robert Stethem was beaten and shot to death, then thrown from the plane. The president and Mrs. Reagan placed flowers at his grave in Arlington National Cemetery on July 2 before going to Andrews Air Force Base that afternoon to welcome the freed Americans home. Reagan told them it was a time of rejoicing but also that the United States would not forget Stethem was murdered — and would not forget the seven other American hostages who had been kidnaped earlier and were held captive in Lebanon.

16
Advice from Dr. Reagan
RR and Gorby
The Geneva and Reykjavik Summits

"I lack words," the letter said, "to express the emotional passion that gripped me when I tuned to VOA to hear the president was to undergo a surgery to remove a pre–cancerous growth in his large intestine. Even though I heard reassuring words from the head of the surgical team, nevertheless, given the vagaries of nature, I felt duty–bound to contribute my quota in prayer and in this worded message. Hence I enclose a card here for the president. . . . It is a card in which I wish him a very speedy recovery. . . ."

Dated July 13, 1985, the letter was from a Nigerian, one of many VOA listeners who sent me get–well cards addressed to the president and asked that I deliver them.

Our listeners were extremely interested in American presidents. Many wrote asking for presidential photos. Others wanted information; for instance, a man in Warsaw asked, "What is Mr. Reagan's favorite car make?" And others sent me messages to pass on, like this one from a man in Budapest, "Please inform the president that I am very happy that he has been chosen again for the next four years."

It is a given, I think, that the illness of any American president is a matter of interest, if not concern, to people and governments around the world. Whenever a president goes to the hospital, even for a routine examination, VOA carries a news item about it. That was the case Friday afternoon, July 12, when Reagan went to the Bethesda, Maryland, Naval Medical Center for what was regarded as a routine surgical procedure, removal of a benign polyp that had been discovered in his intestine during his physical exam in March. But when Larry Speakes briefed us at the White House later that day, we all scribbled furiously in our notepads, then rushed to our phones with the news: "The president will undergo surgery Saturday for removal of a growth in his intestine that is described as appearing pre–cancerous."

Larry told us a larger growth, appearing to be of a pre–cancerous type, was discovered in the cecum, the pouch forming the first part of the large intestine. He said doctors gave Reagan the choice of waiting two or three weeks for surgery, but that the president made the decision to proceed immediately. In reporting what Larry said, I also told VOA's listeners that he "quoted the Navy doctor who will perform the operation, Dr. Dale Oller, as saying the 74–year–old president is in superior condition and chances for a normal and full recovery are excellent."

Saturday morning the White House press operation moved to the hospital, and we reporters worked at a filing center set up in one of its buildings.

The president's surgery lasted just short of three hours. The team of doctors told us afterwards that a portion of the colon containing the polyp had been removed and the president was doing "very, very well." There was no immediate word on whether the growth was cancerous, pending completion of a study by pathologists. If it turned out to be malignant, it was "very likely" that the surgery solved the problem.

While the president was under anesthesia, and then in the recovery room, Vice President Bush was in effect acting president, for a total of about eight hours. Reagan had notified Congress just before the operation that Bush would discharge the Constitutional powers and duties of the Office of President in his stead while he was temporarily unable to do so. The president, I reported, thus was acting in compliance with a Constitutional amendment dealing with presidential disability, although he did not specifically invoke that amendment.

In filing reports while Reagan was in the operating room, I had a dispute with my office. Not about content, but an arbitrary rule — a time limit of one minute for correspondent reports for our 10-minute hourly English newscasts. It was imposed so that the newscasts would have space to carry a full rundown of stories on regional and international developments. On weekdays, we could broadcast longer reports in our 20-minute news programs, but on weekends only the 10-minute newscasts were aired.

I had tried to cram all the information about the operation and the transfer of power to Bush into a minute — 12 lines of copy for the pace at which we broadcast our reports — but I ran over by 20 seconds. A rule-bound staffer phoned me and took me to task for exceeding the limit. I protested vehemently. Here was the president of the United States, the leader of the Western World, the leader of one of the two superpowers, under the surgeon's knife! I insisted that people overseas were interested in knowing about the operation, and in knowing that the U.S. government wasn't rudderless. What's more, there wasn't any other news of great consequence that day. The English staffer later apologized and said I was right. I resolved to do something about the weekend schedule, if I ever had the chance.

That one small flap aside, in reporting the president's illness VOA gave its listeners an extraordinary amount of information, more than any country's broadcast service anywhere in the world has given about the illness of its national leader. This reflected the openness of the American society, and the increasing responsiveness, since Eisenhower's illnesses, to demands that the American public be told in full about presidential health problems. The White House and the president's doctors provided extensive, detailed information. Then, too, there was Reagan himself, whose recovery made reporting easy. On Sunday, the doctors used terms like "spectacular" to describe his recovery from the operation, and Reagan got out of bed and walked twice. Monday morning Larry Speakes said he was making such good progress that the doctors were running out of superlatives.

That afternoon reporters representing news media from around the world, including writers specializing in medical reporting, assembled in a large auditorium at the hospital. We were told the growth contained cancer but the disease had not spread. Briefing us were Dr. Oller, the head of surgery at Bethesda and chief of the president's surgery team, and Dr. Steven Rosenberg, the chief of surgery at the National Cancer Institute, who participated in the operation.

Dr. Rosenberg stunned us when he began his remarks by stating flatly, "The president has cancer." In answer to follow–up questions, he softened the impact: "The tumor specimen that was removed from the president contained cancer. There is greater than a 50 per cent chance that the president now has no cancer whatsoever, that there are no cancer cells in his body and he is completely cured." I reported both his initial statement and his clarification, inserting the tape of his remarks, as well as his saying that an examination of all the internal organs showed they were "completely normal" and the chances were excellent that the tumor would not recur. Before their briefing, the doctors informed Nancy Reagan and then told the president in her company. Dr. Oller said the president's response was, "Well, I'm glad that that's all out."

The next day Reagan was described in excellent condition and excellent spirits. The filing center at the hospital was shut down and press operations moved back to the White House. Bush spoke briefly with some correspondents and, as I reported, said he thought there was "kind of a collective sigh of relief around the world when the operation was successful and then when yesterday's news on balance was very positive."

Reagan returned to the White House Saturday, July 20, one week after the operation. Before leaving the hospital he broadcast his weekly radio address to the American people and said he was feeling great and eager to get back to work. And he had some advice: "But may I say, speaking from personal experience, it's important to go and get a checkup if you think something isn't right. So if you're listening to this right now and it reminds you of something that you've been putting out of your mind, well, pick up the phone, call your doctor or local hospital and talk to someone. Just tell them Dr. Reagan sent you."

My story included that soundbite and noted that in the two or three days after his operation, the American Cancer Society's Washington office alone received more than 2,000 requests for free test kits for colo–rectal cancer. In a later piece I reported that "Dr." Reagan's advice "has been heeded," and a Cancer Society spokesman "says no question about it, there's been a tremendous increase in the number of Americans getting checkups."

Shortly after Reagan's return from the hospital, reporters noticed a blemish on his nose and asked Larry Speakes about it at his briefing on August 1, a Thursday. He said a small area of irritated skin had been removed Tuesday in a brief surgical procedure and that it was a bump that had become irritated by adhesive tape used while he was in the hospital. When asked if the specimen was being examined for skin cancer, he said merely that it was being checked. Later the White House issued a brief written statement, without the usual attribution to Speakes, which said the specimen was submitted for routine studies for "infection" and it was determined no further treatment was necessary. Speakes refused to answer any questions, among them, "Were you told not to say anything more?" The suspicion among reporters was that Larry was under orders stemming from Nancy Reagan, a surgeon's daughter who felt strongly about the privacy of patients and was very protective of her husband.

The following Monday Reagan himself revealed that the tests had shown basal cell carcinoma, which he said was "the most common and least dangerous kind," resulting from "exposure to the sun." Again I phoned the Cancer Society and reported that it "says there are more than 400,000 cases of this type of highly curable skin cancer each year, and no further treatment is required after removal."

The White House briefing room the next day was the scene of a stormy exchange in which Larry Speakes was accused of, and denied, misleading the press when he had been asked about the nose. Most of the questions came from Helen Thomas and Sam Donaldson. Helen: "You pulled an iron curtain down on the truth." Larry: "Exactly right. But I did not lie." Sam: "When did you know that there was a biopsy?" Larry: "I'm not talking about what I knew and when I knew it. . . . You want to call me a liar?" Sam: "I haven't called you a liar. Questions about your credibility have been raised."

A few other reporters spoke, like Joe Ewalt who pointed out that in refusing to answer questions, Speakes had left the impression that the only test that was done was a check for infection. But the most disputatious exchanges were between Larry and Helen and Sam. I told Larry I felt compelled to comment: "I don't think that Helen and Sam should be in a position of being considered alone. We may not agree with them totally but there were many of us who were puzzled by the fact that you were not responsive or forthcoming, as you have been in the past." Larry replied: "Well, I understand that you were and I certainly understood your position. But I told the truth, I did not lie, and I did not mislead. And the reason that I didn't make any further statements is because I did not want to mislead you."

That seemed to me to sum up Larry's dilemma. Sam and Helen, two of the best and hardest working correspondents in the White House press corps and the first reporters on duty every morning, were tough on Larry, but they were really using him as a channel to register legitimate complaints that information had been withheld. The issue was important but I did not file a story on the confrontation, since it would have been of minor interest to overseas listeners, and I had already reported the president's skin cancer.

Reagan resumed horseback riding during an August vacation at his ranch and resumed travel in September, weekly trips to promote his tax reform plan. On these trips other stories often cropped up. For instance, on September 5 in Raleigh, North Carolina, White House officials confirmed a published report that the president was planning a broad review of policy toward South Africa. The House of Representatives had approved economic sanctions against the South African government and the Senate was expected to do the same shortly. Reagan opposed sanctions on the grounds that they would hurt South Africa's black majority. A presidential veto of the sanctions, I told listeners, "is almost certain to be overridden by Congress, where there is overwhelming sentiment against South Africa's racial separation system," and "the administration thus is examining what steps it can take to avoid such a legislative defeat."

In Concord, New Hampshire, on September 18, 1985, the president announced that one of the seven Americans held hostage in Lebanon had been freed. The Reverend Benjamin Weir, a

Presbyterian minister who had been held for 16 months, was released to American officials in Beirut a few days earlier and was reunited with his family in Norfolk, Virginia. The president told the applauding crowd in Concord: "I talked with Reverend Weir on (from) Air Force One this morning and I'm happy for him and his family. But I will not be satisfied and will not cease our efforts until all the hostages — the other six — are released." At the White House the next day, he was asked by reporters about complaints by hostage relatives that the government wasn't doing enough to gain their release, and replied: "Unfortunately, we can't tell even the families all the things that we are doing, so we just have to take that criticism, but it is not justified."

A subject that drew near–constant attention, certainly at VOA, was Reagan's approaching summit with Gorbachev, the first summit of American and Soviet leaders in over six years. The meeting, to take place November 19–21 in Geneva, had been announced 10 days before Reagan's operation. Soon after his return from the hospital he was asked in an interview with *Time* magazine's Hugh Sidey if he felt up to seeing Gorbachev. Yes, he replied, adding that he was looking forward to it. I too was looking forward to getting a look at this new Soviet leader. Gorbachev was 54 — 20 years younger than Reagan — and had gained international attention even before succeeding to power in March. During a visit to London the previous December he had made a favorable impression; Prime Minister Thatcher described him as "a man with whom we can do business." In a subsequent visit to Paris, he continued what was called his "charm offensive."

In late Summer 1985, *Time* magazine reported an extensive interview with Gorbachev, and the White House reacted immediately by suggesting that Reagan should have a comparable opportunity to present his views to the Soviet people through the Soviet media. Speakes, I reported, said the Gorbachev interview was "a prime example of the openness of the American system and the access the Soviets enjoy to the American media." He also said that several months earlier USIA Director Wick had proposed an exchange in which Reagan would be allowed to appear on Soviet television, but that the proposal had not even been acknowledged.

A group of U.S. senators who met with Gorbachev in Moscow agreed that he was an effective spokesman for the Soviet Union, but also pointed to Reagan's effectiveness as a spokesman for America. The senators talked with reporters at our stakeout position in the White House driveway after briefing Reagan on their Moscow visit. Robert Byrd, the leader of the then Democratic minority in the Senate, said: "I'm very upbeat by the president's capability and ability to hold his own with Mr. Gorbachev or anybody else when it comes to being charming and dealing with public relations. He'll do fine. As I said at the beginning, Mr. Gorbachev's to be respected. He'll be a formidable person on the other side, but at the same time he's not 10 feet tall." I used the Byrd tape in a broadcast piece on the pre–summit public relations campaigns being waged by both Reagan and Gorbachev.

In preparation for covering the summit, VOA sent a group of us to a conference at Harvard University featuring experts on arms control, the Soviet economy, the whole range of U.S.–Soviet relations. The sessions provided an abundance of material that I wove into a series of VOA "backgrounders," long pieces with the historical background of events or people in the news. In one of them I reported that "Mr. Gorbachev is said to be still in the process of consolidating his position at home, and in addition has embarked on an effort to improve the Soviet economy. A lessening of tensions would enable the Soviet leader to concentrate on his domestic programs."

Another dealt with how both Reagan and Gorbachev were making use of television in their pre–summit statements: "Television coverage plays an important role in both countries. In the United States, according to the National Association of Broadcasters, television reaches 99 per cent of all households. . . . In the Soviet Union, according to an American expert, there were only 10,000 television sets in 1950, but now television reaches 90 per cent of all Soviet households."

The expert I quoted was political science Professor Ellen Mickiewicz of Emory University in Atlanta, which then was the only facility in the U.S. that received Soviet domestic television at the same time it was being broadcast in the Soviet Union. In telling us the results of some of her studies, Professor Mickiewicz said Soviet television had been "very hard-hitting" in accusing the United States of human rights violations. Obviously, she said, one of the points on the U.S. agenda at Geneva would be human rights in the Soviet Union, and so the Soviet media was making "counter-propaganda pre-emptive moves" in advance of the summit.

The conference was intellectually satisfying, and gratifying because VOA's broadcasts were known to some of the experts and attendees. One participant told me that he had recently been in Afghanistan with the rebels fighting Soviet and Kabul government troops, and that the rebels listened to VOA regularly.

And I loved being at Harvard again, seeing reminders of the glorious year my husband and I had spent there. The old red-brick buildings, the edifices of learning, were as beautiful as they were to Jack and me the first night that we walked through Harvard Yard in a light mist, holding hands. I checked out the street near Harvard Square where we had lived. The row house at 16 Story Street always had the fragrance of "Genuine Old English" furniture oil. The owner, Mrs. Maybelle C. Simpson, doused her dustmop with it for polishing the dark wood floors. She kept her house shining, and made its transient occupants feel it was their home, too. At the front door she put up small plaques etched with the names of her tenants. Mrs. Simpson had sent me Christmas cards for years, but they had stopped; I assumed she had gone to her reward. I still have the Jurey plaque.

For other pre-summit backgrounders, I dipped into recent history and my files. One dealt with the personalities of the two leaders, noting that both Reagan and Gorbachev were "regarded as personable individuals, as well as articulate and strong spokesmen for the differing political systems they represent. When Mr. Gorbachev was nominated to his post, Andrei Gromyko said of him: This man has a nice smile, but he has got iron teeth. When Mr. Reagan was campaigning for the presidency, political columnists and commentators repeatedly pointed out that this man was not to be under estimated."

Another backgrounder dealt with the rhetorical road to Geneva: "There were times when the Soviet Union compared President Reagan to Adolf Hitler and talked about U.S. imperialism, and a Soviet leader threatened to bury the United States. There were times when Mr. Reagan referred to the Soviet Union as an evil empire and asserted that its leaders reserved the right to lie and cheat in promoting their communist philosophy. The rhetoric, however, has been toned down in the past year. . . (and) both leaders have made public statements about wanting to improve relations between their countries."

Reagan gave a preview of his summit agenda on October 24 when he addressed the U.N. General Assembly. On the evening before his speech, he was host at a reception at the Waldorf for heads of state and government and their foreign ministers who were in New York for the U.N.'s 40th anniversary. Among the leaders who accepted invitations was Daniel Ortega, whom Reagan had described as "the little dictator who went to Moscow in green fatigues to receive a bear hug." Naturally, all of us in the press pool covering the reception were eager to witness the Reagan–Ortega encounter when the Nicaraguan leader went through the receiving line. The pool was penned into a roped–off corner of the Empire Room, some distance from where the president, Mrs. Reagan, Secretary Shultz and Ambassador to the U.N. Vernon Walters were welcoming guests, and we strained against the velvet rope in an effort to see. Reagan greeted Ortega with a polite smile and a handshake. Ortega said, "Thank you for inviting me." I filed a brief report on their brief encounter.

In his U.N. speech, Reagan proposed a three–stage peace process for resolving regional conflicts involving the Soviet Union, and said his initiative addressed what would be a central issue at the summit. He listed five countries: Afghanistan, Cambodia, Ethiopia, Angola and Nicaragua. In one of my reports I told listeners that the president's "emphasis on regional conflicts and Soviet involvement in them has been seen as a move to blunt a Soviet public diplomacy campaign," although Shultz and other U.S. officials "insist that's not the case."

Reagan met with Soviet Foreign Minister Eduard Shevardnadze that afternoon, and also had a series of meetings with leaders of other countries during the three days he was in New York. I routinely filed stories on all of them, since each was of interest to one or more of VOA's language services and to audiences for our regionally targeted English newscasts.

The president did get a chance to talk to the Soviet people through the Soviet media, when he was interviewed October 31 at the White House by correspondents of the news agency Tass, the party newspaper *Pravda*, the government newspaper *Izvestia*, and the news service Novosti. The interview was newsworthy not so much because of its content, but because it was the first by an American president with the Soviet press since November 1961, when John Kennedy was interviewed by *Izvestia* editor Alexei Adzhubei, the son-in-law of Nikita Khrushchev. In a backgrounder noting a similarity in the atmosphere that existed before both interviews, I reported that "words spoken by President Kennedy then have been echoed more than two decades later by President Reagan." Kennedy had been asked what he thought of concluding a peace pact between the U.S. and the Soviet Union, and said he thought there should be not only an agreement but that both countries should take those steps which make peace possible. He added that words on paper are not as significant as looking at those areas which provide tension, and seeing if they can dispel that tension. Nearly 24 years later, Reagan was saying the two countries could and should meet in the spirit in which they could deal with their differences peacefully, and that if the Soviets really wanted to live in a peaceful world, more than words were needed.

The president spoke directly to the Soviet people again November 9 in a 10-minute address that he delivered over VOA and was broadcast live worldwide. He told them he hoped for a better relationship with their country and a fruitful summit with Gorbachev that would lead to future meetings. He said he appreciated his recent and rare interview with the Soviet press, but noted that only parts of it were published by *Izvestia*. As I reported, he used his address to explain SDI and to describe his position on other issues he intended to discuss with Gorbachev, regional conflicts and human rights.

The speech was broadcast simultaneously in Russian and other languages of the Soviet Union, and later by the rest of VOA's language services. Speakes said the American Embassy in Moscow reported that two and possibly three frequencies were clearly audible there and probably not jammed. In Leningrad, the American Consulate reported that one Russian language frequency was "loud and clear" and a Lithuanian broadcast was received clearly, although this same frequency may have been jammed in Lithuania. The unjammed English broadcasts "were well received." VOA's audience in the Soviet Union in 1985 was estimated at more than 24 million; worldwide listenership at nearly 120 million.

As with all major presidential addresses in any administration, the advance texts of Reagan's pre–summit speeches were impatiently sought by VOA's language services, which needed time to translate them — especially those services that would broadcast simultaneously with his delivery. The one question I heard most from VOA in the entire time I covered the White House was, "When do we get the advance text?" On some occasions the texts were back–channeled by someone on the National Security Council staff to a specific language service, but I refused to be told anything about such bootleg copies because I felt strongly that I should have access to the texts only at the same time as every other White House correspondent. I might note here that many of us assumed bootleg copies also were given to morning newspapers that printed transcripts of night–time presidential speeches.

When the advance text of a presidential speech was distributed, the White House briefing room was the scene of stampeding reporters reaching out to grab copies from the besieged Press Office staffers. After obtaining my copy and escaping from the herd, I rushed to my basement cubby-hole and immediately faxed the speech to the VOA newsroom, feeding pages into the machine while I read the text, figured out the lead, and started writing.

For the Geneva summit, members of the White House traveling press (207 men/32 women) were given looseleaf trip books, bound in black leather with the presidential seal etched in gray, which contained a message to us from the president. His first sentence was: "Our trip to Geneva is one of the most important of my presidency." This was, I thought, no over–statement. Reagan, accompanied by his wife and top advisors, arrived in Geneva Saturday night, November 16, and in remarks at the airport restated his hope for a "fresh start" in American–Soviet relations despite "deep" differences between the two countries. He was welcomed by Swiss President Kurt Furgler, who said "all eyes throughout the world" would be watching the summit. Certainly the international press would be watching. Approximately 3,600 representatives of the media from around the world were poised to cover the Reagan–Gorbachev talks starting on Tuesday the 19th.

VOA had a 20–member contingent, a big one for us though nothing like those of the American networks, which anchored their evening news programs and morning shows from Geneva. Our group included our resident correspondent, Andre de Nesnera, who was president of the U.N. correspondents association in Geneva; Special Events coordinator Nancy Smart and her deputy Rich Firestone; representatives of the Current Affairs and European Divisions; broadcasters from the Russian, Ukrainian, Polish, Hungarian, Dari, French to Africa, Portuguese to Brazil, and Chinese language services, and three radio techs. When diplomatic correspondent Ron Pemstein, radio engineer Reuel Zinn and I arrived in Geneva aboard the White House press plane, the group was already in operation at the international press center. Radio techs Gary Jaffe, Joe Gallagher and Mike Batho constructed studios for the language service broadcasters virtually from scratch, and then worked staggered shifts transmitting their taped reports and live broadcasts at all hours of day and night during the summit. Paula Wolfson of Current Affairs, who worked on documentaries, joined Ron and me in reporting spot news and Nicolai (Nick) Sorokin of the Russian service substituted for us on a White House press pool at a Reagan–Gorbachev photo op, at our request, so that we'd be sure to have the exact translation of "Gorby's" comments.

Also covering the summit were Radio Marti, which sent its White House correspondent, and USIA's TV service, Worldnet, which sent at least one anchor, but they worked separately from the VOA contingent, and we didn't know what they broadcast. The Marti reporter occasionally came to us for help, but filed her reports elsewhere in the White House filing center, and, NBC complained to us, for a while mistakenly used NBC phones.

Although the summit didn't begin until Tuesday, there was much to cover, such as the flap on Sunday over a Weinberger letter that had been leaked to the press. In it, the defense secretary urged the president not to make a summit promise to continue abiding by the unratified SALT II Treaty, contending that to do so would severely limit options in response to Soviet violations. Reagan was asked by pool reporters if somebody was trying to sabotage the summit. His answer was an emphatic "No." This was followed by: "Are you going to fire Weinberger?" "Do you want a one word answer or two?" "Two." "Hell, no!" Ron Pemstein filed a report for VOA on the exchange.

In the meantime, I was on a press pool waiting to accompany the president and Mrs. Reagan in a motorcade to the Villa Fleur d'Eau, the Flower Water House, the site for his first talks with Gorbachev. At the villa, Reagan tried out the chair he would use, in front of the fireplace, and Nancy sat in the one that Gorbachev would occupy. The fireplace was of significance, as we learned later when the White House tried to have the superpower meeting dubbed the "fireside summit." Some of the media did call it that, but the description really didn't catch fire, at least historically.

American and Soviet officials held press briefings Sunday in what amounted to a pre–summit debate on various issues. The Soviets portrayed the Weinberger letter as an attempt to torpedo the arms control process. The Americans sought to minimize the impact of the letter on the summit, with Ambassador Paul Nitze and others insisting that U.S. policy on SALT II was unchanged, that the

United States would not undercut the treaty if the Soviet Union showed the same restraint.

Gorbachev arrived in Geneva on Monday; the Swiss government had separate welcoming ceremonies for the American and Soviet leaders, and there were more briefings. Larry Speakes told us there would not be joint U.S.-Soviet press conferences during the summit and that each side would report on the meetings as it saw fit. We wondered if we were going to get generalized statements from each side in a propaganda war. And we wondered if the American press conferences would be supplemented by leaks "on background" to favored reporters, leaving the rest of us uninformed and having to play catch-up to match their stories.

At noon on the opening day of the summit, Speakes announced a news blackout. The U.S. and the Soviet Union, he said, agreed there would be no details provided by either side until the meetings were over. He added that only he and Soviet spokesman Leonid Zamyatin would have briefings, and that "only the length of the meetings and (names of) the participants would be provided, nothing else." Zamyatin made a similar announcement.

Although he was pressed by reporters, Larry wouldn't say what the two leaders talked about in their first session. As I noted in reporting the blackout, he told us, "Those who talk about the meetings don't know what's going on, and those who do know won't talk." Now, one would think that the press would object to a news blackout, but in this case I was relieved to hear that we would all be getting the same information. Still there were doubts the blackout would hold. But it did.

I couldn't have said it better than Robert Timberg of *The Baltimore Sun* did when he wrote later (in *Washington Journalism Review*) that it worked to the benefit of reporters covering the summit: "The blackout, which applied not only to formal briefings provided by each side but also to the private backgrounders where senior administration officials disgorge the real story to a select few, created a level playing field on which each reporter's Geneva file largely reflected his or her own energy, wit and perception rather than selectively targeted news leaks served to certain reporters on a silver platter." Timberg also quoted Bruce Drake of *The New York Daily News*: "If it had not been for the blackout, the general run of the press — those outside the magic circle — would have been royally shafted."

Shafted we were not, and despite the paucity of information in the press conferences, we did have news to report, thanks to Reagan and Gorbachev themselves. They had quotable things to say during photo ops, and surprised everyone by holding extended private sessions. Because some of the photo ops were shown on television monitors in our huge filing center at the Intercontinental Hotel, we were able to file stories immediately, starting with the first time they met: "The summit meeting got under way with smiles and a handshake. President Reagan, the host for the first day of talks, greeted Soviet General Secretary Gorbachev at the entrance to a small chateau, Fleur d'Eau, and they stood together briefly as photographers and television camera crews recorded the start of the first U.S.–Soviet summit since 1979. Inside, there was more picture–taking. The atmosphere was, to use Mr. Reagan's word, cordial, and Mr. Gorbachev said he had a good impression."

The first private meeting between Reagan and Gorbachev was scheduled for 15 minutes but it lasted an hour, and, as Speakes told us in a briefing, they talked alone for another hour following the afternoon plenary session, when they strolled to a small lakeside house and, with only their interpreters present, had a fireside chat inside. He described the atmosphere on the first day as "good," as did the Soviet spokesman at his briefing. As I told VOA listeners, Speakes would not list the subjects discussed, in keeping with the blackout, but the scheduled subjects were U.S.–Soviet relations in the morning session and arms control in the afternoon.

That night Gorbachev and his wife Raisa gave a dinner for the Reagans and the two leaders had more comments. Throughout the summit, there were three sets of pools for the photo ops, American–credentialed press, Soviet–credentialed press, and others in the international press corps who were credentialed by the Swiss. Each pool usually had seven members. Reagan was asked how things were going and said, "We're still smiling." Gorbachev was asked why he and Reagan were spending so much time alone and said, "We think it's useful to have face–to–face contact."

My wrapup of the day's events noted that "also drawing attention in Geneva, and in the Soviet media, was a meeting during the summit lunch break between Mr. Gorbachev and a delegation of American citizens from anti–nuclear groups." They included civil rights leader Jesse Jackson, who said, "We're making a moral appeal to him, as we've made to our own government, to put a nuclear test ban as a high item of priority on the agenda." As I reported, Jackson dismissed suggestions the Soviets were using the meeting for publicity purposes, and Speakes said the meeting presented no problem and was the general secretary's prerogative.

Earlier in the day I had tracked down by phone a member of the anti–nuclear group, a coalition named "Women for a Meaningful Summit," who gave me a detailed rundown on the session with Gorbachev, and Nick Sorokin had obtained additional information from the Tass reporters. Nancy Reagan and Raisa Gorbachev also met for tea, and Ron Pemstein and I made brief mention of that in our wrapups. Mrs. Reagan was the hostess, and the two First Ladies had tea again Wednesday, with Mrs. Gorbachev the hostess.

Wednesday's summit meetings were held at the Soviet mission, where a red carpet had been laid at the entrance. Again the two leaders had extended private talks. During the photo ops at the outset, Reagan was asked how the talks were going and said, "fine," and Gorbachev said they were "lively" and conducted "in a frank, businesslike, and, I think, responsible way." Gorbachev also said they'd begun discussing the question of his visiting the U.S. Would Reagan like to see that? "Of course," said the president.

Larry Speakes was asked in his briefing if the president felt equally enthusiastic about visiting Moscow, and said "yes." My report included a paragraph that said: "According to Mr. Speakes as the second day of talks was getting under way, Mr. Reagan told Mr. Gorbachev: 'There is much that divides us but I believe the world breathes easier because we are here talking together.' And, 'Our differences are serious but so is our commitment to improving understanding.' "

That paragraph underscores the importance of attribution, for the quotes had been "manufactured," as Larry disclosed in his 1988 book written with Robert Pack, *Speaking Out: The Reagan Presidency from Inside the White House*. Larry wrote that he had instructed staffer Mark Weinberg "to draft some quotes" for Reagan, after which he "polished" them and gave them to the press. "In retrospect," Larry acknowledged, "it was clearly wrong to take such liberties. " He added, "Luckily, the Russians didn't dispute the quotes, and I had been able to spruce up the president's image by taking a bit of liberty with my P.R. man's license." When his book was published, he received a good deal of criticism for making up the quotes. In reporting what Speakes said Reagan said, I had been careful in my attribution, but in one of my late night wrapups I unfortunately neglected to say again "according to Mr. Speakes."

The Reagans gave a dinner for the Gorbachevs Wednesday night after the two couples attended a reception given by the Swiss, and I was on the White House press pool, giving me the chance to observe the Soviet leader up close. First, our pool had motorcade duty, following the Reagans to and from the reception and then, along with the Soviet and Swiss-credentialed pools, we lined up on the fringes of the driveway in front of the entrance to their residence, an 18th Century country mansion. Altogether, there were 21 of us waiting for the Gorbachevs as snowflakes began descending. After a quarter hour their limousine drew up and the Reagans came out to greet them. The four lined up for a photo: Raisa in a fur jacket and brown velvet skirt, smart-looking and at ease; Nancy elegant in a long gown with geometric pattern, shepherding her guests with smiles and hostessy gestures; Gorbachev, wearing a dark overcoat and confident air (he looked to me like a businessman going to a Country Club event); and Reagan, displaying his usual affability. Poolers shouted questions — any good news to report? Reagan said, "The news is so good, we're going to hold it 'til tomorrow."

The two couples then went inside and, armed with Reagan's quote, we dashed to a nearby restaurant where telephones had been installed for our use. We were to have about 20 minutes filing time before going back to the residence for another picture–taking session. But as we were phoning our pool reports to our colleagues in the filing center, a White House press aide hollered to us to "come quick." The photo op was taking place sooner than scheduled. We ran along a path through bushes to the entrance, and in a mad crush all three pools rushed inside, toppling small potted plants, pushing each other, and being pushed by burly security men. Each pool was to have gone separately into the dining room, where the two couples were seated at the table with four American and four Soviet officials. Under the last–minute change in plans, this orderly procedure gave way to chaos, with everyone trying to cram into the small dining room at the same time. The Reagans and Gorbachevs composedly continued their chit chat, but I thought they must have been horrified at the sight of all these shoving bodies. This was not one of the press's finest moments.

We had very little time for questions. Amid the disorder, I asked the shortest one I could think of as I was propelled past Reagan: "How are things going, Mr. President?" "Fine," he said. Correspondents Barry Seaman and Donnie Radcliffe, who wrote the pool report, said they were told "the reason for the breakdown in pool coverage was because the guests had declined pre–dinner cocktails and had gone straight to the table."

Our pool duties over, we returned to the press center, where I joined Ron in filing wrapups and overnighters to VOA, including the late word that the two leaders would appear Thursday morning at a ceremony in the International Conference Center. According to Speakes, American and Soviet aides worked out the final details while the dinner was going on, and after dinner Reagan and Gorbachev reviewed the report of their foreign ministers and made their decision to hold the joint ceremony. "At the conclusion of their discussion," he said, "they shook hands, seated on the couch before a roaring fireplace."

The auditorium at the International Conference Center was filled with members of the press and American, Soviet and Swiss officials well before 10 a.m., when the two leaders were scheduled to appear. On stage were two adjoining handsome dark wood tables and twin armchairs of similar wood with brown and gold striped upholstery. A few of us asked a White House staffer if the furniture had any historical significance. Sorry, they were of nondescript heritage. We were told they had been found by White House aides who were up all night looking for suitable furniture that matched.

Before the leaders appeared, a joint statement was distributed to the press, and I read it hurriedly, underlining the key passages: "While acknowledging the differences in their systems and approaches to international issues, some greater understanding of each side's view was achieved by the two leaders. They agreed about the need to improve U.S.–Soviet relations and the international situation as a whole." "They agreed to meet again in the nearest future." Gorbachev had accepted an invitation to visit the U.S., Reagan an invitation to visit the Soviet Union. And, "They agreed to accelerate the work" of the talks on nuclear and space arms.

When the two leaders strode on stage, smiles and another handshake. Each spoke briefly, eight minutes in all. The ceremony ended with Shultz and Shevardnadze, seated at the non–historic tables, signing a cultural exchange agreement. Afterwards, Reagan and Gorbachev joined in champagne toasts, and then went their separate ways, planning to see each other again in Washington in 1986 and in Moscow in 1987. In one of my broadcast pieces, I reported Reagan's remarks at the ceremony, that he had come to Geneva "to seek a fresh start" in U.S.–Soviet relations "and we have done this," and that Gorbachev was quoted later as making a similar comment, "It (the summit) gave a new start in the right direction in our relationship." On SDI, I told listeners, "Mr. Reagan did not budge, and neither did Mr. Gorbachev."

Their second summit did take place in 1986, in October, later than had been envisioned, and in Reykjavik, Iceland, instead of Washington. It was billed as a "preparatory" meeting, an interim or pre–summit summit that would lead to a full–scale U.S.–Soviet summit in the U.S., and it came after months of strained relations. The most fascinating aspect of the meeting, to me, was its ending and the "spin" put on it by both sides, so here I will deal only briefly with the events preceding Reykjavik.

In March the U.S. ordered a reduction in the large number of personnel at the Soviet U.N. mission, charging that spies were masquerading as diplomats. The Soviets protested. In late May, Reagan announced the U.S. would no longer adhere to the standards of the unratified and expired Salt II Treaty, on the grounds that the Soviets had violated the treaty. The Soviets disputed that and strongly criticized his decision. In late August, a Soviet U.N. employee, Gennadi Zakharov, was arrested by the U.S. on spy charges. One week later, American reporter Nicholas Daniloff was detained in Moscow and accused of espionage. His detention was met with outrage in the U.S., and the Reagan administration asserted that Nick had been framed in retaliation for Zakharov. The president insisted Nick was not a spy; Gorbachev insisted he was. VOA carried numerous stories on all these developments, and also on the Chernobyl nuclear power plant disaster in April.

On September 29 Nick Daniloff was released, without trial, and he and his wife left Moscow for Frankfurt on their way home. The next day Gennadi Zakharov pleaded no contest to spy charges in New York and flew back to Moscow — and Reagan made the surprise announcement that he would meet with Gorbachev October 11 and 12 in Reykjavik. Reagan said Gorbachev had suggested the meeting in a letter delivered to him on September 19, and that he would not have agreed to it unless Daniloff was released. Reagan also denied that Zakharov had been swapped for Daniloff. Shultz announced that the Soviets had given permission to human rights activist Yuri Orlov, confined to internal exile in Siberia, and his wife, to leave the Soviet Union, and that the U.S. had extended the deadline, until October 14, for the departure of the balance of 25 Soviet U.N. employees who were being expelled.

Reagan flew to Reykjavik Thursday, October 9, preceded by the chartered Pan Am plane carrying the press (203 men/30 women on the White House list), including Ron Pemstein, engineer Hubert Katz and me. Andre de Nesnera had already arrived from Geneva and filed reports on the Icelandic government's preparations for the summit, including the use of emergency powers to take over Reykjavik's four major hotels for housing the American and Soviet delegations. Soviet officials had arrived in advance of the Americans and were holding briefings, which Andre covered. He was a triple–language correspondent, able to broadcast in English, French and Russian. Other members of the VOA team, from the Washington staff, were Moscow–born Victor Franzusoff, at age 75 an institution in the Russian language service; Oksana Dragan of the Ukrainian service, coordinator Rich Firestone and radio tech Joseph Gallagher.

The Icelandic government also had to set up an international press center and accommodate an estimated 2,000 journalists covering the summit. Some were booked into rooms an hour's drive away from the capital. The traveling White House press had no problem; we were housed in the Loftleidir Hotel, where a restaurant–bar was transformed into our cramped filing center–briefing room. The site for the Reagan–Gorbachev weekend talks was a two–story white clapboard house owned by the city government, Hofdi House, which reputedly was once haunted by the ghost of a young woman.

At the first session Saturday morning the two leaders greeted each other with their usual smiles and a handshake. A news blackout, like the one at the Geneva summit, was in effect, and during a photo op they sidestepped questions from reporters on whether they would be setting a date for a full–scale summit in Washington. After their second session, in the afternoon, Speakes announced they had decided to establish two working groups of high–level experts from both sides — one on arms control, the other on humanitarian, regional and bilateral issues — that would begin meeting at 8 that night.

Reagan and Gorbachev were to end Sunday's meeting at noon; Shultz was to brief us, and the president was to leave for Washington at 3:45 p.m. after remarks to American servicemen and their families at Keflavik airport. The session went into overtime, lasting three and one–half hours instead of two, and in answer to shouted questions as he left Hofdi House, Reagan said, "We're not through." They would meet again at 3 p.m. Ron Pemstein and I filed updates, and soon filed again when Speakes disclosed: "The two leaders have made progress in discussions on a wide range of arms control issues. They have narrowed their differences in some cases, in others they have not." Speakes said he felt free to comment on the talks after what he called a flagrant violation of the news blackout by a Soviet official. The official (Yevgeny Vevelikhov) had told the BBC that the two sides were close to agreement on deep cuts in long-range nuclear weapons and elimination of medium-range missiles from Europe. Speakes also said "the president is hanging tough." Still, with progress reported by both sides it was clear Reykjavik was more than a "preparatory" summit. We filed more holding spots in the four hours spent waiting for the final session to end.

Shultz came to the filing center to brief us at 7:20 p.m. His initial remarks were tantalizing: "I've just spent two full, intensive days watching the president of the United States engage with the general secretary of the Soviet Union over the full range of issues that we are concerned about together. The president's performance was magnificent and I have never been so proud of my president as I have been in these sessions and, particularly, this afternoon. During the course of these two days, extremely important potential agreements were reached to reduce, in the first instance, strategic arms in half. . . ." But then he got to the point and said, "So, in the end, we are deeply disappointed by the outcome." The talks had ended in failure because of disagreement over SDI. I rushed to the white line microphone and filed a quick and short report to VOA, and Ron Pemstein followed with a more detailed broadcast piece.

Twelve minutes after Shultz finished his briefing, Reagan spoke at the airport. His remarks were piped into the filing center so we could hear and record them. In a wrapup I reported, "The president made clear he could not agree to a Soviet proposal that the United States believes would have scuttled his Strategic Defense Initiative." Reagan said he had made a counterproposal on SDI but Gorbachev rejected it; the Soviet leader wanted to restrict all work on SDI to laboratory research. As I reported, Reagan also said, "However, we made great strides in Iceland in resolving most of our differences, and we're going to continue the effort." As for a full-scale summit, Shultz had said he didn't see any prospect of one in the next few months. Don Regan was more emphatic in telling network correspondents there would not be another summit in the near future. He disputed a suggestion that the summit was a complete bust for the administration and said, "The Soviets didn't score either. . . . They're the ones that fumbled the ball."

"Reagan–Gorbachev Summit Talks Collapse/As Deadlock on SDI Wipes Out Other Gains," the banner headline in *The Washington Post* reported Monday morning, and "Reagan–Gorbachev Talks End In Stalemate/As U.S. Rejects Demand to Curb 'Star Wars' " was the banner in *The New York Times*. Both papers also carried stories on Gorbachev's post–summit press conference in Reykjavik. The *Post* reported he gave a bleak assessment and the *Times* reported he charged Reagan had scuttled arms control agreements by insisting on developing SDI. Almost immediately, however, both Reagan and Gorbachev began changing their spin and casting Reykjavik in a positive light.

In a speech to the nation Monday night reporting on the summit, the president asserted that the U.S. and the Soviet Union "are closer than ever before to agreements that could lead to a safer world without nuclear weapons." He said his invitation to Gorbachev for a summit in the U.S. "stands," and that American arms control negotiators in Geneva "will work to build on the progress" that had been made. When Gorbachev made a similar report to the Soviet people, Larry Speakes said "we are pleased to note" that the general secretary "stated that the work that was done in Reykjavik will not go to waste and the way has now been cleared for further movement towards significant arms control. This is the view of the United States."

Within a week, I was reporting to VOA listeners that the U.S. and Soviet leaders were waging public relations campaigns aimed at both international and their own domestic audiences. They were trying to justify their positions in explaining why agreements that were within reach did not materialize, but they also were acting "in an apparent desire to blot out the conclusion that the summit was a failure. Each quickly began pointing to the positive aspects of the summit. . . ." Reykjavik did lead to a third Reagan–Gorbachev summit, in December 1987 in Washington. In the meantime, there were other big stories to cover.

Reykjavik also provided a mini-example of global commerce. While waiting for briefings, members of the press had time to look for bargains in shops displaying handsome Icelandic wool sweaters. They were expensive, however, so for a souvenir of Iceland I bought a T-shirt with Reykjavik in ice-blue letters on the front, only to discover when I got home that the label read "Made in Brazil."

17
Arms for Hostages
VOA Controversies and Kudos
My Last Summit

White House correspondents were in Santa Barbara on Sunday, November 2, 1986, when wire service dispatches from Beirut reported that one of the American hostages, David Jacobsen, had been released after being held for 17 months. Reagan was relaxing at his ranch as he neared the end of a campaign tour on behalf of Republican senatorial candidates in the November 4 elections. Presidential aides would neither confirm nor deny the Beirut stories, but finally the official silence ended when Larry Speakes read us a Reagan statement confirming that Jacobsen, the director of the American University Hospital in Beirut, had been freed.

The statement expressed appreciation "to the various parties and intermediaries who have been helpful in arranging this release" and said the United States had been working through "a number of sensitive channels for a long time," but details could not be divulged "because the lives of other Americans and other Western hostages are still at risk." In reporting the news, I included tape of Larry's answer when reporters asked if the administration had changed its policy or made concessions: "We continue our policy of talking with anyone who can be helpful but we do not make concessions nor do we ask third countries to do so."

The next day we switched back to writing about Reagan's "last campaign" and his goal to retain Republican control of the Senate. At his final rally, under sunny skies in Costa Mesa, the president gave a sentimental and patriotic speech, interrupted by chants of "Reagan, Reagan, Reagan" and "USA, USA, USA" from young partisans who filled the arena. The finale featured bursts of fireworks, confetti shot from cannon, an exhibition by sky divers carrying American flags (with their parachutes advertising a brand of beer), and a huge inflatable rubber replica of the Statue of Liberty. Presumably the latter was inspired by the renovated statue's 200th birthday in July, but the imagery collapsed into comedy as the replica lurched grotesquely over the crowd.

Reagan flew back to Washington Tuesday to await the election returns. The press plane followed, and on our arrival we found that the Air Force One pool report contained some intriguing material. Before boarding the plane in Los Angeles, Reagan replied "no comment" when asked by the travel pool about reports that Robert (Bud) McFarlane, "had been in Iran and been arrested." Then Larry Speakes told the Air Force One pool, "We're going to generally not comment on stories of this type from the Middle East — stories involving hostages." Late in the flight, Speakes gave the pool a statement: "As long as Iran advocates the use of terrorism, the U.S. arms embargo will continue. Moreover, the U.S. position on the Iran–Iraq war remains that the fighting should stop and the two sides should reach a negotiated settlement of their dispute. We favor an outcome where there are no winners or losers." Asked if there was still an arms embargo, Speakes said "Yes." He also noted that McFarlane had denied reports that he was in Iran in September.

I phoned the VOA newsroom from the press room at Andrews Air Force Base, and learned that Iranian Parliament Speaker Ali Akbar Hashemi Rafsanjani had confirmed a report on McFarlane's secret trip to Iran, which the pro-Syrian Lebanese magazine *Al Shiraa* had published the day before, November 3, and that Laurie Kassman, then our State Department correspondent, had already filed a story with U.S. reaction. "State Department spokesman Charles Redman," she reported, "refused to comment on declarations by Iran's parliament speaker that former national security advisor Robert McFarlane allegedly was arrested and expelled from Iran last September. Mr. Redman also refused comment on a Lebanese magazine report that Mr. McFarlane traveled secretly to Iran to work on a deal that might free American hostages in Lebanon. The story claims that the Reagan administration then shipped a supply of spare parts for U.S.–made planes, tanks and radar systems currently being used by Iran."

We reporters learned later that the statement given out by Speakes on Air Force One was written by national security advisor

Poindexter, and that McFarlane had traveled secretly to Iran, not in September but in May, with NSC staffer Oliver North and others.

In the November 4 elections, the Republicans lost control of the Senate, despite Reagan's campaign exertions. Up to now, 1986 had been a mixed bag of a year for him. The space shuttle *Challenger* exploded just after launching in January, and a commission headed by former Secretary of State Rogers issued a report in June critical of the national space agency and shuttle scheduling pressures. In February, Reagan reluctantly reversed U.S. support for Philippine President Ferdinand Marcos and recognized the new government of Corazon Aquino, after Marcos had tried to defraud her of her election victory. Reagan won public support for his stand against Libyan leader Muammar Qaddafi in April, when U.S. planes struck Libya in retaliation for what the administration said was Libyan–sponsored terrorism. In Congress, he won approval of his controversial request for $100 million in humanitarian and military aid for Nicaragua's Contras. The Senate confirmed his controversial nomination of conservative William Rehnquist, a Supreme Court associate justice, as chief justice. But he suffered a major defeat when the Senate over–rode his veto of tough anti–apartheid sanctions that Congress imposed against the South African government.

These, and the Reykjavik summit, were all big stories that VOA covered fully. Now we were covering the biggest, most damaging, story of the Reagan presidency, the unfolding arms for hostages scandal. How did we report it? The respected *National Journal* surveyed our output and on January 24, 1987, under the headline, "VOA Handles a Touchy Issue The Way the Other Media Do," wrote: "Has the government's own foreign broadcasting operation favored President Reagan? A review of 453 news stories, 275 correspondents' reports and 20 special programs on the Iran story produced by the VOA from Nov. 4–Dec. 21 suggests not. As Kassman's initial report from the State Department shows, the VOA has aired straightforward news accounts. Further, it has covered the most critical aspects of the many faceted story with persistence."

Many of the correspondents' reports were filed from VOA's basement cubby-hole at the White House, where I was joined by Debi Weinstein, who had succeeded Don Fulsom when he became a VOA anchor. After the Iran story broke, Reagan disclosed in a speech to the nation November 13 that arms had been sent to Iran, but he said they were part of an 18-month-old secret initiative to Iran undertaken for four reasons: "To renew a relationship with the nation of Iran. To bring an honorable end to the bloody six-year war between Iran and Iraq. To eliminate state-sponsored terrorism and subversion. And to effect the safe return of all hostages."

Reagan denied the weapons were ransom payment for hostages, but after his address, criticism of the arms shipments intensified and public opinion polls found many Americans did not believe him. As I reported, members of Congress were angered that they'd not been informed and focused their fire on the National Security Council staff at the White House. They asserted it was circumventing Congress and charged laws were broken. They also criticized the administration for violating the arms embargo against Iran at the same time it was urging European allies not to ship arms.

At a press conference November 19, Reagan again denied weapons were traded for hostages, and insisted the arms were part of his policy to develop contacts with Iranian moderates. On November 25, Reagan appeared in the White House briefing room and announced the resignation of national security advisor Poindexter and the dismissal of Poindexter's staff aide, Marine Lieutenant Colonel Oliver North. He then turned the podium over to Attorney General Edwin Meese, who said he'd discovered that proceeds from the arms sales to Iran had been diverted to Nicaragua's Contras. Meese told reporters: "What is involved is that in the course of the arms transfers, which involved the United States providing the arms to Israel, and Israel in turn transferring the arms — in effect, selling the arms to representatives of Iran — certain monies which were received in the transaction between representatives of Israel and representatives of Iran were taken and made available to the forces in Central America which are opposing the Sandinista government there."

Meese's revelation brought additional criticism that the diversion of funds would have violated a law in effect at the time that barred U.S. government aid to the Contras. Reagan, who said he knew nothing of the diversion, appointed a board to review the operations of the NSC staff. Reagan discussed his Iran policy again in his Saturday radio speech December 6, and as VOA's Dick Chamberlain reported, the president "acknowledged for the first time that mistakes were made in carrying out his policy to seek a dialogue with the moderate elements in Iran."

On the basis of information collected from briefings and reports of congressional testimony, the secret contacts with Iranians began around July and August of 1985. And, as I reported, between September 1985 and Jacobsen's release in November 1986, three hostages had been freed — and three other Americans had been taken hostage in Beirut.

By the end of 1986 Reagan had named a respected government official, Frank Carlucci, as his new national security advisor, and the outgoing NATO ambassador, David Abshire, as his special counsellor in the Iranian matter. Abshire's job was to coordinate White House replies to questions from investigating committees in Congress and the court–appointed independent counsel, Lawrence Walsh. Also, Reagan, Bush and others in the administration were urging that Poindexter and North end their silence and make full disclosure. In a January 1987 backgrounder, I wrote that "the White House strategy in focusing on the two former aides, and in stressing the president wants to find out what happened, was, in effect, to detach Mr. Reagan from the scandal — even if this pictured him as a president who was not aware of things his aides were doing."

In late January, the Senate Select Committee on Intelligence issued a report on the secret contacts with Iranians. It included a paragraph revealing that VOA had been used to send a message to Iran in an editorial broadcast in September 1986. The report said: "According to documents and testimony received by the Committee, the U.S. team told the Iranian official that to show U.S. seriousness, the Voice of America would mention Iran as one of the countries the United States wished to thank for refusing to grant landing rights to the hijackers of the TWA aircraft in Karachi. A few days later, NSC and CIA officials met to discuss a draft of the editorial. Working through State Department officials, the NSC staff convinced USIA that this unusual request came from 'the highest levels' of the government, and the editorial was broadcast over a three–day period."

There were shockwaves at the Voice. Although an editorial, not the news, was involved, this was damaging stuff. VOA of course reported the story, and not only that, our long–form news program, "World Report," broadcast an interview January 30 with VOA Director Richard W. Carlson by anchor Ed Conley, who questioned him about the journalistic propriety of such a message.

Conley: Director Carlson, has VOA gone beyond the bounds of reflecting U.S. policy by becoming actively engaged in a secret diplomatic procedure?

Carlson: Well, I don't think so. I must say, though, that it was a highly unusual request, but it was in my opinion permissible under that part of the Charter which governs the Voice editorial policies. That is, it is our policy to broadcast the opinion of the United States government. This particular editorial was factually correct. It contained no falsehoods of any kind and it was, clearly more than we know I suppose, reflecting the opinion of the United States government at that particular time.

In answer to other questions, Carlson said that the news and the editorials were kept totally separate so that the editorials would not cast "negative shadows" on VOA's credibility. He said VOA and USIA would resist any "nefarious attempts" to use our news broadcasts and would continue to treat the news as "sacrosanct." I hoped, as others at VOA did, that the interview helped repair the damage.

A story in *The Washington Post* the next morning reported that the State Department's chief terrorism expert, L. Paul Bremer, interceded with USIA Director Wick to have the editorial broadcast after the head of VOA's Farsi service, William Royce, and the head of the editorial writers staff, Kenneth Thompson, refused to air it because no explanation was given. (Good for them, I thought.) The story quoted Wick as saying Bremer told him the editorial was of "great importance to national security interests." Wick said he approved putting it on the air after ascertaining it was "factually correct, consistent with U.S. government policy and not in violation of VOA's Charter," the same points made by VOA Director Carlson.

Carlson was the fifth director we had in the Reagan administration and he came to the Voice in 1986 in the wake of another controversy involving VOA. The job of VOA director had become vacant again in October 1985 when Gene Pell, a former NBC correspondent and former VOA news and current affairs executive, ended his brief tenure to go to Munich and head Radio Free Europe/Radio Liberty. To succeed Pell, Wick was planning to name veteran broadcast journalist William Sheehan, a former president of ABC News. It was an excellent choice. But, as *Broadcasting* magazine headlined its story in March 1986, "Helms, conservatives put kibosh on Sheehan VOA bid." Republican Senator Jesse Helms let Wick know that Sheehan was unacceptable. The rightist journal *Human Events* carried stories that conservatives were angry over Wick's choice and that they believed "major sections of the Voice, including the newsroom, are dominated by liberals and/or those further to the left." It also said conservatives felt key personnel changes must be made so that VOA would accurately reflect Reagan views.

"Something is going on that is hurting the Voice of America — something disgraceful," declared John Chancellor in a March 18 commentary on NBC. He said Sheehan was opposed because he "is a political centrist — because he would want the VOA broadcasts to be fair and impartial, which the VOA Charter requires." Chancellor knew VOA well, and prefaced his remarks by noting that he'd served as its director for two years in the 1960s. "What the conservatives want," he said, "is someone who will shape the programs of the Voice to suit conservative views. Bill Sheehan won't get the job. The main asset of the Voice of America is its credibility — the fact that its listeners can depend on it to give them straight news, along with discussion and opinion that reflect all sides of

American life. If any ideological group — liberal or conservative — gets to run the Voice, that credibility goes out the window."

Wick dropped Sheehan and named Carlson, a former prize–winning television journalist in California, as acting director of VOA. Carlson later was nominated and confirmed as the full–fledged director, took office in November 1986, and soon had a controversy on his hands. It involved Reagan's Iran–dominated press conference on the night of November 19, when Radio Marti's White House correspondent, Annette Lopez–Munoz, asked the president a question.

Annette was an aggressive young reporter who tried hard to overcome her inexperience when she began covering the White House. I faulted Radio Marti for not seeing to it that she was adequately prepared for the job. Those of us in the basement press room tried to help her, answering her questions about the NSC, the SALT II treaty and other issues, and lending a hand in recording material for broadcast. She told me a member of the White House Correspondents Association had told her that she could not ask questions in briefings, and then asked me if VOA correspondents could. I explained that we did ask questions about subjects in the public domain and that we tried to avoid even the appearance of collusion.

After our conversation, Annette approached Bill Plante, the president of the Correspondents Association in 1986, who asked me for some historical background. Bill then sent a letter June 10 to Radio Marti's director of news, Jay Mallin, saying that Annette had "asked the Correspondents Association its position on the question of U.S. government employees taking part in White House briefings and Presidential News Conferences." He noted the Association's board had agreed in 1974 that "it would not be proper," but said members of the current board "have unanimously agreed that it should not be the role of the White House Correspondents' Association to decide which accredited reporters may ask questions. We believe this should be a matter determined by the agencies and subject to White House policy."

On receipt of Bill Plante's letter, I was told, a Radio Marti official asked for a USIA ruling on the subject of asking questions at presidential press conferences. Two weeks later, on June 24, the ruling came down through channels. It was passed on to Debi and me at the White House in a memo from Edward J. De Fontaine, then in charge of VOA's News and English Broadcasts, who said that "Director Wick has ruled that VOA will not ask questions at televised news conferences. Questions at briefings and other functions are not ruled out. He does not want to give even the appearance of softball questions, which might not be softball but so interpreted by some reporters on the extremes of issues, and feels the disadvantages will outweigh advantages."

I thought Wick's decision was regrettable and said so in a memo to VOA's assignments desk the same day. "I am sorry," I said, "that neither I nor the USIA wireless file's veteran White House correspondent had an opportunity to offer our thoughts on the matter. I would have preferred that the matter be left as it was — that is, up to us as professionals sensitive to agency concerns and credibility, and journalistic standards." The two VOA White House correspondents, I said, "are just as concerned as any other competent journalists about avoiding even the appearance of softball questions." In the past, I had raised my hand numbers of times at presidential press conferences in trying to be recognized so I could ask a question. There wasn't any objection from other correspondents or from the White House to my making the effort. It was a futile effort, since so few reporters get to ask questions at the televised sessions.

At the November 19 press conference, Reagan recognized Annette. She asked him whether, in view of his "obvious change in policy toward Iran," he would consider changing his policy toward Nicaragua, and if he would consider breaking diplomatic relations with Nicaragua to increase pressure on the Sandinista government. His answer made clear no change in policy and a continuance of diplomatic relations.

Early the next day Helen Thomas broke the story that Annette had been removed from her assignment: "A Radio Marti reporter who quizzed President Reagan at his news conference said today the government station yanked her off the White House beat and threatened to fire her because 'the National Security Council didn't like my question.' " Helen further quoted Annette as saying, "The NSC called the U.S. Information Agency complaining they had absolutely no input in my question. . . that I should have cleared it with the NSC."

Annette was also interviewed by CNN that afternoon, and made no mention of the NSC but said she was told by a Radio Marti official that the complaint about her question was generated at the White House. A White House spokesman said he was unaware of any communication between the White House and Radio Marti. VOA Director Carlson called a press conference in which he said Annette had violated "a longstanding rule" that VOA White House correspondents not ask questions at presidential press conferences.

There was no question in our minds about whether VOA should report the story, and I filed a broadcast piece that included Annette's charges and the VOA and White House reaction. I inserted a tape of Carlson denying that the NSC had called USIA or VOA, and a tape of Annette saying that Radio Marti had not threatened to fire her, but had taken her off the White House beat. And I noted that she made clear she asked the question because she thought she was allowed to do so under the new policy of the White House Correspondents Association.

At the White House morning briefing November 21, Speakes was asked if Reagan had decided in advance to call on Annette at the press conference and whether it was suggested to him that he call on her. He said no to both. One reporter noted that she was "well placed" in the seating arrangement and another noted, "She was in red, too." Did he recognize Annette "on the spur of the moment?" "That's my judgment," said Speakes. "And you believe he did not know she worked for Radio Marti?" "I'd sure bet he didn't know that."

In the exchange with reporters, Speakes repeated that the White House Press Office policy was not to put restrictions on anyone asking questions and that the USIA had made its own decision in the matter. He said the White House Correspondents Association had taken its position "boldly," at which point laughter, some of it derisive, broke out in the briefing room. I couldn't resist speaking up and said I thought the Association "took a very fine stand." Helen Thomas said, "I thought it was a horrible stand." Sam Donaldson said he agreed with Helen and "I don't think government employees should pose as reporters who do not work for the government and ask questions at those news conferences." What should they do, Speakes asked, "carry a flag?" Sam: "Well, yes. If they get up and announce, I work for the CIA, and I want to ask why your policy in Central America is so wonderful, I mean that's fine."

I respected Helen and Sam and I believe they respected me as a reporter, despite our differing views on this issue. This was a matter of principle with them, and I understood that. Their remarks weren't as distressing as those expressed November 23 in a *Washington Post* column by its ombudsman, Joseph Laitin, who in his previous long career as a government spokesman at the White House and elsewhere had earned a reputation as a straight shooter. In a paragraph in his column, Joe referred to "the hullabaloo over the representative of Radio Marti, a Voice of America operation, who was disciplined for questioning the president." Then came the zinger. It was, he said, "to my mind refreshing to hear one lowly public servant, the head of VOA, saying that a government employee has no business asking any government official, much less the president, questions during a news conference. This is the job of the news media."

In a letter to Joe, I expressed concern that the fallout from the Radio Marti affair had been a blow to VOA's credibility, what with his reading us out of the news media and with *The New York Times* editorially asking, "Why pretend government journalists operate by the same rules as the independent kind?" I said the responsible journalists who work for VOA are government employees, true, but we are members of the news media as well, employed by a legitimate news operation engaged in international broadcasting. We take our responsibilities as journalists seriously, I said, and cited the VOA

Charter. In the two–page letter, I noted that we reported presidential troubles as well as successes, pointing out as examples our coverage of Watergate and "the current furor over the administration's dealings with Iran and the transfer of funds to the Contras."

In the aftermath of this episode, Annette stayed on the Radio Marti staff until she resigned in February 1987. Joe Laitin wrote me a very nice letter in response to my letter, and I appreciated it, even though my arguments failed to convince him. Nor did he change my view that the VOA news operation was justifiably part of the news media. We didn't pull any punches because our salary checks were signed by the government. I believe proof of that was provided again in VOA's coverage of Iran–Contra.

The president's special NSC review board — composed of former Senator John Tower, the chairman; Edmund Muskie, and Brent Scowcroft — made its report to Reagan on February 26, 1987. I quickly read through it, and led my story with: "The board's report is a stinging indictment of the president's management style and the performance of the National Security Council staff. In commenting on what it called failure of responsibility, it said the decision–making process was flawed and Mr. Reagan did not seem to be aware of the way in which the Iran initiative was implemented and the full consequences of U.S. participation." The story quoted extensively from the report, including that "almost from the beginning the initiative became in fact a series of arms–for–hostages deals."

The Tower Board also said it knew of "no evidence to suggest that the president was aware of Colonel North's activities" in connection with the diversion of funds to the Contras. In a detailed piece on that, I noted it said North was deeply involved in an operation to provide private support for the Contras during the period that U.S. government support "was either banned or restricted by Congress."

Besides criticizing North and Poindexter, the board said White House Chief of Staff Regan "must bear primary responsibility for the chaos that descended upon the White House" when the Iran initiative was disclosed. There were, I told VOA listeners, "widespread expectations that Mr. Regan's resignation will take place soon." VOA had earlier reported calls by some Republican leaders in Congress for Regan's resignation and press accounts that Nancy Reagan was upset with him and wanted him to leave.

How did our stories compare with others in the news media? The content was the same, though not in as colorful language as those in the newsmagazines, for example. *Time* said Reagan "stands exposed as a president willfully ignorant of what his aides were doing, myopically unaware of the glaring contradictions between his public and secret policies," and *Newsweek* said Reagan "emerged as a careless, remote and forgetful leader, too indifferent to supervise the reckless swashbuckling of his aides."

The day after the Tower Board issued its report, Reagan announced a new chief of staff, former Senator Howard Baker, who, I told our listeners, was considered a moderate, middle of the road Republican. Not long afterwards I received a letter from a regular listener in Nigeria who remembered Baker for his famous line during the Watergate hearings, and quoted it: "What did the president know and when did he know it?" Shabbily, the news that Don Regan was being replaced was leaked to the press before the announcement. He wrote a one–sentence letter to Reagan — "I hereby resign as Chief of Staff to the President of the United States." — and left the White House that day.

Reagan scheduled a prime time address to the nation for Wednesday, March 4, to give his response to the Tower Board findings. On the day before the speech, he named FBI director William Webster to succeed the ailing William J. Casey as CIA director. His original choice had been CIA deputy director Robert Gates, but after some senators said the nomination was in trouble because of the Iran affair, Gates withdrew. Reagan also appeared before reporters in the White House briefing room for the first time in three months to announce the U.S. draft INF treaty being tabled at the Geneva talks with the Soviet Union. And he accepted an invitation to visit West Berlin in June after attending the annual economic summit in Venice.

With a new team of advisors in place, I reported, "the president moved to restore his administration's, and his own, credibility" in his address. He defended his management style as having worked successfully in the past, admitted it didn't work in the Iran–Contra affair and said he had already begun correcting this. The next day Howard Baker told reporters Reagan's speech was "a turning point" and the president now could focus on other issues.

That same day, March 5, Reagan appeared before newspaper executives and presented an optimistic, forward–looking image. In a brief reference to the Iran inquiry, he said enough time had been spent on "inside Washington politics," and he shifted attention to what he called a breakthrough in arms control. He said he'd never felt more optimistic about the prospects for success in strengthening the foundation of world peace, because the Soviets had dropped their insistence on linking an INF agreement to other arms control negotiations. This change in the Soviet position, he said, "is a great breakthrough and shows that in working for the cause of peace, preparedness pays, patience pays, and firmness pays."

Reagan said his administration would remain firm on effective verification of new agreements, and told a story we reporters heard many times: "I'm not particularly a linguist, but in the Reykjavik meeting, I had a Russian proverb that I would say in Russian to Mr. Gorbachev, and I said it, *doverai no proverai* (phonetic) — trust, but verify." On March 6 he announced Shultz would go to Moscow in mid–April to discuss arms control and other matters with Shevardnadze.

Reagan did discuss Iran again, in his Saturday radio talk March 14, admitting he was wrong in ignoring the advice of his secretaries of state and defense not to sell arms to Iran. His purpose, I wrote, was to set matters straight with the two cabinet members. Shultz and Weinberger "were stung by the conclusions of the Tower Board that they'd distanced themselves from the march of events as the Iran initiative evolved rapidly into arms–for–hostages deals." Weinberger in particular was understood to be unhappy that nothing was being said at the White House in defense of him and Shultz. Reagan praised them as men who had never hesitated to give him their unvarnished views on national security issues and said he was "enormously grateful" that he would continue to receive their views in the months ahead. The president's remarks, I told VOA listeners, "served as a signal to the international community" that Shultz and Weinberger "are valued advisors and will stay on in the administration."

The Iran–Contra hearings got under way in Congress on May 5. Besides reporting White House reaction, I kept a chronology of the testimony, comments by Reagan and various administration officials, announcements by independent counsel Lawrence Walsh, and other pertinent developments, for ready reference in writing stories. By the time the public hearings ended August 3 and Reagan made another speech to the nation August 12, the pages of single–spaced typed entries in the chronology totaled 171 inches in length. Here's a sampling:

For June 2, the entries included: Assistant Sec–State Elliott Abrams admits he misled a congressional committee last year (1986) by hiding fact he'd solicited Brunei for $10 million in Contra aid, said he failed to question North about his role with the Contras.

The most eagerly awaited testimony was of course that of North and Poindexter. My entries for July 7 included: North begins testimony in public hearings, said he never told RR about diversion to the Contras but "I assumed the president knew." Said his superiors never told him RR knew about it. "I never personally discussed the use of the residuals or profits from the sale of U.S. weapons to Iran for the purpose of supporting the Nicaraguan resistance with the president. I never raised it with him, and he never raised it with me." And, White House spokesman (Marlin) Fitzwater declined comment, reminded reporters of RR's denial of knowledge of diversion to Contras, said RR didn't have chance to watch North testimony, said conducting business of government is more important than watching TV. Columnist Jack Anderson, who met w/RR, quoted RR as saying he understood from wire service reports that North had exonerated him.

For July 8, one of the entries was: RR made trip to New Britain, Conn. on economic bill of rights, said "all that lame duck talk is for the birds." Protesters shouted "No more lies." RR declined comment on reporters' questions about North testimony.

Among the July 9 entries: Fitzwater reports a deluge of phone calls to White House in first two days of Ollie testimony, overwhelmingly in favor of Ollie and sympathetic toward Contras. Declines comment on Ollie testimony, but it's clear White House is not displeased with Ollie's statements in defense of U.S. aid to Contras. And, White House poll, reported by C–S Monitor, finds RR approval rating nudged up to 54 percent.

July 15: Poindexter begins testimony, said he never told RR of the diversion of arms–sale profits to the Contras. "I made a very deliberate decision not to ask the president so that I could insulate him from the decision and provide some future deniability for the president if it ever leaked out. Of course, our hope was that it would not leak out." Poindexter said he felt he had the authority to make the decision and was convinced that RR, if he'd been told, would have thought it was a good idea. Poindexter said "the buck stops here with me." Poindexter also said he destroyed a secret document that sanctioned trading arms for hostages — a finding that Poindexter said was signed by RR on Dec. 5, 1985 — because if it was leaked it would cause "significant political embarrassment" to the president.

Also July 15: RR, when told Poindexter said he didn't tell him about diversion, said: "What's new about that; I've been saying it for seven months." Fitzwater said RR is gratified that "the testimony confirms" what RR has been saying. Fitzwater asserted RR has said on past occasions that he would not have allowed it if he'd been told about it. Re the December arms–for–hostages finding that Poindexter said RR signed, Fitzwater said RR does not recall signing it or reading it but will not disagree with those who said he did. Fitzwater sought to put the finding in the context of the broader "overture" to Iran.

July 23: Shultz begins testimony, tells of "battle royal" between himself and Poindexter, Casey and others re arms for hostages, and said "there has been guerrilla warfare going on." Shultz disclosed he'd offered to resign three times.

July 30: Former White House Chief of Staff Don Regan testified RR's secret Iran initiative was kept alive by arms dealers, while Iran used American hostages as bait. Regan said he advised RR to end the initiative in February 1986 when 1,000 TOW missiles were shipped to Iran and no hostages were released. "I told him I thought he ought to break it off, that we'd been snookered again. . . . and how long are we gonna put up with this rug merchant type of stuff?"

August 3: Public hearings end, with panel members blasting Poindexter and North for not informing RR of Contra diversion, condemning "secrecy and deception," and noting RR's "corrective" actions. Senator Inouye, summing up, said: "I see it as a chilling story, a story of deceit and duplicity and arrogant disregard of the law. . . ."

In addressing the nation after the hearings, on August 12, Reagan again acknowledged that mistakes had been made and said, "I was stubborn in my pursuit of a policy that went astray." The congressional committees issued their report November 18, finding that "the ultimate responsibility for the events in the Iran–Contra affair must rest with the president. If the president did not know what his national security advisors were doing, he should have."

Reagan's standing in the public opinion polls had plunged immediately after the secret dealings with Iran and the diversion of funds to the Contras were revealed. A CBS News–*New York Times* poll in December 1986 found that 47 percent of those surveyed thought he was lying when he said he didn't know about the diversion. By the end of 1987, however, his approval rating was on an upward swing. A major factor was his performance in foreign policy, in particular arms control.

His rating crept up after a trip to Europe in June when he visited West Berlin and delivered an impassioned speech with the Berlin Wall as the backdrop. He spoke from a platform at the Brandenburg Gate: "General Secretary Gorbachev, if you seek peace, if you seek prosperity for the Soviet Union and Eastern Europe, if you seek liberalization, come here to this gate. Mr. Gorbachev, open this gate. Mr. Gorbachev, tear down this wall." Reagan had called for dismantlement of the wall before, in 1986 on its 25th anniversary, but his specific challenge to the Soviet leader was far more dramatic. It received extensive play in the media then (I watched it on television at home, as Debi covered the trip) and again when the Berlin Wall came down and his "tear down this wall" tape was replayed over and over on TV and radio.

The president announced on October 30 that Foreign Minister Shevardnadze had brought him a letter from Gorbachev accepting his invitation to come to Washington for a summit meeting, beginning December 7. "At that time," Reagan said, "we expect to sign an agreement eliminating the entire class of U.S. and Soviet Intermediate Range Nuclear Forces, or INF."

With only five weeks to prepare for the huge international press corps expected to cover the summit, White House aides went scurrying to find a suitable location for a press center. Space at nearby universities was unavailable or not big enough for the estimated 6,000 news people. Finally a ballroom at the J. W. Marriott Hotel, two and a half blocks from the White House, was settled on, and workmen converted it into a press center on the weekend before the Soviet leader's arrival.

Both leaders were approaching their third summit "with an eye to domestic considerations," I wrote in a pre–summit backgrounder. "Questions about the strength of Mr. Gorbachev's leadership and the pace of his reform programs were raised last month with the dismissal of one of his staunchest allies, the outspoken Boris Yeltsin, as head of the Moscow Communist Party organization. The dismissal was seen as a bowing by Mr. Gorbachev to conservatives in the Soviet hierarchy, and a setback to his glasnost policy of openness." I noted that questions about Reagan's leadership had been raised because of the Iran–Contra affair and the loss of control of the Senate to the opposition Democrats, and added: "Mr. Reagan also has come under fire from his longtime conservative supporters, particularly arch conservatives who have been sharply critical of the INF Treaty and have been accusing him of becoming soft on the Soviet Union and Mr. Gorbachev." Thus both leaders wanted a successful summit, one that would demonstrate their leadership.

Signing the INF Treaty would be the centerpiece of the summit, but the two leaders also planned to discuss reducing long-range strategic missiles by 50 percent, other bi-lateral subjects, human rights, and regional issues, including Afghanistan. In another broadcast piece, I reported that the talks on Afghanistan would be watched closely for any movement toward a resolution of the eight-year-old war. The conflict "has been costly in lives lost, and, for the Soviet Union, costly in the resources it has spent and in terms of world public opinion. . . . The Soviets have found themselves bogged down in what has been called a quagmire similar to the Vietnam war." The estimated 115,000 Soviet troops in Afghanistan, and the Afghan army, had been facing a strong resistance from the Mujahedin. The Soviets were making comments about setting a withdrawal timetable and, one week before the Washington summit, Afghan President Najibulla proposed Soviet withdrawal in 12 months, if the United States and Pakistan cut off aid to the Mujahedin. Reagan dismissed that timetable as too long and too conditional.

As Gorbachev arrived in Washington Monday, December 7, the Soviet Union's red flag with hammer and sickle was flying from lamp posts on Pennsylvania Avenue in front of the White House, alongside the American and city of Washington flags. He was the first Soviet leader to visit Washington since Leonid Brezhnev held talks with Richard Nixon in 1973. At that summit, a giant Soviet flag was put up next to the American flag on the front of the Old Executive Office Building next to the White House. This time a huge evergreen wreath decorated the building for the Christmas holiday season.

In arrival remarks at Andrews Air Force Base, Gorbachev said the summit talks would deal with pivotal questions in Soviet–American relations, questions of reducing strategic offensive arms, and said he hoped he would hear "some new words" on the American side. Two hours after Gorbachev's plane touched down, Reagan presided at the annual lighting of the national Christmas tree and, as expected, referred to the summit: "Peace on earth, goodwill toward men. I cannot think of a better spirit in which to

begin the meetings of the next several days." I filed a wrapup
including tape of that quote and the tape in Russian with English
translation of Gorbachev's "some new words" quote. Reagan later
told reporters Gorbachev would hear them in the morning.

Mikhail Gorbachev and Ronald Reagan sign the INF Treaty December 8,
1987, at a White House ceremony, during which President Reagan
repeated to the Soviet leader his familiar rendition of a Russian maxim,
"trust but verify." (Courtesy, Ronald Reagan Library)

For the White House welcoming ceremony Tuesday morning,
Ron Pemstein was in the press group while I stayed in the VOA
booth in the basement to file a quick spot for the upcoming
newscast. Reagan's and Gorbachev's remarks were "remarkably
similar," Ron reported. "They both talked of progress toward a 50
percent reduction in their strategic nuclear arsenals to go with the
treaty they will sign shortly to eliminate all intermediate–range
missiles. They both addressed their domestic audiences. President
Reagan talked of the American people committed to freedom and

belief in God. General Secretary Gorbachev spoke of the Soviet people united behind his policies of perestroika, restructuring the economy, and glasnost, openness." Later in the Oval Office, Gorbachev said he did hear some of those new words in Reagan's statement.

The two leaders signed the INF Treaty and made brief remarks in an early afternoon ceremony in the East Room and then delivered short messages to the world. VOA carried live coverage of the events, including live reports immediately afterwards by Ron and me and by Victor Franzusoff of our Russian service. My wrapup reported Reagan's and Gorbachev's remarks hailing the history–making treaty and vowing continued efforts to reduce arms and strive for improved relations, and included the tape of a humorous exchange between them:

Reagan: The importance of this treaty transcends numbers. We have listened to the wisdom in an old Russian maxim, and I'm sure you're familiar with it. Mr. General Secretary, my pronunciation may give you difficulty. This maxim is *doverai no proverai*, trust but verify. (laughter breaking in) Gorbachev: You repeat that at every meeting. (laughter and applause) Reagan: I like it. (laughter and applause).

A timetable for Soviet withdrawal from Afghanistan was one of the subjects discussed on the second day, but no breakthrough was announced. Under a U.N.–mediated agreement signed four months later, however, the Soviets began pulling out their troops. The withdrawal was completed in February 1989.

On Thursday, the summit's final day, Gorbachev wowed Washingtonians when he stopped his ZIL limousine at one of the city's busiest intersections, Connecticut Avenue and L Street N.W., and stepped out to greet and shake hands with average Americans. "I'm glad to be in America," he said as he schmoozed the delighted noontime crowds. That afternoon in a departure ceremony on the White House South Lawn, the two leaders, protected by umbrellas from a drenching rain, summed up their meeting. "I am pleased to report," said Reagan, "that this summit has been a clear success."

The visit to Washington, said Gorbachev, "has, on the whole, justified our hopes. . . . A good deal has been accomplished."

Both reported progress toward reducing strategic arms. A joint statement issued later said they agreed to instruct their negotiators to work toward completion of a treaty, preferably in time for signature at their next meeting in the first half of 1988. And what about SDI? The joint statement sidestepped their disagreement. They wanted the summit to strike a positive note, and it did. As for their next summit, I looked forward to covering Ronald Reagan in Moscow!

After the Washington summit, a White House public opinion survey put Reagan's job approval rating at 65 percent. Independent polls showed an increase as well. And the earlier flurry of stories in the press about a president weakened by Iran–Contra had dissipated. On the whole Reagan received favorable treatment in the press. He displayed a jovial demeanor in the company of reporters, although he, like other presidents before him, became annoyed with them on occasion. In the early weeks of Iran–Contra, he accused the press of overplaying the story.

Before that, there was the S.O.B. photo op. It took place February 28, 1986, shortly after his administration granted asylum to Ferdinand Marcos and the former Philippine leader and his family were flown to Hawaii. A press pool was taken to the White House cabinet room to cover Reagan receiving a report from David Packard, chairman of a commission that studied Pentagon procurement procedures. A pool reporter asked Reagan: "Mr. President, there are reports that President Marcos has brought millions of dollars worth of currency and jewelry to Hawaii from the Philippines. Is that appropriate considering the economic problems there?" Reagan said there was "no way for us to know anything about this. This is up to the government of the Philippines and the people of the Philippines." After another question, on whether President Aquino should have released the leader of the Marxist movement in the Philippines, with Reagan replying he didn't know, the pool was ushered out. As its members left, they heard someone say, "sons of bitches," in obvious reference to the reporters. When the pool tape was played on the White House mult, there was no doubt about it, the someone who uttered the expletive was — the president.

In the basement press room, Joe Ewalt decided the event should be memorialized. A few days later he brought in a stack of bright egg-yolk-yellow T-shirts emblazoned with big blue letters: S.O.B. Printed beneath, in very small letters and enclosed in parentheses, were the words: Sons of the Basement. (When I wear my shirt, startled observers seldom notice the small print.) The basement reporters wore the S.O.B. T-shirts to a briefing by Larry Speakes, and gave him one for Reagan. Sarah McClendon wore hers one day when she was on the press pool for several White House events.

The Reagan–Gorbachev Washington summit turned out to be the last summit I covered. On January 30, 1988, I packed up old files and tape cassettes and broadcast my last report from the basement booth I'd occupied for so many years and went back to Voice headquarters on Independence Avenue S.W. to start a new job. Sid Davis, who left NBC to become VOA's director of programs in February 1987, had asked me to return as an executive, and people in the newsroom said they wanted me to come back. I agreed, even though I knew I would miss covering the White House.

A White House correspondent has many "perks," and not the least of them is the chance to see, or at least get a glimpse of, exotic places around the world and to be part of stirring events here at home. One of the stories I loved covering was the celebration of the Statue of Liberty's 100th birthday in 1986. The newly renovated statue was unveiled on the night of July 3 when Reagan pressed a button setting off laser beams illuminating Miss Liberty in all her glory. The nearly three-hour ceremony was an extravaganza of "pageantry, show business glitter, and patriotism," I told VOA listeners, "a celebration of America itself, from the opening fanfare to the dramatic illumination of the statue. . . ."

July 4th was the celebration of America's 210th birthday, and the festivities of "Liberty Weekend" continued with an international parade of modern warships, a stately procession of magnificent tall ships, and that night the biggest fireworks display in the nation's history. I witnessed the fireworks from a privileged location, for I was in the White House press group aboard the aircraft carrier *John F. Kennedy* anchored in New York Harbor, facing the Statue of Liberty. Surrounding the carrier were literally thousands of sail boats, motor launches, and larger ships, a breathtaking sight in itself. I was thrilled to be there, and also felt a bit of home–town pride; among the architects of the fireworks display was a New Castle company, founded in 1921 by Antonio Zambelli, an Italian immigrant from Naples. The president and Mrs. Reagan watched the fireworks from the flight deck, where the Marine Band performed — sort of. The rockets were set off in time to the music. But for the television coverage, the music was pre–recorded so it wouldn't be drowned out by the noise of the fireworks. After filing a broadcast piece, I phoned my mother in New Castle from the aircraft carrier. She, and my sister and brother, were used to my calling them from unusual places. I would miss being in such places, but most of all would miss reporting. I would have to follow events through the reports of others.

In the ongoing Iran–Contra investigation, Oliver North was convicted in 1989 on charges of aiding and abetting obstruction of Congress and two other felonies, but the convictions were thrown out in 1991 when a judge ruled that his trial was influenced by his congressional testimony given under immunity. John Poindexter's 1990 convictions on five felony counts, including obstruction of Congress, were set aside in appellate court in 1991 on the grounds that his congressional testimony, also given under immunity, had been used against him at his trial. Both Robert McFarlane, who pleaded guilty in 1988 to misdemeanor charges of withholding information from Congress, and Elliott Abrams, who pleaded guilty in 1991 to similar misdemeanor charges, were pardoned by President Bush on Christmas Eve 1992. Bush also pardoned four others in the affair. Five lesser defendants pleaded guilty to various charges.

The last American hostages held in Lebanon were freed in 1991, through the efforts of United Nations Secretary General Javier Perez de Cuellar and his envoy, Giandomenico Picco, in complex negotiations with countries and captors that began in early August that year. Edward Tracy, abducted in October 1986, was released by his pro-Iranian captors on August 11. On November 18, Thomas Sutherland, held captive for six and a half years, was freed, along with Church of England envoy Terry Waite, who was trying to negotiate hostage releases when he was kidnaped in January 1987. Joseph Cicippio, held since September 1986, was released on December 2, Alann Steen, captive since January 1987, on December 3, and finally, on December 4, Terry Anderson of the Associated Press, the American hostage held longest — since March 1985. The U.N. negotiations also were successful in freeing hostages of other nationalities held in Lebanon.

In following the coverage of the freed Americans, I was immensely pleased to learn that some of them were allowed, at least in their final weeks or months of captivity, to listen to international radio broadcasts, including VOA and BBC. Thomas Sutherland told a press conference in Damascus on the day of his release that he was "very very moved when I heard on VOA a recording of the bells of Iowa State, which I particularly appreciated hearing when I was a student there on the campus. . . . So when I heard them ring out 72 bells on the occasion of my 72nd month I was extremely happy." Sutherland said he "would like to say an especial thank you to VOA for bringing us those messages that we've received from our families on the shortwave, and indeed on medium wave, in the middle of the night. . . ."

The Voice routinely reported comments by families of the hostages, for instance on anniversaries of their detention, or when relatives, like Terry Anderson's sister, Peggy Say, held press conferences to urge no let-up in efforts to gain the release of their loved ones. VOA also took note of the birthdays of the hostages and broadcast features with news of their families, such as reporting the birth of a grandson for hostage Alann Steen.

I beamed when Sutherland told the press in Damascus that "VOA is an excellent radio station." Then I gasped when he added, "But I'm afraid I have to admit that the BBC has everybody beaten, hands down." However, Sutherland, with the American ambassador standing there, went on to suggest that if VOA had "a bunch of money" and a director were told to "put together the best kind of international radio that we possibly could devise, then you'll come up with something like the BBC. So Mr. Ambassador, my thanks."

That was a goal I endorsed. I wanted VOA to be the best. Sutherland later visited VOA headquarters to say thanks in person, especially to the anchor of the Magazine Show, Barbara Klein, whose broadcasts he had listened to while in captivity.

18
More Grease to the Elbow
Problems and Kazoo-Tooting
The Voice and Tiananmen Square

In my last correspondent report filed from the White House basement, I told VOA's listeners: "I shall miss reporting, but in my new job, where I will be supervising our news coverage, I will be thinking of you. And I'll be thinking too about a saying quoted to me by many listeners in Africa who have wished me well and said keep up the good work. The saying is, More grease to the elbow."

It tickled me that the letter writers had expressed their wishes for a well-lubricated elbow, for when I was growing up, my father had taught me that to do a job well, "you have to use elbow grease." I intended to use it in carrying out my new responsibilities, beginning February 1, 1988, as VOA's editor in chief, in charge of the News, Current Affairs, and Worldwide English Divisions.

I had loved getting letters from listeners. They were reassurance that I wasn't broadcasting into a vacuum. And they were great ego-boosters. Some writers were lavish in their praise, such as a seminarian in Kampala, Uganda, who said: "Allow me to express my heartfelt thanks to you for the service you're rendering to God, USA, and the world at large." Many were curious about my personal life and my role as a White House reporter. A "regular listener" in Sierra Leone asked me if White House correspondents "sleep in the White House, or only work there." I tried to answer as many of the letters as possible, and my reply to this one was that we just worked there, often for long hours and sometimes all night.

Some of the letter writers wanted to be pen-friends, sent me their photos and asked for mine; others requested information on how to enroll in American universities, and some wanted financial help. Many asked for VOA souvenirs, calendars and program schedules. Our audience mail unit, headed for years by Fran LaFalce, sent out the requested items and my replies. The letters came from around the world, even Albania when it was the most tightly closed communist country, run by an isolationist regime. The writer, an elderly man who had worked in Maine and then returned to his native Albania, wanted help in obtaining Social Security benefits he had earned in America. I checked government agencies and the office of a senator from Maine, and regretfully replied that I was told nothing could be done to help him.

When I left the White House beat, I thought the letters to me would stop, but for months mail came in from listeners offering congratulations on my new job. One such letter was from Wuhan, China, in December 1988: "I am one of VOA's millions of listeners," the writer said. "We know you are supervising VOA's news coverage and working for us. In spite of we don't hear your voice now," he wrote, "we are attracted still by VOA's excellent programs. . . . If you can send Voice Magazine to us, we will get a lot of information. It is very useful to us." The magazine was still in existence then, but, as noted previously, was discontinued during the Bush administration because of budget cuts. The budget cuts also forced the shutting down of the audience mail unit for two years. It was resurrected in late 1992.

In bureaucratic shorthand, my bailiwick as editor in chief was NEB, for News and English Broadcasts, which supplied news and program material for Worldwide English and 43 other language services. My mandate was to improve programming and morale. My goal was to make better use of the resources in the three divisions so that VOA would be the best in international broadcasting.

In news, we saw the BBC as our major competitor because of its long–established reputation as a prime source of information. The Voice routinely monitored BBC newscasts, and in international news there was little difference between their story lineups and ours. They were ahead of us in some cases; we were ahead in others. The BBC tended to give more emphasis to events in the Commonwealth countries, and it had the advantage of a large corps of stringers in Africa, enabling it to report more fully than we did on developments there. We also monitored Moscow Radio, which logged more hours in international broadcasting than VOA and carried "news" that was so obviously slanted that one could not regard it as a credible competitor.

My first act was to restructure the newsroom, the heart of the News Division, and the heart of VOA. The News Division had a staff of about 200, including the newsroom's writers, editors, broadcasters and producers; correspondents in our overseas bureaus and in New York, Chicago, Los Angeles and other major American cities, and support personnel. My aim was to ensure that our newscasts were up–to–the–minute in reporting breaking stories. I also emphasized long–range planning for coverage of events and increased live coverage, including going live even on short notice.

One of the first tests of the restructured newsroom was our coverage of a breaking story in Panama on the night of February 25, 1988. Panama's president, Eric Arturo DelValle, had called for the resignation of General Manuel Noriega as chief of the country's defense forces. Noriega, who had been indicted earlier in the month by federal grand juries in Florida for helping international drug traffickers and allowing the laundering of their profits through Panamanian banks, refused. VOA's Central American correspondent Michael Drudge, based in Costa Rica, was dispatched to Panama to cover the crisis. From the airport Mike drove directly to the besieged president's home, found that police and troops had been pulled back, walked in, and got an interview with DelValle in English and Spanish — plus, I was told, a beer and one of Panama's finest cigars. It was satisfying to hear that Mike's reports were way ahead of those broadcast by other media. Our coverage included the administration's reaction to the events and phone interviews with a former U.S. ambassador to Panama, Ambler Moss, and Congressman Charles Rangel, who had been outspoken about Noriega and the Panama–Medellin connection. The newsroom also worked closely with the Spanish service on the story.

One of my major tasks in 1988 was to name new chiefs of the three divisions. Diane Doherty became the first woman to head the News Division, chosen because of her dedication to the integrity of the news. DD was a VOA Summer intern in 1963, joined the newsroom staff in 1967, and served as a correspondent and as deputy chief under Bernie Kamenske. News, of course, was my prime love, and upgrading VOA's coverage was the sunny part of my job. Otherwise, in supervising the three divisions large chunks of my time were spent dealing with budget cuts, personnel and mounds of paper work, instituting electronic wire service delivery — and trying to resolve problems of various sorts. First, some of the problems.

The Current Affairs Division, with a staff of about 50, had come under attack for producing politically biased documentaries. These included programs called "Focus" that were aired each weekday. In reading many of the scripts before I became editor in chief, I found that a majority dealt with subjects dear to Reagan, and some were weighted heavily on the side of ultra–conservative views that went beyond Reagan's policies. A number of these programs, I was told, contained tape excerpts from interviews that were edited to reflect a harder line, by excising a qualifying phrase.

The domestic commercial networks do this sort of thing too, in order to shorten and sharpen soundbites. In one instance I remember in particular, a network TV producer produced a tight soundbite from a Reagan speech by splicing part of one sentence together with part of another. The networks defend such tape editing by pointing out that print media stories contain sentences with fragmented quotes. In print, however, the use of quotation marks makes clear to the reader the separation of one quoted fragment from another. In broadcasting, the soundbite you hear may not always be exactly how the person said it.

The ideological slant in Current Affairs received considerable attention in two articles about the Voice in 1988, one published by *Columbia Journalism Review* and the other by the *Review of International Broadcasting*. The CJR piece was written by a part–time writer on our Special English staff, Carolyn Weaver, and although it caused consternation in VOA's front office, she was not fired and was given an "oral admonishment." The other article concluded that "the Reagan effort to win the battle of words with Radio Moscow" had resulted in "increasing skepticism" about

VOA's integrity. But it added that the skepticism "may be greater" in the United States than overseas and that for many listeners, "VOA is a shining light of freedom and truth."

By the time the CJR article appeared, the Current Affairs chief, Edwin Warner, had been reassigned to the News Division to write backgrounder reports, and I had named former correspondent Steve Thompson, then in charge of the newsroom's evening shift, as acting chief. In overseeing Current Affairs, I reviewed the documentaries, proposed additional topics for them, urged greater productivity, and encouraged use of the expertise of our overseas correspondents. In fairness, some of the documentary writers had been turning out work that met high professional standards, and the Current Affairs feature writers produced pieces of generally good quality. The book reviews and science reports were superior. Science writer Brian Cislak was among VOA broadcasters mentioned in particular by Russian astronomers when they told neighbors of mine, who were attending a 1993 conference in Russia, that they had been listening to VOA for many years.

The Russian astronomers also named the late John Trimble, a newscast anchor; Pat Gates, former host of the English breakfast show (Patricia Gates Lynch later served as ambassador to Madagascar and as RFE/RL's representative in Washington); Russian broadcaster Victor Potapov, and me.

By late August 1988, the three divisions were operating pretty well and I left for a vacation in England and France. It was a mistake. When I returned to work September 13, I found that Steve Thompson had been removed as Current Affairs acting chief by the front office. During my absence, loyalists of Ed Warner had circulated a petition claiming that he had done a fine job producing substantive material and alleging that Steve was not doing so. I was furious that Steve had been removed unjustifiably and without consulting me, and said so, but was told the decision was final and he would have to be reassigned. At that time VOA's East Asia and Pacific Division proposed a new broadcast service, in English, for placement on stations in the region. Steve took on the project and built "VOA Pacific" into a network of stations that received the weekly two-hour program by satellite or through the mail. I listened to it each week before it was sent out. It was a good mix of music and information relevant to the region.

Later in 1988 I announced the selection of a new Current Affairs chief, Kevin Lynch, who then was editor of *Voice* magazine and, before joining VOA, was editor at the conservative *National Review*. Kevin clearly was an excellent editor, and shared my ideas on ways to improve our programs and make more use of talent in the language services. He and his successors did improve the Current Affairs output.

Other problems in 1988 included a disturbing incident on the afternoon of April 22 involving USIA Director Charles Wick and VOA correspondent Ed Conley. Wick and other agency officials, among them the VOA director, had ended two days of talks with a Soviet media delegation headed by Valentin Falin of Novosti on improving communications between the two countries. Wick and Falin were holding a press conference. Conley started to ask a question, noting his VOA affiliation, and Wick cut him off. "Excuse me," Wick said, "we're trying to open this to non-government press at the moment, if you don't mind." Conley tried again and Wick again turned him aside, saying that "we want to give this opportunity to the non-government press."

After the press conference, Wick told Conley he hoped he hadn't embarrassed him and added, "We don't want to be accused of loaded questions." Conley replied that he had a legitimate news question (he had planned to ask about prospects for a breakthrough in an information exchange) and that the incident would be "very demoralizing at VOA News."

We were not only demoralized, we were angered at the treatment of Ed Conley and anguished over the incident's effect on VOA's credibility. In the eyes of those attending the press conference, the Voice had been lumped together with the propagandistic press of the Soviet communist regime. With no objection from VOA's front office, I immediately wrote Wick a letter expressing our feelings and had it delivered by messenger.

Wick phoned me a short time later that afternoon and said that during the media talks, the U.S. side at been "brutally frank" in refuting Soviet charges about the American media. He said the purpose of the joint press conference was to give America's private sector media as much opportunity as possible to raise questions about the Soviet media. And the point he made was similar to what he'd told Conley, that the Soviets might perceive a question from VOA as loaded. He also pointed out that he had been fighting for establishment of a VOA bureau in Moscow. Wick apparently cared enough about the people at VOA to feel that he had to explain the context of his remarks at the press conference. I wrote a long memo to the staff on his explanation, and that calmed things down.

Although Wick was often overbearing and demanding, he made it possible for VOA to begin modernizing its aging network of transmitters, by obtaining increased funding for USIA. He also deserves credit for bringing USIA into the television age, by inaugurating the Worldnet satellite TV service in 1983 and installing satellite dishes around the globe. And as a result of his efforts, Soviet authorities on September 27, 1988 gave their consent to a VOA bureau in Moscow. Geneva correspondent Andre de Nesnera was the logical choice for our first resident correspondent in Moscow, and the bureau was established a year later.

Problems in the Worldwide English Division mostly involved a need for more features of interest to overseas listeners. The 50-member staff produced breakfast and magazine shows; programs on science and communications; "Studio One," a showcase for American culture; and music shows — classical, country western, pop and rock, and the world-renowned "Music USA," hosted by jazz expert and mellow-voiced Willis Conover since the mid-1950s. Musicians in all parts of the world adopted American jazz and swing from listening to Willis. The immensely popular Special English programs were also a part of Worldwide English. These were produced by a small staff of skilled writers who adapted, in effect "translated," newscasts and features, using a vocabulary of only 1,500 words.

The new chief chosen for Worldwide English was John Stevenson, who brought to the post his experience as operations manager in Washington for VOA Europe, and who worked well with his counterparts in the News and Current Affairs Divisions.

VOA Europe was an entity separate from regular VOA. Headquartered in Munich, it supplied news, features and pop music to FM and cable stations in Western Europe. Established in 1985 by the Reagan administration to reach the World War II "successor generation," it was a round–the–clock English service that was structured so the stations could insert commercials, producing revenue for them. VOA Europe had its own staff, budget, and studios in Munich and at VOA in Washington; used VOA program material, and broadcast its own Americana–type features. It carried the first six minutes of VOA's hourly 10–minute newscasts, but produced an evening news show that in essence duplicated VOA's "World Report."

Although VOA Europe was a means of enlarging the audience for Voice newscasts, I thought the duplication in staffs, facilities and programming was wasteful. Costs were reduced when it was moved from Munich to Washington at the end of the 1980s. And its placement on radio stations — extended to include stations in post–cold war Eastern Europe — was integrated into the Office of Affiliate Relations, which works with an expanding network of stations around the world carrying VOA programs. In 1994 VOA Europe's pared staff, except for the pop and rock disk jockeys, was transferred to Worldwide English, and in 1995 the service was earmarked for closure as a separate VOA entity.

The problems I have recounted ought not to eclipse the fact that listeners tuned in VOA because they relied on it to find out what was going on, in the world, in their own countries, and in ours. Now to the sunny side of my job: coverage of the news. The professor of an advertising course that I took at the University of Missouri frequently counseled the class, "He who tooteth not his own kazoo, the same shall not be tooteth." So I did some kazoo–tooting on behalf of VOA correspondents in drafting one of Charles Wick's regular reports to USIA employees, "The Director's

Letter," in the agency house organ, USIA *World*. Among the correspondents cited for stories they covered in 1988 were: Cairo-based Doug Roberts for tracking developments in the Iran-Iraq War, United Nations correspondent Elaine Johanson for her coverage of the talks on the ceasefire between Iran and Iraq, John Schulz in Islamabad for reporting the situation in Afghanistan including the withdrawal of Soviet troops, Costa Rica-based Michael Drudge for reporting Central American peace efforts as well as the Noriega story, Abidjan-based Sonja Pace for her exclusive interview with the president of Nigeria, Mallory Saleson in Johannesburg for her reporting of the four-nation Angola talks, and Jolyon Naegele for his exclusive broadcast interview in Czech with Alexander Dubcek. In that interview, Dubcek discussed what happened to him in the Prague Spring of 1968, recalled a favorite song, and asked that VOA play it for him. Our Czech service did.

Another major story we covered in 1988 was, of course, Reagan's trip to Moscow for a summit with Gorbachev. How I wished I could have covered Ronald Reagan in Red Square! Instead I followed the first-rate reporting of our team of correspondents in Moscow, the stories filed by the newsroom's round-the-clock summit desk, and our live broadcasts that included Reagan's speech at Moscow State University. He called on students to have faith that changes taking place in their country would result in benefits to the Soviet people.

Domestic coverage in 1988 focused on the campaign for the presidential election. Political editor Alex Belida coordinated the output of correspondents and Current Affairs writers, responded to requests from language services for backgrounders on the American political process, and worked with the news-astute producers for our live broadcasts at the national party conventions, Myrna Whitworth and Mike Luehring. I was delighted with our coverage, and with our outside political analysts — who were Jerry Warren and Jody Powell. I had asked them to be the analysts because, as former White House spokesmen, they were known overseas, and I thought they would discuss the election process in terms more understandable to our listeners than the lingo of traditional political analysts. Jerry and Jody enhanced our convention coverage with their insights and thoughtful comments, and they did it for a pittance. VOA couldn't afford to spend much.

On election night, in addition to our live worldwide broadcast covering George Bush's victory over Michael Dukakis and the key Senate, House and governor's races, we provided special reports by phone to radio stations abroad, from the Caribbean to Hong Kong. When VOA went live worldwide, our audience naturally expanded. For Bush's inauguration in January 1989, our listenership was estimated at more than 162 million. Our normal audience in 1988–89 was put at 130 million.

VOA invariably carried live worldwide coverage of space shots. Listener surveys showed great interest overseas in America's space program. After the *Challenger* tragedy, we received many condolences from abroad. One such message addressed to me was from a listener in Tibet, who said, "I express my deep sympathy for the loss of seven space crew members. . . . I'm the sympathizer of American space program because her scientific achievements in conquering the outer space are a matter of great importance to mankind. . . . I never lose the chance of listening on every launching occasion, even at 3 a.m. our time sometimes."

The first shuttle launched since the *Challenger* was the *Discovery* in 1988, and for our live broadcast, anchored in Washington, we deployed a sizable team of correspondents. For the landing at Edwards Air Force Base in California, coverage was by our Los Angeles bureau. The bureau was headed by a pioneer woman network correspondent, Lee Hall Valeriani, who joined VOA after reporting for NBC from Korea, Latin America, the Middle East and the U.N.

In January 1989, VOA started airing 20–minute newscasts on weekends, something I'd vowed as a correspondent to see accomplished if I could. Now our correspondents were no longer limited to filing just brief spots for weekend newscasts, and our listeners were getting the news in detail. We also consolidated our "morgue," our file of prepared obituaries, and brought it up to date. When Emperor Hirohito was lying ill, I discovered that our biography of him was outdated. A newsroom editor, Chuck Flinner, who came to VOA from UPI, quickly got the "morgue" in shape, and we had a complete obit of Hirohito, Japan's emperor for 62 years, when he died in January.

President Bush went to Tokyo for the funeral on February 24, and afterwards visited China and met with Deng Xiaoping. During the stay in Beijing, covered by Alex Belida, then our senior White House correspondent, Chinese authorities prevented a leading dissident, the astrophysicist Fang Lizhi, from attending a dinner that Bush hosted.

By early 1989, I was able to name a Special Projects coordinator, a position I thought was necessary not only for planning coverage of upcoming events but also for developing programs that would be attractive and responsive to our listeners. The Russian and Chinese language services found that their listeners wanted to hear how small businesses in America get started. I assigned Myrna Whitworth to the post and we planned a series with nuts–and–bolts information and human interest stories of individual businesses.

Major stories that we covered in 1989 included the elections in Poland and gains by Solidarity, Bush's visits to Poland and Hungary, the death of the Ayatollah Khomeini, the South African president's meeting with imprisoned Nelson Mandela, the international AIDS conference in Montreal, ethnic violence in the Soviet Union, fighting in Lebanon. The biggest story was in China.

In early April 1989, I met with a delegation from Peking Radio that was in Washington as part of an exchange of visits between U.S. and Chinese broadcasters. The session in my office was very friendly, with the Chinese eager to hear how we went about covering stories. Before the month was out, China was criticizing the Voice for its coverage — of student demonstrations in Beijing and other cities.

Chinese authorities were well aware of VOA's listenership in their country. The Voice had incurred their displeasure earlier, when it reported on a wave of student protests in China in 1986–87. As *Washington Post* correspondent Daniel Southerland reported from Shanghai in December 1986, Chinese students "wanting to know more about democracy and the significance of their efforts" listened to VOA for information on the protests in Shanghai and other Chinese cities. Covering the demonstrations then were our Beijing bureau chief Mark Hopkins and, in Shanghai, a young stringer for us, Maxwell Ruston. Max was nearly mobbed by a crowd of cheering and applauding students when they learned that he worked for VOA.

In 1989 Chinese students again listened to VOA for information on their pro–democracy demonstrations. The demonstrations began April 16, the day after former Communist Party leader Hu Yaobang died at the age of 73. The students had seen him as a reformer sympathetic to their concerns. By the time of his funeral April 22 the number of demonstrators had grown from a few hundred to 150,000 and by some accounts 200,000. They were warned against further marches, but returned to Tiananmen Square April 27.

That day NPR's popular program, "All Things Considered," carried a report on VOA's China coverage by correspondent Ted Clark, who had interviewed some of us at the Voice. Ted began his report by playing a bit of tape of the morning newscast by our Chinese service and listing the lineup of stories: "A demand by authorities that student demonstrations be ended; a crackdown on the *World Economic Herald* in Shanghai, one of China's most liberal newspapers; and an interview about Chinese student activity in the United States." He added: "It's a safe bet that party leaders and student protestors alike were listening to the VOA's broadcast to China this morning. It's a source of information for both sides, but especially for the students who accuse the official Chinese media of ignoring their demonstrations or distorting their message."

Chinese authorities, he reported, were sensitive to VOA broadcasts because it "gets news of demonstrations in Beijing out to Shanghai, Guangcho, Nanjing and scores of other cities. Not deliberately, but inevitably, the VOA becomes a means by which protest is spread." I responded with: "That may very well be true, but are we supposed to ignore the demonstrations? You certainly can't ignore 50,000, 70,000, 80,000, 100,000 students demonstrating." Ted also noted that in 1987 Chinese authorities "seemed particularly upset that the VOA broadcast an appeal for greater democracy from American journalist I.F. Stone, a frequent critic of U.S. policy and a longtime friend of China." I said this was news and added, "We're competitive. We're in international broadcasting and we have some pretty stiff competitors."

Clark's NPR report also contained clips from his interview with the newsroom's East Asia editor, Stephanie Mann Nealer, who said her story selection was based on what's news and not because VOA is a government agency. "I don't look at it as how will this hurt or help U.S.–Chinese relations." Stephanie added that words are chosen carefully in reporting the story: "We can't come out and say 'China has lashed out at student protestors.' The word 'lashed out' carries a lot of baggage with it. We can say 'China says it's not going to tolerate student protests any more.' There's a difference; the information is the same."

Besides running the East Asia desk, Stephanie was taking courses in preparation for succeeding our Beijing bureau chief, Alan Pessin, who was in the final year of his assignment in China. Al, with the assistance of an American stringer in Beijing, Heidi Chay, was working day and night filing stories on the students and doing live broadcasts. And he was preparing for Gorbachev's arrival on May 15 for the first Sino–Soviet summit in three decades. VOA sent Betty Tseu of the Chinese service and Nick Sorokin of the Russian service to join Al in covering the Gorbachev visit. The American TV networks sent large contingents and their top anchors.

Instead of the Sino–Soviet summit, reporters found themselves covering the demonstrations by the students, who had begun a hunger strike in Tiananmen Square on May 13. When Gorbachev arrived two days later, there were so many in the square that the welcoming ceremony was called off, and he entered the Great Hall of the People through a back door. The TV cameras focused on the students, who were willing to have the publicity for their movement. Workers joined the students in a show of support, and the number of demonstrators swelled to a million in Tiananmen Square by the time Gorbachev left for Shanghai. As had been planned, VOA's Betty Tseu and Nick Sorokin went to Shanghai to cover him there, but the Chinese service decided to have her return to Beijing to continue reporting on the demonstrations.

Early on the morning of May 19, the students were urged by Prime Minister Li Peng and the then Communist Party leader Zhao Ziyang to end their strike. Zhao was in sympathy with their goals, as he made clear in his meeting with them in Tiananmen Square. That evening in Washington — when it was May 20 in Beijing, because of the 13-hour time difference — Al Pessin phoned the newsroom that martial law had been declared. His call came as we were nearing the end of our last bloc of English programming to East Asia for the day; we had just finished a newscast and were broadcasting a recorded feature program in Special English. We faded the sound of the recorded show and the announcer went on the air, explaining that we were interrupting our regular programming with a bulletin from the newsroom. I felt certain that many listeners in China, who regularly tuned in the Special English programs, heard the news of martial law from us.

Chinese authorities also shut down television satellite feeds from Beijing on May 20, as shown in dramatic live coverage on TV sets in the United States, where it was the night of May 19. They didn't want the world to see the student protests. Nor did they want the Chinese people to hear what was going on. On the day after martial law was imposed, the Chinese government began jamming VOA's Chinese language broadcasts, which were on the air eight and a half hours a day in Mandarin and a half hour a day in Cantonese. BBC's language broadcasts, aired two hours daily, also were jammed. The VOA and BBC broadcasts in English, listened to by the better-educated among China's one-billion-plus population, were not. Since the beginning of the student protests VOA's audience in China had grown from roughly 60 million to between 300 and 400 million, according to some estimates.

To confuse the jammers, VOA beamed the language broadcasts on additional frequencies, using a transmitter in the Philippines, and increased the Mandarin programs, starting them earlier in the evening Beijing time. Betty Tseu had been filing continuously for the Chinese service but after martial law was declared, its chief, David Hess, told me her voice was not being used on the air. There was concern for Betty's safety. Her press credentials issued for the Gorbachev visit had expired, and it was decided that she should leave Beijing and return to Washington.

Al Pessin and Heidi Chay stayed on top of the story, doing live broadcasts as well as keeping the newsroom informed and filing reports for translation by the Chinese and other language services. In spite of martial law, students continued to camp out in Tiananmen Square, although the number thinned down to about 10,000. They recorded our newscasts as they listened to them, and played them back for others to hear. Al Pessin heard them, too, including his own reports. Chinese army troops remained in and near Beijing waiting for orders.

On the afternoon of Saturday, June 3, I stopped by the office and, as usual on weekends, it was short-staffed. I called in reinforcements and was helping to edit copy when Al Pessin phoned Stephanie Nealer on the East Asia desk with bulletin news: The Chinese army was moving against the protestors in Tiananmen Square. The wire service tickers began erupting bulletins at about the same time. In the hours that followed (early Sunday morning Beijing time), Al kept feeding us information and broadcast reports, and the newsroom writers and editors carefully checked the news agency dispatches and network broadcasts and consulted with Al to make sure our stories were well-sourced, factual and non-inflammatory. I was so proud of everyone.

If we erred at all, it was on the side of caution, using the lower figures when there were discrepancies in reports on the mounting number of casualties. We also were cautious in our choice of words. In one of Al's phone calls to Stephanie, he counseled us against using the word "chaos" in reporting the situation in Beijing, because the Chinese leadership cited "chaos and turmoil" as the excuse for cracking down on the students. It may not ever be known how many were killed by the soldiers on their way to Tiananmen Square and in their attack on the students there. In the aftermath of the massacre, estimates ranged from 500 to 5,000 and even 7,000. Chinese officials said 100 soldiers and 100 civilians, including 36 students, were killed, and praised the army for standing against "counter–revolutionaries." VOA's reporting included the official Chinese statements.

A wave of arrests began immediately in Beijing and other cities. Pessin told me June 5 that an army tank was just 40 yards from his apartment window, and that he and his family had slept the night before in a friend's apartment. We agreed he should send his wife and baby to Bangkok. We dispatched our Tokyo correspondent, Phil Kurata, to Beijing to help Pessin cover the crackdown. Kurata did not have Chinese press credentials so we did not use his voice on the air, but he filed reports, and Pessin was able to get some sleep. We also decided to send our former Beijing bureau chief, Mark Hopkins, who then was our Boston correspondent, back to China. He arrived in Hong Kong June 8 and obtained a Chinese visa the following day. Although he too would be without Chinese press credentials, he told me before leaving for Beijing that he would broadcast his reports anyway. Mark also said he "might have to buy a bicycle," an amusing but, upon reflection, not a bad idea for getting around Beijing.

The Chinese government stepped up its denunciation of VOA's coverage and accused us of telling lies. Almost every day tirades were carried by the Chinese news media, which — until martial law censorship — had reported the pro–democracy demonstrations. In vilifying VOA broadcasts, the Chinese rulers were trying to counter the news we were reporting. Thus they were admitting that VOA was a powerful voice in China.

Just a few days after the army tanks rolled into Tiananmen Square, USIA television cameras were placed in the entryway to the VOA newsroom, where tourists see at one side the glass–fronted studio used for reading our newscasts in English. Now the studio was being occupied by Chinese service broadcasters, for VOA was undertaking an additional way of transmitting our Mandarin broadcasts to China — television. The TV signals were beamed via satellite, and although there were only about 2,000 satellite dishes in China, and these mostly at military installations, VOA Director

Carlson thought televising the broadcasts was worth trying. He said it would ensure that the Chinese army got an accurate account of what was going on. The Mandarin broadcasters were on TV for large blocs of time in the morning and evening, and at other times our newscasters in English were televised.

One of the stories we broadcast was on the U.S. evacuation of American dependents and other Americans wishing to leave Beijing. We also broadcast evacuation notices, which I scheduled at the end of newscasts beamed to the area. Although VOA is not supposed to direct its programs to Americans, I didn't feel we were breaking any law by broadcasting the notices. We could defend them as legitimate; there was concern for the safety of Americans.

The Chinese government had become increasingly critical of the U.S. government, which had deplored the crackdown and loss of life, given refuge to dissident Fang Lizhi and his wife at the American embassy in Beijing, and suspended military sales to China. The Bush administration further announced willingness to extend the visas of the some 40,000 Chinese citizens — students and others — then in the United States. The Chinese students at American campuses flooded VOA, especially the Chinese service, with phone calls and fax messages describing their activities in support of the students back home, and telling us what they were hearing from family and friends in China.

On June 14 the Chinese government ordered Al Pessin and AP correspondent John Pomfret to leave China within 72 hours, accusing them of violating martial law regulations. The authorities alleged that Pessin wrote news stories "to distort facts, spread rumor and incite and stir up counter-revolutionary rebellion." As Pessin said, he "didn't do anything that other foreign journalists didn't do. We made every effort to check facts and give balanced reporting." He and Pomfret were the first foreign journalists expelled from China since the demonstrations began. Mark Hopkins continued covering the story but within a few weeks he was expelled and left for home on July 11.

VOA's reporting to China, I was told in a phone call from Beijing on July 10, "is having such an effect that it is driving the communists crazy." The call was from an old friend, Eric Engberg of CBS, who was just completing a stint covering the crackdown and said he wanted to give us "a well done." He said, "Everywhere you go in the city you meet Chinese who speak English and listen to VOA. All they want to talk about is the VOA." Eric added that the communist press was filled with attacks on VOA, such as, "If VOA were telling the truth, why doesn't the U.S. let Americans hear it?" Aside from being pleased with Eric's call, I have two observations about his comments. First, as reporters and editors, we weren't trying to drive the communists crazy; we were trying to do a straightforward job of telling the news. If that upset China's communist rulers, so be it. Second, Americans ought to be able to hear what VOA is reporting.

Although Americans, except for shortwave radio buffs, couldn't hear our broadcasts, VOA's China coverage was well-reported in the American press, and applauded. Of the many examples of our listenership that were reported, one that was particularly telling was related in the *Washington Journalism Review* (later renamed *American Journalism Review*) by Michael J. Berlin, a former reporter who was in Beijing as a Fulbright lecturer in journalism. He said he was told by a student that "in one small town in Hunan province seven out of 10 people listen to the VOA on transistor radios that cost about $30 — an item that the economic reform has brought within reach of most Chinese families." The economic reform was spurred by Deng Xiaoping, the man whose policies I had thought would be good for the Chinese people, but who chose to abort political reform and crush the pro-democracy movement.

Although Pessin and Hopkins were expelled, Chinese authorities did not close our office in Beijing. Our stringer Heidi Chay, who had press credentials, continued work for us, and we also relied on wire service dispatches. In December China finally accredited Stephanie Mann Nealer as our Beijing correspondent.

By then, I had retired from VOA. My decision to leave was for personal reasons, partly that I wanted to write a book and, at age 61, thought I'd better get cracking. I left the Voice on September 3, 1989. But I can't leave the reader without filing a wrapup.

19
Wrapup

As a news person, this "famous unknown" picked a terrible time to retire. Momentous events were occurring and I was on the sidelines. How I missed being involved in coverage of the reforms sweeping Eastern Europe, the tearing down of the Berlin Wall, the dissolution of the Soviet Union and abandonment of communism. At the same time, I took immense satisfaction in the recognition that VOA received for its coverage, from Eastern European leaders such as Vaclav Havel, and in newspaper stories that reported the influence of VOA broadcasts.

In February 1990, Havel, then the new president of Czechoslovakia, and later president of the Czech Republic, visited Washington and made a special stop at Voice headquarters to thank the Czech and Slovak broadcasters. He said that for many years VOA "has been the most listened-to Czechoslovak radio station." He told the broadcasters, "You have informed us truthfully of events around the world and in our own country as well, and, in this way, you helped to bring about the peaceful revolution which has at long last taken place." Havel also has praised RFE.

Shortwave radio shaped the revolution in Romania, I read in *The Washington Post*, which reported that broadcasts by VOA, RFE and British, French and German stations "helped to undermine the Orwellian repression of the Ceausescu regime." VOA, RFE, and BBC broadcasts won praise for keeping people informed in other European countries under communist regimes. In repressed and impoverished Albania, VOA was singled out for its broadcasts.

In August 1991, during the attempted coup against Gorbachev, a Russian Republic official faxed a message to Washington urging that a speech to the Soviet Army by Boris Yeltsin denouncing the coup be broadcast on VOA. Gorbachev, a virtual prisoner at his vacation Black Sea dacha, listened to BBC, Radio Liberty and VOA to find out what was happening.

After the coup failed, VOA radio tech Reuel Zinn, on temporary assignment in Moscow, told his taxi driver he worked for VOA. The driver thereupon took him to see a message written on the wall of the parliament building, the Russian White House, which faced the American embassy, and translated it for him: "Thank you, Voice of America, for the correct information."

Photo by Reuel Zinn, VOA

Much has been written on the question of "who won the cold war." VOA and RFE/RL broadcasts have been credited with playing a role. But we reporters and editors at VOA did not think of ourselves as propaganda fighters in the cold war. The graffiti on the wall of the Russian White House is precisely the point, providing "the correct information." VOA was reporting the news.

If Americans could hear VOA's reporting, I think they would conclude, as I hope the reader has, that the Voice is not a ventriloquist's dummy relaying only what the U.S. government — that is, the administration in power — says. In striving to report national and international news that is accurate, objective and comprehensive, "telling it like it is," the journalists employed by the government's global radio station demonstrate American principles. Journalism and public service are not mutually exclusive. Both are supposed to serve the public interest. The Journalist's Creed that I memorized at the University of Missouri says that "the public journal is a public trust: that all connected with it are, to the full measure of their responsibility, trustees for the public." So I was comfortable being a journalist and a civil servant at the same time, believing that I was serving the American public by doing my best to cover the news honestly for VOA. I was the same reporter, older, more experienced and reporting to millions instead of thousands, as I was when I worked for *The Southwest Times*, *Roanoke Times* and *Youngstown Vindicator*.

The news reports of a foreign broadcaster, the BBC, can be heard on public radio stations in the U.S., and ABC–TV uses BBC correspondent reports. The BBC's World Service receives government funds and policy guidance from the British Foreign Office, but this hasn't marred its reputation. In international broadcasting, VOA also has a reputation as a credible source of news. The concern that American citizens might be subject to government proselytizing if they heard VOA news ought to be laid to rest. At the least, Americans ought to have a chance to listen to the reports of VOA's overseas correspondents.

A BBC correspondent, by the way, was permitted by the State Department to join the press traveling with Bush's secretary of state, James Baker, on a number of trips overseas — after the correspondent pointed out that BBC broadcasts are heard in the U.S. The VOA diplomatic correspondent, on the other hand, seldom was granted a press seat on Baker's plane. This was a break with tradition, but VOA's protests went unheeded during Baker's tenure. It should also be noted that public radio and television stations in America have received some of their funds from the government, through the Corporation for Public Broadcasting. Yet they have not been regarded as tainted by this connection with the government. I was saddened and angered by a conversation with a news producer at PBS who said loftily that he "wouldn't touch" VOA correspondent reports "with a ten–foot pole." His explanation was that they were broadcast by the government.

This producer was reacting to my suggestion that public radio stations in America ought to be able to carry reports from abroad by VOA correspondents. The stations would benefit by expanding their overseas coverage. And their audiences would benefit from the opportunity to hear VOA's substantive and timely reporting from around the world, especially since the American commercial networks have reduced the number of their overseas reporters.

I have told the reader about some of the letters I received from VOA listeners. One listener, a young man from Somalia, used to telephone me from Abu Dhabi, where he was working. Ahmed not only commented on my reports, he also played back tapes of those he had recorded, to show how they were received via shortwave. They parsed okay and were free of static, I happily noted. He later came to America to study at one of our colleges and, in a visit to Washington, asked to meet me. I suggested we meet at the roof terrace of the Washington Hotel because of its lovely view of the city. Two of my nieces were visiting from Pennsylvania, so I took them along. Patty, a college graduate, and Carolyn, a high school student, found in talking with Ahmed that he knew more about American current affairs and history than they did. His knowledge, he said, came from listening to VOA.

When Patty complimented Ahmed on his dazzling smile, he said that people in Somalia cleaned their teeth with the bark of a particular tree, instead of toothbrushes like the ones Americans use. On return to his country for vacation, he sent her a "Somali toothbrush." Ahmed kept in touch with me as he graduated from college, went to work for a company in Atlanta, and married. After warfare erupted in Somalia, he told me of his fears for his relatives there, then phoned me to report they had left Somalia and were safe. He always asked about my nieces.

I felt a great sense of accomplishment in reporting the news to people overseas. And I am grateful to VOA for the opportunity it gave me to report some of the biggest stories of my lifetime and to see world figures and world capitals. I relished covering the White House, and relished the camaraderie of the White House press corps regulars. On presidential trips, when we were herded through magnetometers and to buses and planes, we poked fun at ourselves by chorusing "baa, baa, baa," or "moo, moo, moo." In this herd environment, however, there was a temptation to go along with the pack in reporting our stories.

There was competition, of course, and some of the reporters were self-impressed because their news organizations were at the top of the White House pecking order. Some were overly officious in their treatment of technicians or White House Press Office secretaries. But on the whole, the press corps was composed of decent people, many of them, like me, from small towns. I liked and respected most of them.

In my 14 years covering the White House, I had the good fortune to be in the company of a great number of very good reporters. I have mentioned some of them in this account, but there were many others. Two of the correspondents were former VOA news staffers, Frank Sesno of CNN and Deborah Potter, then with CBS. Deborah was a fine addition to the growing number of women in the White House press corps.

In telling about presidential trips abroad, I have purposely noted the number of men and women in the traveling press. The reader no doubt has noticed that while the number of women increased, the ratio remained lopsided. The women on the White House beat included not only correspondents and producers but also radio techs, still photographers, and members of mini–cam crews. They all worked hard.

In telling about VOA, I have purposely mentioned a number of women. Women were, I thought, the backbone of VOA, performing the necessary jobs in the newsroom, language services, and various offices to make it function smoothly. When I was editor in chief, the person whose counsel I sought nearly every day was a problem–solver named Eva Jane (Janie) Fritzman, an administrative aide when I first met her, who rose to become a valued assistant to a succession of VOA directors. She knew the workings of VOA and USIA inside out, knew every regulation in the thick telephone book–sized Manual of Operations that ruled our lives as government employees.

The federal government's civil servants are often maligned by political candidates running against Washington. But my experience was that the overwhelming majority of the people who worked at VOA gave full value to the American taxpayers. The Voice had around 2,800 employees and, as is the case in any large workforce, in government or the private sector, there were some who coasted or were of questionable competence. These were a small minority.

In the aggregate, VOA was a collection of talented, dedicated people of many different cultures and professional backgrounds, including authors, playwrights, musicians, and experts in various fields.

The cultural diversity is heady, with broadcasters from all kinds of countries assembled under one roof. But the diversity can be a problem at times. Newcomers in the language services often don't have a full understanding of the American democratic process and free press, and it takes time for them to become adjusted. They couldn't understand why VOA reported the bad as well as the good, and this resulted in disputes between the newsroom and the services. At other times there was an endearing naiveté about some of the language staffers. For example, the newsroom frequently was asked when it would get an advance text of the president's press conference.

Besides the disagreements between the newsroom and the language services over what stories should go into a newscast, there were disputes within a number of the services. These included personality conflicts; with such an assemblage of talented people, VOA does have a share of prima donnas. But the disputes more often were of a factional or historical nature.

VOA's first director, the late actor John Houseman, said in his memoirs that working with the language services gave him "an astonishing insight into the diversity of ethnic prejudices and passions retained and intensified in exile by intelligent and cultivated men and women." Reading that, I nodded in agreement. Houseman also wrote that during his 18 months (1942–43) at VOA he was in "a state of perpetual exhilaration." I found VOA exhilarating, too, though maybe not perpetually.

In spite of squabbles and disagreements and turf battles, however, there is an underlying esprit de corps at the Voice. Its people pull together to meet the challenge and report the news when there is an international or domestic crisis. The esprit is much in evidence in matters of honor — when any attempts are made to restrict VOA's coverage, when VOA is criticized for its reporting of a story, when stories in the American press contain misperceptions about the Voice, when VOA's accomplishments are overlooked, and when VOA is shortchanged in funding the government's overseas radio services. On the latter, it pained me to see RFE/RL and pet projects like Radio Marti, and later TV Marti, enjoy healthy budgets while VOA endured budget cuts. At RFE/RL, the top executives received salaries and additional remuneration higher than those of the top executives at VOA, even higher than the salary of the president of the United States.

After the cold war, RFE/RL and its supporters fought proposals that it be phased out and its assets merged with VOA on the grounds that surrogate broadcasts were no longer needed. In arguing the case for its continued existence, they sniped at VOA's coverage, contributing, sadly, to a perception that VOA is a tool of the State Department. President Bush appointed a task force to make recommendations for the eventual consolidation of the broadcast services. But a majority of the task force took RFE/RL's position that it should continue. In addition, the majority recommended creation of a new broadcast service advocated by influential members of Congress, a Radio Free Asia that would broadcast local news to China and other repressed countries in the region.

The Clinton administration moved toward consolidation in 1993 by presenting a plan to Congress placing RFE/RL and the new Asian service within USIA, along with VOA, Radio and TV Marti, and Worldnet, with all to be under the supervision of a presidentially appointed board of governors. After a compromise worked out between deficit-cutter Senator Russell B. Feingold and RFE/RL defender Senator Joseph R. Biden, the plan was approved by Congress and signed into law by President Bill Clinton on April 30, 1994. Appallingly, the congressional writers of the legislation repealed the VOA Charter. They crafted a general statement of standards and principles instead. After protests from VOA and its alumni and friends, the Charter was restored to law within months.

VOA and RFE/RL began dealing with budget cuts required by the 1994 law and made reductions in broadcasts and staff. The law did envision a phaseout of RFE/RL, but for an interim maintained its status as a corporation receiving grants. The same "grantee" status was applied to the projected Radio Free Asia. Radio and TV Marti continued operating under VOA's director, but with their own bureaucracies and facilities.

My own view, admittedly biased in favor of a single, strong, worldwide broadcast service, is that surrogate stations, like the one-room schoolhouses of the past, should be eliminated, with their resources merged into VOA. Although their supporters argue that they are necessary, the U.S. government, pressed by budget deficits and domestic needs, shouldn't be spending money on specialized broadcast services when it has a global radio service that can do the job.

In making funding decisions for international broadcasting, the government should be looking at the competition from television — from local TV stations in countries around the world, and, internationally, from such enterprises as CNN, NBC and BBC–TV. Television can be used as a medium for extending to viewers the information available in radio broadcasts, as was done in 1989 when VOA newscasts were televised via satellite to China. Since then, great numbers of satellite dishes have sprouted in China, and millions of Chinese have access to foreign TV programs. In September 1994, VOA began televising a weekly Mandarin language public affairs radio program to Chinese viewers via Asiasat. This joint VOA and Worldnet effort could be a model for televising additional radio programs.

While increasing attention should be given to television, the government must not give short shrift to international radio broadcasting. Because of the immediacy, flexibility and intimacy of radio, VOA's shortwave and mediumwave broadcasts should be maintained, supplemented by its broadcasts via satellite TV subcarriers, placement of programs on local radio stations around the world, and the exploration of new ways to extend its reach.

VOA began using one of those new ways in January 1994 by entering the world of cyberspace. It made available to computer users of the international information network, Internet, its daily file of the texts of correspondent reports, current affairs material and features. And as of August 1994, Internet users could hear, through digitized transmission, the audio of VOA newscasts in English and 14 other languages. In a subsequent speech, VOA Director Geoffrey Cowan said people in 61 of the Internet–connected countries had turned to VOA for information. Cowan, a Clinton appointee on leave from UCLA and an author, lawyer and TV producer, had ties to the Voice going back to his childhood. His father, Louis G. Cowan, a network executive, served as VOA's second director, in 1943–45.

The total number of VOA language services, including English, rose to 47 by 1995, but the estimated audience was down from the 130 million in 1989. Based on limited USIA research, listenership to VOA's transmitter–relayed shortwave and mediumwave broadcasts was put at 92 million. This could be attributed in part to competition from new radio stations that have flowered in former Iron Curtain countries. However, the estimate did not include listeners to VOA programs aired on more than 1,000 radio stations around the globe, some with national networks, and to broadcasts via satellite subcarriers. Nor is it possible to get a good idea of VOA listenership in a number of countries, like Iran and Iraq. With the uncounted no doubt in mind, Director Cowan rounded out VOA's total audience at 100 million.

An estimated 20 percent of the listeners to the shortwave and mediumwave broadcasts tuned in Worldwide English programs, with the rest divided among listeners to programs aired in the other languages. That's not surprising. English, after all, has become the language of international commerce and diplomacy. VOA's English broadcasts should be boosted, and Special English and English language teaching programs expanded.

Now to some questions that I pondered while working for the Voice, especially when I chafed at conclusions that VOA wasn't a legitimate news organization and its reporters were somehow tainted because they were government employees. Why should the U.S. be in international broadcasting? Why should American taxpayers foot the bill when the money could be spent on needs at home? And in footing the bill, don't taxpayers have a right to expect that our overseas broadcasts speak on behalf of the United States — in other words, engage in propaganda?

My answers were, and are: The U.S. should be in international broadcasting because it is a superpower, now the only one, and should contribute to world understanding, by telling about America and its institutions and policies, and by reporting what is going on in the world. So American taxpayers should foot the bill, but insist that the money not be spent wastefully. And finally, yes, taxpayers should expect that in telling overseas listeners about America, the purpose is to speak on behalf of America. Am I saying that I engaged in propaganda?

Propaganda used to be defined as the spreading of particular ideas, doctrines and practices. In reporting to overseas listeners about the American political process and the election of presidents, I concede that this amounted to spreading information about our democracy. But in the modern-day, pejorative meaning of propaganda, including use of rumors, allegations and disinformation, I can say I was not a propagandist. I was a reporter and that's all there was to it.

In years past good arguments have been made both for and against separating VOA from USIA, its parent agency charged with informing people overseas about American policies through public diplomacy. I have leaned toward separation. Those arguments are dormant, and new proposals now have been made in the Republican-controlled Congress. So, to update this wrapup as it goes to the printer, here is a summary of proposals that would affect VOA's future.

In March 1995, the new Senate Foreign Relations Committee chairman, Jesse Helms, proposed legislation under which USIA and two other foreign affairs agencies, dealing with arms control and overseas aid, would be disbanded and their functions transferred to a reorganized State Department. VOA (and Radio Marti) would thus be deposited in a public diplomacy unit of the State Department, and the VOA Charter would be more important than ever.

In May 1995, the House of Representative adopted a plan aimed at eliminating the federal government's budget deficit in seven years by dismantling several departments and a multitude of agencies — including termination of VOA. The United States thus would be abandoning an overseas broadcast service that has served America well since 1942.

As someone who spent a good part of her life witnessing the value of this institution, I hope that in the debate over these proposals, VOA will survive — and remain a credible purveyor of national and international news. And I continue to believe the best way for the Voice of America to inform people overseas about American policies is to report the news, not just what an administration says and does, but also what is being said and done in Congress, and whenever possible, the sentiments of the people, as reflected by leading figures in American life and by polls.

As discussed earlier, the editorials broadcast by the Voice are kept separate from the news, but their impact on VOA's credibility was a concern to the news staff, especially when they were strident or inaccurate. An administration has a right, I believe, to present its views in editorials on VOA, just as a newspaper publisher's views are presented on the editorial page. To sharpen the distinction between news and editorials on VOA, I think the editorials should be written, and broadcast, by an official government spokesman instead of VOA employees. They could be done by a White House or State Department official, or in matters of international trade, for instance, an official representing the agency involved. And would it be going too far to think about responsible responses to the editorials, sort of op-ed pieces?

In writing this memoir of what it was like to work for the Voice of America and report news about American presidents, I have tried to tell both the positive and the negative. Beyond that, I wanted to tell the personal as well as the professional aspects of the story. Reporters, and presidents, are human.

I loved being a reporter, whether for newspapers or for the Voice. And as a reporter, I believe VOA has one of the finest news operations in the world. I am proud to have worked there.

Index

Additional copies of this book may be ordered directly from Linus Press.

Mail: LINUS PRESS
       P.O. Box 5446
       Washington, D.C. 20016-5446

Fax: (301) 654-5508

A Basement Seat to History

Number of Copies @ $16.95 _____

D.C. residents, add 5.75% sales tax _____

Shipping & handling: add $2.50 for one
book, .60 for each additional book _____

Total _____

Recipient (please print):

Name _____

Address _____

_____
                    (city, state, zip code)

Payment to Linus Press by check or credit card:

_____ Visa _____ Mastercard _____ American Express

Card number _____

Expiration date _____ _____

Signature on card _____